“OUR PLACE IN AL-ANDALUS”

Cultural Memory
in
the
Present

Mieke Bal and Hent de Vries, Editors

في ٱلمَساءِ الأَخير
على هذهِ الأَرْض

في ٱلْمَساءِ الأَخيرِ على هذهِ الأَرْضِ نَقْطَعُ أَيَّامَنا
عَنْ شُجَيْراتِنا، ونَعُدُّ ٱلضُّلوعَ ٱلَّتي سَوْفَ نَحْمِلُها مَعَنا
وَالضُّلوعَ ٱلَّتي سَوْفَ نَتْرُكُها، هَهُنا . . . في ٱلْمَساءِ ٱلأَخيرْ
لا نُوَدِّعُ شَيْئاً، ولا نَجِدُ ٱلْوَقْتَ كَيْ نَنْتَهي . . .
كُلُّ شَيْءٍ يَظَلُّ على حالِهِ، فَٱلْمَكانُ يُبَدِّلُ أَحْلامَنا
وَيُبَدِّلُ زُوّارَهُ. فَجْأَةً لَمْ نَعُدْ قادِرينَ على السُّخْرِيَة
فَالْمَكانُ مُعَدٌّ لِكَيْ يَسْتَضيفَ ٱلْهَباءَ . . . هُنا في ٱلْمَساءِ ٱلأَخيرْ
نَتَمَلّى ٱلْجِبالَ ٱلْمُحيطَةَ بِالْغَيْمِ . فَتْحٌ . . . وَفَتْحٌ مُضادّ
وَزَمانٌ قَديمٌ يُسَلِّمُ هذا ٱلزّمانَ ٱلْجَديدَ مَفاتيحَ أَبْوابِنا
فَٱدْخلوا، أَيُّها ٱلْفاتِحونَ، مَنازِلَنا وَٱشْرَبوا خَمْرَنا
مِنْ مُوَشَّحِنا ٱلسَّهْلِ. فَاللَّيْلُ نَحْنُ إِذا ٱنْتَصَفَ ٱللَّيْلُ، لا
فَجْرَ يَحْمِلُهُ فارِسٌ قادِمٌ مِنْ نَواحي ٱلأَذانِ ٱلأَخير . . .
شايُنا أَخْضَرٌ ساخِنٌ فَٱشْرَبوهُ، وَفُسْتُقُنا طازَجٌ فَكُلوه
وَٱلأَسِرَّةُ خَضْراءُ مِنْ خَشَبِ ٱلأَرْزِ، فَٱسْتَسْلِموا لِلنُّعاسْ
بَعْدَ هذا ٱلْحِصارِ ٱلطَّويلِ، وَناموا على ريشِ أَحْلامِنا،
أَلْمُلاءاتُ جاهِزَةٌ، وَٱلْعُطورُ على ٱلْبابِ جاهِزَةٌ، وَٱلْمرايا كَثيرَة
فَٱدْخلوها لِنَخْرُجَ مِنْها تَماماً، وَعَمّا قَليلٍ سَنَبْحَثُ عَمّا
كانَ تاريخَنا حَوْلَ تاريخِكُمْ في ٱلْبِلادِ ٱلْبَعيدَة
وَسَنَسْأَلُ أَنْفُسَنا في ٱلنِّهايَةِ. هَلْ كانَتِ ٱلأَنْدَلُسْ
هَهُنا أَمْ هناكَ؟ على ٱلأَرْضِ . . . أَمْ في ٱلْقَصيدَة؟

محمود درويش

"OUR PLACE IN AL-ANDALUS"

Kabbalah, Philosophy, Literature in Arab Jewish Letters

Gil Anidjar

STANFORD UNIVERSITY PRESS
STANFORD, CALIFORNIA
2002

Stanford University Press
Stanford, California

Printed in the United States of America
on acid-free, archival-quality paper.

Library of Congress Cataloging-in-Publication Data

Anidjar, Gil.
"Our place in al-Andalus" : Kabbalah, philosophy, literature in Arab Jewish letters / Gil Anidjar.
p. cm.
Includes bibliographical references (p.) and index.
ISBN 0-8047-4120-4 (alk. paper) — ISBN 0-8047-4121-2 (pbk. : alk. paper)
1. Maimonides, Moses, 1135–1204. Dalālat al-ḥāʾirīn. 2. Philosophy, Jewish. 3. Philosophy, Medieval. 4. Zohar. 5. Cabala—History. 6. Ibn al-Aštarkūwī, Muḥammad ibn Yūsuf, d. 1143—Criticism and interpretation. 7. Context (Linguistics). 8. Andalusia (Spain). 9. Eschatology, Jewish. I. Title.
BM545.D35 A55 2002
946'.802—dc21 2001042906

Original printing 2002
Last figure below indicates year of this printing:
11 10 09 08 07 06 05 04 03 02

Typeset by James P. Brommer in 11/13.5 Garamond

For ʿEylam and Niv

Contents

Acknowledgments xi

Introduction: Declinations of Context in Arab Jewish Letters 1

1 Maimonides, *Dalāla*, Midrash 10

2 "Our Place in al-Andalus, عندنا في الأندلس" 57

3 The Silent Voice of the Friend: Andalusī Topographies of Scholem's Conversations (Mourning Mysticism) 102

4 Reading, Out of Context: *Zohar* and/as *Maqāma* 166

Part ~~1~~: *Zohar* 171

Ibn al-Aštarkūwī's *Maqāma* "On Poetry and Prose" 219

Part 2: Parting Words 229

Notes 249

Bibliography 307

Acknowledgments

Throughout the ambiguous, fragile, and hesitating time that writing bestows, I have had the good fortune of receiving the support of a number of institutions and departments: the University of California at Berkeley (Comparative Literature), Williams College (Religion), and Columbia University (Middle East and Asian Languages and Cultures). I am also grateful for having found, in each of these institutions, friends and colleagues who all affected the work in their own way. Stanford University Press, and most particularly Helen Tartar and the readers for the Press, as well as Andrew Frisardi, have provided a most welcome and positive conclusion to the completion of this project.

This book was written in the wake of Amos Funkenstein's death. His teaching has been and continues to be a true gift. The book could not have come into existence without this gift, nor without the support, guidance, and inspiration of Ammiel Alcalay, Daniel Boyarin, Judith Butler, Nina Caputo, Joel L. Kraemer, James T. Monroe, Amnon Raz-Krakotzkin, Ann Smock, Ruth Tsoffar, and, most of all, Avital Ronell. Expressions of gratitude are always inadequate enough. How much more so here and now.

Le language se définit peut-être comme le pouvoir même de rompre la continuité de l'être ou de l'histoire.

Language is perhaps defined as the very power to break the continuity of being or of history.

—EMMANUEL LEVINAS

Introduction: Declinations of Context in Arab Jewish Letters

> And what if this outside of apocalypse were *inside* the apocalypse? What if it were the apocalypse itself, what precisely breaks in, *fait effraction,* in the "Come"? What is "inside" and what is "outside" a text, of *this* text, both inside and outside these volumes of which we do not know whether they are open or closed? . . . The end approaches, not it's too late to tell the truth about the apocalypse. But what are you doing, all of you will still insist, to what ends do you want to come when you come to tell us, here now, let's go, come, *allons, viens,* the apocalypse, it's finished, I tell you this, that's what's happening, *voilà ce qui arrive.*
>
> —Jacques Derrida, "Of an Apocalyptic Tone Newly Adopted in Philosophy"

> The desire to finish once and for all, or to be done with definitively, is a legacy of the Western logos, promising finite transcendence but also a new, infinitizing start; . . . termination is as much a myth as origin, offering the narcissistic comfort that goes along with closure—who would not want to wrap it up?
>
> —Avital Ronell, *Finitude's Score*

This book offers a reading of texts that raise a historical question, namely, how to read when contexts disappear, when the notion of context itself becomes historical. It is a reading of texts that, central to the history of the medieval Iberian peninsula, emerge from its Andalusī, Jewish and Arabic, cultural sphere: Maimonides' *Guide of the Perplexed,* the rhymed prose narratives (*maqāmāt*) of Ibn al-Aštarkūwī, and the major text of Kabbalah ("Jewish mysticism"), the *Zohar.* They were written in the seventh and eighth centuries of the Islamic calendar (twelfth and thirteenth centuries C.E.), yet, from literary, cultural, and historical perspectives, and although not particularly distant, they appear to have little in common: they belong to profoundly different genres (they have been distinctively classified, located, as literary, mystical [kabbalistic], or philosophical), and are written by people of distinct religions or religious groups; they are even separated by historical walls: the Almohad and Almoravid conquests, the Christian conquests. Thus, although I have just located and described these texts as "emerging from" a geographical and cultural area, and although they "can be brought to rest at the end of this movement . . . [and] can be stabilized into objects of representation,"[1] they are hardly locatable in a common space of some nature. The only feature they share, rather, is that al-Andalus—the general set of circumstances from which they are thus said to "emerge," in other words, their context—disappears or has already disappeared.

This disappearance is historical yet not simply a "medieval" event. It is also a very modern event, one that continues to be inscribed to this day. Hence, Ibn al-Aštarkūwī writes his *maqāmāt* during "the twilight of Arab dominion in al-Andalus";[2] Maimonides composes the *Guide of the Perplexed* when "the age of philosophy in Muslim countries is drawing to its close";[3] and the *Zohar*, the major text of the Kabbalah, appears in the Iberian peninsula shortly after a time in which, "instead of simply dwindling or decaying, Spanish Jewry transferred from the Arabic world to Christian Europe."[4] Al-Andalus is ending, then, it *is* its end, and it has ended in such a way that it foregrounds and renders all that remains of it precisely as such: a remainder, a "legacy" that was reinscribed, celebrated (or mourned), in 1992.[5]

Yet, what if this failure of localization, of finding a stable position, what if the occurrence of the end as the disappearance of context was not simply an external accident, a catastrophe that happened to befall texts that henceforth lost their place? What if the end, which has then to be rethought and reread, was a linguistic and rhetorical occurrence, the occurrence of al-Andalus not simply in but as language? I argue that these texts are written in a language that disrupts the possibility of locating it in a preexisting cultural situation or in a recognizable literary tradition, and of containing it in a particular genre. At "our place, in al-Andalus," language unsettles its localization and repeatedly produces the disappearance of its context. Language allows for a rethinking of al-Andalus as a rhetorical event that is thus not reducible to its contexts, whether literary, historical, or cultural. Here, language indicates that it is itself its "own" place, hardly one, incommensurable because uncontainable, the event of its (failure in) taking place. The unsettling dimension of this language occurs in translation, that which Walter Benjamin calls the "somewhat provisional way of coming to terms with the foreignness of all languages." Such translation can thus be read as a dimension of a specific language in its occurrence, as a provisional visit that relies on the uncertain hospitality of "our place." And language itself becomes both unsettling and hospitable—an irreducible event that, in turn, enables comparison.

"Our Place in al-Andalus" leads me to a reconsideration of what is meant today by al-Andalus as a literary and cultural object of Arab Jewish letters, and to a reconceptualization of its limits and divisions. Al-Andalus, and, similarly, worlds that scholars consider as having ended, as having become lost or vanished abysses that securely divide between historical, cultural, ethnic, religious, and linguistic and literary realms, must be thought otherwise; namely (even if not only), as occurrences that still take place in language, as occurrences to which language—never quite reducible to itself—gives place. This rethinking, which has everything to do with reading and with reading the end, must do justice to the gravity and complexity of such events, and it must do so without reducing their linguistic and rhetorical dimensions.

If the end is near—and the ends of al-Andalus, of Spain, and of Arab Jewish letters are just so, having been repeatedly inscribed and celebrated—its nearing betrays "the desire to finish once and for all, or to be done with definitively,"[6] the uncertain expectation of a present or past present and actual occurrence of the end. If the end is near, its nearing—the nearing of an "impossible passage," a "nonpassage"—has already become an indication of "something else," a future, "the event of a coming or of a future advent," another future in our vicinity, in proximity, "and which no longer has the form of the movement that consists in passing, traversing, or transiting."[7] But why is it that the approach of such a figure and of such a future, as addressed by historiography, most visibly by the discourse on Jewish letters and Jewish history, so systematically translates as eschatology, understood in a restricted sense, as the logic of an *eschaton* that has already occurred in some past present? Why does it translate as a logic of the last and of the end, as a discourse on a vanishing past and on hermetic borders that, having been crossed once and for all, were always left, safely and permanently hermetically-behind? The paradigmatic, though by no means unique, preoccupation of "Jewish studies" with such conclusive ends (and with the end as origin—do not the histories of the "Spanish Jews" almost invariably begin with and from 1492?) also treats the ends of al-Andalus, and the ends of Arab Jewish letters, here and elsewhere, as opening the space of a vanishing, a space of the ends. Along with most efforts to think the question of the Arab and the Jewish together, which invariably focus on questions of territory, land, and place (and on issues of hermetic partitions and separations), the discourses of the ends inscribe a constant and prominent concern with clear and certain locations, with identifiable borders and territories, with determinable places and, indeed, with localizable contexts—and with contexts that are no more.

On the first page of *Against the Apocalypse: Responses to Catastrophe in Modern Jewish Culture*, David Roskies mentions, for the first and last time, a report, a rumor from the thither side of these ends:

> There are said to be Moroccan Jews who have kept the keys to their ancestral homes in fifteenth-century Spain and Portugal. When, in the 1950s, the exiles dispersed yet again—to France, Quebec, and Israel—these metal relics from Seville and Granada, Lisbon and Barcelona, became perhaps their most tangible link to their great Sephardic past. Such keys may not in fact exist; but even so they intrigue as metaphors.[8]

These keys are here the last unverifiable signs, doubtful figures of the end, perhaps even unreadable, decontextualized "metaphors" that nonetheless translate the ends of al-Andalus, of a long-gone, if "great Sephardic past," this collection of lost "ancestral homes" that, being "theirs" and theirs only ("their great Sephardic past") was never, no longer and no more, part of (our?) "modern Jewish culture." These keys are themselves translations from one end to the next ("when the exiles dispersed *again* . . . "), at once the occurrence of a transformation, the alchemical becoming of "metal relics" from "most tangible" into the uncertain existence of "metaphors." In their becoming figures of non-, or doubtful, existence, nonexisting figures, "Spain and Portugal," or "Moroccan Jews" for that matter, are spoken by way of rumors originating in an elsewhere that exceeds the questionable boundaries of their all too finite existence ("there are said to be Moroccan Jews . . . "), accruing the uncertainty of their existence and, a fortiori, of their end. Never again—never again spoken in the rest of Roskies' book, they have always and already truly ended—from the beginning.

The "intriguing" figures, metaphors, and translations—no more than "literature," perhaps, only "literature," but in a restricted sense—open and enable the discourse about, against, and for the end of apocalypse, as they pronounce the unverifiable dimension of their disseminated paradigm: 1492. These are not just signs of an irrecoverable past, then, but uncertain links to another place, the place of the end, which, locked away, is also the time of the end that we do not find: that which is no more opens and closes the place from which the end is spoken, if silently. This too is a dispersed place of uncertain status, ruin of a tangible link, the existence of which is, as they say, rhetorical (ever more in a restricted sense), the nonexistence of which signifies the possibility of rhetoric and its ends, the possibility of a rhetoric of the ends. Hence, having yet to be read, other translations of the "same" dispersed ends described by Roskies have not failed to reproduce themselves as yet more ends, in France, for example, where "in 1968, French Jewry might well have seemed doomed to a literary existence at best."[9] The ends are, therefore, not only rhetorical (signifiers ending themselves, disappearing out of existence, only words and literature, no longer existence, rhetoric at its ends), they are also the beginnings of rhetoric and its enabling conditions.

Eschatological discourses of this sort confirm and undermine the logic of the *eschaton*, and they have shown themselves particularly resilient, from the will-to-bury of the "Science of Judaism" to the "end of exile" and of Arab Jews,[10] the revival and rebirth, and later a more troubled reconstruction of that which had ended badly, of Kabbalah scholarship and its striking articulation in the writings of Gershom Scholem.[11] That Kabbalah, much like the Holocaust, now stands in the middle of these preoccupations with ends (and beginnings as ends), at the center of the discourses of "Jewish studies," partakes as much of a historical, as of a logical, and indeed rhetorical, necessity. Both are constituted by a work of mourning, a "work of death" as Michel de Certeau describes in *The Writing of History*. Paradoxically, this work marks "an effect of impossible or refused mourning (melancholy or mourning)."[12] The histories of Kabbalah scholarship, much like so many Jewish "identities," operate and are constituted around the ends of Spain, be it Islamic Spain or Christian Spain, and the histories of the Holocaust around the ends of Europe, of the German-Jewish dialogue, and more, even when they are uttered "against the Apocalypse."

If the end is near, if a future approaches, it enables and disables the question of its location: it cannot be confined to either side of a separation (the lost voices, the remaining metaphors, the conclusive and concluding end) that it appears nonetheless to draw or posit between past and present, before and after, time and place, and between Jewish and non-Jewish. The end must be read, for it cannot simply mark—without affecting it—the distinction between inside and outside, between language and its others, between rhetoric and its ends.[13] The end must be "inside" the apocalypse that what ends "is," that it repeats and translates. More importantly, if the end is near and nearing, it cannot be figured—it cannot be figured either as an encounter between such poles and across allegedly fixed and recognizable borders (the Arab, the Jew, the Christian). It must already have translated the inscription, the letters, that testify to the end. "There is a problem as soon as the edge-line is threatened. And it is threatened from its first tracing."[14] How is it, then and again, that what here raises the question of alterity—the medieval Iberian peninsula in Arab Jewish letters, in Arabic, Aramaic, Hebrew, and more—was so insistently read and located within the geographically and temporally unambiguous coordinates of the ends? How is it that the end here governs, and indeed safely separates between the discourses of Kabbalah, philosophy, and literature?

Fourteen ninety-two is only the more striking end in a series of ends that inform the representation of medieval Spain in modern historical and literary discourses, Jewish or other. These ends simultaneously mirror the traumas of history and shed light on the discursive processes by which hermetic boundaries are set between periods, communities, and texts. *"Our Place in al-Andalus": Kabbalah, Philosophy, Literature in Arab Jewish Letters* engages the modern representation of the twelfth and thirteenth centuries as the end of al-Andalus. Here, the end works to locate and separate Muslim from Christian Spain, Jews from Arabs, Kabbalah from literature, literature from philosophy, and texts from contexts.

Yet, in order to accept, maintain, or replicate this representation and these divisions, one has to enact—while ignoring—a major dimension of al-Andalus as a historical event: rhetoric, language. By reading mystical, philosophical, and literary texts closely, I show that al-Andalus is a rhetorical event to be read, a language that maintains but also negotiates and disrupts the localizations and divisions established by the end. This event, which fails to take place in a recognizable location, is what I call "place," after the twelfth-century Arab Jewish philosopher Maimonides, who wrote of "our place in al-Andalus." Maimonides' words, written in Egypt and not in the Iberian peninsula, where Maimonides was born and educated, exemplify the unsettling dimension of language at "our place." As al-Andalus, then, midrash occurs as poetry, Kabbalah as *maqāma*, philosophy as literary criticism. And language goes out of context. Al-Andalus is an event of language that takes place insofar as it also fails to do so (this is the end, my friend) "in" the "medieval" texts I read and in the "modern" historiographical considerations of their disappearing context.

I take issue with the modern disciplinary division that governs the study and teaching of so-called Jewish medieval texts, and my critique emerges, revolves around, but also distances itself from the following questions: Is a cultural analysis of the central texts of medieval Jewish letters possible? What conceptions of language and culture are at work in constructing textual and cultural divisions? Why do "mourning and melancholia" govern the reading practices that underlie the current study of medieval Spain? Why is the *Zohar*, the major text of Kabbalah, not studied as part of the rise of vernacular (Arabic, Hebrew, Romance, etc.) literature in medieval Europe? Why is it not even studied as part of medieval Hebrew literature?

What follows, then, is a set of readings of the ends, readings that, while not necessarily conclusive, attend to (thereby also reinscribing if, perhaps, differently) the assertion of loss that confirms and strengthens, but also undoes, the construction, the inscription of hermetic borders. These readings emerged early on as a set of insisting concerns with translation and with the strangely literal notion that sees and construes translation as a unilateral crossing of borders, a crossing that would leave these borders safely in place.[15] Early on, my concerns were accompanied by the deep suspicion that the very limited displacement thus imagined as border crossing was also the anxious affirmation that there were such (literary, ethnic, religious, even—in the "Middle Ages"!—national) borders, and, more importantly, that they could be recognized and localized. The translation of the word

"Kabbalah" into "mysticism" and the localization of the *Zohar* in a narrow textual tradition and in the Romance and Christian world, together with the repetitive announcements of the imminent end of that which was neither Romance nor Christian, not simply so, provided a starting point for a reading of ends as *responses to*—rather than as signs or symbols of—a much more radical displacement, a more radical trans-lation to be read in the texts. Determining the ends and limits, identifying the sources and authorship, locating the place, of the *Zohar* and others, were all, of course, acts of translation on the part of existing scholarship, but more importantly, they were acts that indicated that the texts had already been functioning as a challenge, as a disruption of localization. The assertion of ends, the claim that a text and an event could simply appear and present itself, transparently, as it were, so as to reassure its readers that it had determined and determinable limits and ends (which could be translated as either goals or contexts), paradoxically opened the possibility of describing a different notion of translation as event.

The translation of Maimonides' title into *The Guide of the Perplexed*, the text with which this book begins, provided me with an account of, a provisional formalization for, this notion of translation. Prior to this translation, another translation—the unsettling disruption of localization—was already occurring, taking place in the language of the so-called original. In turn, the (secondary, revealing) translation as the inscription of a determinable location constituted a response to the prior translation, to an indeterminacy that had already translated the reader onto another place, a place which was not one, and that withdrew from localization as it enabled and even provoked the very attempt at localization, at translation. Insofar as the text, its language, is responded to with translation, by way of an attempt at localization and at contextualization that insists on determining "ends," it is already (failing to and) taking place as an event, as the occurrence of a prior translation onto a place that is not one: "our place in al-Andalus."

Against my own prior contextualizing expectations, this event of language that constitutes and responds to the translation that the text already is—the displacement of its place, the withdrawal from localization (literary—as poetry or prose—or other), the declinations of its contexts (in all senses of the phrase: with his own declensions and declinations, for example, Gershom Scholem was declining to attend to anything but a declining context)—is what I turned out to have explored in the texts I had been trying to read. The texts were never representations, never simply effects or even readings of al-Andalus. Rather, the occurrence of their language, its taking place, constituted, if partly, the occurrence of al-Andalus as an event of language, a translation.

Because al-Andalus is not simply a "medieval" object, then, but a powerful modern representation, *"Our Place in al-Andalus"* attends to the conceptions of language that perform and sustain this representation of al-Andalus as a context that has ended. It engages the conception of language that, in my view, dominates the study of al-Andalus (as well as the study of the related field of "Jewish mysticism" and others). This conception considers language to be derivative of its true place, of the context that, having ended, is often silent and lost, and is the occasion of language's occurrence. Gershom Scholem's work (most particularly his writings on Walter Benjamin) offers a striking articulation of this conception of language. Yet, we will see how the intense rhetoric of sadness deployed by Scholem in these texts is only one of many aspects that, providing elements for critique and suggesting alternatives, also illuminate in surprising ways the modern representation of al-Andalus, the mournful operations and affects associated with it, and the reductive conceptions of language that sustain it.

1

Maimonides, *Dalāla*, Midrash

> The *Guide* belongs to a very peculiar literary genre, of which it is the unique specimen.
>
> —Shlomo Pines

> Because there are no fixed points in the Desert, it is not possible to get one's bearings.
>
> —José Faur

> Now incline your ears, and know that praiseworthy poems, delightful riddles, excellent letters, and sharp metaphors possess many paths and many ways in which the "guides of the perplexed, *morei ha-nevukhim*," may go astray.
>
> —Yehuda al-Ḥarizi

Know that if one does not understand the language of a human being whom one hears speaking, one indubitably knows that he speaks, but without knowing what he intends to say. Something of even graver import may occur: sometimes one may hear in someone else's speech words that in the language of the speaker indicate a certain meaning, *tadullu ʿalā maʿnā*, and by accident, *bi-l-ʿaraḍ*, that word indicates, *tadullu*, in the language of the hearer, the contrary of what the speaker intended. Thus the hearer will think that the signification, *dalāla*, that the word has for the speaker is the same as its signification, *dalāla*, for him. For instance [Ar. *maṯal*, Heb. *keʾilu*] if an Arab hears a Hebrew man saying *ʾaba* [Heb. he wishes], the Arab will think that he speaks of an individual who was reluctant with regard to some matter and refused, *ʾabā*, it. . . . This is similar to [Ar. *wa-hakaḏa*, Heb. *ve-khen*] what happens with the multitude with regard to the speech of the prophets, excepting certain portions that they do not understand at all.[1]

Reading Out of Context

For someone who has had to face the difficulties of Maimonides' *Guide of the Perplexed*, even the gloomy reading situation, described in this unsettling passage from the *Guide*, into which one is thrown and to which this chapter is obsessively dedicated, is somehow idealized. Among the towering figures of medieval thought, known as "Rabbi Moses" by Thomas Aquinas, and, according to Jewish tradition, comparable only to Moses himself in his legislating stature, Moses Maimonides (1135–1204 C.E.) writes many an unsettling text. He thus singularly participates in the transformation of the ancient *topics* described by Giorgio Agamben ("In ancient rhetoric, the term *topics* referred to a technique of the originary advent of language; that is, a technique of the 'places' (*topoi*) from which human discourse arises and begins").[2] In a way that is comparable to hearing and reading the speech of another human being and that of the prophets, hearing and reading the speech of the *Guide*, finding or losing oneself at the place of its language, is unsettling in its own manner. It is unsettling because it is both less and more than the (formally, at least) "dialogic" situation described in the *Guide* as occurring between Arab and Jew ("if an Arab hears a Hebrew man . . . "), but also, and more generally, between Aristotelian philosophy and Jewish law, and between text and reader. "Our place" in and of encountering (if it is an encounter) or confronting the *Guide* is, on the one hand, hardly solitary. Yet, Maimonides has a specific way of introducing the chapters of the *Guide*, suggesting early on that each of them is, on the one hand, out of context, disconnected (the obligation to "connect its chapters one with another" is explicitly left to the reader, implying that everything remains out of place, suspended, "prior" to contextualization) and, on the other hand, that everything is at its proper place ("nothing has been mentioned out of its place").[3] Because of this method of composition, which Maimonides explains in the introduction to the *Guide*, and because of the particular setting (or lack thereof) of the text quoted above, "our place" appears never to be "out of its place," and simultaneously seems to have vanished as, and along with, ground, background, or context. This may be why Maimonides' perplexity is related to the desert (perplexity, Ar. *ḥaira*, Heb. *mevukha*, is the situation of the Children of Israel during their wanderings in the desert), and why "our place" is often figured as desert or deserted. More often than not, "our place" when reading the *Guide* occurs, as it does here, as a decontextualized translation of a translation. As we move here between medieval Arabic, Judeo-Arabic, and Hebrew (and modern Hebrew, and English), we are barely given any clues and certainly not enough coordinates. There is too little to provide us with a sense of place, and too much to displace us onto a persistent sense of misunderstanding and abandonment.[4] In many ways, then, reading the *Guide* constitutes the staging and repetition of the accidental, discontinuous, and even paradoxical movement of the *dalāla* in and of the (Arabic and/or Hebrew) word *ʾaba*, between Arab and Jew. This movement is the occurrence of a word, of a language, and it is simultaneously constituted by the eager approach of a wish and the withdrawing reluctance of a refusal.[5] This particular occurrence of language, this text that I have reproduced above, has everything to do with "our place in al-Andalus," and with the place of language in Arab Jewish letters, and it is what I want to explore in this chapter.

Let us consider the accidental movement, and the possibility of accident, *ʿaraḍ*, that Maimonides inscribes here as well as in the opening lines of the *Guide*.[6] It is a possibility that seems, at first, to endanger neither the direction nor the continuity of passage and the transportation between text and addressee, genre and example, and more, the continuity of communication. In spite of the difficulties, then, communication appears to occur. Maimonides' disciple arrives ("When you came to me"), and so do his writings ("your letters and compositions . . . came to me"). And if, for a moment, something seems not quite to reach its goal ("I said however: perhaps his longing is stronger than his grasp"), in the end, there will not have been any problems of communication. But consider that from the beginning of the *Guide*—in the "Epistle Dedicatory" which opens the *Guide* and that I have been quoting in parentheses—by way of its "center" in the passage quoted above, the narrative produced by Maimonides neither leads to, nor ends on, an image of such successful communication. Moreover, what comes under interrogation in that passage is precisely the notion of continuity between two "subjects" (as the unavoidable presupposition of communication) and between two realms (for instance, the example and the general, the figural and the literal, the text and the context, the Arab and the Jew, the original and the translation, the indication and the indicated, etc.). This lack of continuity is underscored, not only by the way Maimonides relates to the tradition (which can hardly be thought of in terms of sheer continuity), but also by the fact that what "mediates" between the alleged poles, here between Arab and Jew, there, between disciple and teacher, what literally "moves" the Arab to read and Maimonides to write, is neither a smooth passage between realms nor the continuity of a presence. Rather, the mediation, if it is one, is the exposure to an absence. Hearing something that has, strictly speaking, not been said, the Arab "responds" with his thought (he thinks about the signification of the word). Similarly, when concluding the narrative of his addressee's education, the story of their communication, Maimonides writes: "your absence moved me, *wa-ḥarakatnī ġaībatuka*, to compose this treatise."[7]

If, then, much like a figure or a translation "which intends to perform a transmitting function," writing here seems to offer itself as a substitute, and therefore as a figure of mediation that would cover the gap of an absence,[8] it is nonetheless the case that, in the few segments of it that I have so far quoted, the text presents itself as a "disjunction," the disrupted and disfiguring effect of an absence (rather than simply, or exclusively, the substitute for a presence), as well as the enactment of an absence that is not simply replaced or covered over. The text thus raises the question, not only of the mediating status of such mediation, but also of the "presence" of two opposed elements or realms between which its language would allegedly mediate. In the words of Jacques Derrida, "Quand le milieu d'une opposition n'est pas le passage d'une médiation, il y a de fortes chances pour que l'opposition ne soit pas pertinente. La conséquence est sans mesure."[9]

Acknowledging at once the dangerous confrontations that isomorphic relationships notoriously invite, I wish to suggest that such an occurrence of language bears analogy with, can be demonstrated as being comparable to, what Derrida calls "the contingent experience of the encounter, *l'expérience aléatoire de la rencontre*."[10] It is an uncertain encounter with, and an uncertain experience of, languages and idioms, riddled and contaminated with multiple possibilities of "accidents."[11] In this case, in or through this experience, the protagonist qua reader more often than not finds him- or herself not only at "our place in al-Andalus"—a place toward which we shall do everything but return in the next chapters—but specifically at the place, the structural position of the "Arab." And this place, which is hardly one, has, as

I will try to show, everything to do with the occurrence of the *Guide*'s language. One not only faces particularly opaque "portions" of a language and of a text, then, but one is also effaced or de–faced, displaced as an understanding listener, and is thus likely among those who "do not understand at all." And while it is not certain that these remarks could apply to the entire text of the *Guide*, even less that they could ever provide a "key" to its interpretation, a return to its meaning, it will become clear how, in the case of the discrete, perhaps marginal, passage quoted above, no contextualization, no introduction, not even Maimonides' (perhaps especially not his), can really guide or facilitate—nor can it, of course, spare one from—an attentive listening to its language, a reading that follows rather than resolves the unsettling movement of the text's language. Even if in a limited and confined way, by staging the occurrence of the *Guide*'s language, the lines of the *Guide* quoted above will therefore prove to be heuristically invaluable, not so much because they will bring us to a new place of knowledge but precisely because they constitute a taking place of the text as un-settling and displacing (cf. the etymological meaning of "trans-lation"). By attending to these lines, what has yet to prove an encounter will both illuminate and undo the place and taking place of the *Guide*'s language. It may, however, also have to unsettle (expectations of) interpretations and localizations such as are now common in the case of the *Guide*.

The text quoted at the opening remains at the center of my concerns throughout this chapter. In it, we are given a few (if contentious) clues as to what occurrence of language, and what relation to the place of language, are to be found in and with the text. These are the clues that seem to me necessary to follow, rather than a larger, contextual frame within which this text could be and has been situated. For it is the very possibility of a relation to the language of the *Guide* that remains, as of yet, suspended; and upon this relation or set of relations, any understanding, contextual or other, of the *Guide*, is dependent. In the words of Werner Hamacher, at this point in the text, "understanding is in want of understanding."[12] This is not a negative or saddening condition, nor is it a situation that can simply be resolved. But it does raise the problem of how to establish a relation between the *Guide*'s language and its place, if we do not consider this language itself as relation and insofar as it itself relates. In that sense, the question of a relation of and to the *Guide*'s language stands prior to (or aside from) the question of interpretation. Interpretation, as "anticipation of sense,"[13] either strives for another place, or assumes understanding, and seeks to reach and return, to determine, the proper place of its occurrence. Such is also true of the disputed question of the genre of the *Guide* (a question that has often paralleled that of Maimonides' identity as a "Jewish philosopher" or what not), part of what Leo Strauss referred to as its "literary character."[14] The question of genre, to which I will turn in more details in the later sections of this chapter, also addresses the question of the place of the *Guide*'s language: into what other group of texts, into what practices of language, does it find or lose its place? And insofar as the difficulty of the *Guide* also resides in its language, it will illuminate the effects and translations of this language on the history of the receptions, as well as the interpretations and identifications of the *Guide* and of Maimonides "himself." But to the extent that such history is also always the history of attempts to answer the question of genre, to determine and to locate the place of the *Guide* (in Maimonides' corpus, or elsewhere, according to precise, philological coordinates), to read it as both defining its own genre and as an example of that genre, it could be said to have already resolved the problem of relating to its language. In contrast, considering these problems of relation and of translation, the occurrence of language as translation, inscribed by Maimonides in the singular passage quoted above, means trans-lating and displacing oneself onto its place, on the side of both question and answer; it is to address and read the problem of access and of translation, the problem of address, of relation, and of destination, and of a passage at "our place."

No doubt, the *Guide*—a text whose explicit, if not sole, purpose (*ġaraḍ*, which also means "genre") is "the science of Law in its true sense, *ᶜilm al-šarīᶜa ᶜalā al-ḥaqīqa*"—*also* sought answers.[15] Hence, it could come to show itself as another imposing figure ("from Moses to Moses, there was none like Moses"), namely a figure of law that towers (if also controversially, as Daniel Silver has documented) not only over the rest of al-Andalus and other Arab Jewish writings, but also over the entirety of "Jewish philosophy" and scholarship to this day (hence Maimonides is considered the most important Jewish thinker and the *Guide* the most significant work of Jewish philosophy ever written). But if the *Guide* is such a figure and is also a translation, then it needs to be read as figure and as translation, indeed, as a complex event of language. In other words, if the passage quoted above, along with an interrogation of the possibility of question and answer, of call and response, also appears to figure a disruption, a disruption of transmission and of history, and if, as the history of its receptions demonstrates, the *Guide* can still be said to figure and translate figures, then it is precisely as such that the *Guide* becomes questionable, worthy of interrogation about the place of its language. Hence, there arises the possibility that the *Guide* also figures and indicates something else, if accidentally, in and as its taking place.

> . . . in the structure of the call we find inscribed the possible intervention of an Other.
>
> —Avital Ronell, *The Telephone Book*

> What translation does . . . is that it implies—in bringing to light what [Walter] Benjamin calls "die Wehen des eigenen"—the suffering of what one thinks of as one's own—the suffering of the original language. We think we are at ease in our own language, we feel a coziness, a familiarity, a shelter in the language we call our own, in which we think we are not alienated. What the translation reveals is that this alienation is at its strongest in our relation to our original language, that the original language within which we are engaged is disarticulated in a way which imposes upon us a particular alienation, a particular suffering.
>
> —Paul de Man, *The Resistance to Theory*

Maimonides, *dalāla*, midrash. Aside from the writer's name, two words have been taken to mark and enable, to figure, the language of the *Guide* as a figural mediation. To be sure, this mediation has been taken as difficult, incomplete, and as producing more perplexity. Yet, this figurative character, and the ensuing notion that what is exclusively at stake here is interpretation—understood here as the passage of and via figurality—has yet to be interrogated. And though it can hardly be doubted that the *Guide* does lead somewhere, that it is implicated in a context that situates it, the language that occurs (only?) in the passage quoted suggests that one needs to engage in a different questioning, namely, a questioning of what Derrida has called the "homogenous space of communication."[16] This is what I try to show, that the space, the place and taking place, the passage of and from language, of and from figurality, of and from exemplarity in the *Guide* as it occurs already in its title, requires such questioning, such reading.[17] This also means raising the question of translation over against, or, more precisely, aside from the question of interpretation, and it has everything to do with reading these two words, these two translations. This is so, not because reading, as it inscribes itself in Maimonides' text, could ever provide (the figure of) an adequate passage, but precisely because reading, as that which addresses the occurrence of language, here raises the question of passage, the question of translation and of the figurative (the "improper" sense) as mediation. Reading (in) Maimonides, raises the question of translation and questions the continuity of its passage, the possibility of access that would be given by a title, or by a translation. Walter Benjamin puts it most succinctly when he writes that "it is plausible that no translation, however good it may be, can have any significance as regards the original."[18] This is not to say that there is no connection between original and translation, but that this connection, this passage, if there is and if it is one, may not be of "significance." Much like Benjamin's translation, Maimonides' opens itself up, therefore, to the "plausible" contingency of not providing, in fact, a connection, a passage—not one, at least, that could be thought of in terms of significance.

Reading translation in this way, then, necessitates an attention to that which (dis)articulates the passage, an "attention to rhetoric or figure" in a sense that would no longer be continuous, and to the "problem of figurative language." It is an "attention to the uncertainly intentional, significative status of the conditions or constituents of meanings—an uncertainty that disturbs the emergence of any recognizable 'face' or figure as the origin or the form" of a work.[19] Incidentally, and insofar as translation is also what "ultimately serves the purpose of expressing the central reciprocal relationship between languages," both translation and the relation to its language articulate precisely what Maimonides' text demands of and teaches its readers.[20] It articulates and teaches the occurrence of language in and as "our place in al-Andalus."

But that all this still needs to be pointed out here and argued means that to attend to the *Guide* in this manner is less about retrieving or redefining its "context," much less its "true intention." It engages rather the unsettling translation (trans-lation) of the *Guide*, and what could be called the interpretations of its translation, either as endeavors that have shown its words as figures, or as interpretations that seek to resolve and arrest figures into meaning (Maimonides, the allegorist). Such interpretations have already located the language of the *Guide* and its Arabic title: *dalālat al-ḥāʾirīn*, as well as the word provisionally translated as "signification" (*dalāla*, from the verb *dalla, yadullu*) inscribed in the text quoted above. *Dalāla* (the word, the title, the book), perhaps a figure, will occupy me as the taking place of translation. It will do so, not so much as a way into the text by way of interpretation—the explanation of the title has already been provided by Maimonides, and, though it seems to have been read quite literally, it already suggests that what is at stake in it is not, or not only, a matter of interpretation.[21] Rather, *dalāla* will provide a set of tracing vectors and indices, indications and demonstrations of the occurrence of its language, its form (and its matter), and its genre—if, in fact, any such thing could be said to be and to be "its" (i.e., the *dalāla*'s) "property." Whether the *dalāla* can be taken as exemplary of an occurrence of language at and as "our place in al-Andalus" is, however, something that cannot yet be fully determined.

Reading the Arab Jew

> Unless being able to read makes the law less accessible still.
> —Jacques Derrida, "Before the Law"

How, then, to read the *dalāla*? How to relate to (its) language and how does this language take place? This is the question that I see the text as addressing, and it is important for what follows to note that it emerges, again, not from the context—not at least insofar as one still thinks of a context as "external" to a text—historical or other, of this text (which has yet to prove readable), but rather, and at least in part, from the question of the addressee in the text: the Arab. The question of the text's audience is the question of the place of its language, and the *legitimacy* of the Arab's answer is raised, understandably enough, by the "law of genre" of the text.[22] It is from his/its language (but which?), inseparable from everything that occupies us here, that many of the concerns that weigh on this study emerge. The Arab, perhaps like the Greeks, who, according to Hegel "only *eavesdrop* on natural objects,"[23] is, in a way, called upon and, in turn, appears obliged to respond by asking (himself?), in order to read the *dalāla*. Yet, "instead of communication, the model might be that of one trying to hear another whose words are not quite audible or contextualizable."[24]

That the Arab also appears as an impossible reader,[25] then, even a reader of the impossible, already provides an illustration of the difficulty of a passage toward that which also indicates and points toward itself, but a "self" that, unlocatable, is not quite an identity (*dalāla*, "our place," reading). It is appropriate, then, if not quite proper, to address both question and answer, and with it the well-recognized difficulties of reading Maimonides' *dalāla*, with a text, not quite a context, and a scene, a staging of reading and its failure, of the taking place of language by and between Arab and Jew.

Consider, then, the importance of a passage in which Maimonides stages reading in terms of a conversation. I write "in terms of" and not "as" because, as with the encounter, some of the problems raised here concern precisely the possibility of asserting whether a conversation actually occurs, whether it is meant to occur.[26] However that may be, it is not insignificant to recall that the possibility of holding a conversation is essential to the course of the *dalāla*, a text that insistently addresses and calls upon its reader as "you."[27] Leo Strauss, undoubtedly the most prominent among modern readers of the *dalāla*, underscores the importance of oral communication for Maimonides.[28] Aside from explicit statements by Maimonides about how conversation is an ideal and exemplary model of communication, Strauss insists that we pay attention to the way in which the text "hints at the essentially oral character of its teaching." In a sense, Strauss further suggests, the *dalāla* may not be a book at all, but a "substitute for conversations or speeches."[29] While this already constitutes a translation of a movement ("your absence moved me") into a substitution, it also suggests a construction of the figural dimension of the *dalāla*. More to the point, for now, it clearly positions the *dalāla* as conversation, as a figure of conversation. Conversation, then, is what Maimonides sees as the most adequate way, as the exemplary way, to teach one how to read.[30]

That the text also comes to teach reading is perhaps too obvious, however. Paradoxically enough, Sara Klein-Braslavy notes that surprisingly little attention has been paid to Maimonides' theory of interpretation, that is, also to the way he *reads* the Bible and rabbinic literature, as opposed to his philosophical, theological doctrines, his so-called "positions." This could already be taken as indicating the complicated movement of the *dalāla*, a movement that stages, or that is followed by, its reading, the movement of a wish approaching and of the withdrawing reluctance of a refusal. This movement, one that exceeds interpretation insofar as it constitutes and enables it, is the occurrence of (the *dalāla*'s) language, and of a relation to it, a movement in which language appears and disappears, showing and withdrawing "itself." By contrast, interpretation would constitute that which counters this double movement by requiring from the text, and/or from what are taken to be its figures, "to produce an identity."[31] Though this may not be avoidable, consequences of interpretation on reading (subsuming one under the other) are momentous, as Avital Ronell shows, most prominently regarding that occurrence in language which she calls "a resistance to signification."[32]

We are only beginning ourselves, and already are faced with such resistance by way of the difficulty of determining precisely whether the passage ends by referring us to an absolute lack of understanding—that is, a situation akin to the one only alluded to at first and where, perhaps, one would not even know that the text "speaks"—or whether, knowing "that there is language" (but which?), one is faced with a lack of relation to, a lack of access toward, that language.[33] What may appear to some, commentators or others, as despairingly clear, is that the scene stages a failure of communication: there is no understanding between Arab and Jew. Yet, even "graver" than the failure of communication (that is, a situation where one knows that one does not have access to the language spoken and does not understand) is what occurs in the case where, not ignorance, but rather the very knowledge of one's *own* language becomes disruptive. Here, one's language disrupts, indeed, worsens and contaminates, communication in such a way that what seems to have occurred is, in fact, the "imparting of information."[34] This situation is graver because presenting itself as a successful communication, it covers the very disruption it articulates. In such a case, one turns around and responds, like the Arab, and assumes—not entirely wrongly, as it were—both a status of addressee, and a knowledge of language, of a particular language. It is precisely this set of assumptions that should cause grave concern. We might say that, here, one already knows (oneself, one's language) too much for one's own good, and the consequences are, in fact, quite extensive.

At the same time, though, we note that it is here language "itself," and its assumed knowledge, that operates in this situation so as to produce a sense of consensus and agreement, even of harmonization.[35] While this already raises the possibility of a relation to language that would not be a "knowing" one, it is with language and, more precisely, with such knowledge that the sense of a binding community of meaning arises: the listener does not so much ascribe an intention to the speaker as much as already appears to know that they have, that they share, the same *dalāla* in common. This figure of a successful communication, which turns out to be precisely its failure, is not simply an effect of a particular language as indication and carrier of meaning, but also engages language—that is, the language of the *dalāla*—as what enables and therefore also disables any encounter, as the condition of possibility and impossibility of an encounter.

Assuming for the moment that we can make "a clear distinction between the place of receiving and emitting,"[36] we are trans-lated, and find ourselves strangely in an Althusserian scene of interpellation, a scene in which it remains unclear who or what is the "good" or "bad" subject.[37] We begin with the speaker: the Hebrew, speaking, I suppose (but Maimonides does not say), in Hebrew, but at any rate "Arab" enough so that he could at least sound, could be situated in (or perhaps torn from?) a frame of reference, a contextual place within which he appears ambiguous enough so as to be understood as or presumed Arabic (and the degree of presumption may or may not be different in each case). This "Hebrew" then addresses or sends a thoroughly decontextualized word to an unspecified listener. The word, or perhaps a rumor ("a kind of assertive rumor that peremptorily answers an inaudible question"),[38] is then received and/or translated, by the Arab. This Arab turns to the word uttered whether he was "in fact" the explicitly addressed audience or, quite possibly—by chance or accident, as it were—simply an inadvertent eavesdropper (but would there be a determinable difference?).[39]

At this point, we have only moved back toward the listener with whom Maimonides had begun. The "Arab" was, after all, introduced first ("if an Arab hears"), and, having received the call, the word and interpellation of the other proceeds to give it a reading, and to consider, perhaps, that communication has occurred. This law-abiding subject then goes on to fall victim to a few "accidents."[40] First, he (mis)perceives the intention of the speaker (as intending/speaking his language). Then, he ascribes the same meaning to the words spoken as to the words heard, assuming in this that he and the speaker share "signification," that they share the *dalāla*.[41] Again, let us keep in mind that we cannot be sure whether the listening audience, the Arab, but also the multitude, perhaps even we, the readers, were in fact even addressed. Nor can it be decided that he, them, "we," were not so addressed. Was an encounter meant to happen? Was the Hebrew calling upon or addressing the Arab? Was the *dalāla* uttered, exclusively uttered, for a Jew, as a "Jewish book written for Jews," as it were?

Were the prophets calling upon or addressing the multitude? Was Maimonides in any way speaking to (us?) readers of his (his?) text? Was that his intention, his "true intention, *kavanah amitit,*" as so many of the modern commentators recurrently put it? With what signification? In what language? Can we presume we know? Can we presume that we were called upon? By whom or what? Should we claim to have such a relationship, such knowledge, given the thematized dangers of relating to language in the mode of knowledge?

Consider that the Hebrew here stands in the position of a text, possibly written in Hebrew script, but "speaking" to us in Arabic and/or Judeo-Arabic.[42] The Hebrew (script) could therefore always be read as Arab(ic), and thus asks the reader to assume knowledge of the Hebrew and his language, but Maimonides does not say which language that is, and so read one must. And the *dalāla* could always be read as either Hebrew and Arabic or both at any given moment. The *dalāla,* in its content and its form, is here therefore already exposed to a multiplied reproduction of the very same problems it both stages and describes, and therefore, restages, and reinscribes.[43] Is an encounter, then, the opening and staging of a relation, what Maimonides describes at all? What kind of relational structure could it be that is already so fraught with possibilities, accidents, doubts, successes, failures, and dangers, so much so that it could go in any number of repetitive and distinct directions, and in which the "sides" that would have to be related are not so easily distinguishable? Is the notion that the text's language stages a relation even relevant? Yet, can such a translation be avoided?

At some level, it would seem plausible to suggest that it is not simply the case, that there is, strictly speaking, no encounter, for the staging that takes place in the text can very well and most plausibly be construed as a situation where one simply overhears someone else and misconstrues the meaning of the words spoken (this would correspond to the view that the *Guide* is a book, then, one that not only limits but even successfully excludes inadequate audiences). No encounter was intended to happen, none was meant to take place, and, true to such intentions, "nothing," in fact, did. Yet, even if such is the case, could the situation here simply be described, negatively, as it were, as a nonevent? Is there not—aside from the obvious narrative construction of the text itself, and even aside from the nonnegligible matter of the words inscribed in the text—a remainder?[44] By chance, accident, or infection, *ʿaraḍ*, something did, after all, reach a, if not its, destination (the fragmented *dalāla*, Maimonides writes, "will reach you, *yaṣiluka*, it will arrive, it will make the connection, wherever you are, *ḥayṯu kunta*").[45] We ("you"? "me"?) have been reading it for some time, some connection—the gesture toward a place that could be "our place"—has been made, even if as the result of unintended eavesdropping.[46]

Most strikingly perhaps, if one assumes that there was, in fact, absolutely no encounter, that no call was made, not to us, what to make of the possibility that such nonencounter is nonetheless said to be "similar to what happens (*yajrī*, what occurs) to the multitude with regard to the speech of the prophets"? Note, however, that "for something to happen does not mean that something occurs within the continuum of time, nor does it imply that something becomes present."[47] Rather, the event, if it is one, is the opening of a certain interruption. And it is the repeated occurrence of such interruption between Hebrew and Arab, the analogy of this perplexing occurrence ("similar to what happens"), that puts the *dalāla* of the Hebrew in the structural position of the law uttered and carried (translated) by the prophets of Israel. Thus, the lawlike dimension of the *dalāla* is made explicit, which is why the stakes are so high regarding its reading, the reading of the law of its genre. It becomes quite crucial, therefore, to attend to what would remain unaccounted for with the dismissal of the situation here described as a nonevent, but which occurs (always? by accident?) when the Arab, and the multitude, begin to read and be read. This remainder is what could be called the encounter in spite of the nonencounter, the relation of a nonrelation, an accidental taking place or event still to be determined and which, for now, we could say to be "figured" here as *maṯal*, the instance, example, parable, or figure, of the encounter with the law (the "speech of the prophets" being a euphemism for Scripture), with and as the *dalāla*, as it occurs for the multitude.

For the *maṯal* invoked by Maimonides does articulate, in its very form and structure, an encounter/nonencounter of its own, the temporality of which is unclear and, as we will see, even contentious. It is a figuration by way of, and that rests on, the instance's own relation to what it exemplifies. More precisely perhaps, the articulation of the example with the exemplified can be taken as another staging of—though by no means identical with—the encounter between caller and called, between reader and text, between law and subject, and between the language of the text and its taking place. This figuration will, therefore, tell us much about a situation in which an Arab is obligated, placed before a call and a law by a "speech," the origin and destination of which are uncertain (Maimonides puts hearing first: "sometimes one may hear"—what? Can hearing already know what it is hearing and about to hear? There remains the unavoidable possibility implicitly raised at first that what is or will have been heard is not necessarily "the language of a human being," that the encounter is with a figure that is not necessarily that of another human: it is with a face that figures language—so much for "subjective" readings of that language).[48] It will also illuminate a situation in which the Arab has already turned and responded to the possibility of being addressed, listening to the Hebrew who could be addressing him (and/or/as a Hebrew) in Arabic. And it will tell us how this situation relates to the reading of the *dalāla.* What is "our place" in this kind of in-stance? What is its relation—assuming it has one—to the lesson Maimonides comes to teach regarding a reading of (the prophets') language?

For Examples

> In other words, it is possible for the divine law—which deals with the perfecting of faith, the providing of true opinions, and the awakening of man to truly know the whole of reality—to be brought by a plagiarizer. Such a situation does not cancel the divine dimension of this law.
>
> —Joel Kraemer, "Sharīᶜa and Nāmūs"

The word here translated as "instance" ("For instance, if an Arab hears a Hebrew man . . . ") and which, although it does not quite seem to come together as a figure, nonetheless articulates the movement of an uncertain figuration, is the Arabic *maṯal* (often used in the plural, *amṯāl*). It translates both "example" and "parable." It does indicate and gesture toward a relation of sameness, yet, as we read, it problematizes this sameness, this passage from like to like. It is also the case that this relation, "the relationship between revealed and concealed can differ from parable to parable."[49] With this inherent ambiguity and difference in sameness, *maṯal* can already be said to mark the place of a difficulty. This is a difficulty that implicates what its relational and referential value is and, more generally, what the narrative's relational and referential value is.[50] The specific moment we are addressing here is articulated in typical rabbinical parabolic form. It is structured like a *mashal*: "*mashal*, *maṯal*, to what is this similar? . . . *kakh*, *hakaḏa*, so it is" (the last part is translated in English as: "this is similar to").[51] But is this the notion of "parable" that Maimonides is working with? As is well known, he himself distinguishes between at least two kinds of parables.[52] The distinction between the two, Maimonides tells us, lies mostly in the necessity of interpreting fully or, alternatively, of refraining from too detailed an interpretation. Is this distinction strictly determinable, however, especially when it comes to figurative narratives such as "parables" that, although famous and prominently figured in accounts of medieval thought, have received surprisingly little attention, namely Maimonides' own parables?[53] There is perhaps more than a matter of lacking the clues to answer categorically and to establish the status of this specific passage. Nor is it enough to recognize with Maimonides that there are two kinds of parables, two "interpretations of interpretation." Rather, and as Samuel Weber has observed, there remains the question of the *relation*, precisely, between these interpretations of interpretation: the question, that is, of "our place," of *maṯal* as the taking place of a relation of language and to language, the "common ground," the in-stance, in which the two interpretations share and upon which they are divided.[54] Let us nonetheless consider the possibility that, with its decontextualized position, the text did provide us with some form of access to this set of questions by way of a strong textual marker, an indication as to how to read, by paralleling the rabbinical, typical structure of a *mashal*.

One could have hoped for a better clue, for it was not long ago that David Stern could still write that "despite all its points of interest, the Rabbinical mashal, like most midrashic forms, has hardly been investigated or discussed in past scholarship."[55] Stern, and others, have done quite extensive work to begin changing this situation. Most particularly, and more directly related to the problem that occupies us here, Daniel Boyarin has addressed precisely the matter of the relation between the *mashal* (as a textual structure, indeed, the "site" of an articulation of *mashal* and *nimshal*, interpreting and interpreted texts) and the text or situation it comes to interpret in terms of the question of reference and exemplarity.[56]

Boyarin shows that in rabbinical parlance the word *mashal*, a cognate of the Arabic *maṯal*, served, as it seems to do in Maimonides' text, as a partial equivalent to the word *dugma.* Like *dugma, mashal* means "example" and it is thus translated as "for instance."

In the Hebrew of the midrash and of the Talmud, the same words mean "example" and "parable." The Rabbis actually use the word "dugma," a normal word for "sample" or "example" as another name for the mashal or midrashic parable, that special kind of exemplary narrative that they deployed as hermeneutic key for the understanding of Torah.[57]

One consequence of this lexical congruence is the profound polysemy of the terms (*dugma, mashal*), what Boyarin describes as "the systemic ambiguity of the operation of the mashal within the hermeneutic practice of midrash" (38) and its "underlying semiotic undecidability" (44).[58] Now, there is no reason to assume that such ambiguity is at work in Maimonides simply by virtue of his place within the rabbinical tradition (a place which, moreover, is more than debatable, as many have argued already shortly after his death).[59] What does apply, however, is that the same questions can be raised about both rabbinical and Maimonidean (at least here) *mashal/maṯal,* if only by virtue of what could be called Maimonides' translation of the *mashal.* In Boyarin's description, the *mashal* is that which, together with the text it comes to interpret and/or illustrate, acquires meaning and significance. The texts "only become meaningful (or their meaning is only understood) when they are shown to be part of a pattern, examples of a class," when they become instances or examples (*mashal*) of a larger class or model (*mashal*) (46). And while Boyarin attributes a lack of meaning, or a certain resistance (in his words, a lack of "transparency"),[60] mostly to the text which the *mashal* comes to interpret, there is reason to believe that the lack of transparency is not simply resolved by the *mashal.*

On one level, Boyarin's own description of the articulation of the two texts problematizes their very distinction. Once there is a *mashal,* in fact, there "are not two narratives [i.e., two texts] . . . but only one" (43), and the presumed "added" story that the *mashal* constitutes "exists only as a shadow double" (ibid.). This double has significance only in relation to a text from which it has become, strictly speaking, hardly distinguishable, raising the question of what was first, the *mashal* or the *nimshal.* Interestingly enough, the question of temporality also articulates the question of occasion: What is the occasion of the *mashal*? Why does it take place? Is it a development that is "internal" to the biblical text, or is it "external" to it? Where does it take place? The opacity of midrashic developments, and what we will see continues to be their controversial status, indicates that all is not resolved, for reasons that, wherever the *mashal* itself originates, are specifically inherent, rather than exterior, to the *mashal* itself. In other words, the lack of transparency cannot be strictly located on either side of the interpreted or interpreting texts, nor can it be reduced to a problem of reception.

Not only is there ambiguity and undecidability (a lack of transparency) in the midrashic interpretation, but along with it is "revealed," and maintained, as it were, an inherent ambiguity and undecidability common to both the biblical and the rabbinical texts, insofar as they are brought together. In the articulation of both—that is in the *mashal* itself as it takes place (the textual structure that includes *mashal* and *nimshal*), in Boyarin's argument—one is exposed to a lack of transparency, an opacity, or, in Ronell's phrase, a "resistance to signification." This is not simply a multiplicity of meanings, but an irreducibility of the text(s) to interpretation. As the text is articulated into an instance of a law of signification (a law that, Boyarin makes clear, is not simply external to its instantiation), it maintains—that is to say, it is and constitutes, at the same time—an unavoidable opacity, a resistance to signification.

This resistance to signification, which also enables (as well as perhaps disables) a becoming meaningful—what Boyarin and others have called "gaps," conceived dynamically—reappears not only in the *dalāla* (to which we are also exposed by way of and in an encounter with, the event of a relation of, difficult texts), but in the very controversy on the *mashal* in which Boyarin's work inscribes itself. For if, as he himself describes, the *mashal* articulates a temporal process through which texts and/or figures become meaningful, through which their meaning comes to be understood, then it is perhaps not surprising that the *mashal* "itself" would not only articulate, but also restage its own articulation in and as (a law of) a genre or class, in critical discourse, in order to become, in turn, meaningful. Restaging the difficulties found in the articulation between *mashal* and *nimshal*, this rearticulation would also take a temporal form, insofar as through it the *mashal* would now acquire an added meaning and itself become meaningful, part of a pattern and member of a class.

It is in fact quite precisely the uncertainty of this relation (that is, the temporal articulation of the *mashal*) that opens one significant site of the controversy. Such articulation is what is at work in the description of the *mashal* as form or genre, and with the distinction in it between "early" and "late," between "unregularized" and "regularized" (44).[61] What this controversy over the rule, the law of the *mashal*'s referentiality (its relation to the text it addresses, and the relation between it and its description) illuminates, therefore, is that the difficulty of classification and of generic description (one may rightly want to say, its contextualization and localization), the opacity or meaninglessness of the *mashal*, remains not only constant (though not static) and irreducible, but is, in fact, constitutive of what the *mashal* is (taken to be). It is a difficulty that occurs quite precisely at the strange temporal moment of articulation, where the referential relation and dimension inscribes itself: the extended (but in which direction?) moment at which the *mashal* refers to the text it addresses or at which the *mashal* itself is made to become both a law and an example, a model and a referent. Strictly speaking, then, the opacity does not precede or follow the text(s); rather, it is the very occurrence of the text in which there is produced the moving frame of an encounter, the becoming of a complex articulating and disarticulating movement—what Boyarin calls the "concretization"—of an *of* in a *mashal* of *mashal*.[62]

Returning to Maimonides' *maṯal*, we can note that as he provides us (us?) with a reading of reading, a *mashal* of *mashal*, Maimonides also produces an instance of a relation to texts—Josef Stern recently wrote that Maimonides "applies the term *parable* (*mathal*, *mashal*) more generally to any text, narrative or not, with multiple levels of external and internal meaning. And not only to texts or discursive speeches"[63]—not so much a continuation, as a repetition, explicitation, and translation of their movement. He addresses this relationship under the figure, if it is one, of an encounter with texts that are themselves, in his claim at least, parabolic, namely Scripture (the "words of the prophets"). But it may be necessary to underscore the way this figuration, this moving set of articulations, appears, here too, to resist signification in its lack of transparency, an opaque remainder of this *mashal* of *mashal*, as a "concretization" of the articulation(s) between its elements. One of these articulations, one site of the resistance of Maimonides' text, occurs at such a moment of "concretization," but because of the way it is staged, it complicates precisely the referential and "contextual" moment, and in the interval, the difficult relation that links the exemplary *maṯal* (Arab and Jew) and the referred reading (multitude and prophets). Maimonides' text, possibly offering itself as a figure of encounter that refers us to reading, also indicates, for us, the interruptions and difficulties of reading-as-encounter, the difficulties of reading the figure of a law of reading, a law that here constitutes the occurrence of its language, its place and taking place. Under the figure, or more precisely, under the *maṯal* of *maṯal*, and of the (failed) encounter, reading, the possibility of a relation to an outside, is indicated, figured, and erased. Like the approach of a wish and the withdrawal of a refusal, language follows the movement of the *dalāla*, it indicates its place only to have it disappear. Language trans-lates, then, it takes place in and as the *dalāla*.

Whether or not there has been an encounter, whether or not the text stages a reading/*maṯal*/dialogue, may still depend, therefore, on how it is encountered, how it is read. As Alfred Ivry puts it in the case of other "examples" invoked by Maimonides, "each example depends upon our understanding of what is entailed by its terms, i.e., by our knowledge of their definition and the function of the substances they represent."[64] This may be an unexpected place to encounter a hermeneutic circle, indeed, for "our place" to be figured as a circle,[65] but one should remember that the text is or stages this circularity precisely in that it articulates a law of reading, an occurrence of language, which may or may not be read but nonetheless obligates its recipient (the Arab) as it takes place, as it is being uttered and inscribed. In other words, this law situates the reader "within" the place of language. At this place, "our place," language and reading do not have so much as they are exposed to a circular structure of response and call. Both remain, therefore, precisely the problem that the text comes to raise and, perhaps, to teach (us?) to read.[66] Still, depending on how we ourselves read, the meaning, even the possibility, of reading and translating will be affected. But the problematic temporality I have alluded to does not allow for either context or reader to be "primary" (consider here Walter Benjamin's famous statement about the "receiver" in "The Task of the Translator"), even if we have seen that it does put this reader under an obligation.

It may be necessary, however, to substantiate this claim (i.e., the non-primacy of reader and context), by considering a certain form of "reader-response theory"—the intense drive to assert the "knowability of the addressee" of the *dalāla*, and to know who the addressee truly is.[67] This is a theory that presumes that the proper encounter will have taken place in its proper place and context and it has asserted itself prominently in the translations of the *dalāla*.

(T)reading the Text at Our Place

> To seek the essence of such changes, as well as the equally constant changes of meaning, in the subjectivity of posterity rather than in the very life of language and its works, would mean—even allowing for the crudest psychologism—to confuse the root cause of a thing with its essence.
>
> —Walter Benjamin, "The Task of the Translator"

It is not difficult to imagine that a reader such as Leo Strauss, for example, would say that the esoteric dimension of the text (its being addressed to a specific and highly contained readership) forbids its direct exposition. No encounter, no simple dialogue can, therefore, take place in a reading of such a text, not, at least, as long as one is not part of the proper community that the text presupposes, those "able to understand by themselves."[68] Marvin Fox would presumably disagree, asserting the communicative dimension of the text and the ensuing possibility, for the larger community of readers to have access to it. In the failure of their own encounter, the dispute between the two readers, the text would emerge once again as a site of perplexity, the taking place of another difficult reading.[69]

One should note that the dispute between Strauss and Fox, between esotericism and exotericism, could obscure what they do share, namely, the notion of a prevailing intent to communicate and to "impart information." That Strauss restricts this communication to a limited group only confirms that for him too Maimonides' translation does "intend to perform a transmitting function."[70] At the very least, Strauss endorses the view that a consideration of Maimonides' work entails what Benjamin calls a "consideration of the receiver" (ibid.). For this reason, the terms in which this is articulated by Strauss, being more extreme (because more limiting) than Fox's exotericism, are most revealing for our purposes. These terms also sustain some of the same presuppositions regarding the "proper addressee" intended by both author and language. Beginning with the assertion that Maimonides is responding to "an urgent necessity of nation-wide bearing,"[71] insisting that he writes with a constant attention to his readership, and underscoring the division of this readership between "the general run of men" and "the small number of people who are able to understand by themselves" (94), Strauss himself trans-lates, and relocates the textual difficulties. He reinscribes them and delivers them to a con-textual "resolution" into and by the hands of the proper reading community. In other words, Strauss figures or translates a textual difficulty into a "social" one. It is not, Strauss implies, that the text and language of the *dalāla* take place in many ways and simply can be read in multiple fashion (Strauss will, at times at least, assert that this is not in fact the case; that the *dalāla* rather actively and successfully prevents a "popular" reading, which is also to say that it enables an "understanding" one);[72] it is rather that there are different kinds of people. Let us note immediately that Strauss is neither "wrong" nor arbitrary here, and that the passage we have been addressing may, to some extent, support this reader-centered interpretation insofar as it, too, emphasizes the position, if we may still use this term, of readers vis-à-vis texts.[73] Were this a necessary reading—one that could anchor the text and resolve its difficulties—rather than a reading that rests on an uninterrogated notion of continuity (a continuity that, to say the least, Maimonides's language problematizes), it would be difficult to argue with Strauss. Yet, since this is not simply the case, we will see that accepting this notion has far-reaching effects on Strauss's reading.

The distinction between "the general run of men" and "the small number of people who are able to understand by themselves" appears, by the end of Strauss's essay, to be a clear and strong distinction, one that supports Strauss's argument for the esoteric dimension, the esoteric literary quality of the *dalāla*. Consider, however, the argument Strauss advances in order to explain the historian's ability nonetheless to understand without presumptuously[74] claiming to be part of that category of people endowed with better reading skills.

> Esotericism, one might say, is based on the assumption that there is a rigid division of mankind into an inspired or intelligent minority and an uninspired or foolish majority. But are there no transitions of various kinds between the two groups? Has not each man been given freedom of will, so that he may become wise or foolish according to his exertions?[75] However important may be the natural faculty of understanding, is not the use of this faculty or, in other words, method, equally important? And method, almost by its very definition, bridges the gulf which separates the two unequal groups. Indeed, the methods of modern historical research, which have proved to be sufficient for the deciphering of hieroglyphs and cuneiforms, ought certainly to be sufficient also for the deciphering of a book such as the *Guide*. (59)

This is where the figuration of a "context" as the social occurs at its strongest, translating and relocating the place of language in some outside, configuring it as a recognizable place in which language serves as no more than the instrument that mediates between social groups. In this figuration, which is nonetheless meant to account for the language (the "literary character") of the *Guide*, the reading of the text becomes not only dependent on but fundamentally determined by conditions that are extraneous to it. Two groups, or communities, the existence of which appears to precede the text, are, if not entirely fixed, nonetheless locatable poles that remain, in spite of the renewed attention to language, the ground and focus of consideration. Further, if they are endowed with a certain flexibility, it is only in order to anchor the possibility of a proper "deciphering," that is, in the end, the adequate reception and understanding of the message sent. For Strauss, then, Maimonides' translation would be intended for its readers. As the determined goal of its guiding intention, they in turn determine the significance of the text. They constitute reading communities that are not, however, hermetically closed to each other, but are located at a distinctive distance from the text that mediates between them. Insofar as this mediation figures an aspect of social relations—if only to resolve them—the construction of what appears as a continuous "bridge" between the groups is therefore important to consider.

There is a transition, for Strauss, or even the possibility of a form of contamination, between the groups he considers. And this very porosity, this mediation, constitutes, in spite of what also appears as an exclusively separating gulf, that which enables the reading of the most secretive of languages. For such language, Strauss tells us, is still "open" to bridging ("method"), to reading, by whatever (member of whatever) group. This method of reading, figured as a deciphering method, is vaguely located by Strauss as neither inside nor outside the text, but it "is" clearly language, and it bridges the "gulf" produced by the language of the text between two communities. Could this method simply and exclusively be located outside of the text, and could this "gulf" simply and exclusively be contained between reading communities? Does not Strauss's argument about the "transition," "bridging," and "deciphering" of the text inscribe the entire landscape of these occurrences as ineluctably linguistic and textual? Do not the very dimensions of the process he describes testify to the way the text "itself" both enables and exceeds (one may want to say, "en-gulfs") both the communities and the reading methods that would allegedly contain it? Strauss's metaphors unsurprisingly appear to inscribe a definite and seemingly unchanging social order, while at the same time figuring the text as the landscape (but this open space is also a "gulf"), which, though divided, does provide the location within which these groups are contained. The text also mediates between social groups, or enables some few individuals to move up the social (and intellectual) ladder. "Winding paths," "precipices," and "depths and caves" figure the sentences of the book as a landscape upon and within which these groups interact (or not). This landscape is traveled by "the leisured and attentive wayfarer" that stands or walks in profound contrast with the "highways, or even motor roads" upon which unnoticing "busy workmen" are "hurrying to their fields" (78). So much for changing the conditions of production and the division of labor on the side of the road. Strauss's own hurried focus away from these paths and caves of language, his trans-lation of the language of the text as leading away from its articulating moments and movements and toward preexisting reading communities, may explain his own use of figural language ("simile" is Strauss's word for *maṯal*).[76] While compellingly reinscribing figurality, Strauss translates this language as less in need of being the object of attentive "leisure" than as something "which may *drive home*"—presumably on highways or even motor roads—or to the fields, closing the gulfs of the "main content" of the *dalāla* for the benefit of "those readers who are more interested in the literary than in the philosophic question" (ibid.; my emphasis).[77]

Again, an explicit recognition that the textual matter is through and through "ambiguous" is at work in Strauss's text. The argument pursued here is therefore hardly to dismiss his interpretation of the *dalāla* as a configuration of opposed meanings between and within which there are found caves and gulfs into which any reader may fall.[78] Yet, the hurried covering of an "inner" distance, while distancing difficulties from the text, the (attempt at) determining the proper place of the text, and the almost exclusive positioning of this place and of its difficulties between reading communities (rather than within them or within the language and the text)—as well as the drive (driving home) to resolve the ambiguities,[79] to cover, or drive away from, the caves and gulfs—although it does open a space of its own between text and reader, ends up effacing the en-gulfing matter of the text, the manner in which, at any given moment, its language articulates and takes place both as wish and refusal (*ʾabā*), as communication and the failure of communication. Strauss's interpretation only figures the hermeneutic circle as a reader's problem (but one "reader" is not reading at all, according to Strauss) in order to configure a path, a method of entry into (but also away from) a text to which he ascribes identity, resolving its figures, and from which he effaces, or rather extracts, the taking place of its language by reading and translating into or under its place, its context.

How could there be any hermetically closed, pure, "secrets" (Strauss's translation for *sirr*, true, or inner meaning) or figures—any texts, for that matter—if the meaning of the very word "secret" and of other words is a matter of contention, if the word itself has no "proper" meaning, as Strauss amply illustrates? More importantly, how can the "sides" (secret/nonsecret, figural/proper, literary/philosophical, understanding/foolish) be so distinctively inscribed if the very inscription they are dependent on is so contentious in the materiality of its language, in its complicated movement? Strauss ascribes to the text a mediating role (a mediation that may also take the form of a lack of mediation when the intention is to conceal meaning), that only supplements a preexisting or anchoring social nature.[80] In this view, the reading of the text, what Walter Benjamin calls its life and afterlife, is reduced to its ("proper") reception, its location and its place as its social existence. But to "translate" in this way the difficulties of the text into a matter of readership or of social constituencies entails a few significant consequences. On the one hand, it reduces or even annuls the distance, even the incommensurability, between the text and any given social order (and it does so by "locating" the text in an outside that remains distinct from it and negatively related to it). And on the other hand, if paradoxically, it maintains a full distinction between textual and social (accidental contamination only occurs between communities, not "in" the text, nor between text and community, assuming, again, that the two would be distinct).

The argument here is therefore not to void the text of all social meaning, nor to argue that texts simply exist "outside" of a context. Rather, it is to interrogate not only the passage (the translation) from inside to outside, but the very terms of that polarity, and to observe that a text cannot only "break with every given context" but can also "engender infinitely new contexts in an absolutely nonsaturable fashion."[81] In that sense, the particular text we are reading can be seen as taking place as a "social" event, as already "having" a social dimension (there is a social scene of reading, one which we are also trying to read), while also exceeding or resisting ("breaking" with) that dimension or meaning, and thus enabling "an effective *intervention* in the constituted historic field,"[82] a field which is also one of nondiscursive forces ("un champ de forces non-discursives").

Yet, the ease with which Maimonides provides for distinct if not necessarily opposed notions of sociality,[83] the ease or difficulty with which his work can be recontextualized, could neither be extracted from nor fully accounted for by the text "itself." This relates, once again, to Benjamin's argument regarding the "plausibility" of the lack of a relation of significance between original and translation. But more importantly, it is the very claim made by Maimonides in the passage we are reading. Hence, the text is both always already social, which is to say that "the theoretical distinction between the social and the linguistic is difficult, if not impossible to sustain,"[84] and, at the same time, it is no longer or not yet social, by virtue of the translation that is the "plausible disjunction," which Maimonides describes as an aural and written "encounter."

The irreducible and difficult movement of the *dalāla* cannot simply and safely be located at some measurable and coverable distance from its linguistic occurrence. Nor can it, in fact, simply and safely be sited at the poles of dichotomies (attentive wayfarer and busy workman, philosophy and faith, theory and politics, reader and text, text and context, etc.), both of which are constituted by and constitutive of its "gulf." The very articulation of the poles, one might say, of the *dalāla* "itself," takes place, therefore, as en-gulfing—"an abyssal dimension that threatens, perhaps even as it makes possible, the constitution of identity"—of text, reader, and path.[85] And it points in too many directions at once. The gulf that separates the figures of Arab Jewish readers, but also of texts and readers, cannot simply be bridged, nor does it simply establish polar and hermetic (or hermeneutic) distinctions between them. Much like the masses in Strauss's reading, and like the Arab reader of and in Maimonides' text, the en-gulfing dimension of the *dalāla* as the taking place of its language, and as the disrupting figure and the figure of disruption, cannot, strictly speaking, be said to have appeared. It could perhaps only be said to have occurred and taken place as what Avital Ronell calls the "phenomenon of [its] own disappearance."[86] The *dalāla* functions as a condition of possibility (and impossibility) of both meaningful sides in their very porosity, and it is this engulfing character that is both figured and effaced, shown and withdrawn in Strauss's text as he attends to the "literary character" of the *dalāla*.

Before arguing that this situation makes more sense than is allowed by both Strauss and Fox (who are here figuratively exemplary: no more, but also no less, than the *amṯāl* of readers of the *dalāla*), beginning with the very title of the text, I want to repeat that their dispute is not simply external to the text (a text which, we have begun to consider, is not identical to itself), but that reading "itself" is here staged in conversational terms, that is, in terms of a nonrelation, in terms of the bridging (of an) en-gulfment. Figures of encounter, *maṯal*, and conversation—the meanings of the latter having been displaced or enlarged onto what occurs in the (non)passage of the *dalāla* I am addressing here—articulate the complex relation, the gulf, that testifies to (signals) and indicates (but also withdraws in and as their constitutive and polar "ends") the figures that stretch across it toward an encounter. "At our place," perhaps "within" the gulf where an encounter may or may not occur, a split figure of Arab Jew, then, is also beginning to disfigure the very splitting of language occurring and failing, its taking place.

Otherwise Than Guidance

> It is a hard saying: for that god "conceals nothing and says nothing, but only indicates," as Heraclitus has said.
>
> —Friedrich Nietzsche, "On the Uses and Disadvantages of History for Life"

The "graver" situation that Maimonides describes ("Something of even graver import may occur") is one in which the problem is not restricted to what happens between two interlocutors (whether or not they are actually addressing each other, something that remains quite obscure in the present case), but extends also to the occurrence within which they "stand," what happens to them in their (non)identity, and to the words "themselves." This is a linguistic event, an occurrence of language, during which the two languages are effectively sundered. The word *ʾaba* or *ʾabā*—which, according to the description that precedes, still qualifies as "one word, *kalima*"—is sundered from its signification, *dalāla*, or, more accurately, signification "itself" is sundered into two *in both languages*. One word is impossibly translated, going in two directions at once, establishing, or rather unsettling and ungrounding (en-gulfing) "our place." An incommensurable difference takes place that is not, strictly speaking, discernible or knowable but that must nonetheless be read. This is also covered over, however, as we saw, since the *dalāla* also marks and affects the very knowledge of one's "own" language. It is that language "itself"—assuming such self-identity is still, was ever, possible—which gets in the way and interferes in the gravest manner, leading one to believe that one knows what one has said, or what one has heard.

Accurately enough, then, Maimonides is right when he implies that "nothing," no knowledge (one may want to say, no signification, no interpretation) is exchanged in the process, since what has been communicated, if at all, is nothing. One does not learn something other (one does not arrive somewhere else), but is rather trans-lated. Nothing went through, no passage nor relation was instituted. This could constitute, in Maimonides' *maṯal*, the possibility of figuration of a circle, indeed, a vicious circle, that remains solipsistically and fully closed upon each or both of its "interlocutors." In this case, all the polar terms we have been addressing would be fully and hermetically maintained. Yet here too we see that this is not simply the case, since translation has occurred. In the occurrence of such "nothing," one's "own" language has been seriously disrupted, traversed, opened to dispute, split.[87] Each language has somehow lost itself in the other, even if it does not appear different—it is the same, one word, just a little different. We are at "our place in al-Andalus," while we do not reside there. This occurrence, which may incidentally summarize both the (de)-constitution and the effects of "our place in al-Andalus" on whatever one considers "Arab" or "Jewish,"[88] and whatever would include—assuming this could be done—our Maimonidean Arab Jewish scene of reading, although its meanings are still in need of much discussion and of much reading, is the taking place of the language of the *dalāla*.

> This indication should not be confused with a statement.
> —Alexander García Düttmann, *Between Cultures*

Such a confusing "state of disruption," as Walter Benjamin called it, constitutes "our place," then, not only that which figures the Arab Jewish text of the *dalāla*, but also the taking place of a splitting, the opening of a place that shows itself and withdraws, an opening that Maimonides "located" in his book and evoked with the notion of perplexity (*ḥaira, mevukha*). Perplexity, precisely the situation of those lost in that place which is not one, the desert, without any or with too many signs and pointers (*ḥaira* at times also translates the Greek *aporia*): "Look how these sons of Israel wander to and fro, *nevokhim hem,* in the countryside, the wilderness has closed in on them."[89] The desert that engulfs by exposing one to too many directions is the very condition that occurs, of all places, in what could be described as the most "locating" moment of Maimonides' book: its title: *Dalālat al-ḥāʾirīn.*[90] It constitutes the figure of a disjunction that also emerges as constitutive of the very notion of signification invoked in the first word of the title: *dalāla.* The double genitive implied by the title as a whole says as much, in which perplexity, the perplexity of the *dalāla* and the *dalāla* of those in perplexity have begun to affect that which it (they?) encounter(s), that with which and as which it takes place.

Dalāla—"commonly translated 'guide,' but actually meaning a gesture pointing to a thing or to a direction: a 'signal,' 'sign-post,' 'indicator,' or 'indication,'"[91] to which we may now here add "sign," "signification," and "demonstration"[92]—is the *dalāla of* the perplexed ones (*The Guide* of ———, *Le guide* de ———), the *dalāla* of those who are perhaps less "in" a "place" of perplexity, than to whom perplexity occurs in and as language, because they have to handle "one" word, two significations, and perhaps more meanings. These are, however, neither fully distinct from, nor simply reducible to, each other. Rather than read the words and parables of the prophets, their *amṯāl, meshalim,* like "an ignorant or heedless individual [who] might think that they possess only an external sense, but no internal one," the perplexed are those to whom language occurs as an unsettling event, in which there are too many signs to follow, and where one does not know whether or not one is addressed by words that have more than one signification, even if there is, as one could perhaps still say, "one" *dalāla,* and "one" *maṯal.*[93] They are those who do not so much know—we have seen the danger of presuming knowledge, especially knowledge of language—but who relate toward language and signification, even as that relation is precisely what has been unsettled, even as the *dalāla* is split, then, and is at least double.

The perplexed ones are those by way of whom it is possible to discern a gesture of and toward a different occurrence of language, a relation that is not one, to language as an un-settling (but not, for all that, negative) taking place. Language as translation. They read and consider some of the times when two becomes almost one (cases where "the internal meaning of the words of the Torah is a pearl whereas the external meaning of all parables is worth nothing, *klum*"),[94] or where two (more or less) meanings of the one *dalāla* remain two (more or less): "Their external meaning contains wisdom that is useful in many respects, among which is the welfare of human societies. . . . Their internal meaning, on the other hand, contains wisdom that is useful for beliefs concerned with the truth as it is" (12). In this double movement of inscription and concealment, even withdrawal into nothingness (*klum*), the *dalāla* articulates, even is, the "phenomena of its disappearance," and it is its movement of en-gulfing opening that becomes constitutive of translating reading, figuratively or not.

Legal Matters

The *maṯal* carried us to the *dalāla*, and the *dalāla* carried us to the *maṯal*. But this double movement cannot simply be described as a question-and-answer conversation, or if it is, "try to remember that the 'answer' to this 'question' would be one that disarticulates such question and answer, such dialogue."[95] This, needless to say, greatly endangers the possibility of recognizing who or what is being questioned, and who or what answers. There are no perplexed ones without the *dalāla*, and we have seen that its language, which may not only be that of a "human being," does not allow primacy to reader, text, or context. Let us approach a temporary conclusion, then, and consider further inter- and dis-connections of the *dalāla*'s translations. We shall remain with the *dalāla* at the origin of its movement, the movement of its origin. This is still "our place," then, though not much of a "context."

Here, too, as was the case with the inevitable surplus and interference of too much knowledge "inherent" in one's own language in the passage quoted earlier, it is a certain excess of knowledge that produces the confusion, the perplexity. Faced with ambiguous words, explains Maimonides, the religious man of sound intellect finds himself in a situation that is structurally identical to that of the Arab hearing the Jew, that is to say that he, the figure that has always been understood as a figure of the "elite" ("those who understand"), finds (or loses) himself in the very position, the place, of the multitude. The perplexed is called twice, it seems, not so much brought elsewhere, perhaps, as unsettled, translated, "the human intellect having drawn him and led him to dwell within its province," and he then hears the Law.[96] He responds to it, considering that he has been addressed by it and feels obligated to it. "He must have felt distressed by the externals of the Law and by the meanings of [its] equivocal, derivative, or amphibolous terms" (ibid.). Such striking parallels between the passage we have been reading—the condition of the Arab and the condition of the perplexed—are only the first sign of a generalization of the "*dalāla* of the perplexed." For this reader is also faced with two incompatible choices and potential conflicts that, although they are presented as potential solutions, now only appear to widen the gulf. Should he "remain in a state of perplexity and confusion as to whether he should follow his intellect, [or should he] *renounce what he knew concerning the terms in question*"? Should he forget that he knows Arabic so as to understand Hebrew? Should he become wary of a knowledge that could lead him to think that he has understood the words uttered? Or should he "hold fast to his understanding of these terms and not let himself be drawn on together with his intellect," refuse translation and remember only the language he already knows (5–6; my emphasis)?

Insofar as he seems fully satisfied with neither possibility, Maimonides could be said to have left us hanging in the suspension of the multidirectional movement of the *dalāla*. Both of these possibilities, Maimonides states clearly, result in a perplexity that frames them neatly ("Hence he would remain in a state of confusion . . . and would not cease to suffer from heartache and great perplexity" [ibid.]). This generalization of perplexity should not go unnoticed, for it inscribes the *dalāla* in and as a space that cannot be contained, or reduced to the options that offer themselves as consequences of perplexity. What the *Guide*, part 2, section 29—which we are still trying to read—has already set in motion, then, is the *dalāla* in perplexity; the *dalāla* as perplexity, the movement of an occurrence of language that (equally?) affects (suspends and decontextualizes) both "the perplexed ones" and the "multitude," whether they "know" it or not. In other words, there would be a perplexity, or more precisely, a *dalāla* of those in a state of perplexity, that would occur "prior" to the specific perplexity experienced by those religious men of sound intellect like Rabbi Joseph and "those like, *amṯāl* [!]" him (4). More precisely, there would be a *dalāla* that is the very occurrence of a language within which "men like these" (but is there anyone else?) read and write.

It is this generalized *dalāla* that makes it possible for the Arab and for the multitude to hear themselves addressed by a language they assume as their "own." It is this *dalāla* that makes it possible for the so-called elite to "encounter" their difficulties and for the speech of the prophets to reach and not reach its destination. Finally, it is this *dalāla* that makes it impossible to separate, strictly and hermetically, one signification from the other, one interpretation from the other, one addressee from the other. Thus the *dalāla* of the perplexed ones reveals, but also conceals, itself to be more and less than one in-stance, one example, and one figure, occurring. It is the language of this *dalāla*—the history, the becoming, of which has yet to be traced and which cannot yet be figured—that constitutes its "own" taking place. This *dalāla*, which is hardly one, then, is the event of a language that enables and disables all indications and translations, including that which has been read as a guiding one, indeed, as the *Guide*. Yet it is also that which enables and disables the establishment, the grounding of any indicative direction or vector that would point in a determined direction, toward a determined place or context. This *dalāla* is therefore both succeeding and failing Maimonides and his readers. Keeping with the metaphor, if it is one, invoked by Maimonides, one may want to say that with and as so many *dalālāt*, the book takes place and, like the desert, commits itself to the abolition of path.[97]

We may wish to escape such difficulties by altogether abandoning the law, model, or example of encounter and dialogue that imposed itself at first as a reading situation, and move on to the next figure, one that articulates light and darkness, instead of Arab and Jew (perplexity and perplexity). I have tried to argue, however, that "our place," the taking place of the *dalāla*, is not only the site of a wish (even if it is a wish to escape), but also that of a refusal and resistance, that it is the moment at which the marked materiality of a figure approached and inscribed itself (Boyarin's "concretization"), and also withdrew and retreated out of reading. To "escape" or "abandon" the peculiar *maṯal* of *maṯal* of the *dalāla* would be likely to repeat, to fall under and translate the movement of the *dalāla*'s "own" retreat. Yet that this would be only part of a more complicated movement is by now quite clear. Moreover, the question of what direction to follow is, of course, the question of the perplexed ones, the question that emerges precisely from the situation that the *dalāla* structures. We can suggest, therefore, that the "answer" would follow the logic of the *dalāla*. This double movement, which a reader could not but repeat, is in the translation and dis-articulation; in what Andrzej Warminski has called "allegories of *of*" (*allégories de de*)—*mashal* of *mashal*, *the* dalāla *of the perplexed*, *the reading of reading*, *an encounter of encounter*, and so on—the peculiarity of what the *dalāla* demonstrates, and which could be read as yet other *amṯāl* (the light of the night, the night of the day, the Arab of the Jew, the Jew of the Arab).

All undercut the exemplarity of dialogue or encounter as translations of reading, most particularly insofar as they are translations that would cover the gulf "connecting," as it were, between the terms the gulf allegedly separates. But before continuing toward yet another *maṯal*—namely Maimonides' midrash—we can note that neither dialogue nor encounter are erased, or entirely withdraw into a simple refusal, as it were. It is difficult to assert that they are exemplary (of what could they be said to be examples?), yet they remain insistently inscribed in their materiality, and still opaque as to their interpretation, resisting signification.

That this resistance is related, if not exclusively, to the very matter of the *dalāla*'s language, to the fact that there is language,[98] to the way in which this language takes place, is strikingly suggested by Josef Stern. We remember that, at the beginning of the text we have been reading, knowing that there is language was said to be distinct from understanding it. It is not impossible, then, that not-understanding, indeed a resistance to understanding and to signification, is constitutive of the language that there is. Stern suggests as much when he writes that, for Maimonides, there is a dimension of words, of language, that "conceals, *maʿalim*," and that functions, in fact, like a "veil."[99] This veil, Stern argues, is the veil of matter described by Maimonides in the *dalāla*: "Matter is a strong veil preventing the apprehension of that which is separate from matter as it truly is."[100] If the *dalāla* is also this veil, it confirms that over against that which "truly is," it is not simply located on another side, in a beyond that would need to be recovered hermeneutically. As thin as a veil that separates and connects, the *dalāla* resists interpretation.

Focusing on Maimonides' discussion of laws, Amos Funkenstein further clarified the question of matter in and of the *dalāla*, bringing us back to the question of the *law* of genre. Funkenstein argues that there is more to matter than a simple exteriority, but rather that it constitutes through and through (and therefore unravels) any "entity" (law, example, figure), as it makes it and prevents it from being "fully" or "truly," as Maimonides puts it, itself determined in its essence ("You should not think that these great secrets are fully and completely known to anyone among us").[101] Funkenstein writes:

> Maimonides developed one of the most original philosophies of science in the Middle Ages. . . . [H]e proved that not only are laws of nature (the ordering structure of nature) in themselves contingent upon God's will; but that each of them

must include, by definition, a residue of contingency, an element of indeterminacy. No law of nature is completely determining, and no natural phenomenon completely determined (*omnimodo determinatum*), not even in God's mind. . . . The purpose can never determine the material actualization in all respects, down to the last particular, a "thoroughgoing determination" is ruled out by the very material structure of the world.[102]

The ruling out of a "thoroughgoing determination" is constitutive of the "very material structure of the world," as well as of the "language of man." That this has been yet another reason for hermeneuts' and commentators' despair is not to be doubted. Yet, the "work" of resistance and its articulation in Maimonides' writing offers itself as a taking place that hardly calls for mourning. The matter of the *dalāla* is not simply some limiting, external garment (although it is often figured as such), nor is it a border that simply encloses that world, that language. Rather, it is the textual occurrence of matter, following the movement of the *dalāla*, approaching and receding, as it also prevents full determination. It is the event of a highly complex (a veil, as Derrida often points out, is woven, like a text) but by no means solely negative or one-sided occurrence of language.

Matter re-lates, and trans-lates, then, (the) *dalāla*. It is the double movement and its suspension that does and undoes the relation, the narrative.[103] And it adds to our account of the added perplexity, the difficulty of a localization and generic classification, the "regularization" of the *dalāla*.[104] Matter itself indicates, *yadullu*, not only a site of the disputes surrounding the *Guide of the Perplexed*, but that very site, the gulf or the "veil" of the *dalāla*, the taking place of language as an exposure to its limit. Matter is not the figure of an outside that would be accessible under different conditions, but another translation of the taking place of a linguistic, figural movement—more, perhaps, than the "substitution" of the *dalāla* alluded to by Strauss. It effaces itself in between, it is a gulf that veils itself as a refusal, yet nonetheless inscribes itself, sustaining and unsettling the very polarities of which it is constitutive. Matter, *dalāla*, trans-lated.

Joel Kraemer has convincingly argued—underscoring that the question is still, and again, if also not exclusively, one of language and of "literary character," the law of the *dalāla*'s genre—that the matter of language (not language as fully determinable entity, then), under the guise of the many Aristotelian discursive modes, is prominent in the *dalāla*.[105] Whether any one of these modes is dominant or not is perhaps determinable, although not fully determinable. This is the *dalāla*'s (and perhaps also Maimonides') success and failure.

In the following sections of this chapter, I wish to take advantage of this difficulty in order to further explore the language and the translation of "our place in al-Andalus" and to continue in the demonstration of comparability "within" this language in terms of its place and its genre ("*Genos* indique donc le lieu," writes Derrida).[106] I want to insist on this difficulty, the difficulty of the "literary character" of the *dalāla*, and to reinscribe a different figurality—the implications of what could anachronistically be called "literature" in the *dalāla*—by raising the possibility of yet another translation—what is, perhaps, no more than a hypothesis, certainly not an attempt at full determination and may even be an error (Maimonides' "own" misreading of the "law of genre"). But insofar as this translation has not entirely refused to offer itself, and has rather begun to manifest itself, it has also inscribed itself with the temporary necessity of a wish. We will address it, therefore, if only in order to consider further the translations of "our place in al-Andalus," and the translation of traditions of "conversations" that may or may not have occurred prior to it. It became relevant under the figure of the *maṯal/mashal*, and it may "be asserted with equal rights," therefore, in comparison with others. Leo Strauss underscored the importance, if not the interruption, of this tradition when he wrote that "Maimonides, while writing the *Guide*, continued the aggadic discussions of the Talmud."[107]

Interrupting Midrash, Poetically

> But whenever we see something wrongly, some injunction as to the primordial "idea" of the phenomenon is revealed along with it.
>
> —Martin Heidegger, *Being and Time*
>
> The activities of thinking were probably profoundly the same as before, but everything had changed. And yet, there had been a non-caesuric change. Nobody could scan the cut because we had experienced an interruption in history altogether different from the ones that had been prescribed.
>
> —Avital Ronell, *Crack Wars*

"It would be no exaggeration," remarks Daniel Boyarin, "to say that Maimonides occupies a place in a specific Jewish literary history and theory analogous to that of Aristotle in the discourse of European literature.

[Maimonides'] reflections on the nature of the Bible and the midrash are the *Poetics* of Judaism."[108] How appropriate, then, that in the translations of the *dalāla* one of its most momentous statements regarding the history of midrash has remained, if sometimes quoted, still very close to unread. To be fair, some kind of reading has been produced by way of translations or even critiques.[109] Hence, it should be clear by now that by "reading" I am alluding to no more, but also no less, than the attention to language that Maimonides' text, the very occurrence of its language, still requires in spite of the extraordinary amount of scholarship on this text. It is, therefore, here too, a matter of addressing the place and taking place of its language. Importantly enough, reading Maimonides' text is beyond the scope of Boyarin's study.[110] Nonetheless, by suggesting that a reading of Maimonides in poetic terms ("Jewish" or other) is yet to come, Boyarin provides us with a rare confirmation that questions about Maimonides' work and its "literary character" are still a worthy endeavor. Most specifically, Boyarin succinctly underscores Maimonides' extraordinary, poetic treatment of midrash—we are still before the law of genre: "Maimonides attempts to establish the genre of midrash" (1). Such an attempt, whether or not it was successful, cannot but situate itself within the history that Boyarin described, a history in which Maimonides—like Aristotle perhaps, and most certainly like medieval Arab philosophers—remains the site of insistently locating interpretations and translations, in spite—in fact, *because*—of a proliferation of readings.

It is plausible to suggest, however, that such a history, such a context, has both begun and has yet to achieve the movement of its appearance, a different modality of its translations. As the following text further suggests, it may also be the case that in order to address the possibility of this history, and most specifically, the way Maimonides translates it, it is necessary for the *dalāla* of the perplexed ones to take place. "Our place in al-Andalus," this unstable occurrence of a place that is not one, the taking place of language that does not necessarily lead one to a new meaning or to a new place of knowledge, implies a relation of and to language in which other linguistic events, namely, midrashic discourses (*derashot*), now have

the status of poetical conceits [Ar. *an-nawādir aš-šiʿrīya*—Munk translates "allégories poétiques"—Heb. *melitzat ha-shir* (Ibn Tibbon), *meshalei ha-shir u-melitzotav* (al-Ḥarizi)];[111] they are not meant to bring out the meaning of the text in question. . . . [They] have the character of poetical conceits whose meaning is not obscure for someone endowed with understanding. At that time this method was generally known and used by everybody, just as the poets use poetical expressions [*al-aqāwīl aš-šiʿrīya*—"locutions poétiques"].[112]

Maimonides' discussion is here, as in much of the *dalāla*, philosophical. More precisely perhaps, its intertext is, to a large extent, philosophical. It is quite important here to emphasize this point, if only to note two things. First, the Aristotelian intertext—an Arab Aristotle, to be sure—regarding the classification of linguistic utterances.[113] Second, the way in which understanding, invoked here as a philosophical requirement, may, in midrash, encounter one of its limits. It is while addressing (the same?) *derashot* that Maimonides writes elsewhere that understanding may, at times, fail us: "Any time an utterance of the Sages appears to us farfetched then we must train ourselves in the disciplines of wisdom until we come to understand the Sages' intent in this utterance of theirs, assuming, that is, that our minds are capable of understanding it."[114] Whether this limitation applies here and whether such limits indicate that a new level of understanding should be sought or that an ultimate, and finite, level has been reached, would require an examination of particular instances of midrashic discourse and of Maimonides' discussion of these instances, as well as a discussion of Maimonides' epistemology.[115] In *Guide*, part 3, section 43, however, it is important to note that "understanding" associates itself with "meaning," whereas the "poetical conceits" are asserted, in a way that has perhaps begun to become familiar, as distinct from, perhaps resistant to, meaning. It is possible, then, that these "conceits" are of an order that is other than understanding, that they partake of a place where understanding would perhaps find a different limit. More importantly for us here, there is an additional dimension at work in our text, a dimension toward which the peculiar intervention of poetry in these lines should provoke careful attention, as should every instance of a philosopher risking an incursion into whatever he deems "literary."

What is extraordinary about Maimonides' words and his conflation of midrash and poetry, is not so much that they invade a realm that strict disciplinary and categorical boundaries may or may not have protected (whether Maimonides is making a "category mistake," in Aristotelian terms, is, therefore, not the important issue here). Neither is the "fact" that he could be wrong or not accurate enough about midrash. Yet the way in which he is taken to be so "wrong" is quite relevant.

Consider, for example, what Isaak Heinemann writes, that Maimonides "does not take sufficiently into consideration the difference between the midrash and stories which are purely fictions."[116] Although we will see that it is not inaccurate to take poetry—in its medieval, Arabic, understanding—as fictional discourse, Heinemann diffuses, or ignores, the historical, poetically, and philosophically precise use of the adjective "poetical." Maimonides, as is known all too well, insisted in an emphatic way on the importance of grasping the preciseness involved in the writing of his words. Simply to equate poetry with fiction would demonstrate, to say the least, a lack of precision and a vagueness difficult to accept in Maimonides' writing. Moreover, assuming that the conflation, the analogy, were to hold, it could not be said to stand without remainder. This is an argument with which we became familiar above. Hence, what is diffused in Heinemann's reading is the other, far more radical and remainder-producing translation of midrash into poetry, not midrash and "creative fiction" or other historically questionable conflations.

In the translation of midrash into poetry, we find, in a historically momentous way, the advent of a significantly new discourse about, a new figuration and translation of, poetry and midrash. Maimonides' translation unsettles both midrash and poetry by demonstrating their comparability.

My suggestion is that if Boyarin's statement about the place of Maimonides in the history of poetics is accepted, it is not so much the context as it is Maimonides' very translation that marks this place itself as an epistemological break. Clearly, this could not be an absolute break ("Nothing is more modern than the idea of the radical break, separating the 'new' decisively from the 'old.'"),[117] but it is nonetheless one that cannot but fundamentally alter the subsequent activity, the subsequent poetics and readings, of any midrashic text. This unsettling consequence, the very taking place of that language, continues to constitute "our place in al-Andalus."

For comparison, one may wish to recall that the only extant book of poetics written by a Hebrew poet and theoretician, Moshe ibn ᶜEzra's *Kitāb al-muḥāḍara wa-l-muḏākara*, worked within a normative definition of poetry that was extremely strict and precise, so much so, in fact, that it did not allow for the inclusion of what otherwise seemed poetical enough in the Hebrew Bible. Poetry, according to Arab (and many other) critics was "metrical rhymed speech expressing a certain meaning."[118] As Raymond

Scheindlin explains, this was a necessary, even if not a sufficient, condition of its being-poetical. Hence, Ibn ᶜEzra was "unable to regard as poetry any literary composition not conforming to the rules of Arabic prosody" (110) and, given the consensus, it is difficult to consider that matters would have been significantly different for Maimonides or for anyone else at the time. Again, as in most medieval poetics, form (meter and rhyme) was not a sufficient condition, but it was a necessary one, in order for a text to be classified as poetical. Even if one allows for the translation to be an assertion about the epistemological status of midrashic discourse, there is still room to wonder how the strict criteria of poetical discourse could have allowed it to be offered by Maimonides within a cultural climate that remains basically the same as that of Ibn ᶜEzra. Something different, indeed, an unsettling rupture, may therefore be seen at work in Maimonides' text and in his translation.

Alexandre Leupin elaborates the familiar notion of epistemological rupture, and points out that even if, and perhaps because, concepts "borrow the same terminological form from one side or another of the rupture, *empruntent la même forme terminologique d'un côté ou de l'autre d'une coupure*," nonetheless, "they designate a different notion, *ils désignent une notion différente*."[119] After what we have read in the previous sections of this chapter, one may also wonder whether this is not, in fact, an accurate, if partial, account of the taking place of the *dalāla*. Be that as it may, the "concept" of midrash has been seriously unsettled from the configuration to which it belonged "prior" to its translation. Midrash has been translated. From the very moment "midrash" is inserted, by Maimonides, into a poetical discourse, it has been thoroughly displaced, decontextualized; it has become the same, yet another "midrash."

Maimonides' translating rupture is decontextualizing on two levels. First, it decontextualizes midrash because it alters its signifying function and situates it within a discursive frame within which "meaning," precisely, is not necessarily any more the primary focus. As Maimonides writes, midrashic texts do not follow hermeneutical modes of readings, they "are not meant to bring out the meaning of the text," and, like the *dalāla*, they may therefore stand aside from hermeneutics. Second, Maimonides' statement decontextualizes poetry, since it addresses it, not as a point of intersection between cognitive and formal elements, as was the case for Aristotle and his medieval commentators, but rather abstracts its particular, poetical, form, and extends its cognitive status to a discourse—namely, midrash—that holds none of the formal elements that make a discourse akin to poetry. From that moment on, midrash and poetry have become comparable, and one can conceivably write poetry without conforming to—though not necessarily independently of—the formal conditions of poetical language. This double movement in which both poetry and midrash show themselves in order to withdraw from the familiar sphere in which they were located, is an unsettling translation in which the place of these "discourses" is no longer the same, neither is it determinably different. Midrash and poetry are not so much somewhere else as much as, like the languages of the *dalāla*, they are both disrupted.

There is another way in which the translation occurs. Maimonides is also translating midrash and poetry, problematizing the distinction between both. As a consequence, therefore, of the break that I am trying to describe, midrash and poetry—which, again, now both mean something remarkably, if not determinably, other—also come to provide, not so much a context for each other as much as they come to appear in the "same" place. As I have already said, they become comparable. In other words, with Maimonides' translation, midrash and poetry take place differently.

As a literary response to the question of what midrash is (but remember what the *dalāla* does to questions and answers, to conversations), Maimonides' "answer" is therefore, if not unequivocal, radically unsettling: midrash is a kind of poetic discourse (and poetry, a kind of midrashic one). The consequences of this answer, assuming it is one, are momentous for a reading of the *dalāla*, especially if we accept part of Strauss's hypothesis regarding the continuation of a discourse of aggadah in the *dalāla*. This discourse is retroactively affected and altered at the same moment, in the same gesture and movement that establishes its "continuity." Since we have, in fact, begun to articulate some of these consequences as they are felt around *dalāla* and *maṯal*, it may be more important at this point to address, if ever so briefly, some of the effects or translations of Maimonides on other, later texts. This is not to reconstruct here some dubious historical continuity, but precisely to follow the breaks of translations and ruptures that have effectively disjointed the tradition. Needless to repeat, such disjointing moments, not their "context," constitute the crux of language and its taking place in and as "our place in al-Andalus."

Translating Midrash, Erroneously

> It is useful to interrogate "improperly" named works: not only does one end up perceiving some kinship between these works and the genre in question, but one also discovers in the "properly" named works, generic properties that one was far from suspecting beforehand.
>
> —Abdelfattah Kilito, *Les Séances*

The Mishnah says: "Shimᶜon [Rabban Gamliel's] son said: all the days of my life, I grew up among the wise, and I found nothing better for the body than silence; not the learning, *midrash*, is the essence, but the deed."[120] Commenting on this passage, Maimonides follows the movement of the rabbinic statement with the analogy it develops between midrash and speech (the latter also implying, as we will soon see, poetry), and he reads this statement as primarily setting up a binary opposition between silence and speech.[121] At first, Maimonides maintains the opposition and concurs, by way of additional rabbinical citations, confirming that silence is, in fact, the higher of the two terms. Soon, however, Maimonides proceeds to complicate the opposition and divides speech into five. With this complication, silence, though for the most part maintained as the worthiest, will begin to place a more differentiated pressure upon speech. Maimonides writes: "And I say that speech is divided according to the requirement of our Torah into five categories: decreed, prohibited, disapproved, suitable (desired), and permitted."[122] This division, although it also includes five categories, appears not to reproduce the discursive classification that Maimonides alluded to in *Guide*, part 3, section 43, and that we considered earlier. Poetry, for example, rather than being one category among others, seems to some extent to transcend or disturb the classification. Neal Kozodoy points out that Maimonides, in fact, "stops to observe a difficulty that may seemingly be posed for this entire scheme by one highly particular form of speech, which is poetry."[123] Rather than simply condemning poetry, Maimonides would argue here that it can belong to any one of the five kinds of speech. Maimonides' position on poetry is still contentious, and resolving it is not my purpose here. What concerns me is, rather, the fact that his discussion, here too, is related to language, to midrash, and to poetry.

As we saw in the Mishnah, Rabbi Shimᶜon invokes midrash as the discourse opposed to deeds, and most importantly, as the structurally parallel term to discourse, as opposed to silence. Midrash, therefore, also serves as the general heading under which language is going to be discussed. The point is not particularly obscure. If a rabbi—for whom midrash is practically a way of life (even if not a practical one)—can posit midrash as the lower term in the binary opposition that links it to silence and to deeds, all the more so with other forms of speech. Confirming that midrash is not just a contingent illustration, we can see, first, that it does more than function—as in the rabbinical statement—qua synecdoche for language. It also appears in Maimonides' text as a recurring element within the fivefold classification that divides language. The question I wish to ask here is parallel to the problem evoked by Kozodoy regarding poetry in Maimonides' classification. Aside from its role as a synecdoche for language, what is the place that midrash holds? Moreover, what does this place tell us about the connection between midrash and poetry?

Midrash clearly does not belong to the second and third category, respectively, "prohibited and cautioned-against" and "disapproved" speech.[124] However, it does participate in, and structure in distinct ways, the other categories. It clearly governs the first category, namely, "the decreed, which is the reading of Torah and learning it and studying its commentary."[125] Maimonides here does not use the term "midrash" explicitly, yet it is quite difficult to imagine that midrash is not what is referred to, even if only partly. Maimonides does add that "there has already been written concerning this learning [of the Torah and its commentary] more than that of which this book could contain even a portion" (ibid.), something that indicates the amount of "learning" involved, and could not but also refer to an extensive part of rabbinical literature. Midrash, however, also appears in the fourth category, the "suitable," even "desired" speech. About this category, Maimonides says that

> if a man were able to speak [this kind of speech] all the days of his life, this would be the desired end, except that he requires with these two things, one that his deeds be fitted to his words . . . and on this matter it is said here, "Not the learning, *midrash*, is the essence, but the deed," . . . And the second thing (which is required) is brevity. (54)

Here reinscribing primacy of a certain kind of language—part of which is clearly the language of midrash itself—over silence, Maimonides further disrupts the binary opposition he had read in Rabbi Shimᶜon's words. He goes back to what seems to be the main dichotomy that Rabbi Shimᶜon had in fact established, and reasserts, if only in passing, that deeds remain superior to words. However, silence does not remain so generally superior, since it is now only opposed to a specific matter. Some words, therefore, can now safely be posited as more worthy than silence. These words are, in fact, fit to be spoken "all the days of [one's] life." Here too, however, midrash functions not only as one of the objects of the classification but also as a synecdoche—a part for a whole. What are those (midrashic and other) words that weigh more than silence? Maimonides describes them as "the praise of rational and ethical virtues . . . , [words that] arouse the soul through sermons and poems, *al-ḫuṭab wa-l-ašᶜār*, and [that] restrain it from (the vices) by the same means" (54; trans. slightly altered).[126] These are not just any words, then, and perhaps not even any midrash. But they do suffice to remind us of, and to reinscribe, in fact, the translation we have read of midrash into poetry (one would perhaps want to say that here is another instance of what is between "midrash and literature").

Something else appears as well, however, and it should not be missed. The two words *ḫuṭab* and *ašᶜār* provide us with a momentous double take on midrash. On the one hand, as I have stated, we have here a repetition, even if a faint one, of the translation of midrash into poetry (not any kind of midrash of course, nor any kind of poetry, but who would not recognize that these too are open to interpretation?). On the other hand, and more importantly here, is that midrash is—among other things—one form of preaching, a form of sermon (*ḫuṭab*). Whether there are grounds for surprise here, or grounds to see any negative valuation associated with this translation, may be left undecided at this point. Understandably enough, one may want to counter the claim made earlier about an epistemological rupture, and assert instead that what is at stake here is a rather banal recognition that the rabbis were also preachers, teaching "the good virtues and removal from base qualities, [what] is called 'the way of the earth, *derekh ereṣ*'" (54). Quite literally what *Tractate Avot* and other rabbinic texts come to teach, "the way of the earth," proper conduct. Yet if things were so simple what would we make of that other, highly publicized instance of translation of midrash into sermons, toward which we will now turn? How would we account for the seriousness with which it has been taken? It is this seriousness that I take as an indicator of Maimonides' impact; an indicator of the continuing, and disjunctive, force of his statement. For it is the added weight of this and similar assertions that reinforces the taking place of language that al-Andalus constitutes, and that I have addressed in these last sections as an epistemological break around the notion of midrash. This is so if only because Maimonides' words prepare the way for subsequent statements that did receive —rightly or wrongly—much more attention from both commentators and scholars. Whether there is anything different in these words than what Maimonides is asserting is, to me, less interesting than the possibility of seeing the latter as a translation of Maimonides' translation.

Romancing Midrash, Forcefully

> No one who has studied the works of Naḥmanides can doubt for one moment that he held Maimonides in very high regard.
>
> —Marvin Fox, "Naḥmanides on the Status of Aggadot"

This translation is a later and famous statement by Moses Naḥmanides, here presenting his own version of the events of the 1263 disputation of Barcelona. Naḥmanides, too, begins with a classification.

> Know that we have three categories of books. The first is the twenty four [books] that are called *Biblia* in vernacular [*la*ᶜ*az*] and all of us believe in it with perfect faith. The second is called Talmud, and it is a commentary of the Torah. For in the Torah there are six hundred thirteen commandments, and there is not one that is not explained in the Talmud. We believe in it with respect to explanation of the commandments. We further have a third book, called Midrash, that is to say *sermones.* [This is] akin to the bishop standing and giving a sermon and one of the auditors finding it favorable and writing it down. This book—he who believes in it, well and good; but he who does not believe in it does no harm. . . . We further call this book Aggadah, that is to say *razionamiento* [*sic*] (stories), things that people tell one another.[127]

The parallels with Maimonides—beginning with the classifying, apodictic tone and concluding with the focus on "conversations"—are quite extensive, and, to a certain extent, even quite obvious. Some of these parallels, however, may have to be emphasized, given that the perspective I am presenting here has, to my knowledge, not been explored.[128] It is important to note that even though Maimonides' categories are, in Naḥmanides' account, reduced to three, they do nonetheless cover the very same range of linguistic artifacts.[129] From the decreed (the "fully believed" Torah), to the suitable ("he who believes in it, well and good"), the prohibited and cautioned-against ("harm" could be done, but not by these three "books"), and down to the attention to literary forms and reception-theory ("perfect faith," "stories that people tell one another"), Naḥmanides thus repeats in very precise terms the originally Islamic classification that we read in Maimonides. More strikingly, perhaps, Naḥmanides' discussion is governed by a term that, even if it does not appear directly in Maimonides, governs all discussions of poetry at the time. Indeed, "belief" is precisely the category that, by separating truth and fiction, also determines a large part of the discourse on poetry in medieval poetics.[130] This determination is negative—but no less potent because of this negativity—and takes the form of an axiomatic principle: "The more deceitful, the better the poem [Ar. *aš'ar aš-ši'r akḏabuhu*, Heb. *meiṭav ha-shir kezavo*]." This is a well-known principle of Arabic and Hebrew poetics, and it is well exposed in Moses Ibn ᶜEzra's own discussion of Aristotelian classifications of linguistic utterances and their relation to truth and fiction.[131]

Be that context as it may, by stating that midrash can be classified on either side of the truth/fiction line, Naḥmanides is intervening in this discourse and concurring with Maimonides' complex categorization of midrash on a level that is not only that of midrash as "sermon" but also on the level of the translation of midrash into poetry as a form of discourse that is not necessarily of the order of truth. As Marvin Fox delicately puts it, Naḥmanides' statement about midrash "indicates an understanding that, in contrast with [the] relation to halakhah [legal discourse], we have here the option, nay, the need, to be selective."[132] This argument, one may recall, is rigorously parallel with the selective judgment Maimonides articulated in relation to poetry, as Neal Kozodoy, James Monroe, and Norman Roth have shown quite convincingly. It is not a matter of endorsing or rejecting poetry (or midrash) *en bloc*, as some have claimed (in medieval and modern times). Rather, one "needs to be selective" and to apply careful criteria in order to establish whether a particular kind of midrash—or of poetry—is desirable, permitted, or disapproved. One could claim that Naḥmanides goes further than Maimonides, that by introducing belief in such an extensive way as the governing term in his categorization, Naḥmanides is opening the door to much more than Maimonides ever could, introducing belief and its suspension as a category in areas that had perhaps not been figured in such terms. However, discussing this opening would take us in directions that cannot be pursued here.

There is no doubt that any discussion of Naḥmanides must address the question of his relationship to Maimonides. Such is the case, however, not only for Naḥmanides but for the whole of Jewish writing "after" Maimonides. The epistemological break that Maimonides' work constitutes was never subject to contention. My suggestion for an "additional" rupture is therefore not an attempt to expand even more the wings of the "Eagle of Córdoba." Rather, and still considering what Benjamin described as the disjunctive dimension of translation, a relation that would not be one of "significance," I want to continue arguing that it is not only in its most explicit achievements that Maimonides' work has effected and affected its translations. The break, and, most importantly, the taking place of a language that fractures and splits the concept of midrash from itself (a consequence that is not independent, of course, of what we saw of the *dalāla*), also breaks from its historical context and demands, therefore, a rethinking of its relation—if a relation it is—to its "context." This is not to say that Maimonides' translations are isolated events that would characterize one individual. On the contrary, the invisibility or, rather, the "phenomena of the disappearance" of the translation of midrash and poetry should lead to a reconsideration of the further unsettling and displacing power of the translations, of the linguistic events we have been reading.

By way of minute in-stances and occurrences of language, we have been led to such a reconsideration of the place and the taking place of the language, of the trans-lations of Maimonides and Naḥmanides, and the different displacements and ruptures they also constitute. These repetitions of an unsettling occurrence of language, contiguous with the double movement of the *dalāla*, cannot, strictly speaking, be described as historical (if only in the sense that they are not and cannot simply be moments within a history that is already known: the history of the Jews, or the history of Jewish poetics, or what have you), rather they *produce or carry, in a double movement, a different taking place and a different history.* This is not a linear history, and it could hardly be phrased in causal, even less in "influential," terms.[133] Rather, these translations open a view into a different notion of history, and a different place of and for language, a place where continuity and discontinuity are refigured, a history in which or with which citations and figures—figures of speech, in particular, which we have seen were at the very center of the break we have tried to describe—have become history-provoking. It is this dimension, this taking place, that Maimonides and Naḥmanides articulate and translate at "our place in al-Andalus." Language takes place in and as al-Andalus, as the double movement of the *dalāla*, as this unsettling dimension of language that is history-provoking even as it is also the "phenomenon of its disappearance."

It does take a peculiar notion of history to argue that one finds not so much *in* history but rather *as* history the traces of a translation, indeed, the very movement and event that the *dalāla* is, that al-Andalus is. To do so suggests that history is, if not an effect, at least part of the "same" gesture and movement I have begun to describe. The problem becomes even more complicated when this history continues to appear (and recede) in additional figurations and disfigurations. What I want to suggest, at this point, is that, at the very least, the taking place of language of and as the *dalāla*, its translations, figural and historical, invites or even requires us to read midrash, poetry, and, indeed, language at "our place in al-Andalus" differently, rhetorically, and patiently, beginning at the moments of its origin; an origin (*Ürsprung*) which, as Walter Benjamin argued, is a tumultuous "crack, *Sprung*."[134] More importantly, we must pay particularly close attention to the taking place of language, to the way it indicates or translates its "own" taking place, the occasion of its occurrence that is less a context than the very event of language taking place. This is even more necessary in the particular instance in which language takes place as "midrash." Such a midrash, namely the *Zohar*, toward which we will eventually turn in the last chapter, was produced, or emerged—but is not locatable—at "our place in al-Andalus," within the unavoidable opening that that origin or crack constitutes. The weight of the complicated co-occurrence of midrash and poetic discourse in this origin does not simply collapse them into one another, as we have seen, nor does it present them as some external "context" from or toward which one should read. Rather, it reinscribes one within the other in terms that are unprecedented, terms that demonstrate their comparability, and which could thus hardly be described by any appeal to "context." The translation of this reinscription, the insistent *comparution* (to use Jean-Luc Nancy's term) of midrash and (and as) sermons, is not simply "later," since it is already the repetition of a possibility that had been opened centuries earlier.[135] But this specific set of textual repetitions and gestures, as the taking place of language, paradoxically unsettles us and trans-lates us onto "our place in al-Andalus"; not so much or not only another scene, then, as much as the disruptive and disrupted moment of its language and translation.

2

"Our Place in al-Andalus, عندنا في الأندلس"

> The parergonal frame detaches itself from two backgrounds, but in relation to each it backs into the other. In relation to the work, which serves as its background, it disappears into the wall and then by degrees into the general text. In relation to the background of the general text, it backs into the work which is set off from the general background. Always a figure against a ground, the *parergon* is nevertheless a form that has traditionally been defined not as setting itself off but as disappearing, sinking in, effacing itself, dissolving just as it expends its greatest energy.
>
> —Jacques Derrida, *The Truth in Painting*

Only the last in a series of "ends" that inform and provide coordinates for the representation of medieval Spain in modern Jewish historical and literary discourses, 1492 illustrates a major mode of appearance of the Iberian peninsula and of its contents. Like earlier "ends" of al-Andalus (Islamic Spain), such historical loci, or, more precisely, framing moments and movements, are constitutive of the peninsula's appearance. This is neither to say that everything has simply ended, that nothing remains, nor that what was has been entirely and purely lost and that it can thus be simply located in an unreachable beyond. Rather, as end, al-Andalus, medieval Spain, appears insofar as it declines and disappears. The end frames and locates al-Andalus ("the old meaning of the word 'end,'" wrote Martin Heidegger, "means the same as place: 'from one end to the other' means from one place to the other").[1] Locating and separating what are assumed to be separate periods or realms, the end is the place and taking place of al-Andalus.

Earlier, in 1090, al-Andalus had already begun its decline. This is one of its many ends, one that occurred when, in the words of Yitzhak Baer, "the foundations of Jewish existence collapsed completely" in the south of the peninsula.[2] The Almoravids—whose army had crossed the Strait of Gibraltar a few years earlier and inflicted a painful defeat upon Alfonso VI of León at the Battle of Zalacca—had "made an end to the small states of Andalusia and to the easygoing and enlightened way of life which prevailed in the courts of their rulers." Although "remnants of most of the Jewish communities, visited by destruction and pillage, did survive . . . many Jewish courtiers of the old regimes were too deeply compromised and were compelled to flee" (60). The life of Moses ibn ᶜEzra, a major Andalusī poet of that time who wrote in both Hebrew and Arabic, illustrates not only the demise of the "courtier-rabbis" described by historians, but also articulates the tropical patterns, the declinations, of the "end." In an often quoted passage, Ibn ᶜEzra responds to the destruction of Granada and of his "native land." He writes:

> I grieved not for the wealth that was plundered, I cared not that it had vanished and gone, I lamented not opulence come to an end, I felt not ill over servants deserting. . . . But the tears flow from my eyes, *aval yizlu ᶜeinay* [lit., but my eyes flow], as I seek to overcome my grief over my loneliness in my native land, *ereṣ moladeti,* without a companion at my side. I am like a resident alien, *ger toshav,* therein, and I see no man about me of my family and kind.[3]

As Ibn ᶜEzra writes, it is the second time over the course of the eleventh century that the Jewish community of the city of Granada has suffered destruction. Rather than putting a temporary end to the Jewish community, however, the destruction is now general; yet, by virtue of its repetitions, the end enacts as well as figures and prefigures, for the historical and belated witness, still other devastations. Everything is again and again severed from its place: wealth is "plundered," it has "vanished and gone," opulence has "come to an end," servants have deserted. The disjunction brought by the events and their repetition is everywhere. Even the poet's eyes appear to desert him, flowing away from him who is separated from all. The poet fails to relate much as he fails to "overcome his grief." He fails to relate to the events as he fails to connect with his loved ones and, ultimately, with the very place in which he resides. Separation and distance constitute his rapport to the land and there are no reasons for him to either leave or stay. Hence, it is "for reasons that are unclear" that Ibn ᶜEzra decides not to depart at this time, whereas, later on, he is "mysteriously compelled to abandon his wife and children" and, this time, to "leave Granada for exile in

Christian Spain."[4] Whether he stays or goes, Ibn ᶜEzra's relations to al-Andalus appear to lack all rationale; they become contingent. And although he notes both loss and devastation, this too is distanced and dismissed as no reason to mourn ("I grieved not for the wealth that was plundered, I cared not that it had vanished and gone, I lamented not opulence come to an end, I felt not ill over servants deserting"). Grief is thus oddly negotiated, both denied and offered as an object of distant, if not impossible, "overcoming." Grief distances and isolates the poet from the place in which he utters his speech, making his relation to place contingent, distancing him from his place, from everything that has vanished, and, apparently, from the vanishing itself. The place, the land, is now distant, and what happens to the poet appears to happen to the land as well. Like everything that has "vanished and gone," yet paradoxically remains devoid of affect ("I grieved not, I cared not"), the poet both remains and leaves, neither remains nor leaves. Following the movement that his words describe, the poet is already distanced and displaced, trans-lated without having "truly" left: he is a "resident alien" in the "native land."[5] No "reason," then, can bind or unbind him and the land. The land itself, or at least all that it contains, ceases from being the place of the poet and of his words, while remaining his "native land." It is a distant and distanced, yet remaining, locus, as well as the declining and vanishing occurrence of a separation: itself a disappearance and a disjunction that, along with what it (no longer) contains, remains the native land. Al-Andalus, this land, appears in this vanishing of itself—and is therefore never, never could have been, quite itself, at its place. It appears to disappear, and it takes place in this particular way in the language of the poet who "saw himself as a true representative of a heritage whose status was declining."[6] The poet and the land decline, then. Neither grieving nor caring, the poet is, like his words, distant: a "resident alien" in his native land, while his words (re)produce the motion of severance, of plunder, disappearance, and vanishing, of and in the land ("the wealth that was plundered . . . vanished and gone . . . come to an end"). Insofar as these words enact and repeat the distancing devastation that befalls the place and its inhabitants, they can be said to articulate a language that points less toward the frame and place of its occurrence—for that place is vanishing—as it points toward itself, toward its articulation. The poet's language, then, would be less a description than a trans-lation, vanishing locus and movement, that occurs not so much, or not only in and to the land, as much as it does, not only to, but as language. By virtue of such a vanishing movement, "language" will, however, be anything but identical to itself.

"عندنا في الأندلس, our place in al-Andalus" cites Maimonides' language. It is an expression used by the Arab Jewish philosopher, apparently to refer to the same place, the same "native land" as Ibn ᶜEzra's, Maimonides' place of origin: the Iberian peninsula. It is a peculiar expression because it occurs even when, as Joshua Blau notes, Maimonides no longer resides in al-Andalus but has moved, in circumstances not unsimilar to those of Ibn ᶜEzra, to Egypt. Blau also explains that the phrase "our place (Ar. *ᶜindanā*)" best translates the French *chez nous.* Understandably, then, the very expression could mislead some readers into thinking that Maimonides is still physically located in al-Andalus at the time he writes at "our place," and that the works of his in which the expression appears are, in fact, written in, and are, indeed, welcoming one into, al-Andalus.[7] In other words, the expression could and in fact has led readers to think that al-Andalus, the geographical and historical entity, is its referent. According to this literal reading, al-Andalus indicates the place and context within which Maimonides' text is taking place. It is the geographical location within which the language of Maimonides can, in turn, be situated. However, that this reading could be, and apparently was, mistaken, begins to indicate the difficulty raised by Maimonides' words. Arguably, such difficulty affects the reading of any deictic ("this," "now," "here," in Hegel's famous examples), any indication in language of the place of language.[8] Yet, in contradistinction to what occurs in the case of most deictics, the expression "our place in al-Andalus" is not abstract. It is rather too detailed and concrete, and it suggests and offers, in this concreteness, the hospitality of a place: such a place, even if not well known, would certainly be available to historical knowledge. Yet, insofar as it fails to make this place available in this manner—because it was not there in the first place—the phrase also suggests that this place appears at the very moment it no longer is. Its concreteness, occurring without its apparent referent, thus recalls Ibn ᶜEzra's language more than his loss, along with his notion of "resident alien." A different reading emerges, then, of the very "place" indicated by Maimonides' expression. In this reading, the phrase "itself," that is, the text written by Maimonides, occurs also where it says it does, namely, at "our place," but in saying so, by locating itself thus, the text disarticulates itself as a distinct relation to place. Not unlike the poet and his words, "resident aliens" in their native land, Maimonides' words do relate (to) their place. However, this place is not the geographical referent that the literal reading takes it to be. Rather, it is the text "itself," neither some sort of immanent completion, nor a locatable inside vis-à-vis some outside ("The recurrent debate opposing intrinsic to extrinsic criticism stands under the aegis of an inside/outside metaphor that is never being seriously questioned," writes Paul de Man).[9] Rather, it is the text as taking place as that which Maimonides writes, Maimonides' language.

In this textual occurrence, the place of the text appears only insofar as, failing to constitute itself, it disappears as context. In other words, the place of the text appears as that which fails to constitute itself as such, and declines, vanishes, and ends, as an "outside" context. Al-Andalus, then, has to be thought not so much, or not only, as a historical and geographical entity, but as the failing and falling event of its language, its declinations, irreducible to ("its") context. If, then, when reading Maimonides and Ibn ᶜEzra, we find ourselves at "our place in al-Andalus," it is because al-Andalus is not merely the distant context that was already in place prior to their writing, but because al-Andalus becomes and also fails to become the context that appears only to disappear: al-Andalus appears and disappears as context. It is the "phenomenon of its disappearance"[10] that appears only insofar as it has already disappeared. It is constituted (and deconstituted) by its very writing, the writing of a text that "is" less, however, as much as it takes place (i.e., also fails to do so) in and as language. "Our place in al-Andalus" thus means that the text takes place as al-Andalus. It means that in this taking place, al-Andalus is inscribed or becomes an event—to be sure, one that has, already and as of yet, hardly any substance—but it is not, or at least not primarily, an event that, external to the text, would provide it with its place. Al-Andalus is the event, the set of events, of its language taking place, a language that indicates and fails to indicate its own taking place, at "our place." It is a language that relates to—or rather trans-lates—place and its place in a singular way, then, and that dis-places expectations of place and of context attributed to this language, to al-Andalus, in the attempt to locate it. And although I hope that this preliminary discussion will soften the dis-placing effects of such language and that it will make "our place" a not too uncomfortable one, it is to this difficult language that I continue to attend in the readings that follow.

My argument is that this contextualization as end—declinations of contexts—has its own history. More precisely, it has its own temporality and movement, a movement of language, and one that fails to become either background or foreground, but constitutively frames—"is" but also "vanishes" (understood as a transitive verb)—al-Andalus. One consequence of this movement is that, rather than seeing context (or history) as the inevitable space within which language would locate itself, I argue that a reading of al-Andalus's texts responds to the specific way in which they are written. This reading occurs as translation: translated into and translating a language that disrupts the possibility of locating it within the coordinates of a preexisting history, cultural situation, or recognizable literary tradition, and of containing it in a particular genre. And note that I write "disrupt," not "abolish."

In this particular case, therefore, the question of reading this language is not that of an alternative between, on the one hand, a "description or explanation that is located at some Archimedean point outside the history I study, . . . some ideal space that transcends the coordinates of gender, ethnicity, class, age, and profession," and, on the other hand, a "history" which, however "thickly" defined or interpreted, remains the only and determining location within which everything else is found.[11] Prior to asserting, therefore, as Stuart Hall does, that "textuality is never enough," it rather seems ever more adequate here to accompany Hall when he asks: "but never enough of what? Never enough for what?"[12] Yet, in spite of his own qualifications and reservations about the issues and insufficiencies of language and of attention to language, and though facing an instance of language the borders and frame of which are hardly secure enough to determine "what" is beyond them, Hall nonetheless reinscribes, if implicitly, not only the traditional question "What is?" but also suggests that what must still and *always* ("textuality is *never* enough") be interrogated is not textuality, not language. Indeed, the assertion that "textuality is never enough" easily enough turns into "enough and away with textuality" even if the borders of that "object" are resisting localization (for if the "what" of that which is not textuality is not determinable, the question of textuality remains; and even more so if textuality, the event of language, is not quite as locatable as al-Andalus appears to be). The pages that follow are therefore less about the general contest of where the "proper" space of inquiry could or should be located. Rather, the *historical* question raised here is one of translation, of how to read when contexts disappear, when the very notion of context becomes itself historical and displaced.

It has become, perhaps, all the more a *historical* question because it already was a "profound" but belated "revolution in historical thought in the sixteenth and seventeenth century" that, Amos Funkenstein describes, provided for "the discovery of history as contextual reasoning." This revolution, however, does not constitute another contextualization. It rather imposes upon us yet another translation in our ways of reading the place of language, for a context—literary, historical, or cultural—would constitute the ground, the place and space, of comparisons, the field within which relations are woven, itself constituted by these relations. A context would not simply be the result but would itself embody "a conception of every historical fact, be it a text, an institution, a monument, or an event, as meaningless in itself unless seen in its original context."[13] "Contexts," then, would establish not only that "facts" are, first of all, "historical facts," they would also confirm the assumption that meaning resides somewhere else. Contexts not only could but would have to be taken for granted, however extensively, in order to generate interpretations. The relation of texts and language (these "meaningless historical facts") to such contexts would be secure enough to enable these comparisons and interpretations. In Edward Said's words, "not the disjunction between a text and its circumstantiality, but rather their necessary interplay," the "field of interaction" that they both constitute is what "generates meaning."[14] That which is external to the texts' language would thus continuously provide the ground, the place, the occasion of their occurrence (Gershom Scholem's work established or, perhaps more adequately, simply reinscribed and reaffirmed, such a theory of language most clearly and most relevantly in Kabbalah studies, as we will see in the next chapter).

However, if al-Andalus, as the place of language, disappears, it also means, as I have said, that it fails to constitute a context: what could be called its "context-function" has therefore to be refigured.[15] In this case, rather than being external to the text, the place of language, and its disappearance as and onto a context remains a function of the text and becomes the very movement that occurs "in" the text. More precisely, the way in which the text takes place must then be shown as disrupting the very distinction of "external" versus "internal." Indeed, if the context can disappear, and if this disappearance does "leave certain aspects intact, . . . this signifies that these aspects can always separate themselves . . . continuing to function in one way or another."[16] This motion of function will have to unsettle the notion of a text as "inside"—another localization that is prevented by a taking place that disrupts localization.

What follows will determine in what way the language of al-Andalus comes to constitute such an event, one that disables as it solicits its reduction to an "outside" or to a context without remaining an inside. Language takes place as a movement that does not relate to a localizable place, but rather unsettles the ground of any localization. Language, then, takes place as translation (in the etymological sense of dis-placement). And al-Andalus, as the taking place of language, constitutes such an event of translation, one that occurs in the texts I address, and it provides, if not the ground, the *dalāla*, the demonstration of their comparability (this phrase was coined by Walter Benjamin, and I will return to it in a moment). Here, language becomes an occurrence, not necessarily a successful one, but, nonetheless, one no longer reducible to a place or context. Language takes place as, rather than in, al-Andalus.

Because al-Andalus is no more, because it has "ended" and nothing remains of it but "itself" as disappearing context (like Ibn ᶜEzra's "native land"), such as could have provided the ground of their commonality, it is not inaccurate to say that the texts I read have nothing in common. Again, though, how do we relate (to) this disappearance of context? What I ask is not whether one could reestablish a common ground, but what to do when the disappearance of al-Andalus as context fails to be exclusively "external" to the texts. This question is also suggested by Maimonides, by the *dalāla*, which brought together the textual categories that interest me here without providing the ground of their commonality (if there ever was any). In the *Guide*, we saw that Maimonides commends his addressee and student for having journeyed from far away in order "to read texts." He then explains his high opinion of his student by referring to what he observed in the student's poems, *ašᶜār*, letters, *rasāʾil*, and compositions in rhymed prose, *maqāmāt*. How are such texts brought together in a text with such philosophical demands as the *Guide*? Is the *dalāla* suggesting that "literature" may function as a (pedagogical) condition of the possibility of philosophy? How are philosophy and midrash, midrash and literature, prose and poetry, brought together? What do these categories consist of, and are they, in fact, carried away and brought together? Are they, or do they become, comparable?

In this chapter, I address the notion of the place of language, the relation between language and its place and context, and the singularity that al-Andalus constitutes as a linguistic event. I learn most, therefore, from readings that "attempt to break out of the simple dichotomy of an immanence and interiority of language/text versus an outside reality that haunts many theories of realism and of language,"[17] and that see in the relative independence of language ("not . . . that everything is language," as Rainer Nägele explains, "but that language extends onto everything")[18] less a predicament than an opportunity to rethink ethics (understood here as the relation or nonrelation to place) and culture. In the next chapter, however, I will engage in more detail the conception of context and language that I have begun to explicate here, and that, in my view and for reasons that can be accounted for rhetorically, dominates the study of al-Andalus (as it dominates the related field of "Jewish mysticism"). This conception considers language to be derivative of its true place, the context that, often silent, is the occasion of language's occurrence. Gershom Scholem's work, most particularly his writings on Walter Benjamin, constitutes a striking articulation of this conception. The final chapter will continue to follow the translating movements of the first by engaging in close, rhetorical readings of two texts at "our place," texts that also raise, in distinct ways, the question of language, the question of its place and taking place.

How does language relate? How does it continue "to function in one way or another"? How does it relate to the place of its occurrence? If language is, and also fails to be, the place of its occurrence, its taking place, how does this affect reading? What kind of events are such texts? And what do we learn about al-Andalus as the taking place of these events? Read together, these chapters constitute a response to these questions, a demonstration of comparability, where literature is in question and where the possibility of comparison appears to be lacking at "our place in al-Andalus."

Declinations of Languages in Letters

> This is what I want to show by deporting you as swiftly as possible to the limits of a basin, a sea, where there arrive for an interminable war the Greek, the Jew, the Arab, the Hispano-Moor. Which I am also (following), by the trace.
>
> —Jacques Derrida, *Glas*

Although, like Ibn ᶜEzra and other Arab Jews, this is not the only language Maimonides knows or practices, he writes "our place in al-Andalus" in a language that—over against that place upon which are inscribed quite a number of historically contentious names (Hispania, al-Andalus, Iberia, Spain, . . .)—has, strictly speaking, no name, no name of its own.[19] Judeo-Arabic, as it is now called, "has no proper name in the different Jewish dialects." Its speakers, however, "are fully conscious of what distinguishes [it] from the neighboring non-Jewish dialects. When this distinctive opposition must manifest itself in the Judeo-Arabic discourse, it translates itself by way of the term 'our Arabic.'"[20] There is perhaps nothing peculiar in that fact, since "Arabic" itself is a plural language within which many idioms, dialects, and languages are called "Arabic." However, the multiglossia of Maimonides' language may have added to the difficulties of considering it as one language. If it is one, it is, in any case, a language that has its singularities, prominent among which is its Hebrew script (the expression "our place in al-Andalus," then, is written as follows: ענדנא פי אל-אנדלס). To be sure, we do not know whether this script was always and continuously used, but it is clear that, in manuscripts, its Hebrew letters are clearly recognizable as being shaped in a manner very close to Arabic letters.[21] This neither adds to nor diminishes the specificity and close relatedness of Judeo-Arabic ("a" language that has many variants) vis-à-vis other Arabic languages or idioms. Yet, what is important to note is that because it has no name of its own—no name that singularizes it as what it is, as the event that it is—that language only indicates its specificity by effacing itself onto indicators of its place of occurrence, as it itself takes place. In both its content and its form, then, in and as the place of its own language, the expression "our place in al-Andalus," although it could always be read as a reference to its geographical context, also suggests that to be at "our place" has less to do with a geographical location and more to do with a linguistic one—conceding for the moment that the two could be strictly distinguished. But if al-Andalus "is" such a linguistic place, the place or taking place of its language, it becomes necessary to ask whether its occurrence as such can be noted, or, more precisely, whether the modes of its occurrence can be read.

On the one hand, then, "our Arabic"—as thoroughly distinct as it is from Arabic (a language that, like the other languages and dialects of al-Andalus, is hardly identical to itself and raises immense problems of classification and localization)[22]—has no name. On the other hand, its name is Arabic. Let the ambivalence of that last phrase maintain itself and consider that the naming of that dialect or language takes place in its being written and spoken. The name is not external to the language but is the language that, in its occurrence, is indicating itself as what it is at the same moment that it does so in "our Arabic." The very writing of "our Arabic" in Hebrew letters is distinctive of this occurrence of Judeo-Arabic but it is not unique to it. Much as Judeo-Arabic reaches a cultural high in the Iberian peninsula, so does *aljamía* (or *aljamiado*). Hence, in spite of the repeated assertion that Arabic was not known in medieval Castile, it should be noted that much as in the case of Judeo-Arabic, there developed in the Iberian peninsula "a new Arabized Spanish . . . the literary language of the Muslims; specialists generally refer to it now as *aljamía.* One of the features of *aljamía* is usually that it is written in the Arabic alphabet."[23] *Aljamía* shares with Judeo-Arabic a problem of naming, for whereas it now serves in scholarly discourse as a name for the Arabized Spanish that was used by Muslims and Mozarabs in the Iberian peninsula, it appears to have also meant simply Spanish in the language of its users.[24] This suggests that, in the manner of Judeo-Arabic, speakers of *aljamía* were referring to it by "our Spanish."

A language that indicates that its place is not simply to be found in another place, in a context that is external to it, would have to defy any container, including itself. If it is not to be found in one place but is, rather, its own taking place, it cannot be anchored in any easy way. To some extent, one could say that this is the very condition of language, which many critics have described as a modern predicament. Yet, not only is the burden still ahead of demonstrating that such would already be the case in this way in the language of the texts I am addressing, the very notion of a language taking place "outside" of any fully determinable context (that is to say, taking place not simply or not only in a place that is external to it) is a notion that implies that this language occurs in a singular way—as Derrida says, it continues to function in one way or another—which then needs to be explored in its specificity. Moreover, if the place of language that indicates itself is tenuous to the extreme, effacing itself and even disappearing under the expected concreteness of a geographical, historical, and cultural context, such as it seems to do in Maimonides' expression, it requires a reading that attends to it so as to address its occurrence in and as language.

The texts written in the twelfth and thirteenth centuries, "our place in al-Andalus," could always have been said no longer to "reside" in al-Andalus, to be "resident aliens" in their native land. As their context, al-Andalus is close to disappearing, or has already done so. But my argument is that they relate (to) al-Andalus as an occurrence of language. And in their relation of that "place" of their own occurrence, and to the occurrence of language and its place and taking place, they have yet to be read together. What I want to show in my readings is that the singularity of such an event or set of events of language constitutes and deconstitutes al-Andalus, and continues to do so even where unexpected. Again, in this event, al-Andalus is less a geographical location (although it is also that), and more the linguistic occurrence of and as that event. Here, language does not, or does not primarily or exclusively, refer to an outside (geographical, historical, or other), but articulates rather a more complex relation to its place, to itself as its taking place and as the location of its own occurrence. The readings of the texts that I propose set as their task to describe the structure taken by this event or set of events, and to explicate the relations within this structure. Extending a reading that attends to such events and texts written in Arabic (Ibn al-Aštarkūwī's *Al-Maqāmāt al-Luzūmīya*), Judeo-Arabic (Maimonides' *Guide of the Perplexed*), Aramaic and Hebrew (the *Zohar*), Hebrew and most or all of the above (al-Ḥarizi's *Taḥkemoni*, but also that other Andalusī linguistic event that the *muwaššaḥa* is),[25] it becomes possible to address the singular, yet plural, event that al-Andalus constitutes without collapsing it or even reducing it to its geographical, historical, social, or cultural dimensions. It also becomes possible to consider that al-Andalus is and testifies to the unsettling of place, of locations and borders (national, ethnic, cultural, historical, disciplinary, generic, etc.) that are commonly ascribed to it when viewing it from the perspective of such "dimensions."

If, as in the case of "our place in al-Andalus," the language of these texts becomes its own taking place, showing itself and its place also in its disappearance as and onto the very location of its occurrence, then the question of this occurrence's limits becomes highly important but also particularly difficult to determine. As complicated as it is to locate "our place" outside of Maimonides' language, it is even more complicated to understand its language, or simply to read it. As a result, and remarkably so, what surrounds al-Andalus and its language is most precisely and most recurrently an attempt to locate it in the most determinate way, an attempt to assess its location, its limits, origins, and ends, both temporal and geographical. This is one of the reasons why al-Andalus keeps "ending," as we have begun to see. One prominent and, for what follows, guiding example of such a stringent localization coagulates around the second holy book of the Jewish tradition, namely, the *Zohar*.[26] Here, al-Andalus has not only disappeared from all relevance, the text itself is assigned to a particular place and context ("Christian Spain," the Jewish tradition, "mysticism") without taking into account the way its language may oppose such gesture. As the occasion of a discourse of localization and contextualization, the language of "Jewish mysticism," which follows and translates the difficult taking place of the *Zohar*'s language, provides an important moment against which the language that takes place as al-Andalus may be illuminated.[27] We will return shortly to the general drive to localize, to contain, and to assert the "end," the telos and ends of, al-Andalus in some of its most visible forms. It is sufficient to note that the specificity of language at "our place in al-Andalus" can also be addressed, because of the way it takes place and is put into place, by reading the language of its ends. For now, the question of the place and the taking place of language as it is raised about the *Zohar* deserves a separate discussion, toward which I now turn.

The Place of the *Zohar*

> By the end of the thirteenth century, the condition of Spanish Jewry was on the decline.
>
> —Daniel Matt, *Zohar: The Book of Enlightenment*
>
> In a way, *ein-sof* displaces all levels by one square, including nothingness, which will be thus humiliated in its claim to be the very first. There is truly no first, says *ein-sof*.
>
> —Charles Mopsik, "Notes complémentaires"

Kabbalah studies is, of course, not the only discourse within which the question of language and its context, of language and its taking place, emerges as being of particular interest. Yet insofar as the *Zohar* guides many of my readings, and insofar as the matter of al-Andalus has begun to be raised in it (albeit translated as the recurring question of the—historical or "mystical"—"origins" of the Kabbalah), Kabbalah studies articulates something of a privileged site. Recent discussions within it, moreover, suggest that questions of place, of the place of language and its taking place regarding the *Zohar*, are, in fact, worth pursuing.[28] The work of Gershom Scholem, and its particular relation to place, to the exposure that a taking place of language constitutes—or rather (de)constitutes, as Philippe Lacoue-Labarthe puts it—will occupy us later on in more detail, but for now, it should suffice to mention that Scholem underscored what he called the kabbalists' "superabundantly positive delineation of language."[29] That such positivity has become, by now, a common place, may not only suggest that it has been too quickly and uncritically accepted, it may also and paradoxically have led discussions away from the question of language and of its taking place.

This is not said in order to cancel or diminish the importance of the illuminating insights at work in the discussions that take language as their topic. Rather, it is said to acknowledge, first, that the two disciplines (namely history and comparative religion) that still govern the modern study of the *Zohar*, the central textual corpus of Kabbalah have, indeed, positioned the matter of language as being central, and continue to do so.[30] But, second, that the character of the ensuing attention to language—for the most part, a philological and hermeneutical attention—necessary as it remains, has been insufficient. In order to substantiate this perhaps polemical assertion, I want to address here zoharic texts that are, in singular ways, no more than decontextualized "words" (although such status itself is not unproblematic, as we will see). With these "words," then—namely *ein-sof*, *zohar*, and *peshat*—and with their ensuing translations by modern scholars, I wish to indicate in a preliminary way the urgency of the specific questioning I am trying to engage.

Here, translation (reading out of context) continues to illustrate the modes of diverse and specific events of language that take place in and as these words, in and as translations at "our place in al-Andalus." I take the works of Charles Mopsik, Yehuda Liebes, and Elliot Wolfson on these words as essential translations, then, crucial indicators of the unavoidable difficulties of reading "our place," not so much, or not only, out of context, as in the very taking place of the text, the very event of its language. Such translations, themselves unavoidable, provide a temporary point of departure as well as an illustration of the difficulty of distinguishing between them and any alleged "original." It is therefore also toward these translations that I turn here and in the other chapters, in my readings of al-Andalus and of the taking place of language it (de)constitutes.

In his discussion and explanation of the complex zoharic notion of *ein-sof*, Charles Mopsik makes two distinct assertions.[31] On the one hand, "*Ein-sof* stands elsewhere than in discourse and each element of discourse designates it, *En-Sof se tient ailleurs que dans le discours et chaque élément du discours le désigne,*" (520), and, on the other hand, "it is, in language, the sign of what exceeds it, and it is this only, *il est, dans le langage, le signe de ce qui l'excède, et seulement cela*" (521). As a result of the limited amount of instances in which the *Zohar* mentions *ein-sof,* the very place of *ein-sof* is, therefore, and from the very start, contentious. In a way, Mopsik, like his "theme," must be read out of context, if only for lack of context. But even if we were to fully clarify the distinction between language and discourse, Mopsik's oscillation as to the "place" of *ein-sof* in or out of language would nonetheless suggest that we should give greater weight to the second assertion, insofar as it is because of its place in the language of the *Zohar,* and thus in language, that the difficulty arises. *Ein-sof* re-lates to and in language: Even in the first assertion, *ein-sof* "stands, *se tient*" elsewhere, but it is also "designated" which implies that it is also, in whatever mode of signification (*ein-sof* is, after all, *un signe*), "in" language, precisely what the second assertion makes clear.

Rather than pursuing further the intricacies of this textual difficulty, and to address the way the text's own language produces it, Mopsik—who rightly criticizes those scholars' permanently seeking the "essence cachée" behind the texts (522)—surprisingly maintains Scholem's inscription of a "silent voice" at the heart of Judaism (more on this in the next chapter) and reads this silent voice as *ein-sof,* as the obscure center out of which language emerges.[32] Mospik locates *ein-sof* (and what he elsewhere calls *le principe ineffable*) at the origin of a process of emanation, the coming into being of language that parallels the coming into being of the divinity and of the world.[33] He thus distances *ein-sof* from considerations of language by locating it before and outside of language. Thus, Mopsik "translates" the *Zohar*'s statements about *ein-sof,* statements that merely assert its unknowability and concealment, into statements about ineffability.

In order to assess the weight of this translation, it becomes important to note that all the citations brought by Mopsik that refer to the unsayable are, in fact, Neoplatonic sources, not zoharic ones.[34] But why is the concealment, the difficult place, of *ein-sof* that which makes it "close to the notion of the Unspeakable in Damascios, *proche de la notion de l'Indicible chez Damascios*" (525)? And how do we read this closeness? At what place? This is not simply to invoke the proverbial garrulity of a text that would affirm that which cannot be said, but to note that its assertions not only say the word *ein-sof,* they also refer to it quite explicitly as a *name* by which different dimensions of the divinity are called.[35] Clearly, the linguistic dimension of *ein-sof* cannot be said to be of the order of communicative language (the zoharic insistence on its concealment and secrecy makes this clear enough).[36] Yet, this neither amounts simply to ineffability nor does it exclusively situate *ein-sof* outside and at the external source of language. To paraphrase Walter Benjamin, given that language is far from being exclusively human for the *Zohar,* even if humans could not say the name *ein-sof,* this inability would hardly make it ineffable (similarly, that the angels do not know God's place, *meqomo,* does not mean that God has no place, nor that God's place is not a place, even if of a distinct kind). Rather, the *Zohar* may suggest that *ein-sof* demands what Benjamin calls a "reading of what has never been written," and that it belongs, therefore, to the "language of names" or "pure language."[37]

Mopsik does provide us, in fact, with fundamental elements that prove valuable in order to read after Benjamin and to rethink the taking place of language that occurs in the *Zohar.* It may already be worth considering here a description provided by Giorgio Agamben, whose work I address below, a description that provides an account of changing conceptions of "nothing," such as they emerged around the ninth century C.E. Agamben writes that

> nothing is a sort of limiting dimension within language and signification. It is the point at which language ceases to signify the *res,* without, however, becoming a simple thing among others, because as pure name and pure voice, it now simply indicates itself. Inasmuch as it opens a dimension where language exists but signified things do not, the field of meaning of nothing appears close to that of the shifters that indicate the very taking place of language, the instance of discourse, independently of what is said.[38]

That both "nothing" and "shifters" determine the taking place of language in the *Zohar* hardly needs to be pointed out. The development of a long tradition of reading deictics and the translation of this tradition in the *Zohar* has been followed, in fact, most closely and convincingly by Betty Rojtman[39] (note that Rojtman also argues that the register of signification as it is transformed in the *Zohar* is "radically cut off from the context of the utterance or act of utterance, *radicalement coupé du contexte d'énoncé ou d'énonciation*").[40] But the question is whether *ein-sof*—which rightly appears, as we will see, as a kind of place—can be situated as an origin that would precede language, that would in fact be external to language. In that case, the coming to be of language would perhaps have to be rethought in terms of a coming into sense of language, indeed, as what Jean-Luc Nancy refers to as *la venue au sens.* We will see that Mopsik's own descriptions, yet prior to his translation into ineffability, already suggest that *ein-sof* functions as a limit "at which language ceases to signify the *res,* without, however, becoming a simple thing among others, because as pure name and pure voice, it now simply indicates itself."

It is one of Mopsik's most important contributions to the reading of the *Zohar* that he not only begins a rethinking of the notion of *ein-sof,* but also links this notion to the distinct relation to materiality and sexuality that operates in the *Zohar.* Mopsik writes that *ein-sof* is not only a limit of thought, but that, in the *Zohar,* this limit is also the occasion for an opening of "a path toward a mode of relation to things of the senses, to matter, a mode of relation that no longer implies resentment toward matter, *un chemin pour un mode de rapport aux choses sensibles, à la matière, qui n'implique plus de ressentiment à son égard.*"[41] This opening or path, which the *Zohar* explicitly designates as a "place" or as having a place (*atar de-ein sof, Zohar* I: 16b, 21b; and see how *ein-sof* is often referred to as by way of spatial attributes, situated, for example, "above," *le^cela*), is however not to be thought of as a simple or static position. As Mopsik argues, "the negative particle *ein* does not negate a quality, but, quite precisely, a localization, *la négation* en, *en hébreu, ne prive pas d'une qualité, mais très précisément d'une localisation*" (526). What is made clear, then, is that the interrogation of the notion of place is fundamental to the writing of the *Zohar,* and to the zoharic reflections on *ein-sof.* The function of *ein-sof,* in the *Zohar*'s "own" project for a translation, implies a necessity for a rethinking and a rereading of the taking place of language "in" it. Accordingly, Mopsik offers a radical translation: "rigorously understood, *ein-sof* could be translated as: there is no position of the end, *rigoureusement entendu,* en-sof *pourrait être traduit par: il n'y a pas de position de la fin*" (ibid.). *Ein-sof* would therefore be that place which is not one, a place that, for the *Zohar,* radically undoes (Mopsik here writes *déplace*) any possibility of writing of inside or outside, early and late, and so on.

Strictly speaking, then, both assertions of Mopsik with which we began could be said to be true and not contradictory. This is so because *ein-sof* appears to be the place of language and its occurrence ("something unexpected occurs that is called *ein-sof, il se passe quelque chose d'inattendu qui s'appelle En-Sof*" [537]), an event of and in constant displacement that occurs, *se passe,* and, moreover, astonishes and surprises. *Ein-sof* is a place, then, insofar as it "stands elsewhere than in discourse and each element of discourse designates it" (520), but, on the other hand, it cannot strictly speaking be distinguished from language, insofar as "it is, in language, the sign of what exceeds it, and only that" (521). If it could admit the possibility of property and propriety, *ein-sof* would more "appropriately" be described as an event, and as the "taking place" not so much of language "itself"—since *ein-sof* displaces the possibility of speaking of language "itself"—as much as of sense "in" language.

Hence, it is not language that comes to be, but *ein-sof* as language is also the taking place of language and the coming to sense (the "bringing of language to language") of language. Insofar as *ein-sof* is the taking place of language, it is also its trans-lation, and, as Mopsik strikingly puts it, a *déposition* ("le *En-Sof* dé-pose le désir" [526]), a *dé-saisissement* (ibid.), an exposure of thought (and of language) to its limit, the opening of a different kind of relation of and to language, but also a relation as language. It cannot be situated, not simply because it is a distinct taking place, but also because its temporality prevents it from being seen as simply early or late, as prior or posterior.

Mopsik beautifully explicates the intricacies of such temporality when he describes how the zoharic "one" (to be distinguished from the Neoplatonic "One") is both hidden and the event of a work of unification ("the one occurs by way of a work of unification, *l'un advient par une œuvre d'unification*" [531]). Given that the biblical text begins with the Hebrew letter "Beth" (the numerical value of which is two; it is also the second letter of the Hebrew alphabet), it posits two, rather than one, at its origin. Mopsik writes: "since the primary position belongs to the two, it designates the very fact that the one is not here. The one is therefore what the two, as initial position, forces to unveil, *la première position revenant au deux, elle désigne par là même que l'un n'est pas là. L'un est donc ce que le deux, comme position initiale, force à dévoiler*" (ibid.). However, "its unveiling [i.e., the unveiling of the 'one'] will be nothing else than the command to make that which is two into one, in other words, to uni-fy. . . . After the one is made, it will still not be, but immediately exposed to the risk of undoing itself, it calls upon us from the depth of its retreat, without coming out of it, *son dévoilement ne pourra . . . être rien d'autre que l'exigence, le commandement de faire un ce qui est deux, autrement dit d'uni-fier. . . . [U]ne fois l'un fait, il ne sera toujours pas, mais aussitôt exposé au risque de se défaire, il nous enjoint du fond de sa retraite d'où il ne sort pas*" (ibid.). "One," therefore, *is* not, though it can be said, retrospectively, to have been hidden. But it "is" so hidden without denying to the two its initial position (but both of these terms—initial, position—have already been suspended), while still robbing it of its primacy. "The one in retreat is an impossibility from the point of view of logic that endlessly demands a primary position for the one, *L'un retiré est une impossibilité du point de vue de la logique qui réclame sans cesse pour l'un la première position*" (ibid.).

What Mopsik makes very clear, then, is that it is precisely a thinking of positions that is de-posed by the zoharic language. So much so, that any position, any "one" is thus de-posed, revealed, and made as something else than what it is, only in a concealment that "is" not. Needless to say, this initial position that Mopsik elsewhere also ascribes to the "silent voice" (that is, the "voice that keeps silent, that stands silent")[42] cannot be maintained as having the status of an origin nor that of an ineffable outside of language. For it is precisely origin and place that are thereby de-posed.

Whereas Mopsik goes on to find, in this relation of de-position, the mark of a different attitude toward the materiality of sexuality (the "two" seems to always appear as a heterosexual couple and it is this sexuality that would be celebrated by the *Zohar* at micro- and macrocosmic levels—but there is room to question the exclusivity of the heterosexual dominant as well, as Elliot Wolfson has now convincingly shown), I merely want to point out that what has been called the "materiality of language" deserves, as a consequence, no less consideration.[43] This means continuing to read the taking place of language that can be discerned as occurring here without diminishing other dimensions, but, most importantly, also without reducing language to these dimensions, without reducing language to something else, even to itself.

Note, however, that there is no need to distinguish hermetically between the materiality of sex and the materiality of language. But it may be that, as I have already suggested, the construction of ineffability (which may be the minimal and necessary requirement for the text to "graduate" to the class of "mystical texts") functions so as to push language aside (this, of course, was always possible—declinations of contexts—since neither language, nor anything else for that matter, could claim any primacy). Hence, when Mopsik—whose work has also been instrumental in establishing the importance of performative and theurgic dimensions of language in Kabbalah—comes to discuss a zoharic interpretation of the utterance of the prayer Shemaᶜ ("Hear! O Israel"), he focuses entirely on the process of unification that is enacted in it insofar as it occurs between man and wife, not in the words of the prayer "itself." Again, it is clearly not that the significance of the language of prayer is lost on Mopsik, but, I suggest, that the role, or more precisely, the event, of language becomes somehow secondary and even more derivative in his notion of materiality.

Having earlier collapsed *ein-sof* with ineffability, Mopsik here collapses prayer onto its sole "intention," in order to translate the words (prayer as action) onto intending, acting, sexual bodies. As he showed earlier, however, it is not simply the intention (*kavanah*) in the sexual act, but indeed, also the materiality of this act that produces the unification toward which the *Zohar* strives. Mopsik had elsewhere written, if ambiguously, that

> body and soul . . . play the same part, to the extent that it is in the matter of engendered bodies that the "dazzling light" of the divinity is supposed to encrust itself . . . thanks to the movement of the thought of the parents at the moment of their union. As if this thought alone had the power to produce the incarnation—let us risk this word overly laden with implied meanings—of the divine in the midst of procreated bodies.

> le corps et l'esprit . . . jouent la même partie au point que c'est dans la matière des corps engendrés qu'est censée s'incruster la lumière éclatante de la Divinité . . . grâce au mouvement de la pensée des parents au moment de leur union. Comme si cette pensée avait à elle seule la force de faire s'incarner—risquons ce mot trop riche de sous-entendus—le divin au sein des corps procréés.[44]

Clearly, intentions (whatever is meant by that other contentious word in the *Zohar*) are important, but not only are they not exclusively so, they are never sufficient (in spite of the possibility of locating power exclusively in them). The entire thrust of Mopsik's argument (and of others with him) has been precisely to show that the embodiment (what Mopsik hesitantly calls here "incarnation" and elsewhere *engendrement*) of these intentions is, in a way, primary (although recall the logic of the "one" above).[45]

But what, then, of the "incarnation" of language? What of the linguistic dimension—not as a metaphor or sign for sexuality or for anything else, for that matter (that would hardly qualify as more "material," given that language—although not communicative language—is the very "stuff" of creation)—but as a distinct, if not quite stable, dimension? What of the distinct and multiple dimensions of unification (*unifiée sans être uniformée*), a unification which is not simply achieved but rather takes place (*advient*)?[46] "To make the one, to uni-fy does not mean . . . to posit the one at the end of the path, *Faire l'un, uni-fier, ne signifie pas . . . poser l'un en fin de parcours,*" (538), nor does it imply, therefore, that the modes of materiality here at work should collapse onto one. Mopsik makes clear that nothing "about" *ein-sof* could simply be translated into an "idea" that would then resemble a Kantian ideal; it is rather the very idea of an end and of means to that end that becomes, and is thus displaced as, such an untenable ideal ("En-Sof, 'sans fin', indique que l'idée de la fin du parcours n'est qu'une idée" [ibid.]).

Not only sex (which includes, but is not restricted to, procreation), then, but language as well, taking place, here begins to echo with what Giorgio Agamben calls "means without ends" (more on this below). Needless to say, the taking place of the text of the *Zohar*, articulated as it is as a walking upon roads and pathways (elsewhere briefly noted by Mopsik as the "essential difference" between rabbinic and zoharic texts), will therefore require an attentive reading.[47]

> The world of the Kabbalists is the world of the mouth and of speech; there is none above it.
>
> —Yehuda Liebes, "Zohar and Eros"

By highlighting in turn the word (if it is one) *zohar*, Yehuda Liebes follows a direction not unsimilar to that of Mopsik and orients us as well toward sexuality as the prominent realm within which the zoharic writings need to be rethought and reread. Although Liebes also makes clear that the different dimensions of unification are intricately connected, it is important to note that the taking place of language, the relation of the text to text, to textuality, and to language—which seemed at first to be Liebes's primary interest (Liebes goes so far as to describe parts of the *Zohar* as a kind of *ars poetica* [78])—later recedes and declines, and becomes derivative of the primary, founding dimension (Heb. *ᶜiqar*, a word that appears repeatedly in Liebes's text), namely: sex; or—in Liebes's constant translation effort (mostly into Greek)—*eros.* So it is that the *Zohar* is translated, or, more adequately perhaps, rebaptized as "The Book of Eros" (70, 99). Liebes does not so much minimize the linguistic, literary dimension of the text,[48] as ascribe to sex a primacy that is at times so great that language cannot but be diminished and reduced.

To be sure, the materiality of sex, affirmed throughout and constituting the material relation to the text (both in its "creation"—to use Liebes's word—and in its reading), does become deflected when this sexuality runs the risk of being understood too literally. Yet sexuality, even in its diminished or "sublimated" version, does remain one step removed from language as it continues to determine, rather than be linked to, the textual practice. What seemed at first to have been as material (as sexual) as other sexual practices, namely writing and reading, is presented as a "sublimation" and, instead of "sex," we are referred not to poetics anymore but to "eros in the wider sense, *eros be-muvano ha-raḥav*" (104). Though there are additional reasons for this "sublimation" to occur in Liebes's text, reasons that hardly suffice to consider that gesture "deliberate" or even intentional, it is notable that, in his text, even the issue of "comparative literature" seems to hang on the possibility of showing that the "force" of love governs the *Zohar* much as it dominates Plato's *Symposium*. Hence, if the word *zohar* indicates, or even is, not only a recurring word (75), but also a central notion (*ᶜinyan* [68]), and, finally, the very book called *Zohar* (85), it is striking to consider that *zohar* is also represented by Liebes as the motivating force that is both behind and within the writing.

Hence, *zohar* is the "soul of the *Zohar*" (68), it is that which "gives its name to the book" (ibid.), it is said to be at work "in both" human and divine creators, *bi-shnehem* (73). It is the "prophetic inspiration, *hashraᵓa*" (74), and "the force of creation, *koaḥ ha-yetsira*, [that] throbs in the soul of the creator and gives him life" (75). In short, if *zohar* is the very word (*ha-milah*) that, inscribed in the text, marks, like a beating heart, a rhythm that "returns and strikes like a call or proclamation" (Liebes also associates *zohar* with music and melody), it is also the origin of the *Zohar*, that which "arouses and encourages the interpreter" (ibid.), the writer, and "creator, *yotser*." But in that construction, rather than addressing language and sex in their *com-parution* (which neither means that they are identical, nor that they are absolutely distinct, of course), the place of "eros" (if not always sex—in the "narrow" sense) is constituted as that of a determining "force" from which all other dimensions would be derivative. To that extent, it may be plausible to suggest that it is not so much the materiality of sex that Liebes advances, as much as what he himself calls its "mythological" dimension, a dimension that, however vague, appears as neither simply bodily nor as simply transcendent.

Consider, however, that much as in Mopsik's discussion of *ein-sof*, there seems to be an ineluctable difficulty in Liebes's text, in localizing *zohar* as either "behind" or "within." Insofar as *zohar* is also the book "itself," neither the word nor the book can ever be entirely dissociable from each other (my own rather conventional use of upper-case *Zohar* versus lower-case *zohar* for clarification is absent from Hebrew, and from Liebes's text as well). Yet, beginning to address this difficulty as the occurrence of a distinct and specific event of language does require that we refrain from collapsing the materiality of sex onto the materiality of language, and that we consider the latter neither as absolutely distinct from, nor simply as a "sublimation" of, the former—however "powerful" in Liebes's terms. Once we do so, *zohar* (and its language of names) becomes the event of its "own" taking place,[49] something that, as Liebes writes, can hardly be defined (70), but which remains the world and the word of the *Zohar*, the world of (its) language (it is the "world of the mouth and of speech" [71], but also the "written Torah" [85]).

In other words, what one finds when reading *Zohar* is not so much that language substitutes for sex; rather, and as Elliot Wolfson puts it, "what one finds is nothing other than the *peshat*, i.e., the text as it is"—the text as such, utterly unidentical to itself, but unalterable and irreparable.[50]

In much of his work, Elliot Wolfson uniquely turns the discussion of sexuality to its textual, linguistic dimensions, reading the former (in contradistinction from Liebes) as derivative of, or as equivalent to, the latter.[51] This turn allows far more complex readings, but it is a turn that, it should be noted, is not simply the gesture of Wolfson's writing. This linguistic turn is rather the very movement that, followed by few readers, had earlier suggested the word "incarnation" to Mopsik, the coming to being refigured as a coming to sense, at which there is always already language (albeit not necessarily a language of communication, neither the communication of meaning nor the communication of force as theurgical activity).

Wolfson follows a distinct direction in this figural movement, further showing the difficulty of localization that we have already encountered.

His argument is thus quite important (and, along with Rojtman, quite uncommon, in Kabbalah studies) toward our understanding of the place and taking place of language in the *Zohar*, since it affirms not only "the precedence that the *Zohar* gives to the graphic over the phonetic,"[52] but also that "in zoharic literature engraving letters, or more generally the process of inscription, is a decidedly erotic activity" (68). And although this suggests that "eroticism" may, in fact, be prior to writing, Wolfson makes clear that the two are either co-constitutive or that they are equally derivative.[53] Wolfson writes, for example, that "the play of sexuality is the most appropriate . . . expression to convey something of the nature of the infinite Godhead in the first phases of creativity" (69).

Pursuing his attention to zoharic language, in "Beautiful Maiden Without Eyes" Wolfson turns to hermeneutics. Against the dominant view of zoharic hermeneutics as a multiplicity of expandable layers or shells that may be disregarded in order to reach the core (the "nut"), he argues that the governing metaphor is not the nut, but the garment or veil. Hence, although he does not "deny that in some of the most important statements in zoharic literature" there is a "hierarchical view" of interpretation (168), one which the image of the nut strongly suggests, Wolfson does go on to argue that this is so only "from the perspective of . . . the uninitiated or unenlightened" (169). Rather than discard the various "shells" of textuality, then, one should develop a different mode of vision and see "the inner light (the esoteric matter) shine through the external shell (the literal sense) of the text" (ibid.).[54] In other words, what Wolfson explains is that the place one reaches "at the end" of the reading process is not fundamentally different from (although it is hardly identical to) the one from which one began. This would already tend to confirm Mopsik's translation of *ein-sof*, "there is no position, no place, of the end," as "situating" (if one could still use this word) the event of zoharic language, or, more precisely, as "being" the taking place of zoharic language. Moreover, Wolfson's remark affirms the necessity of preserving, indeed, of relating positively toward the (textual) veil itself as that which not only conceals but also reveals: "the secret is hidden from everyone by the garment but it is only from within the garment that the secret is revealed to the wise" (ibid.).

But a difficulty that is by now familiar arises again, putting into question the possibility of speaking of "the veil itself," as if it was identical to itself. For what is the "place" that this veil constitutes, and what is the place of the reader "in" it? Note that the phrase "from within" equally suggests that one is behind the veil (within the enclosure it protects and/or facing the veil since the veil hides "from everyone"), but also that one is within the veil itself—a "position" that is perhaps made only slightly more imaginable if the veil is multilayered. At the very end of his essay, Wolfson makes the difficulty of "position" quite explicit when he writes that "the wise one will see the inner light *in and through* the very garment that at the same time conceals it from the purview of everyone else" (190; my emphasis). And a few pages earlier, he writes that the *peshat* "is not a shell that is to be broken or a garment to be discarded, but rather a veil to be penetrated so that through it one can behold the mystical insight—in the words of the *Zohar*, to see the secret matter from within its garment" (18).

One would expect that after a penetration of the kind here described, there would hardly be any veil left—or perhaps that enough of it would be left behind—so that there would no longer be any need to still gaze through it. We then find ourselves once again oscillating between an inside and an outside of and in the text, both of which suggest that the (impossible?) (dis)placements we have already encountered continue to disturb the possibility of ever finding oneself "in" the *Zohar*, or in any one place. Indeed, any such place turns out never to be quite identical to itself. These displacements, I suggest, have inscribed themselves, translated themselves, onto the texts of the readers of the *Zohar*, they have taken place in their own texts.

If such is the case, however, it may well be that Liebes is correct when he criticizes Wolfson for ascribing too much passivity to a text that would have only to be penetrated and formed by its interpreter, and for not sufficiently considering the active dimension of the "letter" of the text.[55] Yet it also appears that the dis-placing taking place of the *Zohar*'s language can be read, if only translated, within Liebes's own text as well as within the text of the *Zohar*'s other readers. In that case, the distance, in fact, the very distinction between text and reader, may not be as determined or determinable as both Liebes and Wolfson seem to see it. For if the readers cannot quite decide which side of the veil they find themselves on or "in" (and again note that there would be three sides to this fourfold interpretation: in front, behind, within), it is because these readers are already caught within the movement of trans-lation that the text "is."

This condition does not necessarily suggest that one should attempt to provide more precise coordinates for the text, more of a context to situate it. Rather, it suggests the importance of reading the text as an event, as the taking place of language, a reading that would take seriously, not only the text "itself," but also the way in which it has withdrawn from localization in some of its most important aspects in the occurrence of its translations and its readings. We "are" still at (though we do not exactly "return" to) "our place in al-Andalus."

The Place of Language

> The modern idea of a *lived reality* that the poet must express in his poetry . . . is born precisely from this misunderstanding of the troubadour (and later *stilnovo*) experience of the *razo.* (The equivocation that persists in assigning a biographical experience to the dimension of the *razo* is so old that it already forms the basis of the first attempts at explaining Provençal lyrics).
>
> —Giorgio Agamben, *Language and Death*

A language that occurs as its own taking place rather than in a definable place would then have to articulate a frustrating limitation to its reading, insofar as it would have to displace and upset precisely the setting of limits that understanding is—but reading is, as we saw, never simply about understanding. Paradoxically, such language would likely provoke and even justify attempts to set limits to it, but it would not be contained more successfully for these attempts. It would necessitate something else than an interpretative gesture that seeks to understand by locating. Again, there is nothing particular in the gesture and attempt to set limits, definitions, and containments. Here too, what needs to be shown is the specific way in which such an attempt functions, the way it reveals itself as a particular occurrence, a particular instance of language.

This is why a reading of the language of and as al-Andalus must address itself precisely to such instances (literally, in-stance, standing in and at a particular place, taking place) where it has become so uncontainable as to altogether disappear from view. Whether they are separated by definitions of genre or metagenre (philosophy, Kabbalah, literature, *adab*), or by definitions of place (Muslim Spain, Christian Spain), and by borders of time (before or after the Almoravides, before or after the Christian conquests), the texts I am attending to in this book are, as I have said, so far apart that they cannot be said to share a place, much less a common ground. This is a question of comparative literature, then: these texts have nothing, almost nothing, in common and they have not been studied together. The task I have set myself, however, is neither to put them in the same place and to show them as one, nor to engage in the classifications and comparisons that have already been more than entertained: between "mysticisms" or "religions," "cultures" and/or "literatures." Rather it is, as Walter Benjamin puts it, to "demonstrate that the texts are comparable."[56] The comparison itself may have to wait, but what I show (and what, one would think, would need to be shown), is what Benjamin came to call the "relatedness of two languages, apart from historical considerations," apart from context.[57]

This relatedness is not to be found "in the similarity between works of literature or words" (13/E74), but in "the mode of intention, *die Art des Meinens*" of language, the way in which language indicates. Having problematized the relation between original and translation, between language and context, Benjamin turns then, with this expression, to the relation of reference ("The words *Brot* and *pain* 'intend' the same object, *ist das Gemeinte zwar dasselbe*, but the modes of this intention are not the same" [14/E74]). Benjamin insists that, in order for this relation and for the relation between languages to be explored, the mode of intention, the way language relates, must be distinguished from the referent, from the intended object (ibid.; note however that, as Christopher Fynsk emphasizes, Benjamin doesn't use the word "object": "there is no 'object' expressed").[58] The prerequisites for a demonstration of comparability do not involve denying that there is a context, or a referent, but suggest rather that one addresses a dimension of language in which "meaning is never found in relative independence . . . Rather it is in a constant state of flux" (14/E74). Such a constant state of flux, the specificity of which needs to be exposed and addressed in each case, is what I take to be the occurrence of language in the texts I read, its taking place at "our place in al-Andalus." It is a state that inscribes the historicity of language but does not reduce it to a history that would determine and locate language in its context. In other words, in these texts, language has a history and a movement of its own and it becomes comparable to "itself" insofar as it takes place, not independently, but as that which entertains a singular relation to place and to its place.

Yet the way in which this language locates itself disturbs the very possibility of locating it in a preexisting context. It indicates that it is "itself" its own, incommensurable (because uncontainable) place, the event of its taking place. Moreover, and not surprisingly in the light of Benjamin's words, I read the way in which the unsettling dimension of this language occurs in translation, this "somewhat provisional way of coming to terms with the foreignness of all languages" (E75). Such un-settling, trans-lating dimension of language is its occurrence, the event of a provisional stay in the hospitality of "our place," while not residing there. It is a different negotiation of grief, a place which is not a "common place," and it articulates itself, after Maimonides, as the taking place of language at "our place in al-Andalus."

What, however, is meant by the place and taking place of language? Giorgio Agamben's work provides the terms that inform much of the preceding (and following) discussion. It is from his work that I borrow the notions of the place and taking place of language as they facilitate an important clarification regarding what displacing occurrences are that take place in and as al-Andalus. Agamben describes a movement that "transports the object not toward another thing or another place, but toward its own taking place."[59]

Agamben argues, moreover, that a hiatus in history (mostly the history of the West, but a West that already begins to look considerably different from what it is usually taken to be) enables the question of language and of its place to be asked. Agamben writes that, whereas at that time "the ancient topics—inasmuch as it was especially concerned with the orator and his constant need for arguments at his disposition—eventually eroded into a mnemonic device, conceiving of the 'places' as mnemonic images"; and whereas, therefore, "the *inventio* of classical rhetoric presupposed the event of language as always already completed," there also occurred a renewal of the rhetorical tradition. It was a renewal that brought about a different understanding of *topics* and rather conceived of "its duty as the construction of a place for language."[60] Rather than "recall arguments already in use by a *topos*," and thus to situate language in a place (*topos*)—even a linguistic one—considered to have already been existing, the texts articulate a new desire, or the re-articulation of an ancient one: the "wish to experience the *topos* of all *topoi*, that is the very taking place of language as originary *argument*, from which only arguments in the sense of classical rhetoric may derive" (68).[61] This different experience is an undergoing of language in its relation, one in which language relates and takes place differently. Here, language finds its very place, and occurs as its place. Rather than relating and referring to an elsewhere, an other place and a geographical location within which it could be located, there emerged therefore a "duty" to address and read language not as self-sufficient, but as its own taking place.

Beginning with his work in *Stanzas*, Agamben makes clear that more than an Arabic "legacy" constitutes the twelfth and thirteenth centuries in the western Mediterranean. He implicitly interrogates the representation of Arabic culture as little more than an empty passage—a translation too but as a passing on and away—between ancient Greece and Europe. By affirming the events of language of the period, Agamben also participates, in his own way, in a celebration of the other ninety-two, not 1492 this time, but 92 A.H. (= 711 C.E.; Ṭāriq ibn Ziyād's crossing of the strait that will be named after him, "Jebel Ṭāriq," Gibraltar). He illuminates to a great extent that which can still be called "our place in al-Andalus," even if one no longer resides in it. In al-Andalus, then, as Agamben reads it, the place of language is rephrased, which argument constitutes. Language occurs differently and would have thus generated an experience that went beyond the classical *inventio* that only built on preexisting *topoi.*

What kind of a place, of a new place, does argument now come to constitute? It is important to note what the term *argument* means in order to address this question. "The term *argumentum* derives from the very theme *argu*, found in *argentum* and signifying 'splendor, clarity.' *To argue* signified originally, 'to make shine, to clarify, to open a passage for light.' In this sense, the argument is the illuminating event of language, its taking place."[62] Following Agamben, the meaning of the word *argument* could thus recall the occurrence of that other, "splendor, *zohar*" and "shining light, *zohar*," and lead to a reconsideration of the occurrence of language. Language itself comes to be experienced as love and illumination.

Agamben explains elsewhere that the theory of the poetic sign held by the medieval poets is also their theory of love. "By conceiving of poetry as the dictation of inspiring love," the poets were able to abolish—to come close to abolishing—the fracture between "corporeal and incorporeal, sensible signifier and rational signification."[63] In the poetic word the separation between loving the image (the phantasm) of the loved one and the corporeal figure of the loved one is, in a way, overcome. "Poetry is then properly *joi d'amor* because it is the *stantia* (chamber) in which the beatitude of love is celebrated" (128). The text, the poem, indeed, the *stanza* (strophe, but also room, which Agamben reads as a translation of the Arabic *bait* [130n9]), becomes the site of language, and language becomes its own—though again, not identical to itself and to this "own"—taking place.

This suggests that a fundamentally positive relation of and to language is at work, one that does not reduce language to its (external) place by seeking to locate it, nor one that considers language only insofar as it refers to such a place.[64] Agamben raises doubts as to whether this is actually the case at this time, whether such positivity can be asserted without qualifications. He observes that "this experience of the taking place of language as love necessarily included a negativity that the most radical troubadours—following contemporary theological speculations on the concept of *nihil*—did not hesitate to conceive of in terms of nothingness."[65] Going back to the ninth century, as we have begun to consider earlier with the *Zohar*, conceptions of the nature of nothing had begun to change and had become, by the twelfth and thirteenth, common-places, *topoi* of their own. Even here, Agamben seems to suggest, "nothing" functions as an "end," in and as language in a way such that language remains, but also declines at, the place of its own occurrence. Agamben writes, and the passage bears quoting again, that

> nothing is a sort of limiting dimension within language and signification. It is the point at which language ceases to signify the *res*, without, however, becoming a simple thing among others, because as pure name and pure voice, it now simply indicates itself. Inasmuch as it opens a dimension where language exists but signified things do not, the field of meaning of nothing appears close to that of the shifters that indicate the very taking place of language, the instance of discourse, independently of what is said. (73)

If the limit of language takes place "within" it, if language itself "opens a dimension where language exists but signified things do not," in other words if language occurs in a dimension that is no longer located in the realm of existing things, then the "very taking place of language" constitutes itself into a history of its own and, as this history, "now simply indicates itself." And although the event of language may still be thought of in negative terms, as the event of an end and loss (because "nothing" may still be conceived as being "external" to language), it would certainly constitute a difficult exposure to a limit, to itself as a limit. Such language would represent a challenge (and most likely also a powerful enticement) to situate and locate it, indeed, to limit it by negating the limit that it itself constitutes.

What is sufficiently clear, at any rate, is that this language constitutes a doubly particular event. As an event of its "own," it suggests that the cultural sphere within which it occurred is still in need of being read in its linguistic dimension. And, simultaneously, as a linguistic event, it disrupts its very localization into an external sphere, cultural or other. The interruption or disruption of signification and the particular experience of that event by the troubadours and other Andalusī writers is therefore momentous. With it, and with the attempt to "*live the topos itself, the event of language*,"[66] that language, the language that is "our place in al-Andalus," shows itself as presenting its readers with the task of displacing themselves onto the specific linguistic dimension that it produces, and that, insofar as it takes place, still requires reading.

Moreover, such an event enables shifting the discussion away, if only for the moment, from the questions of al-Andalus (or "Spain") as either an "historical enigma, *un enigma histórico*" (Sánchez-Albornos's famous title), or as a cultural product that is determinable or locatable within different cultural spheres. It suggests that al-Andalus (which may very well be also the things that historians describe), is a linguistic event, the occurrence of which is still to be explored. By focusing almost exclusively on the troubadours, however, Agamben also raised the question of comparison that Benjamin addressed. Can the texts to which Agamben refers here be demonstrated as being comparable to other texts written at "our place in al-Andalus"?

> . . . in consecrating all necessary forces to make without respite *that which is designated as the "beyond" of the world pass back into the world.*
>
> —Jean-Luc Nancy, *The Sense of the World*

What would a language be, the relation to which would not be restricted or dominated by a negative one, that would enable relating to it as an occurrence that "no longer refers to any unsayable foundation . . . and in which words are no longer distinguished from any other human practice"?[67] What would such a language be whose significance would emerge, not simply or not exclusively by referring to a location that is external to it (and is thus seen as "unsayable" because fully distinct from language), but rather insofar as its own occurrence would be its very (taking) place? Agamben provides only limited answers to this "certainly difficult to imagine" question (ibid.), and, in two distinct instances, he does so by evoking the

Zohar. In both instances, Agamben offers significant steps for the demonstrations of comparability toward which Benjamin directs us. Indeed, it is plausible that Agamben mentions the *Zohar* in such key places of his later work to preserve or renew his earlier discussion of the taking place of language that suggests itself in and as al-Andalus.

Explicitly addressing Jacques Derrida's work (otherwise echoing through much of his writings), Agamben comments on the sin of Aḥer (the "cutting of the shoots" described in the Talmud, treatise Ḥagiga, 14b ff.) as interpreted in the *Zohar.* Agamben reads the separation and isolation of the Shekhinah from the other divine "shoots," the *sephirot* (of which Shekhinah is the last) as the "mortal risk implicit in every act of interpretation," the risk of separating word from voice (two distinct *sephirot* in the *Zohar*), and language from its context, language from its referent.[68] "The cutting of the shoots" constitutes a relation to language, but to a language that operates so as to separate "speech both from the voice and pronunciation and from its reference. A pure word isolated in itself, with neither voice nor referent, with its semantic value indefinitely suspended" (ibid.). Agamben, who sees in such a linguistic event also the linguistic condition of modernity, suggests that the limits and historical boundaries of the taking place of language, and the hiatus of which he wrote, are still to be explored. This has everything to do, then, with "our place in al-Andalus."

Agamben does not, however, make facile comparisons or invoke easy analogies (as they were and are still pursued elsewhere) between, for example, Derrida and the Kabbalah.[69] On the contrary, he insists, the comparison is possible only if one can, assuming one could, demonstrate comparability. And he suggests that such demonstration could only occur after we recognize the specificity of the occurrence of language that takes place in both the texts of the *Zohar* and those of Derrida ("all thought defines itself above all through a certain experience of language," writes Agamben).[70]

The second time the *Zohar* appears, Agamben slightly expands on what he means when he refers to the linguistic condition of modernity. He suggests that the "society of the spectacle" documented by Guy Debord, may be the "final phase" of a process that the *Zohar* had earlier described.[71] Language's separation from referent and from context, Agamben explains, is similar to the separation effected by the spectacle, which "is nothing but the pure form of separation."[72] When "the practical power of humans is separated from itself and presented as a world unto itself," even communication (the very image of the media as means of communication) ceases being shared and the very notion of sharing is altered in a movement of translation and expropriation: "what is being expropriated is the very possibility of a common good" (80). Yet in spite of its violence, the spectacle, as language's isolation and communication into a remote and separate place of itself, as a decontextualized world, "retains something like a positive possibility that can be used against it" (ibid.).

Along with the "isolation of the Shekhinah" described in the *Zohar*, the possibility that Agamben mentions is that language, now (de)constituted as a quasi-autonomous, if not quite enclosed sphere or location, "no longer reveals anything—or better, it reveals the nothingness of all things. There is nothing of God, of the world, or of the revealed in language. In this extreme nullifying unveiling, however, language (the linguistic nature of humans) remains once again hidden and separated" (81). This dis-placing event, Agamben continues, may constitute a "devastating" experience, but it is crucial because it brings "language itself to language" (83). With this devastation that also constitutes a translation, then, and that opens the possibility of a different relation to the place of language and to its taking place, we are recalled to Moses Ibn ᶜEzra's "resident alien" and to "his" native land.

The Sense (of the End) of the World

> It should be known that the world of the elements and all it contains comes into being and decays. This applies to both its essences and its conditions. Minerals, plants, all the animals including man, and the other created things come into being and decay, as one can see with one's own eyes. The same applies to the conditions that affect created things, and especially the conditions that affect man. Sciences grow up and then are wiped out. The same applies to crafts, and to similar things.
>
> —Ibn Khaldun, *Muqaddimah*

Al-Andalus disappears in a figural movement, a figure of decline. Al-Andalus is its disappearance and its end, its mode of being and of appearing, such that it recedes into the background and becomes its absence from itself, and becomes, in Rina Drory's phrase, a "hidden context."[73] L. P. Harvey paradoxically writes that "nothing indicates that Arabic was spoken in Castile much north of Toledo, but Arabic was the written language of the *aljamas* [the Muslim quarters] for religious and other purposes." Only after more time went by, "Arabic became difficult to sustain even for purely religious purposes, because of the lack of educational facilities. There are many remarks in manuscripts in *aljamía* lamenting the loss of Arabic."[74] Considering the impact of Arabic onto Spanish, it may be interesting to consider what the said loss or the "end" of Arabic may actually mean (this is one of the numerous "ends" of al-Andalus), whether it does not reproduce, for example, a disavowal of the very much found effects and operations of Arabic in Spanish, in that which follows the "loss." Aside from this, one should consider—without diminishing in any way the damage done by the Christian conquest and the slow process of eradication of Arabic and Muslim culture throughout the peninsula (a process that becomes slowly comparable—but *only* comparable—at times, to the eradication of Arabic and Islamic culture in Algeria by the French colonial powers in the nineteenth century)—that the decline and loss of language is itself a *topos* well known from Andalusī literature in all of its languages.[75] In the light of more nuanced understandings of cultural dynamics in colonial and postcolonial conditions, the "namelessness" of the languages of al-Andalus (and "Romance," "Latin," "proto-Spanish" [?] are part of these) should prevent hurried translations that maintain contrived or even bizarre notions of cultural ends.

Recent historical research has begun to question the dominant model of such cultural ends by considering the continuation of relations (from cultural translation to literal citation, from extreme violence against each other to violence perpetrated together in crime) between Christians, Muslims, and Jews in al-Andalus.[76] The tendency, quite laudable in itself, has however been to focus on specific locations, whether social (only the elite would have known Arabic) or geographic. This has to do with archival remains and with the recognizability of the places in which one may search and research. But be that as it may, there is sufficient evidence, not only that earlier Andalusī cultural relations continue, but also that its languages are repeatedly and obviously translated (even if through different kinds of translations) well into the fourteenth and even fifteenth centuries (perhaps less obvious, later translations have also barely begun to be treated). Translations from Arabic were still being made in the fourteenth century (for example by Shem Tov ben Yitzḥak Ardutiel, the famous Santob de Carrión);[77] Qurʾānic verses were inscribed on the walls of a fourteenth-century-built synagogue;[78] populations inhabiting quarters that were never hermetic were in constant and daily interaction.

Beyond the empirical record, what needs to be asserted is not, or not only, the continuity of Andalusī *convivencia* so much as the particular, "multicultural" (which does not necessarily mean nonviolent, as David Nirenberg makes very clear),[79] and repeated translations that are taking place in al-Andalus. The argument I follow regarding the taking place of language does not deny this cultural dimension, it is not simply ahistorical, but it addresses rather the specific history of linguistic events, the occurrence of multiple translations throughout a historical period of political and military shifts in the twelfth and thirteenth centuries in the Iberian peninsula. Whether these are parallel histories is a question that can only be answered by attending to the specificity of each.

Nirenberg recently wrote that "virtually no work has been done on Muslim-Jewish relations under Christian rule in the Iberian peninsula, so that we know little of the material infrastructure of these relations."[80] In spite or because of that lack of knowledge, al-Andalus is not an object of knowledge, as much as the unsettling and unsettled (dis)figure of a fall that shows itself first by endlessly ending, appearing only to disappear. This is not reducible to a historical event, but marks rather the interruption of a history—a history and an interruption (indeed, a series of interruptions)—that operate and/or take place in different modes of translation. It is not accidental, then, as Américo Castro points out, that "the name *español* is of Provençal origin" and that "in Castilian . . . *España* meant, within Spain itself, the zone of the Peninsula occupied by the Moors."[81] The translations of "Spain" and "Spanish" seem to have occurred both outside and inside, in and through al-Andalus, not so much to replace or substitute for an original, but to repeat the gesture that consisted in belatedly naming that which never quite came into its "own" in spite of repeated and enormously violent attempts to do so.

The innovative dimension of translation, as well as a recognition that no original is thereby simply erased (for it would have had to be there in the first place), enables a discussion of "Spain" (a name which has carried national and political agendas quite far) in yet another translation, as al-Andalus. This is not meant to heal or cover over the discontinuity that constitutes the sixth and seventh centuries A.H. not only in cultural terms ("il faut . . . voir les confins du XIIe et du XIIIe siècle comme ce que nous avons appelé une période d'acculturation"),[82] but also in terms of the repetition of violence done to and exchanged by entire populations over this time.[83] Al-

Andalus, then, is also the mark of transportations, deportations, and more. It cannot be "identical" to or even simply continuous with Islamic Spain before and after 1250 C.E. Yet, to emphasize this difference does not quite amount to saying only that al-Andalus "fell," "declined," or ended. This is so not only because al-Andalus (however it could be narrated, understood, or translated) was never identical to itself, but also because it is also in itself a repetition of multiple translations.

Al-Andalus is an event of language that marks a disjunction. It takes note of the way recurring translations have engaged, paradoxically enough, in asserting an absolute break (the "end"), as well as in constructing a continuity that could cover that break (the history of Spain, of the Jews, etc.). Here too, the structure of distinct yet insistent figurations and translations is operating, and it is therefore worth pausing, as we will do shortly, to consider more of its various and detailed aspects. Al-Andalus is not reducible to a historical event or set of events, for it translates and marks—it *is* also —a displacement of its place and taking place as "past." The practice that constitutes its object as lost by pushing "it" into the past, indeed, in this particular case, by mourning it ostentatiously, is familiar enough not to warrant further discussion here (though I will return to it in the next chapter), except to indicate two things.

First is the question raised by the very term "end" when dealing with cultures, and second is the way Arab and Arab Jewish cultures (as well as their variants, such as "Hispano-Arab," "Sephardi," "Western Islam," etc.) seem to require the repeated inscription of their being "past" and their having "ended."[84] Insofar as both these gestures continue to imply an attempt at contextualization, the very language of al-Andalus, its very occurrence, can be seen as still taking place—not in its entirety, of course, but nonetheless significantly. The burden of this book is to further underscore this occurrence.

Describing the disputations that took place in the late thirteenth century in the Iberian peninsula, Yitzhak Baer writes: "On the soil of historic Spain approaching the end of the Reconquest, and in the part of the peninsula closest to the classic centers of the Inquisition and the persecution of the Catharist sectarians, an indication was given of the direction the war against the Jews was to take during the next two centuries."[85] The foreshadowed end of a world whose insisting "legacy" recurrently inscribes its demise by staging the repetition of political, economical, religious, intellectual, and cultural ends also articulates what remains marked as the history of a grounded ("the soil") and "historic Spain."[86] Given that "Spain," either as nation or as "idea," still has to constitute itself (assuming it ever does), it matters little whether one reads here a belated translation of wishful thinking on the part of self-proclaimed "Spaniards" or "Europeans" who thus sought to "recapture" (2) that which would never have ceased to be their property (hence the repeated use of the term "Reconquest," a term that echoes the belated nationalist narrative of a return to a land waiting patiently for the "return" of its rightful and manly owners) and that would thus never have ended nor been interrupted by 750 years of Muslim and Arabic culture ("the soil of historic Spain");[87] or whether one reads this as the continuity of a process of "foreshadowing" in which one tries "to make sense of a historical disaster by interpreting it, according to the strictest teleological model, as the climax of a bitter trajectory whose inevitable outcome it must be."[88] However that may be, what does remain to be read is the insistent inscription of decline, what can be called the (de)constitution of al-Andalus.

Following Baer, Bernard Septimus goes on to assert the "brutal abruptness" with which "the end came . . . in the middle of the twelfth century,"[89] whereas Rina Drory writes of the thirteenth century as the "final phase of Jewish cultural contact with Arabic."[90] Both seem to suggest that whatever is "Jewish"—much like whatever is "Spanish"—nonetheless remained "intact" after such momentous change. As Septimus puts it, indicating that "Spanish Jewry" had come into existence even before "Spain" had made its own trans-lation into "Europe": "instead of simply dwindling or decaying, Spanish Jewry transferred from the Arabic world to Christian Europe—and it did so as a community, with its collective identity more or less intact."[91] This is and is not the end, then. "The Christian victory at Las Navas de Tolosa [1212 C.E.] ended once and for all the Almohad threat to Christian Spain and hastened the decline of the Almohad empire."[92]

Even a sharp critic of Baer and of his followers writes about the historical process that carried Jewish identity through the Middle Ages, that it continued "even after the decline and total disappearance of Judeo-Arabic culture from Andalusia."[93] Such a figuration of decline *cum* continuity, as well as the assertion of "total disappearance," is all the more striking when made by a historian whose explicit purpose is to bring a much needed corrective to the fact that "not much research has been conducted on the cultural impact of the Andalusian Jewish migration to the Hispanic [i.e., Christian] kingdoms" (ibid.). A few pages (and centuries) later, note how decline inscribes itself again. In the sixteenth century, the "decline of Sephardic culture would be resumed in many parts of the new Diaspora, as the inevitable result of the general cultural decline of the Islamic world" (124).

The word "decline" does seem to impose itself with peculiar force, then, in the description and the deconstitution of al-Andalus. So much so that it is inscribed even when it is not relevant: "Poets, philosophers, scientists, historians created a Golden Age in the eleventh century. Even though the atmosphere tended to be more repressive during the domination of the Almoravids and Almohads, there was no substantial decline in intellectual and artistic activity."[94] No decline, then? Not quite so, since on the next page, the events of the fifth and sixth centuries A.H. (eleventh and twelfth C.E.) are said to have "contributed to a substantial decline in the Mozarabic communities of al-Andalus" (306).

Who could doubt, then, the inexorable, if highly rhetorical, movement of a fall—that which "in retrospect . . . appear[s] as the beginning of the actual downfall of the Iberian-Arabic society"[95]—when a tradition is so insistently made "out of mourning the passing of things we never had time really to know"?[96]

Hence, no questioning is intended here of the factual accuracy of these descriptions, insofar, at least, as the defeat at al-ᶜIqāb (609 A.H./1212 C.E.) was "the worst suffered by the Muslims, [and that it] is considered to represent the real end of Muslim power in al-Andalus."[97] Yet, what criteria and what means would enable not only linking such an event to the "rest" of its time (Walter Benjamin reminds us that "we cannot conceive of a single empirical event that bears a necessary relation to the time of its occurrence"),[98] but also dissociating its occurrence from the rhetorical effects of such descriptions upon the figuration of al-Andalus as a "period of decline"? This too requires a distinct relation to language.

A different experience of the taking place of language at "our place in al-Andalus" suggests a different mode and negotiation of mourning, or, more precisely, a different (relation to) rhetoric. It suggests a less melancholic relation to a different object along with a different notion of relation, indeed, the affirmation not so much of decline, which always implies continuity, but rather of separation and of disjunction, of difference. This is why the purpose of a reading of al-Andalus could not be a "reconstruction" (such a favorite term these days) or a recovery of a lost context: not because it is impossible (though the historical work that would begin to translate this possibility into a concrete one has yet to emerge), but because the requirement of thought that imposes itself most urgently here is that of a reading, the reading of al-Andalus as a linguistic event. In this event, a mediation, a mode of relation constituted by disjunction and translation demonstrates itself along with, and as, decline.

> Alas for those mosques that have been walled up to become dung heaps for the infidel after having enjoyed ritual purity!
>
> Alas for those minarets in which the bells [of the Christians] have been hung in place of the Muslim declaration of faith [being announced for them]!
>
> Alas for those towns and their beauty! Through unbelief they have grown very dark!
>
> They have become strongholds for the worshipers of the Cross and in them the latter are safe against the occurring of raids.
>
> We have become slaves; not captives who may be ransomed, nor even Muslims who pronounce their declaration of faith!
>
> Hence, were your eyes to see what has become our lot, they would overflow with abundant tears.
>
> So alas! Alas for us! Alas for the misfortune that struck us, namely harm, sorrow, and the robe of oppression.
>
> —Anonymous; trans. from Arabic by James T. Monroe

Rethinking the place of language in the disappearance of context, the loss of a world within which language would "make sense" can be further illuminated with the notion of writing as exposure, writing as inscription and exscription to the world, *au monde*, as Jean-Luc Nancy puts it in *Le Sens du monde*. Nancy, who also alludes to Derrida,[99] makes clear that the taking place of language does not at all imply a hermetic closure, but precisely an *exposure* (hence, *exscription*). This exposure to the loss of sense, to the loss of the world as making sense (Ibn ᶜEzra's "devastation"), implies a distinct negotiation of loss and raises the stakes of writing at the limit of sense. Nancy explains that, in this situation, the stakes of style and writing are about configuring "the space of a tracing of sense. A space itself traced by the passage to the limit of significations, the exscription of thought into the world, *l'enjeu du style ou de l'écriture configure l'espace d'un frayage du sens. Un espace lui-même tracé par le passage à la limite des significations, par l'excription de la pensée au monde.*"[100]

This exscription, or exposure to the finitude of sense, that is also a coming to sense, *la venue au sens*, to a sense that is never present but whose absence does not make sense, is what Nancy explores in different ways throughout his work (touch is perhaps the most notable one, as Derrida suggests in his "Le Toucher").[101] Most importantly for us, with this thought Nancy suggests that writing exposes itself to its taking place to the extent that the world has lost its sense. We are referred or sent back, *renvoyés*, to a world that has vanished as having sense, a world that has no sense, and in which a relation of sense to the world remains precisely what is missing. All that remains, then, is the world "itself" (*le monde lui-même*). "Thus, the world *no longer has* a sense, but *it is* sense, *alors, le monde* n'a plus *de sens, mais* il est *le sens*" (19/E8). Writing (thought) loses itself in its exposure to the world, exscribes itself to it, *s'y excrit*. It "lets sense carry it away, ever one step more, beyond signification and interpretation, *laisse le sens l'emporter, toujours d'un pas de plus, hors de la signification et de l'interprétation*" (19/E9).

Hence, Nancy presents us with a notion of writing as "une exploration de l'espace," a space to which one finds oneself exposed to the widest generality of sense, a space that is both "a distended, desolate extension—the 'desert that grows,' *une étendue distendue, dévastée—le désert qui croît*," and "a broadly open, available extension, *une étendue largement ouverte, disponible*" (20/E9). Much as Agamben suggests a way to rethink al-Andalus, by suggesting that the "spectacle" and the "cutting of the shoots" open futural possibilities, Nancy leads us to think of al-Andalus's "ends," and what we may now think of as its exscription. Here, the growth of the wasteland, of the desert where we already found and lost ourselves earlier, could reveal an unknown space, an unknown and excessive aridity of the sources of sense (44/E24).

If such loss of sense, the vanishing of a world and the "isolation of the Shekhinah," is not—in fact, if it could not be—the first time such an exposure, such an occurrence of language as described here, takes place, would it further imply that something has yet to be read or translated from al-Andalus? If so, such reading could clearly not be attempted in the name of a return to a prior "truth" of writing, but would rather have the form of a demand not simply historical (which does not mean ahistorical), a demand not past us so much as still in front of us. As Pierre Alféri puts it, "a demand—and less than any other, a demand of thinking—is never merely historical. What prescribes, prescribes thought and onto thought, must precede by a distance that is not measurable in terms of history, in order to point toward that which can remain untimely, to come and to be thought."[102] Whatever occurrence of language takes place in and as al-Andalus, if it does indeed demand thought, is neither timeless nor essential. It must precede us; it must still remain before us.

Agamben's *Stanzas*, although it does no more than temporarily raise the possibility that the occurrence of language in the troubadours' writing does articulate a hiatus, a partial break from the negative relation of Western thought to language, emphasizes that this experience is an experience of love.[103] Agamben shows how fundamental the experience of love is, along with developments, in Arabic thought, of theories of the imagination, and suggests ways in which it affects, or rather how it comes into play in the *Roman de la rose* (discussed explicitly and extensively in *Stanzas*), the *Zohar*, and the *Libro de buen amor*. Agamben, however, emphatically criticizes both the suggestion that there is any "mysticism,"[104] any ineffability, here at work, and the interpretation of that experience of love as a "lived reality" that a subject would have experienced, for both mysticism and love, understood as a subject's experience, presuppose precisely such a subject's preceding its "expression" in the poetry. Agamben argues that there is here a "misunderstanding" that fails to recognize the "experiencing of the event of language as love."[105] Much as the poem does not take place in the chamber, but is rather that very chamber (*stanza*), the poetic word is the event of the experience of love, not a previous experience's expression. Love, as the relation of and to language I am trying to describe (what Agamben calls *experimentum linguae*), is therefore both subjectless and presuppositionless—or, more accurately, it is its "own" presupposition. It can thus be read in the manner of the decontextualization and the interruption of reference that operates in the "isolation of the Shekhinah," as a "bringing language itself to language."[106]

This translation is not to be seen as language's return to itself; it is, rather, language's exposure to its limit. Love functions therefore as another name for the way "any language can be transformed, how language differs from language" in translation, a translation of translation.[107] For translation sets out neither to (re)produce nor to recreate a context, but rather renders explicit, by breaking from it, language's being-transformed. Viewed in this way, love is also a name for the opportunity to see something in its being-thus, in its occurrence as such, "like Dante and the author of the *Zohar* . . . who, in culturally diverse situations, made of the margin between truth and its transmission their central experience."[108]

Love, like the translations of the writings that occupy me in these chapters (and the two are not necessarily distinct), is "seeing something simply in its being-thus—irreparable but not for that reason necessary; thus, but not for that reason contingent."[109] As Nancy puts it, love is therefore the exposure to

> this "self" that is neither a subject nor an individual nor a communal being, but *that*—she or he—which cuts across, *traverse*, that which arrives and departs. The singular being affirms even better its absolute singularity, which it offers only in passing, which it brings about immediately in the crossing, *qu'il l'entraîne aussitôt dans la traversée.*[110]

By calling translation "a critical-poetic act *par excellence*," Agamben raises the notion of "means without ends"[111] that resonates with the idea of a love that does not presuppose an experience, certainly not that of a subject, but is "rather love as the experience of taking place in a whatever singularity."[112] Love, recast such as it is at different moments of Agamben's work, is that experience, rather than its presupposition or effect, suspended away from and exposed to an outside, the existence of which is neither denied nor affirmed: whatever being ("being such that it always matters").[113]

Translating History

To suggest the plausibility of a recognizable and continuous link, a mode of relation and of signification, between periods and places, and even more, between periods and language, between texts and contexts, would be everything but historical, insofar as it would disregard the singular historicity of language. It would also ignore what Walter Benjamin referred to as the "disjunction" constituted by translation. In other words, an experience of language that considers "history" at its source (and hence continues to relate to language negatively), that reads language as an expression of a prior reality, an expression that follows its presupposed "place," suggests that language has no history of its "own." Language's history cannot be reduced to culture's history: not because language would be "independent" or autonomous, but because language, a particular language, has its own historicity (which is also something else than the history of its changes). As valuable as historical research is, history cannot be taken for granted in its status as the place of language. Moreover, in its own dependence on language, history can also be read as an effect of language. Much before any "linguistic turn" in history, Walter Benjamin addressed this issue along with the specific question of other, different "periods of decline," while rethinking the taking place of language.

Reminding us, along with Agamben and Nancy, of the possibility of a different relation to language and its place, Benjamin characterized "so-called periods of decline, *die sogenannte Zeiten des Verfalls*,"[114] as periods "possessed of an unremitting artistic will," if "not so much . . . of genuine artistic achievement." These would be ages in which "the form as such is within the reach of this will, a well-made individual work is not."[115] Asserting that such is always the case in periods of decline ("So steht es immer um die sogenannten Zeiten des Verfalls"), Benjamin continues his description: "To this should be added the desire for a vigorous style of language, which would make it seem equal to the violence of world-events. . . . Glory was sought in devising figurative words rather than figurative speeches, as if linguistic creation were the immediate concern of poetic verbal invention" (235/E55). Such linguistic creation occasionally takes the form of "the most arbitrary coinings . . . especially in the form of archaisms." (Similar coinings, it should be noted, play a prominent role in translations, an activity that dominates al-Andalus, even after its "end.") In the "state of disruption" (within which language becomes "equal to the violence of world events"), Benjamin continues, "arbitrariness is always the sign of a production in which a formed expression, *ein geformter Ausdruck*, of real content can scarcely be extracted from the conflict of the forces unleashed, *dem Konflikt entbundener Kräfte*" (236/E55). With this reference to "forces" in relation to form, its production, and "linguistic creation, *Sprachschöpfung*," Benjamin, who addresses the question of representation and form throughout the entire "Epistemo-Critical Prologue," repeats his earlier injunction to attend to linguistic form as neither the product nor the effect of external forces, but rather as the very event of these forces. Benjamin clarifies that what may have appeared at first as a historical categorization ("so-called periods") is to be understood as a linguistic event. With his insistence on language and form, Benjamin's elaborations suggest that the historical descriptions of al-Andalus, which we have considered, would be indications and translations of linguistic events. The relation between history and language is thus displaced, and could even be said to collapse, to the extent that history "becomes equal to signification in human language."[116] Language having acquired the violence of world events, history now "becomes equal" to language. Hence, Benjamin offers what he calls "a conceptual treatment" as an alternative to "literary-historical analysis."

In literary-historical analysis differences and extremes are brought together in order that they might be relativized in evolutionary terms; in a conceptual treatment they acquire the status of complementary forces, and history is seen as no more than the colored border to their crystalline simultaneity. From the point of view of the philosophy of art the extremes are necessary; the historical process is merely virtual.[117]

That Benjamin's "conceptual treatment" does not establish the continuity of tradition and of "evolutionary terms," the terms of an alleged progress, is perhaps already too much of a commonplace. It is therefore important to note that the complementary forces, *komplementäre Energie*, here alluded to are described a few pages earlier as conflicting forces and power whose aftereffect is history. Samuel Weber explains how these forces are figured "as a *vortex* or maelstrom, which draws (literally tears, rips: *reißt*) the raw materials of emergence, *Entstehungsmaterial*, into its force-field."[118] These "raw materials" and the forces which draw and tear them apart, are inseparable from linguistic form, but they do not constitute its "context." They remain, therefore, at the center of our attention and, keeping in mind that Benjamin considers translation first and foremost as a form, they translate and help read the occurrence of that other singular figure—al-Andalus—not so much as a historical period, but as a linguistic event, as the textual matter, a maelstrom of "conflicting forces" and "linguistic creation" that constitutes, in singular ways, the taking place of (its) language.

Note, then, that Benjamin writes of "so-called, *sogenannte*, periods of decadence" and not of "periods of so-called decadence," as the English translation has it. It is, indeed, a matter of their name (as periods and as decadence), the product of an activity of naming the period as such, an activity in which the "period" itself may be said to participate and which has little to do with its referential—some might say, historical—truth, aside from the movement of rhetoric. Such naming has been made most notable by the sorrows of Moses Ibn ᶜEzra and the other descriptions of devastations we have briefly seen.

Like Maimonides, this naming "our place" translates al-Andalus, a translation that occasions more than sadness. Such sadness also figures in the description of bygone days by Yehuda al-Ḥarizi, in the early thirteenth century, and later on in the writings of Ibn Khaldun, who makes decline into a historical necessity. Yet these and other writers write an al-Andalus that is also, but not simply, falling and disappearing, declining. Today, even if the naming of such a fall has received considerable qualification, it has hardly stopped from affecting contemporary thinking on al-Andalus.[119] Repeated calls to reconsider the role of Arabic on literary and nonliterary history, and the sense that each of these calls emerges from an ever more isolated and desolate wilderness, should make that clear enough.[120]

In the course of the remainder of this book, I intend less to raise anew the question of historical context (however necessary that question may also be) than to address the meaning and force of the naming of al-Andalus. I read al-Andalus as an occurrence of language, and raise the question of whether it is meant to indicate a lost, previously attained wholeness or unity, or the impossibility of such unity. I read the place of its emergence, in singular occurrences, as the taking place of language. To evoke Paul de Man's words, commenting on Benjamin—words that significantly recall the kabbalistic theme of the "breaking of the vessels" and the question of Benjamin's relation to "Jewish mysticism" that will occupy us in the next chapter—the question is less whether there was any vessel in the first place, whether we have any knowledge of this vessel, any access to it, but rather what the relation is of any "work" to language, even to "pure language."[121] This is to question the conception that any given so-called period, area, or community is an organic, coherent, and symbolic unity (a whole "vessel"), and to suggest instead the necessity of reading "our place in al-Andalus."

3

The Silent Voice of the Friend: Andalusī Topographies of Scholem's Conversations (Mourning Mysticism)

> In its silence, the voice of the friend, *die Stimme des Freundes,* speaks to Dasein of its death.
>
> —Christopher Fynsk, *Heidegger: Thought and Historicity*[1]

> In a sense, Conversation disrupts the possibility of a simple history because it dispenses with a personal or universal narrative in favor of what could happen to us between ourselves when we expose ourselves to this space, which belongs to neither the one nor the other.
>
> —Avital Ronell, *Dictations*

> But surely in all these years there was the chance for people like me to pursue our cause, *unsere Sache*—which, God knows, originally had nothing to do with Englishmen or Arabs, *die weiß Gott nichts mit Engländern oder Arabern originär zu tun hatte.*
>
> —Gershom Scholem to Walter Benjamin, 1 August 1931

My argument has been that al-Andalus does not simply provide the context of the texts I address in this work, the location of the linguistic events that were produced in it, but that the very taking place of their language is also al-Andalus. To say that al-Andalus is this occurrence rather than the context of these texts implies, however, that there is an alternative view that does consider al-Andalus as such a context. In this view—one that, in the example we saw in the previous chapter, would explicate the Maimonidean expression "our place in al-Andalus" as referring to the place within which Maimonides wrote—al-Andalus is a geographical or cultural location that precedes the writing of Maimonides. And although it was not the case in the particular instance of Maimonides' writing (neither the expression "our place" nor the *Guide of the Perplexed* were written in the Iberian peninsula), one would not necessarily conclude that al-Andalus, as the place of Maimonides' language, disappears from relevance. I have already alluded to the way al-Andalus does, in fact, disappear and "end"; part of the purpose of this chapter is to show further that such disappearance takes place, and how, and that this disappearance is constitutive of the becoming-context of the place of language.

Still, and prior to this disappearance, consider that even if deemed relevant for a reading of Maimonides, al-Andalus remains a place, and Maimonides' language remains distinct from, and negatively related to, that place: Maimonides' language is not its place. This negativity can take two forms. Either one considers that the language of Maimonides is lacking, that it cannot be understood outside of its context, in which case all one is left with are "only words," or language is taken as autonomous, as not being determined by its context in any way. In the latter case, the place of language becomes its essential meaning, a meaning that is, paradoxically, "extractable" from the text and that is therefore "presentable, even if incompletely and not exactly, in paraphrase."[2] In this case, language is said to refer to Maimonides' "true doctrine," which, being hidden "in" its language, continues to function as exterior to and distinct from it. Language here, like the national entity that is presumed to speak it, is therefore seen as even more hermetically distinct from, more negatively related to, its location. In both cases, at any rate, the distinction is maintained and language remains distant from its place (even when it is the closest, literally standing on, taking root, as the organic view has it, "in" its place).

What, then, could it mean to say that the taking place of Maimonides' language (and of the language of other texts) *is* al-Andalus? To answer this question is my purpose in this book, so rather than engage it directly here, it seems more urgent to consider the way in which the alternative view ("al-Andalus is a place and Maimonides' language is not that place") also constitutes a linguistic argument, indeed, a linguistic event that itself takes place and is not reducible to an external context. In other words, to say that al-Andalus is the place that is not language and within which, or out of which, language emerges, is also an argument about language, an argument about what constitutes a linguistic event, and about what happens when language takes place. In turn, this argument is itself a linguistic event that must be read, not so much, or not only, in order to contextualize al-Andalus, but precisely to consider how al-Andalus has already taken place in a determined mode of language, how it has come to be considered as, how it has come to be reduced to and even to disappear as a *contextual* location.

> So far we have hardly considered melancholia from the topographical point of view.
>
> —Sigmund Freud, "Mourning and Melancholia"

The combined writings of Walter Benjamin and Gershom Scholem must articulate one of the most profound set of reflections on language that were produced in the twentieth century. Yet Scholem's contribution to these reflections, and, along with them, to the reception of Walter Benjamin's work, is perhaps not as readily known. It is more often "illuminated" by—less read and studied than—his contributions to the study of Jewish mysticism and, by extension, to the study of the language and culture of al-Andalus (and its translations and transformations). But Scholem no doubt achieved, throughout all of his writings, that for which he credited Benjamin; namely, a unique synthesis of a philosophy of language and a philosophy of history. What I argue is that this synthesis illustrates and, more importantly, profoundly affects, the way al-Andalus (and "Spain") is still constituted in language.

That there would be a common thread running through Scholem's synthesis and that it would in turn illuminate, in particular, the notions of event and of language held by him, is perhaps not surprising. I want to question the source of that illumination, and consider in detail how Scholem's writing on Benjamin is the occasion for a striking version of his conception of history and of language. Further, I will show that this writing, this event of language, provides an account of the occurrence of al-Andalus and of the place of language in it. Scholem's writing tells us much about the place Benjamin occupies in its language, the way Benjamin occurs in language (something which will occupy me in the larger and later part of this chapter). It also tells us much about the way al-Andalus ("Spain"), "mysticism," and finally, language itself, occur in this language (this will be addressed in the first section of the chapter). This occurrence, the event of language that constitutes these "objects" of Scholem's writing (Benjamin, Spain, mysticism, language), is ostensibly marked by a rhetoric of sadness, a language whose logic may have yet to be exploded, the labor of which we also know nothing about but that bears partial comparison with Freud's account of "mourning and melancholia."

Here, language enacts a constructive labor, a figuration (hence, rhetoric) and a mourning of Spain, a figuration and a mourning of mysticism, and, most legibly, a figuration and a mourning of Benjamin. It is not, therefore, that the loss is simply not known, but that what is lost in it remains at work, indeed, still labors. If such is the case, and I argue that it is, it becomes possible to show that what Giorgio Agamben calls "the sadness of the scholar" is a linguistic occurrence that structures the founding writings of Jewish mysticism—itself a major instance of language "on" al-Andalus—and that it structures this field to this day.[3] Most importantly here, it becomes possible to argue that the rhetoric of sadness determines the language and the place of "al-Andalus," that it still determines the place of its language as its "contextual," that is, its external and thus negatively determined, location. Finally, and as a temporary conclusion that may facilitate our exploration of "our place in al-Andalus," a reading of Scholem's rhetoric of sadness continues to open the possibility of a different notion of the place and taking place of its language.

In the Name of the Voice

> It is important to observe here how the "conscience" of Western philosophy rests originally on a mute foundation (a Voice), and it will never be able to fully resolve this silence.
>
> —Giorgio Agamben, *Language and Death*

There are, in Gershom Scholem's writings, two distinct narratives of the relation between history and language, a relation in which an occurrence in the full sense of the word is constituted. The narratives are divided into normality and crisis, and as such they articulate two basic courses that history can and has, in fact, followed. Both narratives illuminate the connection between language and what is taken to be its place, its context. This connection, one toward which Scholem returned on many occasions, can be seen most strikingly at work between language and a series of originary events that are repeatedly posited as that to which language relates and in relation to which it takes place. Such originary events, it should be noted, may not always be described as "historical" by Scholem. They are not simply nor only located as temporally anterior to that to which they give rise. Rather, they may best be described as providing the context, the place and occasion for the occurrence of that which emerges out of them. Such events, such contexts, then, are "history-provoking," or, as Scholem puts it, they are always "meaning-bestowing."[4] This is the case, at least, to the extent that language's connection to these events is maintained, that is to say in the first of the two narratives.

In this first narrative, the originary event is a senseless occurrence of tremendous, often cataclysmic force: it is the voice of God, the mystical experience, or a catastrophe of another kind, which, in time, gives rise to a historical chain of utterances and interpretations ("tradition"). This tradition constitutes language; it is language. It is that which gives meaning to the originary voice, word, or event, and it is figured by Scholem as a kind of conversation, a linguistic interaction and communication. This constant conversation between the original event and its later interlocutors is what constitutes and maintains language, what continues to provide it with its context and to maintain it in its integrity. The originary event resonates, or, more precisely, it must resonate in the later conversation that language is, which otherwise turns into an isolated, decontextualized monologue. The occurrence of this monologue describes the second of the two narratives, the narrative of "crisis."

In crisis, the connection between the originary event and the later chain of utterances is broken, and language itself turns silent. Words "are stripped of their customary communicative function" and their "covert existence is certified by their manifest absence," indeed, by silence.[5] What this silence consists of can be explained by way of the break that is the occasion of silence's occurrence, since this break reveals the true nature of the originary event. In crisis, language, the chain of tradition, appears in fact to acquire the very attributes of the originary event. By breaking from what was its original context, language turns into or repeats and reproduces that context itself. In a striking and concise version of the dual narrative I have been describing, Scholem explains that the "tradition, which has its own dialectic, goes through certain changes and is eventually delivered in a soft, panting whisper; and there may be times, like our own, in which it can no longer be handed down, in which this tradition falls silent. This, then, is the great crisis of language in which we find ourselves."[6] What is here described, then, are the two states of language produced by or in two different historical conditions. In the situation of normality, the conversation occurs, tradition is "delivered in a soft, panting whisper." In crisis, on the other hand, "it can no longer be handed down" and thus "falls silent." To the extent, however, that there is still language ("this is the great crisis of language"), this falling silent can be described as a monologue, in contradistinction to the dialogue or conversation that takes place in normality.

There are a few "originary events" for Scholem, most of which are well known, and they all follow the double pattern I have described. From the experience of revelation to the catastrophe of the exile from Spain, and from the mystical experience to the loss of a friend, the structure of the historical occurrence includes an abyssal (often ahistorical) event, a meaningless, even silent, voice, word, or name, which later becomes audible and resonates in language (still later, it may fall silent again). This voice is at times described as a "nothing," and like the other figures of originary events, it is then worked and processed in language, in the chain of tradition. Language, then, constitutes a series of interpretations and conversations that translate and figure the originary event into history by maintaining it as audible. Often, the conversation stops, and the voice of the originary event is no longer audible. Scholem describes this state of crisis, the break between tradition and its originary context, in terms of a dramatic transformation of language. In doing so, he nonetheless implies that the relation between language and its context (the originary event) is not to be thought of as a complete break.

According to one of the most important of these descriptions, namely that of revelation, insofar as tradition remains akin to the originary voice of revelation it can remain historical and meaningful. By breaking from its context (i.e., from the voice of revelation), on the other hand, tradition "becomes hollow and takes on a ghostly character." As David Biale explains, "without tradition, the 'voice, *Stimme*' of revelation necessarily loses its force."[7] Scholem writes:

> The voice which we perceive is the medium in which we live, and where it is not [the medium], it becomes hollow and takes on a ghostly character in which the word of God no longer has an effect, but instead circumvents. . . . The residue of the voice, as that which in Judaism is the tradition in its creative development, cannot be separated from it [the voice].[8]

Scholem thus makes clear that the voice constitutes both the originary event and that which becomes transformed in the state of crisis ("it becomes hollow" when it is no longer the medium). The break between language and the voice of the originary event is thus also a transformation, even the ruin ("residue"), of the voice which had previously served as the context, "the medium in which we live."

At the time he writes these very lines, Scholem also makes his famous and momentous epistolary complaint to Franz Rosenzweig about the state of the Hebrew language.[9] The complaint throws an important light on language and its place in Scholem's writing. According to Scholem, the Hebrew spoken in the streets of Palestine—a "secularized" language that seeks to rid itself of the originary treasures and abysses that fill it—has parted from its original context. Hebrew, says Scholem, has become a "ghastly Volapük, *gespenstische Volapük*" and "a ghostly language, *eine gespenstische Sprache.*"[10] Again, it seems clear that what I have been describing as a break of language from its originary context (the continuing event of tradition) is a condition in which the connection between language and its contextual, originary event is not absolutely broken. Rather, it is a transformation, perhaps a translation, at any rate a new condition (a "dialectical" one, as Scholem has it) in which the voice of the originary event is no longer heard (which does not mean, therefore, that it is absolutely absent or eradicated). In crisis, in this new condition, then, language becomes as meaningless as the originary voice would be if and when such voice were to be found by itself (remember that the originary event is a senseless one: "this communication" writes Scholem about the event of revelation, "is incomprehensible!").[11] When the voice ceases being the context, being the "medium in which we live," language is displaced and, although it remains a language, the originary voice no longer resonates in it. Language becomes "hollow and spectral." And while this is so perhaps only for those who cannot hear the originary voice, nothing could diminish the catastrophic dimension of that becoming. In this, too, the break from the originary event constitutes a repetition since this event is, as we saw, often enough cataclysmic.

In another description of the break of tradition represented by one such cataclysmic event, Scholem's language continues to follow this pattern. Here, the originary event constituted by the exile from Spain is an event that led to "ultimate values which differed widely from those of the rationalist theology of the Middle Ages." That which, under the mode of a "wide difference," follows and breaks with the originary event, also leaves another voice behind. Up to that break, "Aristotle had represented the essence of rationalism to Jewish minds; yet his voice, which had not lost its resonance even in mediaeval Kabbalism despite its passage through a variety of media, now began to sound hollow and spectral to ears attuned to the new Kabbalah."[12] The structure here—although less dramatically, perhaps, but not significantly different from what we have already seen—remains one in which a vocal tradition, a tradition that continuously emerges out of a voice, loses its context. This context had earlier constituted a more forceful voice and had sustained language and tradition as a vocal rather than silent ("hollow and spectral") event. This voice was conversed with, and interpreted in, language. It is a voice within which language remains located even if their relation has become more remote. Language, now distant and out of the context of this voice, and having therefore lost its "resonance," can only (re)produce and repeat that voice, but as meaningless chatter. Language comes to hear only, it itself becomes, a "hollow and spectral voice."

What is the value of such a "hollow and spectral" language, one that has lost its place and resonance in such a way? Scholem surprisingly and paradoxically asks this question in the future tense, indicating perhaps the extent of the loss. For on the one hand, it would seem that we (Scholem never says who "we" are) are not yet in crisis, that language is still connected to its originary context. But to the extent that "in our times" only those who do, perhaps, hear the voice could answer the question of the value of language as it is now, in fact, in crisis, this question itself becomes futurally remote:

> What the value and worth of language will be—the language from which God will have withdrawn—is the question which must be posed by those who still believe that they can hear the echo of the vanished word of the creation in the immanence of the world. This is a question to which, in our times, only the poets presumably have the answer. . . . And poets have one link with the masters of the Kabbala. . . . This link is their belief in language as an absolute, which is as if constantly flung open by dialectics. It is their belief in the mystery of language which has become audible.[13]

At the conclusion of his most sustained inquiry into the matters of language, it is notable that Scholem inscribes the aural and the ability to hear the voice, as the most central—indeed, the most crucial—element of language with which "our times" must measure itself, and which we, along with our belief in it, may have almost entirely lost (save for the possibility of a future question). Scholem had opened his inquiry by stating that "under the system of the synagogue, revelation is an acoustic process, not a visual one; or revelation at least ensues from an area which is metaphysically associated with the acoustic and the perceptible (in a sensual sense)."[14] By the end of this inquiry, Scholem once again underscores the centrality of the voice as well as the way kabbalists (and poets) are among the few that remain attuned to it. They are those who can still hear a voice that may well have been (or have become) inaudible, but that is a voice nevertheless, whose echo may then continue to resonate even in a language that has lost that voice as its necessary context. Against that "hollow and spectral" language, then, and whether or not he himself has faith (whatever that could mean), Scholem consistently maintains the notion of the Kabbalah's privileged access to its abyssal source:

> Mysticism does not deny or overlook the abyss; on the contrary, it begins by realizing its existence, but from there it proceeds to a quest for the secret that will close it in, the hidden path that will span it. It strives to piece together the fragments broken by the religious cataclysm, to bring back the old unity which religion has destroyed, but on a new plane, where the world of mythology and that of revelation meet in the soul of man.[15]

Mysticism, then, is the history of language and of tradition that preserves the connection between human language and the originary event that constitutes its necessary context. Mysticism is a linguistic process, but it is one of construction, as it builds unity and establishes, across the abyss, the unifying connection with "the old unity." This constructive and reconstructive project consists in piecing together the fragments that emerge out of the abyss, out of the originary event that remains, therefore, both ground and center to this construction project. Such is also the history of human language, a language that sustains the voice of the abyss by building out of it a solid unity, and by "closing in" and enclosing, even encrypting, that which provides it with the place of its occurrence. This constructive and reconstructive dimension of language will highlight the figurative and the rhetorical in the sections that follow.

I have already suggested that human language separated from its context, separated from the originary event that is its context, takes on the attributes of the originary event—the voice, word, or abyssal catastrophe that lies beyond and provides the place of language's occurrence. Another of Scholem's momentous descriptions of the occurrence of language out of its abyssal and cataclysmic origin can be found in his description of the "symbol," the central rhetorical figure around which Scholem based his analysis of Kabbalah. In a manner that parallels language and tradition, the symbol can be described as a conversation, the communicative exchange and understanding within which resonates (i.e., must resonate so as not to turn into "allegory") the voice of and as the place that sustains its occurrence. Note that, strictly speaking, what is communicated remains "nothing," that is, something occupying a sphere that precedes language and functioning in the way of the originary event we have considered.

The symbol "signifies" nothing and communicates nothing, but makes something transparent which is beyond all expression. Where deeper insight into the structure of allegory uncovers fresh layers of meaning, the symbol is intuitively understood all at once—or not at all. The symbol in which the life of the Creator and that of creation become one, is—to use Creuzer's words—"a beam of light which, from the dark and abysmal depths of existence and cognition, falls into our eye and penetrates our whole being." It is a "momentary totality" which is perceived intuitively in a mystical *now*—the dimension of time proper to the symbol.[16]

What Scholem describes, then, although here he departs from his usual and dominant emphasis on the vocal and the audible, is a conception of history and of language that seems to have remained consistent throughout his writings. This dual conception constructs and maintains a close connection between history and language by facing the abyss, "the dark and abysmal depths" (the "nothing," or the "something transparent") that constitute and separate the poles of the conversation, and close it in. It is a philosophy that also conceives of language as double: on the one hand, the most significant of all originary events are, to some extent, linguistic. God's voice, the inaudible utterance of his word and of his name, is the most prominent of these events. And, on the other hand, language is also that which, maintaining the silent echo and resonance of the originary voice and event, builds across and around the abyss of that event, and closes this abyss, this "vast gulf which can be crossed by nothing but the *voice*."[17] The voice, which is also nothing, is therefore both the context of language as tradition and that which enables tradition to maintain itself ("the medium in which we live"), otherwise dooming it to become as empty and meaningless, even as spectral, as it is by itself.

Scholem's dual narrative is revealing of a most fundamental and recurring structure of the historical occurrence, where the place of language is not language, or at least not human language. This place is that which, although a voice, is "beyond expression," and, although it is itself "enclosed," is always also and necessarily open to the possibility of being separated from language.

As such, it remains distinct from the language spoken and, most often, written, even by kabbalists (and poets). In opposition to the originary voice, this later language remains derivative, often turning "hollow and spectral" if and when it is separated from its originary context, from the originary voice and event. Yet that voice, if it were to be heard alone, would apparently be as hollow and spectral, even if it is deemed to be the source of all forces of language. This originary voice is, as Scholem also writes, the "true" language that cannot be spoken, from which our derivative language is or can always be exiled.[18] This silent voice as originary event, rather than as history (which is the history of human language and of human action, for Scholem), provides the necessary context and place of tradition as language. And because it can always be lost, it is a voice that cannot but be mourned and longed for. So it occurs that language is ultimately located in that which has always already been lost. So it is that the place of language, the "context" within which Scholem's language takes place, vanishes and becomes constitutively lost (a "nothing," a silent voice that is both "hollow and spectral"). So it is that tradition becomes a heritage and a legacy to something that is no more, and that language becomes a language of sadness and mourning.

> From what are the phenomena to be saved? Not only, and not so much from the disrepute and contempt into which they have fallen as from the catastrophe that a certain kind of tradition, *Überlieferung*, their "valorization as heritage, *Würdigung als Erbe*" very often entails—They are saved through the disclosure of the breach, *die Aufweisung des Sprungs*, the showing of a leap or crack in them. There is a kind of tradition that is a catastrophe.
>
> —Walter Benjamin, "N" (trans. slightly altered, following Samuel Weber)

> The indissoluble link between the idea of the revealed truth and the notion of language . . . is presumably one of the most important, if not the most important, legacies bequeathed by Judaism, *das ist wohl eine der wichstigsten, vielleicht sogar die wichtigste Erbschaft des Judentums*, to the history of religions.
>
> —Gershom Scholem, "The Name of God"

Emphasizing the affinities as well as the differences between Scholem and Hegel, Nathan Rotenstreich explains that in Scholem's work the abyss that is constitutive of the occurrence of history and of language is never speculatively sublated. In a striking formulation, Rotenstreich writes that, for Scholem, "dialectics is a mode of transformation, but does not become a mode of reaching a synthesis, in the speculative sense, between the universe and God."[19] There can never be produced a higher unity that would cancel the gap of ineffability (the "gulf that can only be crossed by the *voice*") that provides the event of language with its place and context. Rather, the question remains of "closing in" the abyssal distance by both reproducing it empirically (the "mystical experience"), and by speaking it symbolically, by making it "resonate." This remains, therefore, a linguistic occurrence, as Rotenstreich perceptively notes, a continuous riddle: "the question of the essence of [the mystical] experience and how it is adequately to be described is a great riddle, which the mystics themselves, no less than the historians, have tried to solve" (300). The impossibility of "making the bridge reach the transcendent pole" (292), of completely achieving the constructive and reconstructive aim that would provide for a full synthesis, remains insistently inscribed. The place of language, which is also the object of desire (mystical or scholarly desire, since it is that of "the mystics themselves, no less than the historians"), remains less out of reach than constituted by and constitutive of a language of failure and loss.

How serious such mournful and recurring loss is for a genealogy of the field of Jewish mysticism, the history of its language and its conception of the place of language—rather than for psychologically doubtful speculations or biographies—is difficult to evaluate. Its seriousness would be underscored, however, by the claim that a full synthesis, the solution of the riddle, had been achieved (such a claim can be witnessed in the recent attempts to assert that the abyss was worked over, that it was built and bridged by Jewish mystics in *unio mystica*). Moreover, the repetitive inscription of loss in distinct textual instances suggests that the scholarly language of Jewish mysticism is a language of sadness. I want to suggest that this language or rhetoric of sadness is, in fact, quite readable, if perhaps not as audible as Scholem and others would have it. The sadness of the scholar—which, insofar as it is attributed to the mystic, is not entirely the scholar's "own"—is a linguistic event of its own, one that may be explored in the language of Jewish mysticism, not only in Scholem's writing but also after it.

One prominent instance of this rhetoric of sadness is, of course, that which I seek to account for, namely, the place of al-Andalus and its becoming-context. In the previous chapters, we have begun to consider how "Spain" continues to makes its appearance as significant only at the moment of its "End,"[20] only at the moment, in other words, of its disappearance (in terms of "Jewish history," of course) in 1492. Like the stars, which, following Benjamin's description, "never appear in the writings of Baudelaire—or if they do, . . . they are always in the process of fading or disappearing,"[21] the significance of Spain remains constituted by its vanishing. Declinations of context. Spain's disappearance, or rather the repeated assertion that it is disappearing, and that, having ended, it can only bequeath its legacy, is perhaps the clearest inscription, not only of yet another originary event, but also of the rhetoric of sadness that marks the language of Jewish mysticism. This rhetoric determines the context of language not so much as the very occurrence of it as constitutive of what remains our encounter, if an encounter it is, with "our place in al-Andalus." This has also been called "the lachrymose conception of Jewish history," at the center of which figures the "catastrophe" and the "monumental legacy" of "Spain" and, occasionally, of Hispano-Arabic culture (and thus of al-Andalus) that was celebrated and mourned in various festivals and commemorations during the year 1992 C.E. —"Spain's" importance, again, residing mostly, if not exclusively, in 1492. It also constitutes the consolidation of Spain's "proper" inheritors and ethnic boundaries (hence, in the words of one scholar, "impressive achievements and lofty values [were] bequeathed to us by Spanish Jewry").[22]

Moshe Idel perceptively notes another occurrence of the rhetoric of sadness and attributes it to a personal condition. The image that Idel fastens upon is precisely that of a distant place, a piece of land from which would emerge something like a voice (Sinaitic echoes are of course recognizable here). Idel writes that Scholem "attempted to approach the 'mountain,' namely, the core of [metaphysical] reality. He waited, as he himself confessed, to receive a hint coming from that core."[23] Yet that very "core," Idel suggests, remained distant and silent.

Features of Scholem's language to which we will return are consequently underscored. Expressions of longing and melancholic self-deprecation—in short, a rhetoric of sadness—are already apparent when Idel reports that Scholem "was, in his own eyes, rather a failure qua mystic, yet one who longed for mystical experience" (ibid.). The personal interpretation of that language by Idel (and apparently by Scholem himself: "in his own eyes") follows a pattern of reading that insistently puts the emphasis on biographical and psychological dimensions, on authorship and authorial ("mystical") experiences. Such reading has its limitations, although it is, of course, not "wrong." Yet it would be a profound mistake, I think, to leave this language to stand as the derivative expression of an exclusively personal plight, a piece of biographical and psychological trivia the relevance of which is not only doubtful but also already situates the ground of a language elsewhere, in a remote outside. Again, such an elsewhere continues to function as the place of language, and it is moreover reduced to the psyche of the author. I suggest that, with the insistent inscription of longing and melancholia, we are rather reading a recurrence of a dimension of the scholarly discourse on mystical experiences, its rhetoric of sadness. In this language, objects and experiences that constitute the occasion for the occurrence of language (and this includes not only the mystical experience, but the entire psyche and life of authors), are repeatedly constituted as lost in an unattainable beyond: beyond language and/or beyond apprehension. This beyond is the place of language and its context. It is not language but the distant and always already lost place of its emergence.

Clearly, the assertion of this lost place and context cannot simply be taken as a personal "failure" of Scholem. In fact, a few pages later, Idel himself inscribes—and subscribes to—a very similar condition of loss as being unavoidable. Idel reinscribes, then, the rhetoric of sadness. He writes that "at its best, the mystic's testimony is a veil covering a psychic process that as such must remain beyond the scope of textual studies."[24] Whether it "must remain" that way because of a singular limitation of "textual studies," because of an absolute impossibility, or because it should so remain in order to preserve it from being further lost by way of the multiplication of words, is not quite made clear. What is clear, however, is that the mystic's language, his "testimony," is taking place elsewhere, in what is here described as "a psychic process" that appears abyssal. Idel, being openly less interested in textual than in experiential matters, seems easily to cope with the longing provoked by the loss of this language. Hence, he suggests that the loss of written testimonies is "not so great" when compared to a more important reason to mourn (20).

Like Scholem, who could not hear the voice of the mountain, Idel writes a language of longing for the voice, and for the much greater loss of the oral teachings of the great kabbalists (ibid.).[25] Idel further inscribes the rhetoric of sadness around the distance that separates the scholar from that which constitutes its object. Idel writes that "the mystical experience, the most important source and trigger of mystical literature, is unfortunately beyond the direct reach of those who are interested in fathoming the nature of mysticism."[26] Although Idel also argues that the scholar should focus on "the phenomenology of unitive language rather than a typology of the experiences,"[27] his language seems to both lament and affirm the inaccessibility of an object that remains the grounding foundation of experience: "Experiences that were transformed into words are the raw material for learned analysis" (27). Language is therefore inscribed as derivative of an originary event (the mystical experience), and, in its scholarly derivation, it appears to carry the memory of its place, a place that is external to it and remains remote and distant, even silent. Still, it may remain unclear whether the experience or the word constitutes the proper object, if not the "raw material," of the inquiry. This lack of clarity may be explained by a feature of Idel's language that confirms that the language of sadness is not simply the expression of a personal state of mind or feelings.

Idel's language inscribes, in fact, a curious inability to fully identify with the very notion of loss that remains otherwise inscribed. Hence, it is only "according to this conception" (which may be or not, therefore, Idel's own) that "the core of the mystical phenomenon is . . . inaccessible to the scholar" (ibid.). Whether or not this suggests that the scholar's sadness is here considered "curable," if one were to stop or to transcend one's being a scholar, it remains plausible to conclude that here, it is the very inscription of the loss, as well as the loss of (the conception of) a loss that is occurring in language. With these repeated, if distinct, losses, we learn not only about the rhetoric of sadness, then, but also about the taking place of language as originating in a place that remains distant from it, a place that remains "unfortunately beyond" and that continues to be thought of as "the Voice . . . the unthinkable on which metaphysics bases every possibility of thought, the unspeakable on which it bases its whole speakability."[28]

Mysticism Mourning

> Conversation strives toward silence, and the listener is really the silent partner.
>
> —Walter Benjamin, "The Metaphysics of Youth"
>
> Friendship does not keep silence, it is preserved by silence.
>
> —Jacques Derrida, *Politics of Friendship*

The text, story or history, *Geschichte,* of Scholem's relationship with Benjamin, construed from the beginning as conversation, and, more precisely, under the negative model of Gustav Janouch's *Conversations with Kafka*, immediately appears as placed under the sign of a voice.[29] It is the story of a friendship that is figured as a sustained relation to Benjamin's voice, a figuration of Benjamin that opens with and unfolds toward the vanishing of that which was the occasion of its occurrence: Benjamin's end and Benjamin's voice.[30] Located in and as the record of voices exchanged, as extended conversations, *Gespräche*, it is also the story of a becoming of language, one in which language both constitutes and remains distant from its place, a place of sadness, devastation, and loss. Distinct from a silencing or eradication, this movement does not contextualize, but rather constitutes the very occurrence of a text that gradually figures Benjamin, and ultimately "true" language, as *a silent voice*. This voice, both origin and end of History and of the story of the friendship, finds its own (distant) place in sadness, and, as we will see, only slightly less emphatically (less audibly? less visibly?), in "Spain." This occurrence of language, the figuration of the place of language in and into a silent voice, demands a reading that extends beyond the necessity to rethink the history of a friendship, but also involves the continued occurrence of language and its place as it takes place in Jewish mysticism.

Scholem's assertions about the science of Judaism, *Wissenschaft des Judentums*, the nineteenth-century discipline against which he polemicizes, already indicate the pervasiveness of the rhetoric of sadness that dominates and constitutes the field he "created" (as Martin Buber, who may have been a contender for that founding role of Jewish mysticism, puts it: "only Gershom Scholem has created a whole academic discipline").[31] In the *Wissenschaft*, Scholem sees a discourse that drives its readers to despair, *zur Verzweiflung zu treiben*.[32] And although he writes in response to this despair, Scholem inevitably locates his scholarly endeavor at a distance from, but also in relation to, this despair. Despair becomes the occasion of Scholem's attempt to prevent the "liquidation of Judaism as a living organism," for in many ways the irreparable has already happened. Scholem responds or converses with (the possibility of) such a devastating event, one that provides the occasion for (his own) language. He thus shows more than what Benjamin had elsewhere described as a "narrowly prejudiced thought," even if we could already note that Scholem's attachment to "organic" unity is not entirely remote from the prejudice about which Benjamin writes. Insisting against all odds on naming "life" as that which is "limited to organic corporeality" and that could thus be located at a safe and unbridgeable, though determining, distance from the devastation of death, Scholem distances but also grounds his language in sadness and mourning.[33] Insofar as this language is a forceful response to and as sadness, insofar as it opposes itself to the cataclysmic event of a liquidation, a dissolution and limitation (which, sadly but relevantly enough, was, in one instance, to take the form of "a decent burial, *ein ehrenvolles Begräbnis*"), it already finds its "place" in despair and sadness.[34]

Scholem's language can thus be read as a distinctive kind of work, a constructive building, that paradoxically finds its place and distances itself from what appears as a "dark ground," all the while construing and figuring, piecing together a "living organism." This is a "life" of a peculiar kind within the logic that governs Scholem's discourse, since it is one that nevertheless insistently continues to bequeath an afterlife, a will, and a legacy.

The figures of "dark ground"[35] and "fields of ruins," inscribed at the very opening of Scholem's *Major Trends in Jewish Mysticism*, both locate and strikingly articulate the rhetoric of sadness and longing that constitutes, in turn, the study of mysticism. This language of sadness situates itself by figuring and distancing itself from the "true" language (namely silence), and from the source of its speakability.[36] It also prefigures the recurring gesture that Scholem himself did so much to firmly establish, and that places "the catastrophe" at the center of Jewish history, as its ultimate context. This cataclysmic event is also one that would have affected more than the "living" ("The concrete effects and consequences of the catastrophe of 1492 were by no means confined to the Jews then living" [246]). Thus, *Major Trends* could be said to open by (dis)placing its readers "in the midst of . . . far-flung ruins and debris, *zwischen . . . weitverstreuten Trümmern*,"[37] exposing them to sadness, devastation, and destruction, and to "objects" for which there was no burial, for which no grave has been found. As we will see to be the case with Benjamin, and as we have begun to see with mysticism "itself," here too, sadness is worked and processed, its fragments being built and pieced together into language. The occurrence of this language is thus one of reconstruction and of consolidation, and it articulates sadness as its place and context.[38] Along with the assertion of its own new perspectives ("this gradually unfolding conception differed not inconsiderably from the views hitherto current in the literature published on the subject"),[39] this productive prospect can therefore be seen as structuring the trajectory of the scholar and of his "field," from an "early" exposure to a cataclysmic, originary event on and toward constructive and figurative productions. Language thus reveals itself to be located in the field that constitutes this event, indeed, in the place of a traumatic loss, the loss of a "nothing" as object.

Let us consider closer the peculiar configuration, the place of destruction, loss, and severance (de-cathecting) within which *Major Trends* inscribes itself from its very beginning, in its 1941 preface.[40] Scholem somehow emphatically situates the place and the construction project it carries. He writes of wrestling Jewish mysticism away from "a field strewn with ruins" ("the task which confronted me necessitated a vast amount of spade-work in a field strewn with ruins"); of buildings built "on shaky premises" ("Rapid bird's-eye syntheses and elaborate speculations on shaky premises had to give way to the more modest work of laying the secure foundations of valid generalization. . . . [O]thers had . . . erected some lofty edifice of speculation"); and of the necessity of "clearing the ground of much scattered debris" ("I found myself constrained by circumstance and by inclination to perform the modest but necessary task of clearing the ground of much scattered debris and laying bare the outlines. . . . Needless to say, like all spade-work, the task gradually imposed on my mind") (vii).[41]

What is the field of devastation from which the constructive, if also repeatedly "modest," language of Jewish mysticism emerges and within which it finds its work place in the very first pages of the book?

Note first that these words, written in the preface to the book, are dated twice, at the beginning of the preface ("More than twenty years have passed since I began to devote myself to the study of Jewish mysticism") and at its end: "May 1941." The book is thus clearly located in terms of its temporality, being written in the time span that covers the history of friendship toward which we have already begun to turn. It is also written at a time when, as Scholem tells us in the narrative of this history, he is already heavily engaged in an attempt to inscribe and reconstruct the "true" figure of Benjamin, to preserve his memory, the memory of his "real self": "Six months after his death, I tried to induce Dora, his former wife . . . to write down what she knew and had witnessed of his life and his real self."[42]

Second, in the preface, Scholem describes how, although this was not his primary purpose, he insistently "sketched the historical connections" that contextualized and linked the various systems of thought he discussed in the book.[43] There is, however, a major exception, one that is of momentous consequences for our reading of "our place in al-Andalus" (otherwise, and anachronistically enough, called "Spain" in the book) and the *Zohar.* Having apparently given himself a categorical "rule" to sketch historical connections, Scholem writes of his singular breaking of this rule: "Only in the lecture on the Book Zohar and its author have I departed from this rule" (ibid.). It is not clear, at this point, whether the *Zohar* is here said not to have been contextualized, whether the connections between the *Zohar,* Spain, history (of a friendship or other), and whatever else there is that should have connected, were more or less than "sketched" in this particular lecture (the fifth lecture out of nine in *Major Trends*). It also remains unclear what precisely is departed from when the rule is thus broken.

Readers who are already familiar with this lecture may recognize, however, that in it Scholem does delve at least as extensively as in the other chapters into historical details concerning the *Zohar.* If there are more contextualizing details, they concern not so much the *Zohar* itself, but rather, as in the history of a friendship, its author, the vocal origin of the text. The lecture thus follows what I have already noted as the privileging of biographical details (though it should be noted that information on the *Zohar*'s alleged author, Moses de León, is, in fact, quite scant).[44] This may further indicate what kind of "life" is considered to provide the "context," to constitute the historical connections within which a language is to be situated: the most striking fact about de León's life relates most directly to his death, which is described in a strange testimony that says that he died suddenly, before showing what he claimed was the original, ancient manuscript of the *Zohar* in his possession.[45] Be that as it may, what is even less clear in this preface, in which Scholem also asserts that he distanced himself "from the confusing welter of fact and fiction" that offered itself to his "spade-work," is whether one should or should not, in fact, read this lecture. On the one hand, Scholem writes that the *Zohar*'s importance is "generally acknowledged," but, on the other hand, he suggests that some readers "will miss little by skipping the fifth lecture" (vii). A strange indifference, then, if not the inscription of a melancholic self-deprecation, a seemingly uncharged and dis-affected connection and a "departure," a severance from something that will not be missed, all appear quite strikingly to coagulate in the language that articulates itself around the "Spain" of the *Zohar.* What remains, therefore, is a strong sense of separation, the repeated inscription of a rhetoric of longing and sadness that is also figured as hard, constructive, and reconstructive work, and a striking instance in which Scholem himself tells his readers that he "departed."

Consider that the *Zohar* remains significantly marked by the rhetoric of sadness throughout Scholem's writings. The *Zohar* is "departed" from, and it too goes through a process of reconstruction. It takes place upon the ground of the traumatic realization of a loss, namely that of an object that may not have been there in the first place, the loss, in other words, of another cataclysmic "nothing." This is what Giorgio Agamben referred to as "the sadness of the scholar."

In a later short piece, Scholem confirms that the *Zohar* "itself" may, in fact, be added to the list of originary events. Scholem also sharpens his descriptions of such events, whether they are nonobjects (he writes of *Gegenstandslosigkeit,* purposelessness or objectlessness), objects, or persons.[46] As in the case of the symbol, the relation to this "nothing" may be by way of a voice, but it is not necessarily discursive. The nonobject, toward which knowledge cannot cross over, which it cannot penetrate, *die Erkenntnis kann nicht herausführen,* appears, at any rate, simply to be found by or taught, *gelehrt wird,* to some anonymous consciousness, out of the first pages of the *Zohar* (a book earlier described as "written somewhere in the heart of Castile").[47] As he addresses the "character of knowledge" of the Kabbalah, Scholem discusses the tradition in which the *Zohar* situates itself.

This tradition is, as we have seen earlier, a "medium" within which every thing, almost, remains connected. Note that the tradition is "useful," "applicable," and, finally, "transmissible," only to the extent that it is "oral": "anwendbar wird sie nur, wo sie 'mündlich', das heißt aber tradierbar wird." Scholem extends the structure of the cataclysmic, originary event to the text he reads. He clearly locates his own reading as wanting out and elsewhere, one that longs for its source, "die Kreatur von ihrem Medium aus zu ihrer Quelle vorzudringen sucht," and his writing as emerging from a context that is as sad and as irreparable as it is infinite. Scholem is the clearest on the question of place when he inscribes a rhetoric of sadness that is not (that cannot be?) the kabbalist's. Scholem writes: "There is something infinitely disheartening to the assertion of the purposelessness of the highest knowledge, as is learned from the early pages of the *Zohar, es ist etwas unendlich Trostloses um die Aufstellung der Gegenstandslosigkeit,* objectlessness, *der höchsten Erkenntnis, die auf den ersten Seiten des Buches* Sohar *gelehrt wird.*"[48] Now that Scholem explained that there is no way out, that God is not outside, that God is the medium, the tradition, where the creature must remain in order to be with God (the creature must remain, "unabwendbar im Medium bleibend, denn noch Gott selbst ist ja Tora, und die Erkenntnis kann nicht herausführen"), it is hard to understand why the kabbalist would still long for an elsewhere, how the rhetoric of sadness could be his. The history and the occurrence of language that I am trying to read is that by which the occasion of a loss becomes also, for Scholem, the inscription of a language of sadness. Again a (cataclysmic?) despair-provoking nothing, a nonobject is figured as the place, the source and context that comes to be lost, that comes to be learned as being lost and nonexistent. This is also the history by which this loss has already become part of a production process of recovery and restoration, a process that would reconstruct and piece together its fragments into an integral whole, a figure of completion that remains marked by loss and lack ("there emerged from the confusing welter of fact and fiction a picture, *Bild*, more or less definite though not at all points complete").[49] This process is history and it is language. It translates and reconstructs an originary event which, like the *Zohar*, "at first sight seems to be pure nonsense" (167). This is the event of a dispersal, of a linguistic dispersal, "a rainbow picture of linguistic eclecticism" (164) that is constituted by "a multitude of writings of apparently very different character, loosely assembled under the title 'Zohar'" (something that seems, at first, "to leave no argument against the view that they do in fact belong to different writers and different periods" [159]). By the end of this process, the figure is in place, its language fully clarified. It emerges from a field of infinite despair, dispersal, and devastation, and it comes to be reconstructed and established as "the real *Zohar*" a book that "can be definitely asserted" as being "the work of one author" (163).

That, in turn, "Spain" as the place and context of the language of the *Zohar* and of much of what is called Jewish mysticism would be heavily associated, invested with and divested of the value of departure, exile, and longing, even of a certain unattainability, is hardly surprising when one considers the construction of Jewish history around that insistent lost object, the "legacy" of which keeps being reinscribed. Yet it could already be noted that this *topos*, this "common-place," takes the form, in Scholem's language, of the appropriation, even incorporation of another's departure ("I departed"). Benjamin, it is well known, never quite completed his departure, and never reached, never made it into Spain. He was buried at its border, in Port Bou, Spain, which in the twelfth and thirteenth centuries was neither a unified, "complete" country, nor bore the name "Spain." Spain appears now, more than ever, as a highly distant—in fact, unattainable—object, a distant place and context as *Gegestandlosigkeit,* that provides the occasion for something that "readers will not miss." Spain is also worked into a figure and a locus of distance and separation that is hardly even connected to itself. Spain is therefore also an occurrence of and the occasion for the rhetoric of sadness in the history of the friendship. We now turn toward a more detailed exploration of this rhetoric, language, and history.

Conversations with Benjamin

> What I am able to offer here is the story of our friendship and my testimony.
>
> —Gershom Scholem, *Walter Benjamin*

The dual story and history of a language that takes place in sadness comes together around the events that surround Benjamin's death as Scholem relates them. Scholem meets Benjamin for the very last time—though he could only know that at the time he wrote, or at any rate, belatedly—in Paris in 1938 while on his way to New York to deliver the lectures that would become *Major Trends in Jewish Mysticism.* Having returned to Jerusalem, Scholem later learns of Benjamin's suicide on November 8, 1940, when already at work on the printed version of these lectures.[50] Aside from the figures of loss to which I have already alluded, Scholem then inscribes, at the very beginning of *Major Trends,* what can be considered the last chapter in the history of the friendship. Insofar, however, as Scholem would delay writing that history for another thirty-five years, this last chapter could also be read as the first installment of that history. The temporality thus remains, as we have seen, one that transcends historical order, and what I am referring to as a chapter already acquires a major attribute of the originary events I described earlier, the context and place of all the language that follows.

For now, upon the first page of what is to become his magnum opus, the book that remains the grounding text of the study of Jewish mysticism, the founding scholar of Jewish mysticism writes the first and the most impressive instance of the rhetoric of sadness, one that also situates, if negatively, all the work that follows. Scholem writes a commemorative monument, a sort of permanent memorial, a stele or tombstonelike *Andenken* to Walter Benjamin's memory, indeed, to Benjamin's silent memory.[51]

Why silent? Benjamin is never mentioned again, let alone quoted, in the book, and only very rarely in all of Scholem's subsequent works, all of which are basic texts for the study of Jewish mysticism.[52] Benjamin is thus firmly located, kept not only isolated and concealed, but even sealed off, in a separate portion of these works, the salvaging and reconstructive endeavor to which the story of a friendship, along with the editing of the correspondence, is itself testimony.[53] Buried and not buried in an otherwise unmarked and unfound grave, Benjamin appears to remain, henceforth, almost absolutely silent.

In the particular case of *Major Trends*, Benjamin's spectral and silent presence at the very opening of the book is more than an occasional intrusion of life as death into a scholarly work. It even becomes conspicuous, not only because, as Eduardo Cadava points out, Benjamin had anticipated his burial in his "own paper graveyard,"[54] and not only because of the way Benjamin and Scholem continue to be perceived, for the most part, as kindred spirits (at least regarding their affinities on the subject of "Jewish theology").[55] Rather, and most strikingly, it becomes conspicuous when, in a rare acknowledgment of his intellectual debt, Scholem belatedly (and almost secretly, in a note consigned exclusively to the 1957 German edition) inscribes what seems to be the first occurrence of Benjamin's name in print in any of Scholem's writings. Up to that inscription, and aside from the *Andenken* of *Major Trends*, Scholem had apparently left Benjamin completely *out of print*. In this note, however, Scholem describes Benjamin's study of the Baroque mourning play (*Trauerspiel*) as a "most significant" source of his own discussion of allegory and symbol, a distinction that has often been recognized as governing much of Scholem's own work. We are, however, in 1957: Benjamin has been dead for seventeen years, Scholem is still seven years away from publishing his first essay on Benjamin ("Walter Benjamin," 1964),[56] and the original lectures of *Major Trends* have already undergone three revisions (1941, 1946, 1954; the last revisions were made in 1960, but the 1957 German "update" on Benjamin never made it into English).

Consider, however, that the knowledge of their friendship hardly rendered necessary the note of the German edition in order to read Benjamin as being an important occasion of the occurrence of Scholem's language, as providing, to some extent, the place and context of this language. Still, aside from this isolated note, there appears to be no philological evidence, in Scholem's work, of Benjamin having played any role in his scholarly endeavor. Benjamin is left out of this and other moments in the study of all trends of Jewish mysticism (as if he had had nothing to say about any of it—and whether or not he did is part of what is at stake here). Benjamin becomes a context, then, a historical and bibliographical connection, that may and therefore has already disappeared from the writing of Jewish mysticism. Benjamin and Benjamin's language (as well as Scholem's language on Benjamin) withdraw, depart, and disappear precisely as context. This figuration and disappearance as context is finalized in an added turn downward, an added trope, when Benjamin himself must in turn be contextualized. Benjamin is repeatedly subsumed under the dominant voice of Scholem, and of others who seek to label and figure him out as a "mystic," or to assess his place and position vis-à-vis an "object" ("Jewish mysticism"), which, strictly speaking, did not exist prior to Scholem's foundational intervention.[57] At this point, Scholem remains throughout the major, if not the only, but at any rate the most vocal, authority as to how to locate Benjamin, as to what is Benjamin's relation to Judaism, and as to whether Benjamin is or is not a Jewish mystic, whether he can be contextualized in the Jewish mystical tradition.

The habit of citing Scholem as an unavoidable proof text finds here its origins, though it may have become a strikingly standard practice only with Habermas's discussion of both Walter Benjamin and Jacques Derrida as "Jewish mystics."[58] It hardly begins to clarify anything, however, let alone Benjamin's place, his taking place in the language of Jewish mysticism. Considering the recurrence of the word "mystical" in what has been written by and on Benjamin, the question of his relation to and position in Scholem's work, as well as in Jewish mysticism, deserves much more attention that it has drawn so far. Aside from a reading of Benjamin that is already under way,[59] this entails a double task, the first part of which is to further explore what the "place" is that Benjamin already occupies, how he figures in the language of Jewish mysticism as it occurs in Scholem's work. This would further illuminate the rhetoric of sadness in this language. It would also render possible a second task, namely the emergence, not so much of a context, then, but of a different taking place of language, the possibility of considering other linguistic occurrences of Jewish mysticism, but also of the language of its texts, and of the language of "our place in al-

Andalus." This is an endeavor that would demonstrate that the texts ("Benjamin," "Spain," "Jewish mysticism") are "comparable."[60] And it necessitates a reading of the way language and its place(s) are already constituted and a reconsideration of the way this "place" is also, in fact, a linguistic, textual one.

What is at stake here is therefore not an argument about the "silencing" of Benjamin (or about the "erasure" of an alleged proper "context" for a study of "our place in al-Andalus"). Rather this is an attempt to show that the taking place of language in Jewish mysticism, and Benjamin's mode of "presence" in it, is determined by a deep-seated phonocentrism and an uninterrogated notion of "life" (which requires that be shown here what Jacques Derrida has called the "systematic and historical solidarity" of such phono- and biocentrism).[61] It is also an attempt to illuminate the taking place of language, the function of a disappearing "context" and place of language, and, in its very figuration, the rhetoric of sadness that is constitutive of this language. My argument therefore is that Benjamin, and the relation to him that is inscribed in the language of the history of a friendship, becomes an originary event that also unsettles the rhetoric of sadness. The intensity of this event needs to be read carefully, for it is an intricate and complex construction, an event of language that comes to constitute its place only insofar as this place, the occasion of its occurrence, is lost. As an indicator of the place and taking place of this language, as one of its striking originary events that, for Scholem, constitute the place and context of language, Benjamin is articulated, figured, and constructed in and by the rhetoric of sadness. He is an occurrence of this language that is also related to the figure of "Spain" and its "legacy."

Beginning with *Major Trends*, then, but brought to what will first appear as a stable, restful, and silent position by way of the history of a friendship, Benjamin can been located in but also as a "place," the context of the event of language written by the scholar of Jewish mysticism. This place parallels and illuminates the conception of history and of language that we have begun to see the scholar of mysticism as construing and building, from the originary silent voice to the "hollow and spectral" voice of silence. As "immensely sad eyes dominate the landscape prearranged for them, and the auricle of a big ear seems to be listening for its sounds," Benjamin becomes a figure of silence, a silent voice.[62] An allegory of the originary events of the Jewish tradition, Benjamin becomes as alive, abyssal, and distant, as voiceless (a mute voice and a mute word) and ineffable and finally as lost, as the object(s) of Jewish mysticism.[63]

Is Benjamin, however, such an "object"? Has he become, in fact, a site, a commonplace, and a figure of mysticism "itself," and of Jewish mysticism in particular? Although I believe that repetitive references to and discussions of Benjamin's mysticism, messianism, and even Judaism are evidence enough of this figurative role, one of the purposes of this chapter is to show that his "place" in Jewish mysticism functions as the place of language, as the originary event out of which language emerges in the "field" of Jewish mysticism. I am not implying that this figuration has been universally accepted, nor that all uses of these words imply an uncritical attitude. Yet I do want to consider the way Benjamin has become constituted as such a "mystical" figure in the very writings of the founder of Jewish mysticism. This implies nothing more, as I have said, than the "demonstration of the comparability" of Benjamin as such an object, as the figure of an originary event, a context of and in Scholem's language, its comparability with other objects and originary events of and in (the language of) Jewish mysticism. I seek to account for the following: if it is indeed the case that Benjamin is such a figure of an originary event within which Scholem's language is situated, how did he become so? How does this becoming, this occurrence, take place? What indications can we learn from this taking place regarding the place of language in Jewish mysticism (i.e., in the discourse of Jewish mysticism)? To paraphrase Philippe Lacoue-Labarthe, the question here is: what is the figure that Benjamin already "was" in order for him to become a figure of Jewish mysticism? Or, again following Lacoue-Labarthe, what is the "idea" of Jewish mysticism that could be figured as Walter Benjamin?[64] The purpose of these questions is not only to continue our considerations of "our place," the notion of "context," and the place and taking place of language at "our place in al-Andalus," but most specifically, to raise the possibility of considering that neither Benjamin nor "Spain" constitutes simply a "context," that language—the language of Jewish mysticism, the language of al-Andalus—does not, or does not exclusively, find its place in such an extraneous context. In other words, if Benjamin has become a figure of Jewish mysticism, a site of its occurrence as a linguistic event, it is because he corresponds to a certain idea, indeed, to a certain occurrence of language that is constitutive of Jewish mysticism, an occurrence that takes place in sadness. The rhetoric of sadness articulates the language of Scholem as a *Trauerarbeit*, a work of mourning and incorporation. The figuring of language, of its place, and most legibly, of Walter Benjamin, is a work of agony and mourning. It is a construction project that leads toward Gershom Scholem's *Major Trends in Jewish Mysticism.*[65] In the very occurrence of this language, both the figure of Benjamin and the "nothing," indeed the silent voice—which emerges out of Scholem's text and that becomes, as we began to see, the foundation of his thought, and the place of language in this thought—imprint themselves, becoming both tradition and history.

The nothing and the silent voice also show themselves, however, in their disappearance, in their coming to an *end* in tradition and in language, becoming and disappearing out of language, as it were, as the place and context of language's occurrence. I am not suggesting, as I hope is clear, that such originary events are, in fact, prior to language, but rather that they are so construed, following the logic of the originary events that we have seen earlier. On the one hand, Benjamin disappears from the discourse that concerns itself with and maintains Jewish mysticism, while nonetheless figuring that very discourse (the *topos*, the "common-place" of Benjamin-the-Jewish-mystic); and, on the other hand, "Spain" disappears (or "ends"), while nonetheless figuring as the historical "context" or place out of which the main text of Kabbalah, the *Zohar*, emerges along with other texts, the texts that I address in the other chapters of this book. Hence, insofar as the figurations and translations of Benjamin are doubled by his disappearance (remember that we will see that Benjamin "ends," that he becomes silent, a silent voice), Benjamin (much like "Spain" and other originary, cataclysmic events that are constitutive of but also always already separate and vanishing from, the language of Jewish mysticism) is also clearly inscribed onto the topography and construction, the language of Jewish mysticism. In the remaining sections of this chapter, I will closely read Scholem's text as a topography where language (figuration, translation, and writing) and the appearance of Jewish mysticism, of Benjamin, and of al-Andalus, constitute this "phenomenon of a disappearance" (Ronell). Since no account has been provided for what could then be called a dual "phenomenon of disappearance," I suggest that an attention to this series of linguistic occurrences will illuminate our understanding of the language, the place and taking place of language at "our place in al-Andalus."

> This belongs to a cryptological reading of our haunted rapport to Benjamin.
>
> —Avital Ronell, *Finitude's Score*
>
> . . . by reading the writing couple whose sustained encounter takes place on the grounds of a catastrophe.
>
> —Avital Ronell, *Dictations*
>
> Installation, in technology, is therefore both provocation and stele.
>
> —Philippe Lacoue-Labarthe, *Typography*

At Spain's very border, where he died, Benjamin's grave was never found. Scholem reproduces Hannah Arendt's report, in which Arendt describes how she failed to find the grave a few months after Benjamin's death: "It was not to be found; his name was not written anywhere, nowhere did it stand, *Es war nicht zu finden, nirgends stand sein Name*."[66] But the name, though neither standing nor, perhaps, speakable, will find itself inscribed. The rhetoric of sadness, of loss and mourning, was already inscribed, as we saw, at the very opening of the book *Major Trends*, which consists of a series of lectures delivered in New York, beginning in February 1938. As already mentioned, it was while on his way to give those lectures that Scholem had his last encounter with Benjamin.[67] The conclusion of this encounter (i.e., the moment of departure and separation) is, significantly enough, never narrated, never related by Scholem. It was at times a difficult meeting and the conversation did not always go smoothly. Scholem explains that he had planned to see Benjamin once again, on his way back from New York, but that meeting did not take place, so the two friends never saw each other again. Less than two years later, stranded on the Franco-Spanish border at Port Bou, and following his failure to have his visa of entry into Spain recognized, Benjamin, Scholem tells us, took his own life on "September 26 or 27" 1940 (226). With the inscription of this ultimate departure, *Major Trends* begins where the story of a friendship ends, opening in fact with and as a wound. Intensely associated with the unattainability of Spain, it locates most profoundly the rest of the book, from the very first page. This wound provides the book with the most literal of openings. *Major Trends* opens with the dedication to Benjamin, the memorial of his death and unfound grave.

In Port Bou, where Benjamin is buried, the coffins are not put into the ground, Hannah Arendt also reported; rather, they are placed in terraces and "are pushed into . . . stone walls, *Steinwälle*," walls which, judging from the numerous photographs, appear to be as white and as silent as stones.[68]

Note that in this dedication, the departure is that of a disjointed figure (the tripartite division into capitalized figures of "Metaphysician," "Critic," and "Scholar" evokes Kantian distinctions, as well as the bridging of the "immeasurable gulf" that separates the Kantian realms of cognitive faculties).[69] It marks a separation that irreparably distances not only the possibility of "unity" itself (in the later German version, Scholem will figure this lost union as that of an encounter, a *sich treffen*), but also renders the "Scholar" ever more remote, whose (dis)appearance is once again associated with a language of sadness. Most importantly, the dedication reads like a tombstone. It inscribes the name of Benjamin, it makes it stand again, and encrypts it somewhere rather than nowhere (*nirgends*), atop a thick volume that will continue to serve as the founding and cornerstone, the indispensable place and context, of Scholem's edifice ("Jewish mysticism"). This "stone" and with it the book upon which it stands cannot be perceived henceforth but as grave and crypt, the "dark ground" in relation to which the edifice, that construction of language, necessarily stands. In this construction, the lost and fragmented unity broken by a cataclysm is pieced together, and the gulf is "closed in."

The echo of ruins, dear to Benjamin, the impossibility of synthesis that underscores the object's loss, and the unattainable dimension of a Spain placed in parentheses, are now all inscribed as being lost, as having ended, and each "object continues to recall the fact that something else was lost."[70] Consider that parentheses are the only marks of punctuation inscribed on the page; they mark the finite temporality of Benjamin's years, and they mark, in the same way, the finite dimension of "(Spain)." Everything is now as distant and as lost as the unifying ability of the genial friend, as lost as the "Spain" of the *Zohar* (remember that this is where Scholem tells us he "departed"). These losses, clear indications of the rhetoric of sadness, are both brought together and dispersed forever, in this impossible stele and place—this "commemorative monument" in which the object "betokens the place, the dates and the circumstances in which desires were banished"[71]—in the abysses of separation (made even more apparent by the absence of closure, one that could have been provided by an ostensibly absent punctuation—save, again, for the parentheses) that are made visible in the white space that situates and surrounds (the taking place of) the dedication and that which

TO THE MEMORY OF

WALTER BENJAMIN

(1892–1940)

The friend of a lifetime whose genius united the insight of the Metaphysician, the interpretative power of the Critic and the erudition of the Scholar

DIED AT PORT BOU (SPAIN)

ON HIS WAY TO FREEDOM

follows it.[72] Like the inscription of a name that is unbearably absent even in its presence (*nirgends stand sein Name,* nowhere does his name stand), substituting for a grave that was never found, yet marking the very place of that grave, *Major Trends in Jewish Mysticism* testifies to the place of language. It is itself an event of language that emerges out of the tomb and entombed, mourned, dead friend. It testifies to and marks the impossible "closing in" of the tomb, but it also constitutes that tomb as that which encrypts and locates, and perhaps "resonates" in, the language of Jewish mysticism.

> The photographs before me clearly indicate that this grave, which is completely isolated and utterly separate from the actual burial places, is an invention of the cemetery attendants. . . . Visitors who were there have told me that they had the same impression, *Eindruck.* Certainly the spot is beautiful, but the grave is apocryphal.
>
> —Gershom Scholem, *Walter Benjamin*

That an originary event from which Scholem's words are definitely separated needs to be constructively repaired, and that a definite unity, which though remembered, is now inscribed as lost is clearly not something that begins with Benjamin's death. Nor does the necessity of reinscribing this loss necessarily end with that death, or stop from being governed by the voice. Arnaldo Momigliano notes, for example, that "Gershom Scholem has carried on a dialogue with Benjamin . . . that not even death has interrupted." Truly, then, "these men . . . possess an extraordinary talent for communication,"[73] all of which should continue to make us reflect on the distinctions between life and death upon which Scholem's language otherwise seems to insist. Incidentally, then, and possibly without this ever affecting the conversation, Benjamin may have always already been lost. He may at least have "died" much earlier.

Scholem writes in fact, that almost ten years earlier, in 1931, "Benjamin was at peace with himself and had finished with his life, *er war mit sich im Reinen und hatte mit seinem Leben abgeschlossen.*"[74] Benjamin has already closed and concluded his life, and at that early point he is said to be already dead. This may explain why two years later Scholem writes: "I am happy that you are still among the living, *daß Du noch lebst,* that you still live, and I hasten to assure you that the same holds true for me."[75] Scholem thus repeatedly implies that his letters, his language, may always already be taking place "on the grounds of a catastrophe." Indeed, he alludes to the fact that both he and Benjamin may have been dead, and that his own being alive is no less surprising, no less in need of confirmation than that of Benjamin. It is never obvious, then, nor can it be taken for granted by either of them, that the occasion of their conversation is, in fact, life. Consider how this was already confirmed by Scholem's opening of this other major book. We have seen, in *Major Trends*, that Scholem's language of beginnings certainly held a strong rapport to the devastation of death, but he begins here, with the following words, the history of the friendship: "Not many people are still alive, *Es leben nur noch wenige Menschen*, who remember Walter Benjamin."[76]

Both Benjamin and Scholem may, therefore, always already be dead. The occasion of their conversations is already located not in life, but precisely on the grounds of devastation. This explains why they share a common interest in another language of sadness, namely, "lamentations, *Klagelieder*—a subject I [this is Scholem speaking] occupied myself with intensively" (84/E65). This too, paradoxically, provides the ground for further conversations. They have "numerous conversations about laments and lamentations, *unserer vielen Gespräche über Klage und Klagelied*" (106/E82). This bare living, even barely living, that articulates the context for the first of Scholem's auto-bio-graphical writings, is perhaps less remarkable for its recurring preoccupation with, if not resolute anticipation of, death and mourning, than for the fact that it underscores Scholem's strange inability to write the story of his life.

Seemingly incapable of bringing himself to write a language that would not be one of sadness, that would not find the occasion, the place, and context of its occurrence in the devastation of death, Scholem never quite brings himself to write a bio-graphy, neither auto- nor allo-biography. Scholem thus ends that which will have to qualify as (the story of) his life, his *Jugenderinnerungen*, even earlier than the story of his friendship, with the very years that mark another of his departures, this time his definite departure from Germany (1923–25) and from the world he shares with Benjamin.[77] Whether this is a further indication that Scholem considers that he too, at that time, is "finished with his life" may be difficult to assess (the English version of *From Berlin to Jerusalem* ends with "Thus began my academic career," a career in which the "end" of Spain and "the catastrophe" of 1492 will, of course, loom large).[78] Be that as it may, in his "testimony"—

one that appears more and more as what Jacques Derrida calls "an allo- and thanatography"[79]—Scholem does make clear that he is "seeking a stable position, *einen festen Ort*," a position which, fittingly enough, has to produce and reconstruct a restful totality.[80] His "efforts to understand Judaism," Scholem thus hopes, could be pieced together; they "would more clearly fit together into an integral whole, *zu einem Ganzen fügen würden*."[81]

Whether this whole is, in fact, made less or more remote by Benjamin's suicide is also not something that can be clearly established. It should be noted, however, that the revelation of this ideal (the fitting together into a whole, a restful place) comes after the extension of one of the many and lengthy, all too lengthy, separations that mark the friendship ("After all, four years was a long time in the lives of young men" [130]). Once again, a wounding distance and separation seem to provide a relation (or lack thereof) with the occasion of later conversations. These too, however, can turn to monologues. In 1927, knowing that Scholem is arriving in Paris to meet him, Benjamin is also compelled to stage his own departure. He decides to "defer" their meeting, almost running for his life: "If Scholem were not arriving today, I probably would not have gone," Benjamin writes. "But I fled, *aber ich bin geflohen*. Right now I could not bear his sometimes rather ostentatious self-assurance."[82]

On the other hand, and precisely because of repeated departures, separations, and demises, there should be no doubt as to the importance of a project of unification in *Major Trends*, a project I began to discuss earlier. This is a scientific project, to be sure, if not a univocal one, and it bears here added relevance. For if, as we saw, Scholem always stresses that a certain distance is characteristic of Jewish mysticism (Scholem, we saw, writes of an "abyss" between God and man "which can be crossed by nothing but the *voice*"),[83] his description of mysticism as the ultimate stage of a tripartite dialectical process is—Rotenstreich's analyses notwithstanding—quite revealing of an insistent drive to close the gap. Note, for example, the descriptions that Scholem quotes approvingly, descriptions that involve "immediate awareness" or "immediate contact with God."[84] Here too, then, we may wonder at what landscape of devastation is figured, what unity has been lost and what traumatic wound has been opened that mysticism would have been exposed to and that it would come to close and heal. Scholem once again shows the exposure in order to "proceed" and efface it, to construct over it, thus maintaining the structure of the "originary event," out of which language is constructed. This passage, which we have already considered, must be quoted again.

> Mysticism does not deny or overlook the abyss; on the contrary, it begins by realizing its existence, but from there it proceeds to a quest for the secret that will close it in, the hidden path that will span it. It strives to piece together the fragments broken by the religious cataclysm, to bring back the old unity which religion has destroyed but on a new plane, where the world of mythology and that of revelation meet in the soul of man. (8)

Mysticism, then, is what responds to the abyss, but it is also that which, "striving" to "close it in," engages in a reconstructive project that would "piece together the fragments broken . . . to bring back the old unity." Mysticism both opposes itself to the abyss and finds in it its place and context. It therefore opposes itself to that which does not strive for the same closure. It opposes itself to "a religion which has severed all links with the mythical" (22), a religion that does not maintain a strong connection to its source. Mysticism, under the (re)constructive figuration of the symbol, wants to connect with that which it recognizes as being distant. Seeking to resolve a dialectical tension and doing so on a "new plane" (26), it opposes itself to allegory, an allegory that also finds its place in the abyss, but relates to it, it would seem, differently. Allegory, writes Scholem, "arises, as it were, from the gap which . . . opens between the form and its meaning. The two are no longer indissolubly welded together" (ibid.). It is therefore not only that the abyss, the gap, is the occasion, the place, and occurrence for language (allegory or symbol), but also that the distance must be asserted, integrated, and, most importantly, resolved and covered within language (as was apparently the case before: the gap is said to have "opened"—past tense—and the terms are "*no longer* indissolubly welded together"). So it is that the symbol, rather than the allegory, inscribes most forcefully the rhetoric of sadness, while allegory is chastised for not registering the same sadness, the same mourning. Allegory does not relate to its place under the mode of negativity. Everything that is associated with mysticism is figured as solidly linked by such "welded" relations, connections that secured and "strengthened [the Halakhah's] hold over the people" (29), over against allegory and philosophy. Philosophy "has no relation whatever to the Halakhah itself" (ibid.), and, like the voice of Aristotle, it may therefore "sound hollow and spectral to ears attuned to the new Kabbalah" (249). Like allegory, philosophy is criticized for achieving no more than a false synthesis with Halakhah; and, even when benefiting from the genius of Maimonides—an Andalusī "genius" that, unlike that of the "friend of a lifetime," did not "unite" nor unify anything—such false synthesis cannot produce nor construct anything. It must "remain *sterile*, and the genius of the man whose spirit moulded [the two] into a semblance of union cannot obscure their intrinsic disparity" (29).

If the disparity is intrinsic, however, it only confirms that the abyss is constitutive of language. Mysticism is exposed to the abyss of this failed unity, but it wants to stand on the other side, it wants to construct its own voice as a bridge over the abyss and to be on the side of relations that are "strong and unbroken" (30). Like Scholem facing the despair of the *Wissenschaft*, mysticism desires a home that remains distant from its language. It is governed by a constant drive for unification that is threatened only by everything that allegory and philosophy (and Spain!) are made to stand for. Much like the logic of the originary event and of the tradition that is disconnected from it, that which is separate acquires the attributes of that from which it is separated. Allegory and (Hispano-Arabic, Judeo-Arabic) philosophy thus become figures of the abyss. They become the context, the occasion, for the emergence of the Kabbalah. They are also figured as that which can be reconstructed and worked into the totalizing language of the symbol.

As the insistent mark of the cataclysm that Scholem's mysticism comes to heal, allegory, at any rate, remains "marked by a specific vocabulary of anxiety."[85] Scholem clearly joins Goethe and others for whom, Rainer Nägele describes, allegory is placed within "an associative chain" along with "notions of dismemberment, dissolution, and sterility." Allegory is "a threat to the wholeness of life, body, and beauty" (ibid.). In *Major Trends*, and by the added virtue of allegory's "infinity of meaning," which arbitrarily—as David Biale explains[86]—"attaches to every representation,"[87] allegory is also the figure of Walter Benjamin, who had—how could Scholem, how could anyone ignore this?—"defended" it in his *Trauerspiel* book. Threatening the integrity and unity of the place and context that is the occasion of language, threatening the construction and reconstruction of the whole, allegory is also the Benjamin "whose harmonious view of the world was shattered and in disrepair, *gesprengt und verfallen war*."[88] As that which also threatens beauty, allegory is the unacceptable sign of the irreversible separation from the friend, from the genius and the voice of the friend, from the cataclysmic sterility of Spain, and from the astoundingly beautiful picture, the figure that Scholem draws of the friend. With this description, we turn toward specific dimensions of the figuration of Benjamin, his becoming a figure in language, an originary event's figure of speech that is not only shattered, but shattering. Benjamin becomes another figure of repeated devastations.

> I shall certainly be the last to deny that [Kabbalism's] representatives often lost their way and went over the edge of the precipice.
>
> —Gershom Scholem, *Major Trends*

Although Scholem's description is too long to be reproduced here in more than just fragments, it may be enough to mention that it functions so as to preserve and maintain, and more precisely, to produce a full image and figure, *Gestalt,* of Benjamin, including that which is—Benjamin himself had noted, in one of his statements about physiognomy—rarely accounted for: the gait, *Gang.*[89] In this detailed description, Scholem also alludes to the place of language. Scholem writes that Benjamin's mouth is "full." This appears to be more than an odd detail, and rather indicates the prominence of Scholem's—by now familiar—attention to the voice. We turn, then, to the way Benjamin's voice is going to constitute and be constituted as a major occasion, a prominent location for the occurrence of the history of the friendship. What I want to address here is the way in which Scholem's relation, his connection to Benjamin and to his voice, inscribes itself in the story's language. Benjamin, sadness, and the voice, in relation to which the language of the history of the friendship is constituted, are thus positioned as originary events. They are located as the occasion for the occurrence of the storytelling, for the occurrence of its language. What kind of "place" this originary event articulates and what relation it bears to Scholem's language is what we are continuing to explore.

"Benjamin had a beautiful voice, melodious and easily remembered" —the German highly emphasizes beauty by putting it first—*Schön seine Stimme, die melodisch und einprägsam war,* the voice imprints itself, it gives rise to a further chain of events that will often be rendered as impressions. Let us take note of such impressions, therefore, as they too are going to reinscribe themselves in many more places, and as they indicate the mode of the relation to that which is the place of their occurrence. Impressions are the tradition, a tradition which, as oral as it is, will appear to "resonate" with the voice only to the extent that the voice's imprint remains marked, only to the extent that it remains, as it were, *in print.*[90]

When Benjamin took off his glasses, something he did in fact quite often in conversation, *im Gespräch*, he revealed "a pair of striking [*sehr eindrucksvoll*, making an impression again], dark blue eyes. His nose was well proportioned, the lower part of his face still very gentle at that time, the mouth full and sensuous, *sein Mund voll und sinnlich*." Except for his mustache, "his face was always clean shaven and slightly pink in color; otherwise his skin was absolutely white. His hands were beautiful, slender and expressive, *Die Hände schön, schmal und ausdrucksvoll*."[91] Although this figure, insistently impressive and expressive as it is, may appear fragmentary, perhaps even dismembered, it is important not to lose sight of it as the figure of a further fullness (like the mouth) and, again, of a whole.

Not only Judaism but also a certain silence together provide the occasion for Benjamin's "fullness": "taken as a whole, his physiognomy was definitely Jewish, but in a quiet, unobtrusive, *stille*, silent way, as it were, *der Gesamteindruck*, the whole imprint, the whole impression, *der Physiognomie war durchaus jüdisch, aber auf eine stille gleichsam eingezogene Weise*" (ibid.). Benjamin, whole but (dis)membered and already silent—already a figure of Jewish mysticism—cannot be named, he is not what one can name, *was man nennen könnte*, beautiful, and although the fame of his photographic portraits would perhaps indicate the contrary, "no one would have called [him] handsome, he was not what is called handsome, *Benjamin war nicht, was man schön nennen könnte*" (ibid.). Who makes the call for handsomeness? And what is called, *was heißt*, handsome? And can it prevent Benjamin from appearing as an insistent figure, a very impressive if also time-frozen image of a beautiful whole, a totality that recalls a restful, certainly quiet, and Jewish place? Can it prevent him from appearing as a full mouth out of which sense may emerge, but where hardly any meaning can reside?[92]

We have begun to consider that Benjamin also appears in Scholem's language as the disruption of a figure, if not solely as a figure of disruption, and of allegory. Substantiating this argument will take us back to Benjamin's "gait." For Scholem certainly shows himself to have been well aware of Benjamin's position, or, more precisely, of his "posture, *Haltung*, at any one fraction of a second of taking a step."[93] Benjamin himself writes that only photography can open up the space in which one could become aware of this posture. This suggests that Scholem, who mentions photographs at the end of his account of Benjamin's "physiognomy," is writing in an isolated and decontextualized space such as photography is, and also that he has quite an arresting vision. It further suggests that Scholem is describing Benjamin as a kind of photographic image, an arrested figure and a frozen *Gestalt.*

Yet it is precisely here that Benjamin appears as a disruption, disturbing the speed of a continuous, speed-wise stable, at times even frozen and arrested, temporality.[94] The image is not entirely static, it does not only suggest a restful posture or position, but appears rather as a complicated motion (Scholem also provides some details about his own posture, his place and position in relation to Benjamin, and one should note here that, in spite of his self-asserted speed, Scholem is not always ahead). Benjamin, Scholem says, "did not like to walk fast, and it was not easy for me, who was much taller, had long legs, and took big, quick steps, to adapt to his gait, *seiner Gangart anzupassen,* when we were walking together. Very often he would stop and go on talking. He was easy to recognize from behind by his peculiar gait, *von hinten war er an seinem Gang leicht zu erkennen*" (16/E8).

The language is quite clear and it gives us more than strong hints. In order to be preserved as a restful, undisturbed, "living," but quiet whole in the language, both the image and Benjamin's speed have to be adjusted. Whether too slow or too outspoken, something is out of joint, both stopping and going, and it has to do with Benjamin's figure and with his language ("he would stop and go on talking"). The relation to the occasion of the conversation, to that which constitutes its necessary place, must be altered to fit this context as Scholem sees it. More importantly, and in a way that may have a lot to do with Scholem's insistence on bringing Benjamin into the Jewish fold, Benjamin himself has to be confirmed in what is otherwise unobtrusively quiet: his Judaism. More precisely, Benjamin is rendered both more Jewish, and, in the same movement, more quiet (recall that Benjamin's physiognomy was unobtrusively, quietly Jewish and that it is when he speaks that Benjamin forces Scholem to slow down), more unnameable and unspeakable by way of his figuration. In order for the *Gestalt,* the figure, to be worked into a conversation that would take place within the right temporality, in order to become a symbol (in which things happen "in a momentary totality") as quiet and unobtrusive, as "alive" perhaps, as a silent voice and as a mystical experience—terms that Benjamin's entire oeuvre is engaged in disrupting, indeed, even destroying—Benjamin has to become a silent voice. It is therefore interesting to note that between the *Story of a Friendship* and *Major Trends* (for that is the chronological order the narrative establishes) the originary silence of the mystical nothing will itself come to be figured as the Jewish (silent, *still*) "legacy, *Erbschaft*," the "voice" of revelation, a voice, moreover, that means and says nothing outside of the history of its reception.[95]

Between Men

> And hence the following words of Holy Scripture now apply to you: "Arise my friend, be swift as a gazelle on the mountain rocks."
>
> —Scholem to Benjamin, 25 January 1939

> If the heterosexual denial of homosexuality results in melancholia and if melancholia operates through incorporation, then the disavowed homosexual love is preserved through the cultivation of an oppositionally defined gender identity. In other words, disavowed male homosexuality culminates *in a heightened or consolidated* masculinity, one which maintains the feminine as the unthinkable and *unnameable*.
>
> —Judith Butler, *Gender Trouble* (my emphases)

> The long history of Jewish mysticism shows no trace of feminine influence. There have been no women kabbalists . . . [Kabbalah], therefore, lacks the element of feminine emotion which has played so large a part in the development of non-Jewish mysticism, but it also remained comparatively free from the dangers entailed by the tendency toward hysterical extravagance which followed in the wake of this influence.
>
> —Gershom Scholem, *Major Trends*

From September 8 to 10, 1921, Benjamin and Scholem spend "two memorable days in a fine old house," the previous owner of which was the bishop of Bamberg.[96] At this time, then, the bishop is no longer the master of the house, and the house is now owned by a teacher and a common friend of Benjamin and Scholem: Ernst Lewy. Though Lewy is a professor of philology, there is little to suggest that he ever provides Scholem, at least, with an overwhelming love for written texts. At any rate, if such a love does develop in Scholem's heart, as his later career would seem to suggest, it is in no way comparable to his enduring fixation on voices and their silence. Such fixation will now illuminate under a different, more gendered, light, Scholem's relation to Benjamin, his work of agony, and the construction of Benjamin's figure, that we are here reading.

Early in the stay Scholem seems to feel disturbed by the power dynamics inside the Lewy household. Using terms that recall what we previously encountered as the "quiet and unobstrusive ways" of Benjamin,

Scholem writes that "Mrs. Lewy dominated her husband in a strangely quiet, silent way, *Frau Lewy beherrschte ihren Mann auf merkwürdig stille Weise*" (ibid.). The strange but powerful effects of that voice of silence are prefigured when, a few lines earlier, Scholem describes how he reads the books of a peculiar author, the style of whom borders, we are told, "on the pathological." During one of Benjamin's visits, Scholem reads to him "a long preface to one of these [books], which sounded like a voice from another planet, *wie eine Stimme von einem andern Planeten klang*" (134/E105). It is not the books so much as what they sound like when reading them out loud that has surprising dimensions.

The peculiarity, even uncanniness, of this strange and distant voice then comes to be attached to the figure of Mrs. Lewy. There is "something uncanny, *etwas Unheimliches*, about [Mr. Lewy's] wife, who spoke slowly and little, *die nur langsam und wenig sprach*: she had the attracting power of a swamp, *Sumpfig-Anziehendes*, the magic of an orchid, and the sucking and frightening quality of a clinging vine" (ibid.). Such description may begin to provide us with an account of some of Scholem's misogynistic stereotypes,[97] but it may also fill in the decontextualization, the unsettling displacement of the world of Scholem's work at Bamberg (the femininity of the dark ground that stands or lies there, its slow speed, its silent, meaningless voice being uncannily, *unheimlich*, attractive). Such a "displacement of works," which has been described by Martin Heidegger as occurring at the Bamberg cathedral (presumably where the good bishop officiated), where "the world of the work that stands there has perished," seems to constitute the condition in which Scholem finds himself on the next morning.[98] Before we turn to this next morning, however, we should slow down and remain at the unsettling site of the house at Bamberg, or at least in the neighborhood of feminine swamps and silences.

Earlier, Scholem describes another uncanny figure of silent femininity. Here, it is in the case of Dora—Benjamin's at this time not yet ex-wife—that we find another possibly haunting and swamplike figure, an even more silent presence/absence. By the time he knows her a little better, in fact, Scholem turns to Dora's case; he makes, about Dora, his own analysis of a case of hysteria: "I began to grow aware of the hysterical elements in Dora's behavior, *hysterische Elemente in Doras Verhalten*, which were sometimes suddenly triggered by the most insignificant events, *bei unscheinbarsten Anlässen*" (87/E68). Some things, barely phenomenal, *scheinbar*, cannot even be seen as appearing. More precisely, it is insofar as they do not appear, that is, only in their disappearance, that they possibly begin to make any impression. Like the missing hysteria of the kabbalists, it is to the extent that an event does not appear (like a silent voice) that Scholem becomes able to exercise his perceptive apparatus. Still, it is possible that Scholem merely wants to hear something else.

Remember that Scholem has earlier made many efforts ("*bemühte ich mich,* I worked hard") to bring Dora to speak, to reveal the secrets of Benjamin's "true self, *sein eigentliche Selbst,*" but this Dora, too, does not want to speak or write, at least not in that way, so that Scholem's "efforts" are "unfortunately not successful, without result, *leider ohne Erfolg*" (7/Eix). It is as if, by this point, Dora herself has given up even trying.

We return, then, to that other place of silence, the house whose previous owner was, undoubtedly, a man, namely, the bishop of Bamberg. We (but who, we?) are at the beginning of a new paragraph, even a new chapter in the story of this friendship. This new chapter provides some of the elements that would illuminate the investing and divesting within which we found Scholem engaged. Whereas Scholem had told us that some things may not be missed, we have already begun to notice that such things are not necessarily the less invested in (*besetzt,* cathected). The unsettling confrontation in which Scholem finds himself, however quickly, is therefore worth dwelling upon.

"We were housed in a large room with a huge double bed, *mit einem zweischläfrigen Riesenbett.*" There is obviously a lot of space, wherever and whoever "we" are, for we do seem to know where we are and where we—if not our names—stand. Most importantly, we are not too close in this large room in which we stand and this huge double bed in which, so it turns out, we lie. "When we awoke in the morning, Walter said to me"—note that, even though it has been a few years that Benjamin and Scholem have been on a first name basis, Scholem rarely refers to Benjamin in the text as "Walter." Most often, in fact, it is when there may be some confusion in the description as to whether Benjamin is addressing Scholem, in particular, or someone else who may be there at the time. This time, though, even if there is a lot of space in the room, there does not seem to be anyone else there as Walter and Gerhard are waking up on that morning (Benjamin always calls and writes to Scholem as Gerhard, addressing him only by his German given name, never by his Hebrew one). Walter, then, says to Gerhard: "When I opened my eyes just now, if you had been a woman lying there, *wenn Du jetzt*, if you now, *als ich die Augen aufschlug*, as I opened my eyes, *als Mädchen dagelegen hättest*, had been (as) a woman lying there, I would have thought I was the bishop of Bamberg, *würde ich geglaubt haben, ich sei der Bischof von Bamberg*" (135/E106). So Walter would have believed, so may almost have been his new faith, *Glaube*, had Gerhard been, that is, a woman. Scholem, who is not a woman but does stand there in that room, and may have lain there as a woman, does not remain lying there for long. Whatever cataclysmic event he is here exposed to, Scholem does not let it resonate for long, nor does he seek to produce an interpretation that would constitute that event as the origin of a tradition. And although Benjamin's words often force him to stop in his fast tracks, this time Scholem does not even pause to reflect on how he could have never been robbed of his masculinity, since, had he been a woman, he might never have lost that particular object. Keeping to his habit of making big and quick steps, failing once again in his goal of synchronizing (himself with) the slow gait and speech of Benjamin, Scholem moves speedily away from this particular morning, away from a day that flashes by, in fact, so fast that we immediately find ourselves transported straight onto the very next day. Indeed, in the limited space of one line, Scholem moves very quickly and he marches on as if the world of the work that stands or lies there at Bamberg has not, in some way, perished, as if he has not irreparably become what Laurence Rickels calls "the widow of his heterosexuality."[99] "The next day [Benjamin] presented his ideas on the nature of *Angelus*" (ibid.). The *Angelus novus* is the journal Benjamin is preparing to edit at that time, a journal that is named after one of Benjamin's famous angels—the sex of whom is, it is well known, unknown.

At this point, things are not working out too well, as Benjamin attempts to enroll Lewy as a contributor to the *Angelus*. The uncanniness of the house previously owned by our good man the bishop reappears: "the uncanny atmosphere, *das Unheimliche der Atmosphäre*, that surrounded the Lewy family really got on Benjamin's nerves, and especially on the last evening he became jumpy and irritable. In such things he was very sensitive, *Er war in solchen Dingen sehr sensitiv*" (137/E107). It is not clear whether this "sensitivity" to the uncanny (that was marked earlier as feminine, under the figure of Mrs. Lewy), echoes what we will soon discover as Dora's "strong gift for receptivity, *starke Gabe der Rezeptivität*" (31/E20), or whether it is meant to reestablish and consolidate Scholem's masculinity. It does, however, tell us that Benjamin is attuned, perhaps as receptive as Dora, to the uncanny, in ways that Scholem does not necessarily share. We need to follow more of the thread of Scholem's consolidation and construction project throughout the story of a friendship, the story of a relation and a translation, the unsettling of a ground and of a place, one of which is the place of Scholem's masculinity and that of his language.

> Has there been such a man, *hat es so einen Mann gegeben*? Or would you be man enough to be that man, *oder wärst du Manns genug, dieser Mann zu sein*?
>
> —Benjamin to Scholem, 4 February 1939

Exposed as he repeatedly has been, and perhaps not as unaware as he suggests, Scholem has quite an amount of work to do in this building project, not only because of what he sees as the impression Walter makes but because of Dora as well. I have already alluded to the importance of such impressions, and we will continue to return to them in some detail, but for now and as we closely follow the operations of Scholem's work of agony and of his phonocentrism, it is important to note that another strong impression is inscribed as being made by Dora's speech. Dora, Scholem writes, is very good with languages; her English, for example, is excellent, *ausgezeichnet*, "but her greatest talent lies in her ability to absorb, *eine überaus starke Gabe der Rezeptivität*, appropriate, and keenly respond to anything she deemed important. Her speech was very animated, *Sie sprach*, she spoke, with strong Viennese inflections; she had a knack for stimulating conversations, *Gespräche aufzubringen*, or steering them around to different subjects" (31/E20). Obviously Dora speaks, and she too has an impressive voice. Being very musical, she is reported later on as singing.

Yet, and aside from her resistance, her receptivity, and her silence, it would nonetheless seem that among her most significant interventions in the story of this friendship are those made under the guise of letters of baby Stefan (the Benjamins' son) to Scholem. Dora writes these letters, baby Stefan dictates them, and Walter is perhaps participating. Strictly speaking, they are Stefan's letters, but they are written in "Dora's handwriting, *in Doras Schrift*," and they are produced with Walter's knowledge and "possibly even his participation, *nicht ohne Walters Wissen und vielleicht auch Zutun geschrieben*" (88/E68). This makes it difficult to know whether, for Scholem, Dora actually says anything of her own, whether she is simply absorbing and redirecting, and/or whether she is here too simply conversation-enabling (or perhaps "meaning-bestowing"?). However that may be, Dora has, perhaps, the impressive and attractive dimension of a swamp since many people are, in fact, "greatly impressed, *sehr beeindruckt*, by her and a little in love, *verliebt*, with her" (31/E20). Scholem, always open to such impressive effects, also writes that Dora "made an excellent impression, *sie machte . . . einen ausgezeichneten Eindruck*," upon him (39/E27). Dora is "a decidedly beautiful, *eine ausgesprochen schöne*, elegant woman" and she takes "part in the conversations, *beteiligte sie sich an den Gesprächen*" (ibid.). Like Benjamin's mouth, Dora is described as "sensuous, *sinnlich*"; she is "a very sensuous, *sehr sinnliche*, woman" (122/E95). Dora shares therefore quite a number of features with the figure of Walter Benjamin, and, by virtue of this sharing, underscores not only that her being-together with Benjamin was highly significant, but also that the force of this significance did not fail to impress Scholem doubly.

> . . . the mouth was full and sensuous, *voll und sinnlich*.
>
> —Gershom Scholem, *Walter Benjamin*
>
> After all, four years was a long time in the lives of young men.
>
> —Gershom Scholem, *Walter Benjamin*

As we read Scholem's work of consolidation, we have considered the association of Benjamin with voice, and the investment of Scholem in voices and the impression they make. Benjamin's voice, Scholem writes, is a "beautiful voice, melodious and easily remembered, impressive, *einprägsam*" (16/E8). Benjamin's speech, as it centrally impresses itself upon the figure of him that is constructed here, makes, in its form, *Redeweise*, its own lasting impression upon Scholem, who writes that it "greatly influenced, *stark beeinflußt*," him and that he consequently "adopted a good number of his mannerisms, *seiner Manierismen*" (18/E9). Lest we think of locating Scholem as simply lying there under the sway of Benjamin, things have already been safely clarified: no such harm has been done, and the rightful owner of the conversations, if not of the house, may remain undoubted and unharmed. "To be sure, in one sense I was his equal in my conversations with him, *ich mich im Gespräch mit ihm schadlos halten konnte*, I was unharmed, did not lose a thing to him" (17/E9). The impression cuts deep, but no damage is done.

Such attempts on Scholem's part at (re?)asserting not only the wholeness of his body, but also a dubious, even doubted, equality ("in one sense, I was his equal"), and at times even superiority, are not infrequent in the story of this friendship. We have considered some of what this may indicate in the (gendered) terms of the relationship, but it further implies that Scholem also has his doubts as to whether Benjamin has what it takes to make a more forceful impression. This is something that could be confirmed by a strange assertion made by Scholem later on, to the effect that Benjamin "was not tough enough, *nicht hart genug*, for the events of 1940" (279/E224).

Scholem often enough builds his own appearance as "tough" and shows himself as most driven upon consolidating his masculinity. Clearly, this phenomenon is no longer separable from the fact that it comes as a response to a loss, that it is a language of sadness akin, in its structure, to the originary event. This is what we have seen provides the occasion for the occurrence of language, an occurrence that takes the form of a construction and a figuration for Scholem. Consider further that Scholem engages most ostensibly in this kind of reconstructive activity when facing, indeed when exposed and responding to, *both* Dora and Walter. The intense investment that Scholem puts in those whom he figures throughout the story as being most impressive (and as having the most impressive of voices) is what deserves attention here. For what he construes and even builds is not only himself as "man," but also the figure(s) of (and as) what makes an impression, over and against which he must locate, consolidate, indeed, figure, (his) language and himself.

In one particular instance, Scholem writes a strange, somehow isolated paragraph to suggest that, during the years of their "growing friendship," he always won at chess. "During my visits we played chess several time" (46/E32). This also has to do with the speed, not of his walk, but of his game, for chess is a game at which Scholem is "a much faster player, *ich viel schneller spielte*. I played much faster." Benjamin, however, turns out to be, yet again, a figure of disruption, and even of a certain dismemberment. Benjamin is not only "monstrously slow, *ungeheuer langsam*" but also desperately lacking, even wounded, since, like Oedipus, he is "playing blindly, *sichtlos*, and took forever to make a move; as I was a much faster player, it was virtually always his turn" (ibid.). Only one time does Scholem report a different scene, but he makes sure to provide us with elements that would prevent us from thinking that this loss alters his masculinity, especially since, this time he clearly was at a disadvantage. Scholem continues and writes: "I lost one game, in which Dora and he [Walter] joined forces against me, *Ich verlor eine Partie, die Dora und er zusammen gegen mich spielten*" (ibid.).

Yet, although he inscribes forcefully the way in which no harm or loss was done, Scholem does lose, if perhaps otherwise, when, on another occasion, he is faced again by Walter and Dora, who together, *zusammen*, as they enter into a violent argument, play again, if not against him, certainly opposite him. Their inconsiderate behavior, not hiding when they are fighting, and their exposing Scholem to their violent disputes, all appear to produce great harm this time. Testifying to this harm in his diary, Scholem writes, "I am not asking for any [consideration] and shall never say a word, *werde [ich] nie ein wort sagen*, but it bothers me that it doesn't occur to them to think of me" (99/E77). Scholem breaks down but does not remain entirely silent. Rather, he continues to uphold the need to testify, to maintain the tradition in front of the cataclysm: "I am the only witness to these things, *ich bin der einzige Zeuge dieser Dinge*" (98/E76); earlier, Scholem refers to the entire history of the friendship as his "testimony, *Zeugnis*" (7/Eix).

Scholem thus demonstrates his ability to figure silence while also continuing to suggest that words and silence are not necessarily opposites, that one might resonate in the other. Having sworn that he shall never say a word, Scholem is thus not necessarily breaking his promise when he cries out, "After all I am not a eunuch, *Ich bin doch schließlich kein Eunuch*, conclusively and definitely not one, to whom one exposes and bares oneself as one wouldn't to anyone else, *vor dem man sich entblößt*, even strips, *wie man es sonst vor anderen nicht tun würde*" (99/E77).

This strange, but philologically sound and documented assertion (it is quoted in all candor from Scholem's own diary of November 5, 1918) to the effect of his having been exposed, marks, then, another momentous instance of the rhetoric of sadness. Consider how Scholem is saved from the traumatic and senseless event that just befell him. He writes: "Without the moving sonnets that echoed within me through it all, *die mir dazwischenklangen*, I would have despaired completely at such togetherness, *wäre ich ganz an solchem Zusammensein verzweifelt*" (ibid.). Wounded by the Benjamins' exposure, Scholem would have been split by despair in front of the event constituted by the Benjamins' *Zusammensein*, their being-together.

This *Zusammensein* does not quite hold things or fragments together; and much like a game of chess in which they together vanquish him, it would here have repeated the offense by splitting Scholem in two. Were it not for the sound, *Klang*, of the voice of the sonnets that remained within (or between) him, the being-together of the Benjamins would have separated him from his own togetherness.

But what is the voice that now saved Scholem from despair?

It is the voice of the friend, the voice of his friend Walter Benjamin, who earlier had read some (unheard? *ungeheuer*, monstrous, also translates the French *inouï*) beautiful sonnets ("he read us some really beautiful sonnets, *er las einige ungeheuer schöne Sonette vor*" [98/E76]). These sonnets had already constituted a language located in a traumatic event: they addressed the death of Benjamin's childhood friend Fritz Heinle. What saves Scholem, therefore, is the sheer sound of Benjamin's voice resonating, *klangen*, with the voice of another friend speaking to him of his death that, within and between Scholem, constitutes the sound of a silent voice (the sound of the voice of the silent, dead friend). It is the silent voice of the friend that holds Scholem together, when faced with the cataclysm that splits him and throws him into the abyss of despair. This astounding occurrence of language is also an instance of the rhetoric of sadness, and it situates Scholem and his language, as exposed. By working it through, by letting it resonate, the field of devastation within which Scholem's language will take place can be reconstructed in a series of activities of construction and (masculine) body building which we have partly considered. His language, Scholem himself, are saved from a split of despair by Benjamin's silent voice, the silent voice of the friend that remains *dazwischen*.

Surely, Scholem is not a eunuch, though Amos Funkenstein suggests that he may well be a voyeur.[100] Yet insofar as he forcefully needs to reassert this fact, insofar as he needs to reassert a wholeness and totality that would not have been harmed, insofar as he needs to hold onto the silent voice of an experience of unity (the reading of poetry that was immensely beautiful, through which "everything was good, *es war alles gut*" [98/E76], the wholeness of his masculinity, or the wholeness of *unio mystica*), one may wonder at this occurrence of language that occurs with and as the sadness of the scholar. In the face of an exposure to finitude and in the face of catastrophe, this sadness and despair is what Scholem responds to. What he finds is a voice, Benjamin's voice, a voice that saves him from that very despair. Sadness and despair are thus inscribed in Scholem's language when exposed to the devastating *Zusammensein* of the Benjamins. This *Zusammensein* may, however, also rob him of understanding.

This *Zusammensein,* to which Scholem refers in quotation marks as a "triangle," is only difficultly shared with the Benjamins. In it, neither Scholem nor the Benjamins fuse or participate—in Jean-Luc Nancy's terms, this is a *partage des voix,* not a *participation mystique*—but their respective distinctiveness does become doubtful. On the same page, Scholem reports that on November 9 he wrote in his diary about "our relationship," thus making his own additional contribution toward bringing yet more to light.

> Yesterday and the day before I was at Walter and Dora's, and it was very nice. After a half-year of being, living together, *nach einem halben Jahr des Zusammenlebens,* our relationship—the most decisive one of my life (with a man, at any rate), *Unser Verhältnis, das Entscheidendste meines Leben, jedenfalls zu einem Mann*—appears in a clearer, purer, light, *in reinerem Lichte,* to me. (99/E77)

Whether this clearer light will have shone upon the reader is to remain undecided (note that in German, as in English, a decision, or a most "decisive relationship," may not be unrelated to an incision, a cut). Yet, if a purer light took its time to shine upon Scholem, it may indicate that some obscurity, even some nonsense, remains ("I am sure I have written a lot of nonsense, *viel Unsinn,* about it in these pages, and in essence that is all wrong" [ibid.]). Who is it after all that is here said to have lived together? What kind of being-together is a *Zusammenleben*? Wasn't Scholem visiting at the Benjamins while renting his own room? Has he moved in with them? Is he locating and inserting himself in this difficult household? Who, once again, is the "we" of "our relationship"? If "we" are, in fact, in a relationship "with a man, at any rate," does it imply that Scholem and Dora are, at this time and in this particular game, a "we"? And is this "we" a relation, *Verhältnis,* that would be different from, less despair-provoking than, a *Zusammensein*? Would it be a togetherness that would be more easily comprehended? In it (if one can be "in" it), are Scholem and Dora joining forces, playing this time "against" Benjamin, or are Scholem and Benjamin doing this? These questions may tear apart too many things, splitting them into too many directions, too wide a dispersal of fragments. By now, it is unsurprising how there would be, once again, reason for yet another voice of silence: "one can only keep silent about it, *man es nur verschweigen kann*" (ibid.). Scholem may also be suggesting that things are, like the wasteland, growing silent, becoming ineffable and nameless, even when, like the sound of a silent voice that reads a *ungeheuer schön* sonnet, they are spoken or read aloud.

In the case of sonnets, at least—the voicing of which had earlier saved Scholem from despair—language may, once again, not always mean the opposite of silence. The translation from one to the other, the conversation between one and the other, may even be quick and easy. Scholem carries us from one to the other as fast as his quick gait and game allow: "My sonnet for Benjamin was my only foray into language, *der einzige Schritt in die Sprache.* I am beginning to grow inexpressibly fond of Dora again, *Ich beginne Dora wieder namenlos lieb zu gewinnen*" (ibid.).

Out of a "triangle," upon which Scholem reflects later, emerge another inexpressibility, a namelessness ("nowhere did his name . . . "), an unspeakability, the image of an indubitable resistance, and the impossibility of continuing to respond. The "triangle," the impossibility and absence of a certain experience that remains the place of Scholem's language, also articulates a different halt before "words buried alive, *des mots enterrés vifs,*"[101] questions without answers, refigured silences, and unattainable objects or countries, yet more (un)veiled secrets.

> Was it (as it sometimes seems to me in retrospect) that three young passionate, gifted people . . . had to use one another as release mechanisms in the private sphere? Were there in this "triangle," of which we were unaware, unconscious emotional inclinations and defenses that had to be discharged but which we were not able to recognize in our "naiveté," that is, owing to our lack of psychological experience, *infolge unseres Mangels an seelischer Erfahrung*? I could not answer these questions even today, *Ich könnte es auch heute nicht beantworten.* (112/E87)[102]

It is, of course, a very different moment of Scholem's life (or was it his career?)—one in which he is not necessarily the one being silent and/or lacking the answers—that Harold Bloom translates when he writes that, for Scholem, using "the language of Freud, . . . would imply that Kabbala ensued from . . . compulsiveness, from an obsession that had its origin in prohibitions or atonements, symbolic negations of desire or substitute gratifications. Scholem of course rejected all Freudian reductions of Kabbala."[103] This lack of interest in Freud (Jung remains much more popular in Kabbalah studies to this day) and the phenomenon of disappearance (and ensuing reconstruction) of what the Kabbalah may hold in a more disjunctive, disrupted and disruptive relation, and to which it too is exposed, may begin to explain why Scholem inscribes his language at the site of the unsayable. As we shall still see, not everything is unsayable, however, including "our place in al-Andalus," and the reconstructive activity in which Scholem engages his language and his masculinity is still more complex.

Scholem, we have already noted, rarely misses an opportunity to clarify the respective places or space he and Benjamin occupy, and to assess his own size vis-à-vis Benjamin. In fact, Scholem goes quite far in this matter and even gathers, albeit inadvertently, information from Benjamin's wife, Dora. Scholem seems almost forced to listen to Dora's voice, which, at this point, begins "to speak about features that had never been voiced between us, *die vorher nie zwischen uns zur Sprache gekommen waren*" (122/E95). This voice that comes from what perhaps should have been silent describes "her experiences in the marriage" (ibid.). In this reference to yet another limit of his experience in a determinate between, *zwischen*, Scholem nonetheless provides us with what he seems to judge crucial information, insofar, at least, as it may consolidate different vital hypotheses. Here comes Benjamin's first name again: "Walter's intellectuality impeded his libido, *seine Geistigkeit stünde seinem Eros im Wege*" (ibid.). For a spiritual man such as Benjamin (someone who at one point may even have believed himself to be a bishop—a *geistlig* and *geistig* person, then, if not quite a man), Eros is not quite walking the right way, does not quite have the right gait. That, however, is not scientifically proven—who could be sure that Dora's voicing of such matters actually means something rather than nothing? Scholem cannot "really corroborate this diagnosis on the basis of [his] own experience, *ohne es aus meinen eigenen Erfahrungen wirklich bestätigen zu können*," not really and effectively: that is, not scientifically. Something about that experience too seems to have remained remote. There are ways of being together that unsettle Scholem's way of knowing, that seem to be lost on him. Benjamin, not quite standing, perhaps even lying there, speaking of matters of the spirit, is in the way, in the way of an experience that could not go all the way. Scholem himself would not know, then, at least not from experience, which is why he needs to do precisely what many have since criticized him for not doing enough, namely, less textual and more anthropological work. Scholem here does do fieldwork; he works that field of ruins in order to gather additional information. In other words, Scholem becomes a participant-observer and tries to fill the picture with the help of additional informants.

Later I spoke with several other women who personally knew Walter Benjamin very well, including one to whom he proposed marriage in 1932. They all emphasized that Benjamin was not attractive to them as a man, *daß Benjamin als Mann keine Anziehung auf sie ausübte*, no matter how impressed or even enchanted they were with his intellect and his conversation, *von seinem Geist und seinen Gesprächen beeindruckt oder gar entzückt waren.* One of his close acquaintances told me that for her and her female friends he had not even existed as a man, *er habe . . . als Mann gar nicht existiert*, that it had never even occurred to them that he had that dimension as well. "Walter was, so to speak, incorporeal, *Walter war sozusagen unkörperlich.*" (122/E95)

What is here being established is not only that Scholem (*als Mann*? *als Mädchen*?) is far more than a philologist, but also that he is among the few people (alive?) who have been the most intimate with Walter Benjamin, the voice of whom remained for him *dazwischen*. This is the case to the extent that Benjamin, if he has ever actually been impressive, has been so only insofar as he is a *Geist*, insofar as he has (and is) a voice and conducts conversations. If Benjamin has ever been able to imprint some form of corporeal effect, he is no more bodily than his sheer voice, nor has it been demonstrated that he, in fact, exists outside of this vocal "presence," at least not as a man, *als Mann*.

It appears, then, that the "verdict of reality" regarding Benjamin's existence is therefore suspended. Incorporeal as he is, it is doubtful to what extent one can, strictly speaking, continue to write of Walter Benjamin as a figure. If he is, nonetheless, a figure, Benjamin is the figure of a voice, for regarding other corporeal dimensions, Benjamin whom we know has "tried to formulate the laws governing the world of premythical spectral phenomena, *die Welt des vormythischen Gespenstischen*" (79/E61), is, according to reliable testimonies, body-less and of uncertain existence, a *Geist*, then, a spirit and a ghost.

> We speak a ghostly language.
>
> —Gershom Scholem to Franz Rosenzweig

The rhetoric of sadness that inscribes the originary event as its lost context is here coming to its expected conclusion. Scholem's exposure to Benjamin, what he suggests as being a continuous series of "conversations," appears therefore not only as a series of exposures to a voice that constitutes a cataclysmic originary event, but also as exposures in response to which Scholem's own language emerges. It is striking, however, that the originary voice of Benjamin would be figured as "ghostly," a ghostliness that fills or heals a field or space with the impression it leaves. In this, too, Benjamin joins the spectral voice of Aristotle in Spain. That the voice is always marked as impressive reveals most legibly its figurative status insofar as it confirms that it is, to some extent, "bodily," that it has, in other words, bodily, impressive, effects. More importantly, however, what is thereby offered to be read constitutes the forceful inscription and construction of a rhetoric of sadness that finds its place in a "living organism" that undoubtedly and repeatedly shatters any simple notion of "life" (and of manhood) that Scholem could hold on to, but in the face of which he embarks on his construction project. This other vanishing trace and vanishing place, Benjamin's *Geist*, less bodily than a voice even, and never quite described by Scholem as having made an impression, is not to be fully distinguished from the voice, but it may be more legible in its disappearance as it seems even less open to a figuration. More precisely, it becomes more legible as the occasion of a figuration that is a reconstructive measure.

Plausibly enough, the "tradition," the language that follows the originary event, also takes on the very attributes of the occasion of its occurrence. Here, this voice without body that constitutes the place within which Scholem's language, as he conceives of it, takes place, leaves Scholem, in turn, perplexed, *ratlos.* Later in the story of the friendship, Scholem quotes Benjamin as having said that some words leave one "as perplexed as the speech of ghosts, *ratlos wie Geisterrede*" (278/E224). In the English translation, *ratlos* is rendered as "disconsolate." It would be difficult to argue that this is a wrong translation, for it continues to mark Scholem's rhetoric of sadness, his exposure to a perplexing, uncanny, cataclysmic event.

Indicibles Exposures

> The name of God can be addressed but not pronounced. . . .
> The "true" language cannot be spoken.
>
> —Gershom Scholem, *Judaica 3*

Something about Benjamin's and Dora's way of speaking and their voices repeatedly strikes Scholem, from the time of their very first encounter. It is not insignificant, then, that in this first encounter Benjamin appears as none other than a voice: a speaker-lecturer. By the time of the second encounter, Scholem writes: "again I was struck by his characteristic way of speaking, *er mir wieder . . . bei seiner Rede auffiel*" (13/E5). We have seen that Scholem is never insensitive to the impressions made on him by conversations, even, and perhaps especially, if he is conversing with silent voices, the meanings of whom can always be unfolded later, figuring and imprinting themselves in a history of reconstructions. At this point, however, it becomes increasingly relevant to consider the distinct possibility that it was in and to their writing—another modality of *Zusammensein*—that the Benjamins were exposing Scholem. This exposure constitutes an event that would be the taking place of language, rather than language conceived as that which occurs in a place ("Spain") to which it is negatively related. Rather than to their voice, silent or not, this event, if it is one, would not have had to be heard so much as it would have offered itself as *legible* (even, and perhaps, because, it would not make that much of an impression).

Not, of course, that the Benjamins would have had nothing to say, but it is likely that Scholem's governing concern for voice and impressions would have led him to miss such an occurrence if it were to have taken place. In the remaining pages of this chapter, I want to address the possibility that language may take place other than in a context, a place to which it would be negatively related, a ghostly voice and ground. I want to suggest that such a language, such a taking place of language was given by the Benjamins to Scholem to read, and that this took place in writing. Not that the Benjamins reify the difference between writing and voice; rather, they seem to want to alert their reader to that dimension of language that is the opening of language's place, language as its own taking place.

This place which is hardly one is the occurrence of language between writing and voice, but also between language and its imprint, between writing and the impression it makes. I do not argue that the Benjamins are substituting writing for Scholem's voice. The writing of the Benjamins intervenes neither as ground nor as a figure. Rather, the difference they introduce is a disruption, the taking place of a disruption of and as language. Marking the indirectness of communication, the Benjamins' writing exposes Scholem to a marked, if not imprinted, difference. The question that I then want to address is whether this difference, this "writing out of print," can in fact be read as an alternative to Scholem's rhetoric of sadness. Were this to be the case, there would be, of course, a certain irony if one considers that writing out of print is not unrelated to the enormous corpus of Kabbalah manuscripts that the scholar of mysticism reads, catalogs, and, indeed, prints. Hence the necessity of addressing in more precise terms what the difference is that the Benjamins would be indicating and offering to read.

First, there is one of the letters we have mentioned earlier, from baby Stefan Benjamin to Scholem. This letter is not unrelated to a definite longing, one that may have gotten the better part of Scholem's earlier testimony of fondness, even love, *Lieb*, for Dora. Consider the pedagogical, somewhat authoritative tone of this letter, written by Dora, in which Stefan sternly addresses Scholem.

It's hard for me to tell you, for I wouldn't want you to believe that your relationship with my Mama isn't all it should be, *als sei Dein Verhältnis zu meiner Mama nicht wie es sein sollte.* It is quite all right but only on its own terms, as it were, *aber sozusagen nur wenn es sich selbst ansieht,* for you would like it always to be something else, *denn Du möchtest immer etwas Anderes haben.* What you want from my mother, *was Du von meiner Mutter verlangst,* she cannot give you, because you don't love her, *weil Du sie nicht liebst*; she has known too many people who did [love her] to be mistaken about this. You could, however, get a great deal from her, but you don't realize this, *was Du aber nicht siehst,* because you want, even long for, other, *weil Du nach Anderem verlang,* inadequate things. That's why she has no time for you, for now this would be lost time, *denn jetzt wäre sie verlorne*; there would be quarrels too often, for the aforementioned reasons. (96–97/E75)

Scholem, Dora's handwriting explains, is not paying close attention to the relationship such as it is; he is always longing after something else, always already wishing for other things. Whereas Scholem appears to want to take things elsewhere, to settle somewhere else, Dora's handwriting exposes him to a difference. This is not so much the difference between what there is and what Scholem desires, as much as the difference between what he wants and what there could be. At the same time, Dora's handwriting does remind Scholem that he may be wrong in thinking that their relationship "isn't all it should be."[104]

Whatever the relationship is, Scholem appears unsatisfied. Obviously, it is not that he does not listen, for as we know, he was quite impressed with voices, even with silent ones, and certainly by Dora's voice. Yet the letter would remind him, on the one hand, of the difference writing makes, and, more importantly, it would be explaining to him that there are alternatives to longing for an elsewhere and for "inadequate things." The letter introduces and constitutes its own difference by telling Scholem, in writing, that he does not take the relationship on its own terms.

Finally, and though here more than ever one should refrain from assuming continuity between question and answer, the letter does suggest that Scholem had expressed some desire for time. But this is precisely what he cannot receive. It seems plausible to suggest that there is a connection between the other things and the time after which Scholem longed and for which he would have asked. Scholem's longing would be the consequence of his inability to stay at the place of a relationship, a being-together, a *Zusammensein* that does not fit his ideas of unity. Strikingly enough, the letter appears to be a kind of farewell, one in which Dora informs Scholem of an interruption of their time, an interruption of time, insisting that whatever time there will or would be, it is already lost. Dora's handwriting, then, informs Scholem both that their relationship is what it should be and that their time is lost. In this way, the letter may be suggesting that loss is the only mode that Scholem's way of being-together enables. In its inscription, at any rate, Dora's handwriting could and will not imprint itself in the course of time. In fact, it refuses itself to time, raising the possibility of a different relation to loss and to time. This *Zusammensein*, however, appears not to constitute the kind of relationship for which Scholem longs.

True to a mode of perception that repeatedly emphasizes the voice and impression it makes in time, Scholem may have difficulties reading Dora's handwriting. Scholem appears to find himself exposed to that which he does not care to see. At one point, in fact, he reiterates some of the doubts we have seen and testifies that he is, if not a man, then, like a man, *wie ein Mann*, but that when faced with Dora's and Benjamin's exposure, he is "like a man who has seen more than he cares or loves to see, *Ich kam mir vor wie ein Mann, der mehr gesehen hat als ihm lieb ist*" (88/E68). This may explain why he is now told that he does not love, *lieb*, enough, which would then confirm that Scholem does not want to see, much less to read.

This reticence to reading is documented, in fact. Earlier, Dora's handwriting had already offered itself to be read, and Scholem, always on the hear-out for other things, appears to have missed it. Stefan reminds him of this when he writes in the letter we have been reading: "I believe I already even wrote you about it, *ich schrieb Dir glaube ich auch einmal darüber*" (96/E74). Recalling the tone of the passage above, one may consider the letter as that of a teacher gently but firmly reminding a student of an important bibliographic reference: is it possible that you still haven't read . . . ? Earlier still, and using the same tone of authority that suggests the importance of texts, Stefan had given an ambiguously addressed order, perhaps directed at himself, perhaps directed at Scholem. Underscoring how complicated, and at times hardly distinguishable, the members of that unintegral *Zusammensein* may have been, Stefan told him(self) to start a book, not one of those that one prints, but one in which one writes and takes notes: "start keeping a little book in which you note everything down, *schreibe schon jetzt ein Büchlein wo Du Dir Alles anmerkst*" (88/E68). Like the verdict that time is always already lost, the imperative to write a book may have been disruptive, giving Scholem something to read and write just when he remained so insistently concerned with voices. Scholem would be reminded that by longing for an elsewhere, he does not love (to see, to read) Dora, nor perhaps her handwriting. In fact, he himself should practice his handwriting.

> Something went wrong with my eyes. I had to undergo an operation and wasn't allowed to write at all.
>
> —Gershom Scholem to Walter Benjamin, 6–8 November 1938

A few weeks earlier, Walter Benjamin is said to have reacted quite passionately, even angrily, to yet another demand made by Scholem in an open letter of his own. Scholem has begun to recover and he is writing again, learning how to do so. The letter he writes is (perhaps un-)surprisingly entitled "Farewell, *Abschied*," and it marks the differential split of separation in more than one way.[105] To begin with, although Scholem and Benjamin had considered maintaining a definite being-together, planning on cosigning this letter, Benjamin takes to his typical gait, and starts to walk at a speed and in a direction that, once again, differ from Scholem's. "Benjamin withdrew from the idea, *Benjamin trat aber von dem Gedanken zurück*, he stepped back, walked away from it" (94/E73). Then, anticipating in his own way this gesture of severance and withdrawal, Scholem himself had meant his letter to be a "farewell," his dismissal of and severing from the German Jewish Youth Movement. Actualizing the risks about which he had been warned by Dora's handwriting ("there would be quarrels too often"), Scholem's letter becomes the occasion of "violent arguments." Benjamin ends up angrily telling Scholem that the letter would not accomplish its goal, for in it Scholem is ordering the usual, he is "loudly demanding silence with a loud voice, *mit lauter Stimme das Schweigen forderte*" (ibid.; Scholem quotes Benjamin here). Using an authoritative tone with which we have begun to become familiar from other members of the Benjamin family, Benjamin here seems to want to educate Scholem about silence, but this too is a lesson that, although it does not seem to fall on a deaf ear, may be too ambiguously addressed. Benjamin's lesson reaches perhaps neither the right eyes nor ears, since it is again a matter of a difference in writing, and then, of course, in reading. "In the *methodos* of silence," writes Benjamin, who would know about silent, and even Jewish, unobstrusiveness, "silence itself must not occur, *darf das Schweigen selber nicht vorkommen.* One writes this sort of thing to free oneself, but one does not print it, *aber man druckt es nicht*" (ibid.).

What Benjamin is teaching Scholem, then, is the difference that, for Scholem, constituted all "crises." A voice that, however loud, would be disconnected from the originary event of silence, would be a ghostly voice. This is precisely what Benjamin tells Scholem to practice. He tells him that rather than a voice and a figuring that tries to piece together and build a bridge over the abyss, there is or there should be a writing that remains distant from both silence ("silence itself must not occur") and from print. Benjamin is not teaching Scholem about constructing impressive figures, he is teaching him about writing out of print. Along with Dora's handwriting and Stefan's handwritten book, Benjamin is reminding Scholem of the difference between writing and printing, between writing and imprinting.

In the light of Scholem's recurring considerations of impressions, those figures and constructions that immediately follow (longing after and trying to connect with the loss of) a cataclysmic event or a silent voice—and must so follow in order to produce a language that would be in its proper place—the notion of "writing out of print" appears to drive a wedge, to open a difference. This is a difference that may recall the "disjunctions" of Benjamin's essay "The Task of the Translator": whether between the work of art and the receiver ("In the appreciation of a work of art or an art form, consideration of the receiver never proves fruitful"),[106] the disjunction (which is also a connection) between translation and original ("no translation would be possible if in its ultimate essence it strove for likeness to the original" [73]), and the definition of kinship (*Verwandtschaft*) which "does not necessarily involve likeness," and "cannot be defined adequately by identity of origin" (74). Rather than considering a relation that would "piece together," build bridges, and connect by way of figurative constructions, Benjamin writes of a distinct kind of being-together and suggests that one relates to "pure language" in a different way (Benjamin also writes here that pure language is "fully formed in the linguistic flux" rather than external to it, and is also "expressionless, *ausdruckslose*, out of print, and creative" [80]).[107] Pure language, the relation between languages, is not an external place of language, nor does it constitute a lost unity to be recovered.

Even the occasion for that event of language that the translation is, namely, the original, "has already relieved the translator and his translation of the effort of assembling and expressing what is to be conveyed" (78). Rather than "closing in" that which is the occasion of the occurrence of language, the translator is relieved of the effort of assembling and his task is "to release in his own language that pure language which is under the spell of another, to liberate the language imprisoned in a work in his re-creation of that work" (80). The task of the translator is not to print, imprint, or figure, but to liberate, even to redeem language out of print, *Druck*.

Commenting on Benjamin's history of photography and what he calls his "photography of history," Eduardo Cadava concisely explains the difference to which Benjamin exposes Scholem: "what structures the relationship between the photographic image and any particular referent, between the photograph and the photographed, is the absence of relation."[108] Walter Benjamin, in fact, the Benjamin family, would thus be exposing Scholem to the difference constituted by a difficult *Zusammensein*, a being-together that is not a relation (or more precisely, in Maurice Blanchot's phrase, "a relation without relation, *un rapport sans rapport*") and that is not to be looked for elsewhere. It is a difference that operates so as to "teach" Scholem that, although one may read or write a book, and perhaps even speak (Scholem was, after all, demanding silence with a loud voice), in none of these should difference (even if a devastating one) be ignored or responded to hurriedly with a constructive, figurative, or impressive project. (One should note that it is not impossible that Scholem did, in fact, take this advice literally. Thus Benjamin would have remained out of print until 1957, he would have been figured out of print in Scholem's work, receding onto and as the context that, like "Spain," declines and disappears.)

In a repetitive way, both Dora and Walter Benjamin, or at least their handwriting, expose themselves therefore, bare themselves, offering something to see, something in writing that exposes itself and exposes Scholem to a difference that, as we saw, splits Scholem in two and throws him into an abyss of despair. This takes place "in" the Benjamins' writing to Scholem about a difference that is not to be longed for elsewhere (Dora), or by indicating a difference between voice and silence, between the voice and its imprint, and between writing and the making of an impression, the construction of a figure (Benjamin). One could even suggest that what happened at Bamberg, in the house previously owned by the bishop, is part of that "education" in difference. However that may be, the Benjamins teach Scholem about difference by exposing him to it, whereas Scholem himself, encountering and recoiling from a certain limit, does not seem to recognize himself as their addressee.

Scholem, whom we know to have felt strong longings, is always engaged in a reconstructive project of consolidation and figuration. He reconstructs his masculinity, like a man, *wie ein Mann*, not as a woman, *als ein Mädchen*, and he seeks to close up abysses of difference and build anew upon fields of ruins. Scholem, though he is exposed, seeks not so much to settle in this field (not at least if such settlement does not involve construction and buildings), to let it take place. He does not want this exposure, nor does he want to maintain a *Zusammensein* with fields of ruins that would not be a being-together of reconstructive figuring. Scholem does not want to see or read where writing exposes itself and exposed him, and he asks rather for the continuity of longing and of other relations, loudly demands silence, and paradoxically figures names and languages as unspeakable and continuously imprinting upon history (which would never be lost time, then, but always the time of a loss). Scholem is always after, demands only to hear, a silent voice, a voice that is insistently figured as something that would have made a big impression, a solid construction that may be worth printing, even if later in history. Dora and Benjamin, however, obstinately writing, expose him to a different occurrence of language, and they teach him both how to read and write, and the difference it makes. It becomes plausible to assume that we are here provided with some of the reasons why Dora, perhaps out of despair, later turns Scholem down and refuses "to write down, *aufzuschreiben*, what she knew and had witnessed of his life and his real self."[109]

> Ye heard the voice of the words, but saw no similitude, no image; only ye heard a voice.
>
> Deuteronomy 4:12, quoted in Scholem, "The Name of God"

Paradoxically enough, then, Scholem would seem to have paid much less attention precisely to the (at least written) words of those whose voice he deemed most impressive. This suggests more than the phonocentrism we have been considering; it indicates also a determined reticence concerning both the taking place of language and the differential dimensions of that language "itself." I write that this is paradoxical because along with Dora and Walter Benjamin's manner of speaking and their voices, what seems to have most impressed Scholem is, in fact, Benjamin's philosophy or theory of language. Leaving little room, this time, for those whose attitude toward the mystical is limited to a negative or nonexisting (objectless) knowledge, Scholem often and quite inexplicably (he himself, at least, does not explain) refers to this theory of Benjamin as "mystical." At an early point in his life or career, Scholem decides to write his own doctoral dissertation "on the linguistic theory of the Kabbalah, *über die Sprachtheorie der Kabbala*,"[110] but he admits to have been able to bring this project to completion only forty years later, that is to say very close to the years during which one may assume he was working on the story of his friendship.[111] In this late study of language, Scholem writes, again, of an "indissoluble link." In bequeathing a legacy of its own, Judaism itself quietly joins other living (?) organisms ("Spain," etc.).

> The indissoluble link, *die unlösige Verbindung*, between the idea of the revealed truth and the notion of language—is as much, that is, as the word of God, *das Wort Gottes*, makes itself heard through the medium of human language, if, otherwise, human experience can reach the knowledge of such a word at all—is presumably one of the most important, if not the most important, legacies, *Erbschaft*, bequeathed by Judaism to the history of religions.[112]

Scholem continues and says that, aside from communication, which is a kind of consolidated building,

> there is something else vibrating, *schwingt etwas*, which is not merely communication, meaning, *Bedeutung*, and expression, *Ausdruck*. The sound upon which all language is built, *der Laut, auf den alle Sprache gebaut ist*, and the voice which gives form to the language, *die Stimme, die sie gestaltet*, forges it out from the matter of sound, *Lautmaterial*; these are already, *prima facie* beyond our understanding. (8/E60)

This, Scholem says, constitutes the background, *der Hintergrund*, of the "undecipherable character of language, *des Unenträtselbaren in der Sprache*" (ibid.). Considering that there are also echoes of Benjamin resonating here, echoes of a pure language that is expressionless and where meaning fails, we nonetheless meet once again a buried voice, a voice in and of (and to) the ground, a voice that, though seemingly devoid of materiality, makes, indeed builds and forms, its own history as the history of great impressions. It is therefore only in its effects, in the history that follows it, that this voice is accessible. Fundamentally, then, one can only speak about consolidated things, buildings, impressions, or masculinities. At most, one can refer to the ground of these buildings and figures, a ground that is not a figure or a construction, but a voice.

Scholem affirms the difference between the voice and its history, between ground and building, but not only does he never seem to question the continuity (the indissoluble link?) between that voice and its history, he also clearly separates between the voice as the place of language, and the taking place of language "itself." In this view, the relation of language to its place remains negative, and the difference only consolidates the exteriority of a "context." In spite of the possible analogies, then, one should be careful not *hurriedly* (speed—whether walking, talking, or reading—is, after all, essential in the history of the friendship between Scholem and Benjamin) to equate Scholem's meaningless voice and Benjamin's many times printed notions of communicability and pure language (remember too that, at times at least, Benjamin was "monstrously slow"). Insofar as Scholem conceives the voice as an unspeakable foundation, this conception remains, in fact, a construction and a figure, even if an impossible one, that seems hardly to be found in Benjamin's writing. With this figuration of that to which his own writing was exposed as a voice in and as a ground, Scholem not only continues to engage in his construction project, he also fails to relate to that which Benjamin suggests is, in language, writing out of print.

Scholem's "The Name of God" presents us with the final, or at least most developed figuration, the consolidated image of the originary event, the "nothing" of revelation, the ineffability of such connecting but declining and disappearing experiences that "Spain" and "mystical experience" came to be. And it confirms, if it does not consolidate, the history of a friendship as the narrative of the becoming mute of something that may well have held, as Scholem himself writes toward the end of a history of the friendship, a definite danger. "Something had remained mute that had not been designed to be so, and like everything thus unspoken, it was dangerous, *Es war irgend etwas stumm geblieben, was nicht dazu bestimmt war, und wie alles derart Unausgesprochene, gefährlich.*"[113]

What Benjamin, Dora, and even baby Stefan were trying to show and give to read was not necessarily dangerous in the way Scholem seems to consider, although, like the paradigmatic originary and cataclysmic events, it may have been so perceived by him. It was neither a voice nor an impression that testified to the exteriority of a place of language. Rather than a voice, silent or otherwise, or a writing of a recognizable kind, Scholem did not have to long and listen, but, like the children of Israel, *to see the voices,* that is to consider a different, or, more precisely, a differential occurrence of language, to read that which only wrote itself by exposing itself, that which, rather than being an expression and making an impression—producing an exteriorization, and even an imprint—was instead "writing out of print," the event of language as the space of its taking place. Whatever such writing—which is neither impression nor expression—is or could be, if it has ever been (Benjamin, Scholem wrote on another occasion, "was overwhelmed by what he called *das Ausdruckslose,* the expressionless"),[114] it could hardly be construed, consolidated, or reconstructed as the recovering of a voice, not at least insofar as any attempt so to recover or restore the voice would likely remain, like Scholem's, the consolidation of a desperate (and loveless?) longing and search for something else. Such an attempt at restoration would continue to write a language of sadness, it would continue to inscribe a longing for "nothing," for a silent voice, and for the history of the expressions and impressions it had or had made. The possibility of turning away from such a voice, of freeing oneself from it, as Giorgio Agamben suggests, may therefore lead one to acknowledge that Benjamin may have been and still be very quiet (though one should not dismiss here the possibility of a *cri écrit*), but also that he may have insistently been giving us something (not necessarily something else) to read.

Much earlier, Scholem himself had noted about Benjamin that "even then, he occupied himself with ideas about perception as a reading, *die Wahrnehmung als ein Lesen,* in the configurations of the surface, *in den Konfigurationen der Fläche.*"[115] Keep this perception in mind for a few more moments. Benjamin "himself" may have been unable to use his "voice and gesture to support individual sentences, *in Stimme und Mienenspiel die einzelnen Sätze . . . standzuhalten,*" he may even have been unable to have his sentences, and even his own name, stand—*nirgends stand sein Name*—as Hannah Arendt had written. The writer, occupied with writing and reading surfaces, aims however "not to carry the reader away and inspire him with enthusiasm, with spirit, *kein Ziel mitzureißen und zu begeistern.* This form can be counted successful only when it forces the reader to pause, *einzuhalten,* and reflect."[116] Writing out of print demands, therefore, that one not merely long for an elsewhere, or for a spiritual, even ghostly, unification. It demands rather that one slow down and read, read difference, read the difference that "Spain" makes. Writing out of print remains, therefore, to be read.

No doubt, the opposition between voice and writing, between depth, impression, and surfaces, can no longer be maintained any more than can the opposition between ineffability and language,[117] these oppositions seem to have remained, on the reading we have been following, uninterrogated. Most importantly, the taking place of these oppositions, much like the taking place of language "itself," seems to have remained buried and figured precisely as ground to be built upon, and insofar as it continues to function as the determining experience of language it also recedes onto its outside. It is therefore not erased so much as it shows itself in its disappearance. Scholem's text therefore raises the possibility of the remaining task, that of reading (with) Benjamin that which has already indicated the site of an exposure and (as) the taking place of language. The scholar's rhetoric of sadness and his figurations thus also provide a way to interrogate what *reading* means. Avital Ronell—who showed that Benjamin and his "destructive character" had very sensitive ears, being open to all kinds of noises and rumors when walking the surfaces of the streets[118]—has argued that we may not yet have understood what perception as reading means, and with what organs one should read. Consider, then, that we are still reading about perception as construction and/or perception as reading.

Just as a person lying sick with fever, *wie ein Kranker, der im Fieber liegt,* transforms, *verarbeitet,* all the words which he perceives, *alle Worte, die ihm vernehmbar werden,* into the extravagant images of delirium, so it is that the spirit of the present age seizes on the manifestations of past or distant spiritual worlds, in order to take possession of them and unfeelingly incorporate them into its own self-absorbed fantasizing, *um sie an sich zu reißen und lieblos in sein selbstbefangenes Phantasieren einzuschließen.*[119]

Reading, therefore, may be quite distinct from an attempt to listen to voices, silent or other, but it may nonetheless require that, as Ronell suggests, we also learn how to "read with our ears."[120] As we begin to do so, and are thus neither approaching nor departing from "our place in al-Andalus," reading suggests the possibility of a different, if a more unsettling, experience of language. Before we finally turn to the *Zohar*'s language, it is appropriate to begin, rather than to conclude here, with this text by Benjamin, whose attention to details was exemplary.

With his diagnostic ("Just as a person lying sick with fever"), Benjamin incidentally also provides us with the clearest appreciation of what was addressed in this chapter. As he writes here of a Hegelian "spirit of the age," one should take note of Benjamin's difficult words. In a way, he encourages us to acknowledge a debt to Scholem. Most importantly, Benjamin emphatically warns us away from the possibility of considering the texts and problems discussed here as reflections of a personal fault or, worse, as an individual, psychological "illness" (a lack of love, *lieblos*, unkind, as Dora and Stefan had diagnosed it, could never be a strictly personal problem) on the scholar's part. This would clarify why the "sadness of the scholar" has been understood here as an occurrence of language, a rhetoric of sadness, rather than as a matter of individual, psychological dimensions. Benjamin reminds us also that the rhetoric of sadness gives to read the complexity of the constellation that "connects" less than it translates the event of language, the life and works of the "age." This has nothing to do with recovering an original, then, nor about reconstructing a lost context. It is neither about longing for an elsewhere nor about an outside, another voice or another text. If the event of language of the scholar is determined by the desire to stand and build elsewhere, to want something other and to be on its side, on the side of the beyond and of a health that would be strictly opposed to and uncontaminated by illness, what Benjamin suggests is rather that language taking place ex-poses, unsettles, and translates, out of context and at its place, the taking place of language at "our place in al-Andalus."[121]

4

Reading, Out of Context: *Zohar* and/as *Maqāma*

> It is the collapse of the representation into a face, into a "concrete abstraction" torn up from the world, from horizons and conditions, incrusted in the signification without a context of the-one-for-the-other, coming from the emptiness of space, from space signifying emptiness, from the desert and desolate space, as uninhabitable as geometrical homogeneity.
>
> —Emmanuel Levinas, *Otherwise Than Being or Beyond Essence*

> Why does "our" "era" have nothing other to suspend itself from than the treading movement of a step? Why would the step, *pas*, of a *démarcheur* be the final judgment today? And why would *Dasein*, "our own," have to constitute itself as a *démarcheur*?
>
> —Jacques Derrida, *The Post Card*

Rabbi Yose and Rabbi Ḥiyya were walking on the way.
While they were walking, night fell; they sat down.
While they were sitting, morning began to shine; they rose and walked on.
Rabbi Ḥiyya said, See the face of the East, *anpoi de-mizraḥ*, how it shines!
Now all the children of the East, *bnei madinḥa*,
who dwell in the mountains of light, are bowing down to this light,
which shines on behalf of the sun before it comes forth, and they are worshiping it.
Of course once the sun comes forth, there are many who worship the sun;
but there are those who worship this light,
calling this light, the God of the shining jewel
and their oath is, "By Allah of the shining jewel, *ve-uma'a di-lehon be-Allah de-margela de-nahir.*"
Now you might say: This worship is in vain!
But since ancient primordial days they have discovered wisdom through it.
(*Zohar* II, 188a; trans. Daniel Matt in *Zohar*, 134–135)

The trans-lation of al-Andalus, its displacing dimension, as I have tried to address it in the previous chapters, both fails to and succeeds at constituting an event, or set of events, of language, a language that occurs in distinct manners, in different texts. Although it can be described in general terms only with difficulty—thus adding to the failure of its localization—it appears that by way of this very difficulty one can account for the translation and transportation, the repeated attempt at localization (if not quite successful relocation), of al-Andalus. If such is, in fact, the case, the production of the ends of al-Andalus is less about a later and "external" imposition that would have failed to recognize the truth of al-Andalus by virtue of having located it, but constitutes rather a repetition and translation of the complex rhetorical movement of al-Andalus as an event of language, of the displacing and translating movement that articulates a search for, and an inscription of, its declining contexts, its withdrawing limits.

It has now become possible to consider another instantiation of this displacing movement, an early occurrence of al-Andalus (which, once again, ends as, and translates into, "Spain") as trans-lation: the already meritorious activity of travel in Islam (*riḥla, ṭalab al-ᶜilm*, the search for knowledge) had a particular importance in the writing of al-Andalus. Travel, *riḥla*, and the search for knowledge, *ṭalab al-ᶜilm*, became "both an adventure and a religious duty," and, as Sam Gellens explains, the "central feature of Spanish [*sic*] Muslim intellectual life." It gave rise to "several thousand biographies," all of which "trenchantly document the significance of *riḥla/ṭalab al-ᶜilm* for Spanish Muslims." This "most important aspect of Spanish learning" constituted "a multi-faceted intellectual endeavour" and "occupied a very special position in Spain in that those who traveled (*ahl al-riḥla*) represented a distinct category of individuals." "Those who traveled" became themselves objects of praise, and their reputation increased when they "made a trip and, in addition, returned with a new or rare text previously unknown in Spain."[1]

The *Zohar*, itself "a new and rare text previously unknown in Spain," inscribes itself in the Andalusī and Arab Jewish tradition of displacement literature, a tradition that never quite achieves the status of "genre" insofar as it takes place between the biographies mentioned by Gellens, geographical writings, and *maqāmāt* literature.[2] Yet the ubiquitous insistence on place and localization that permeates and surrounds the *Zohar* does not simply locate it in this tradition. Rather, it constitutes a reading of the displacing, trans-lating dimension of that tradition within the text. It is a recurring displacement, one that we began to consider earlier in its specificity in the taking place of *ein-sof*, and a larger movement that affects literature "itself." This movement has already begun, then, now taking us—were these poles, strictly speaking, locatable—from mysticism to literature, from religious fervor to the emergence of secular writing (not yet literature[3] but already vernacular), and from "ontology" (a favored term of Kabbalah studies)[4] to rhetoric, a set of translations that already occur in (or rather as) the *Zohar*. (Something very different and in an altogether distinct direction will end up bearing the weight of another translation. This translation takes place in the Andalusī *maqāmāt*, toward which I turn in the second part of this chapter.) I write here of "displacement" rather than of "travel"—although the latter is far from irrelevant—because the notion of travel literature limits the range of the translations that al-Andalus carries and is carried by. Travel, moreover, may overly suggest a leisurely dimension (and, perhaps, a teleological dimension as well) which, we have already seen, was not always at work at "our place in al-Andalus."

The emphatic "sense of place" found in Andalusī travelers' accounts is as significant as the "basic wanderlust" to which they testify; but, as Abdelfattah Kilito explains in his work on the *maqāma*, a peculiar affectlessness materializes prominently in the peregrinations of a "déplacement [qui] ne connaît pas de fin," such as occurs in *maqāmāt*.[5] Our "*protagonistes avancent au milieu d'un paysage certes changeant, mais toujours familier*, protagonists go forward in the midst of a landscape that is indeed changing but always familiar" (21). This *paysage* that the text constitutes, "our place," understood here as a taking place and as a displacement, therefore has less to do with affect, the emotions of the characters (be it the "lust" of "wanderlust," sex, and/or love—as in Ibn Ḥazm's *Ṭawq al-Ḥamāma*, the *Libro de buen amor*, the *Roman de la rose*, and, in distinct ways as well, in Ibn Zabara's *Sefer Shaᶜashuᶜim*, and in al-Ḥarizi's *Taḥkemoni*). Rather, the *paysage* in motion is meant to emphasize the occurrence of this motion as language, indeed, as trans-lation in the etymological sense. This translation constitutes the text as displaced and articulates the movement of Kabbalah into literature. Insofar as this movement leaves a crucial mark in the very act of withdrawal, it demands a reading.

As familiar as the background *paysage* for readers of *maqāma* literature, the narratives of the *Zohar* are stories of displacements, relating the adventures of traveling rabbis, of older, *saba*, and younger, *yanuka*, men who, repeatedly preaching in their wanderings, keep transforming their appearance. The movement of flux and transformation is continuous, hiding no "essence" behind such shifting grounds. The generations of men organize their discursive trek around a core emptiness and asserted essencelessness. Meaning and concealment give way to acknowledged emptiness. There is little place for a transcendental semantics where the unavailable and irretrievable truth of their speech is asserted, and where language is seen as playing tricks ("I know that there is nothing in his words . . . his words are empty non-sense . . . empty words," says Rabbi Yose, recounting his encounter with "an old man, a donkey driver, who kept asking me riddles the whole way")[6]—an "empty rhetoric" that, like the travels described (and as Orientalists have complained both about *maqāma* and Kabbalah), hardly leads anywhere. The rhetoric of the road where it turns into a way makes way or creates place without claiming territory or reifying particular and regional determinations of land—the precarious status of this sacred highway has everything to do with the turning of Kabbalah into literature. The *Zohar* (including, but not reduced to, its famous narrative of *Saba demishpatim*) and the *Maqāmāt al-Luzūmīya* enact such events in distinct and, what follows will show, not easily comparable ways.

Not easily comparable because the *Zohar* is not, or not simply, narrative. In the same famous gesture, the *Zohar* dismisses (but paradoxically also encourages) the comparability of (its own) narrative developments and, at the same time, appears to oppose narrative as such, putting aside even the possibility of reading the biblical narratives as narratives: "Woe to the human being who says that Torah presents mere stories and ordinary words!"[7] And yet, the *Zohar* articulates itself as a "narrative frame" and as a set of narratives adding a conspicuously unread irony to its particular brand of literary criticism.[8] The translating, displacing movement that I address in what follows already takes place when the *Zohar* presses on and explores the possibility of comparison, the possibility of reading as narrative, and of repeating the rhetorical movement of the biblical narratives. If the Torah did tell "mere stories," the *Zohar* writes, "we could compose a Torah right now with ordinary words and better than all of them!" (ibid.). The *Zohar*'s "own" narratives, disseminated by "those who possessed the booklets"—(not) "secular compositions, *quntresim*"[9]—were they to be read, would therefore have to articulate a complex movement of translation, the displacement according to which the *Zohar* exceeds narrative and, indeed, "refashions the Torah's narrative into a . . . novel."[10] The *Zohar*'s language, taking place as a rhetoric of trans-lation, is therefore narrative and more than (but also no more, no longer) narrative, indeed, *plus d'histoire*, and also, as Derrida says, *plus de métaphore*, and, we will see, *plus d'une langue*.

Part ~~II~~: *Zohar*

> Jewish mysticism is not poetry.
>
> —Richard Cohen, *Elevations*

> Uniformity is also the mark of the [*Zohar*'s] illustrative or explanatory proto-excursions into story-telling. The same small number of literary motifs is juggled in all of them. The figurants change, but the story remains the same.
>
> —Gershom Scholem, *Major Trends*

> On the other hand, some of the lines commented upon are extracted from their context in such a manner that the latter is, at least apparently, without any relation to the topic under discussion.
>
> —Charles Mopsik, "Avant-propos"

Giving Place at Our Place on the Way

Dependent for its essential meaning on figural language, the *Zohar* has never been considered according to the criteria by which literature is traditionally read. To the extent that the *Zohar* is not studied in departments of literature, the question of its "official" rapport to literature remains suspended. Largely obliterated, the negative site that literature constitutes has given way to a narrow range of other determinations that have dominated the field of Kabbalah studies. In lieu of rhetorical or genealogical analyses, the text has been submitted to a logic that tends to privilege categories associated with kabbalistic, mystical, or symbolical classifications from which literary aspects would be at best derivative. These classificatory gestures—whether institutional and curricular or philological and hermeneutic—have maintained limited views on the *Zohar*'s cultural significance and literary provenance. Moreover, they have left basic principles of reading uninterrogated only to bolster the general resistance to the *Zohar*'s literariness. Yet, the *Zohar* itself has something to say about the reception that has accrued to its history. Prior to institutional control and policing—of a religious or academic nature—the *Zohar* displays its relatedness to literature, allegorically staging how it should be read. In so doing it reveals literariness as its essential trait. This trait stands in excess of the historical responses that have emerged from its readings and generated the most significant attention. By analyzing this trait and reviewing other, less acknowledged responses, I point to what I see as the main reason for the *Zohar*'s continued exclusion from crucial literary considerations. Among other things, the *Zohar* sets in motion a literary practice that inscribes it within a different tradition (so-called "secular" literature, specifically and historically, Arabic and Arab Jewish literature), a practice that, relocating it and recasting its genealogy, demands, finally, another reading.

The second—and last—sacred Jewish text, the *Zohar*, unlike the Bible, may have been deemed too fragile to let itself be exposed to literature. The Bible can withstand literary incursion and rhetorical analysis, but the *Zohar* had to be shielded from its own literary determinations. In this instance, the text's status as sacred seemed to depend upon a disavowal of literature, which is doubled in the suppression of its literary provenance.[11] These acts of disavowal can be related to the intense historical anxiety out of which the *Zohar* emerges, and to its own efforts to preserve both reference and memory, to produce an alternative memory bank, as it were, to mere historical recounting. For the *Zohar* responds to catastrophic expulsions and gets subsumed under loss. It is as though it were compelled to prevent a history of loss from dissolving into fiction. Yet in good faith, the *Zohar*, we could say, knows that the one genuine and authentic way to name loss is by taking recourse to the literary. Already as a textual entity and event, the *Zohar* is obsessed with the question of how to read. At the very least, the *Zohar* tells us how it reads itself, how it wants to be read.

Prompting the question of how to read, "Rabbi Eleazar opened his discourse with the text: 'Lift up your eyes on high and see: who hath created these things?' [Isaiah 40:26]. 'Lift up your eyes on high': to which place? *Rabbi Elᶜazar pataḥ: Seᵓu marom ᶜeinekhem u-reᵓu mi bara eleh. Seᵓu marom ᶜeinekhem—leᵓan atar*?"[12] Reading, and the question of reading the language of the *Zohar*, emerges from the *Zohar*'s early pages as this question of place. It is a question that takes the verse at its word and orients the gaze toward a specific place in order to discover the act of creation. The searching look orients itself by moving from a "who" (who has created?) to a "which" (to which place?) by turning toward a place that is not merely one place, but gets complicated by a difference asserted between a way (*oraḥ*) and a road (*derekh*). Reading is essentially linked to walking, and it seems right that the subsequent exegeses be structured according to peripatetic motifs, engaging an activity that occurs on the way. It is therefore not by accident, Abraham Azoulay explains, that the rabbis utter the words and the gift of the text on the way.[13] But one quickly reaches a hermeneutic fork and is confronted with the weighty decision of choosing the right path.

"The way, *oraḥ*, of the righteous" [Proverbs, 4:18]: What is the difference between a way, *orah*, and a road, *derekh*? It has been established [elsewhere]. But a way has now been opened, uncovered, and made in a place where feet have never previously pounded. A road, as it is said: "as if you had trodden the winepress" [Isaiah, 63:2], for the feet of anyone who wishes pound there. Upon this, for the righteous it is called a way, for they are the first to open this place. And this is not about any place, *ve-la ʿal kol atar hihu*, but rather, even if it is a place other persons walk upon, now that the righteous walk on it, it is a new place. Now it is a new place, as if no one else had ever walked on it before. The righteous make anew this whole place with many high words.[14] And in them, the Holy One, blessed be He, is aroused. Moreover, the Shekhinah walks in this place, something which was not so earlier. Therefore, it is called "the way of the righteous." For with it is hosted a high and holy guest. "Road" is open to all, and is walked by all who wish, even if they are sinners. "Road": this secret "he made [lit., gave] a way through the sea, *ha-noten bayam derekh*." [Isaiah, 43:16][15]

Neither the place nor the act of walking, the *Zohar* tells us, can be stabilized or reduced to an absolute locus. Rather, each depends upon the difference that is asked about in this passage: it is a matter of establishing the difference between a way and a road. The way makes way for a new place, for disclosure and opening. The place occurs as new in association with language, "with many high words." Moreover, because of a subtle and uncertain difference, both the place and the walking fail to emerge into full view and repeatedly occur only in the movement of vanishing: the way is mentioned at the beginning of an exegetical impulse and then disappears in the discursive unfolding. Thus, the text raises doubts as to whether its question propels or arrests the way of inquiry: "after a man by means of inquiry and reflection has reached the utmost limit of knowledge, he stops at *mah* (what?)."[16] But this arresting point is presented as only the failed beginning ("What, *mah*, have you understood? What have you observed? What have you inquired into? Everything remains as concealed as before") of an itinerary that will lead to *mi?* (who?). Hence, although it is not clear whether there is at all an answer to this "what?" the *Zohar* does makes clear that there is another, the same but distinct, place, and another question—the difference between "who?" and "what?" is asserted but never quite defined, nor can it be thought simply in terms of a distance that could be covered—that is not only even less likely ever to be answered but even reached by a path that has already been arrested: the question *mi?* (who?). Giorgio Agamben acutely comments on this passage that "having reached the limit of the *who?*, it is clear that thought no longer has an object; it experiences the absence of a final object."[17] That this absence resonates but also translates the peculiar notion that there would be a place, *atar*, where there is "no position, no place, of the end" (Mopsik) has perhaps become slightly more familiar from our earlier discussions of *ein-sof* at "our place in al-Andalus." And what I want to show here is that the doubling of the question (who? what?)—which seemingly only carries the reader onto another place, without opening a coverable or recoverable distance, and where "thought no longer has an object"—does not remain in a place that would be beyond, at a distance from, the object. Rather, it multiplies objects and prevents each "one" object (who? what? the road? the question? the place? *which*?) from becoming identical to itself. The "object" is therefore not absent in some beyond that would be no place, but it is "absent" insofar as it exceeds its oneness while remaining both "less than one and more than double,"[18] *plus d'objet.*

The many narratives conveyed by the *Zohar* ambivalently maintain the importance of the way upon which the rabbis constantly travel. It is as if, by introducing its elaborations with a quasi-formulaic description of the rabbis on the way, the text were constantly signaling, however discreetly, the importance—and the question—of place and of the text as (taking) place. The *Zohar* repeatedly calls itself a way while undermining the very narrative gesture that makes the claim that the way exists at all. It at once establishes the road-way as a privileged locus from which rabbis and messages are sent en route, and expresses a need for suspending this road-way as a proper analogy for discursive insight. It is as if the text were thus reading literally (but we will have to return to this matter of literal and figural) "the ways of Torah" upon which it reflects or, indeed, treads. This, the place of the text, is not simply locatable within or outside the text. That is, it does not occupy a place in a serene or sure way. Instead, it continually shows itself as taking place and then as suspending the sanctity of place.

What is thus disabled is a notion of the text that would be fully coextensive with place, if only because the text—or the place—is never identical to itself ("the righteous make anew this whole place with many high words"), even if "the feet of anyone who wishes pound there" at the same time that it is "a place where feet have never previously pounded." This is the *Zohar*'s modus operandi, to take away the place it takes. But when it finds a way, with the influx of "high words," the *Zohar* endeavors to make place for itself, *to give place*, among the sacred texts.

In one of the *Zohar*'s numerous "road" narratives, the following anonymous teaching is offered:[19]

> A person who sets out upon the way
> must prepare [and be ready] for three things:
> for [giving a] gift, for [conducting] a fight, for prayer.[20]

Prior to the introduction of this teaching, two rabbis are depicted as having themselves "set out upon their way." The anonymous teaching is spoken, cited, by one of the rabbis in order to provide what appears to be a measure, a standard for recognition, perhaps a means to locate, to answer a "who" or a "what" as they see something or someone approaching. The rabbis are in need of such a measure since, on their way, they have encountered someone else, an other person (*bar-nash*, no gender is specified at this point), who is also walking upon the way, and whom the rabbis wish to know or, more precisely, to read. As they try to read the signs carried by the other, they seem to reach a quick conclusion: the person fulfills two of the three requirements provided by the anonymous teaching. First, s/he is armed and therefore ready to fight; second, she or he wears a prayer shawl (*talit*) and, therefore, is ready to pray. However, beyond this hasty, dual recognition, there is a third element that emerges insofar as it fails to show itself. This is the giving of a gift. The rabbis say: "Here is this person, who is walking on his way, covered in his *talit*, he is ready for prayer. And with him [also] are his weapons for fighting. Since these are two [of the requirements], we need not inquire about the third." The gift of the way that is not any place cannot—or, more precisely, need not—be asked about ("What have you observed? What have you inquired about?"), either because knowledge is not the purpose or because its (non)object can already be assumed to be found. More precisely, one can already assume that one is "at this place," the place of the gift, a different place, to be sure, but which, like a gift, only appears insofar as it has failed to do so.

That the text later turns out to have proved the rabbis both wrong (a moment of gift-giving, namely the giving of greetings, fails to materialize) and right (the person nonetheless turns out to have brought or even "been" a gift, teaching the text and giving it to read) only renders more difficult the way in which to read the place of the gift. Indeed, what kind of necessity is articulated in the requirement to be ready, to approach and let approach what is coming, along with the giving of a gift? What does reading mean if it also means reading as gift?

The three "requirements" translate, each in their distinct way, modalities of reading in giving, reading at the place of the gift, and it seems fairly clear that there is more to read with these ways of reading. Yet, what interests me here is how the question of the gift, and here the place of the gift, and of the way as gift, articulates what Christopher Bracken has called a complex "zone," a "textual zone where the marking of limits is impossible."[21] The purpose of addressing it here, then, can be neither to resolve this complexity nor to answer its question (not at least insofar as responding has taken the form of locating). What I rather wish to point out is that the peculiar lack of discussions of the status of both the way and the gift, of the way as gift ("at our place" raises the question of hospitality, on the way that, if not quite locatable, remains nonetheless a place), already testifies both to the evocation of place, to the drive to resolve it, and, on the other hand, to the peculiar way in which the "zone" articulated by the way and the gift withdraws from attention, withdraws and declines.

Precisely at the moment where the possibility of locating the place emerges, and where the insistence of the text on place is at its strongest, the assertion is also made that this giving place (rather than—but not entirely distinct from—taking place) does not manifest itself, but offers itself to be read in its differing from itself: "even if it is a place other persons walk upon, now that the righteous walk on it, it is a new place. Now it is a new place, as if no one had ever walked on it before." This movement of withdrawal (the place, the way, is no longer what it is) does not constitute an absence in any simple sense, but rather offers itself as new, gives itself as a walking that only emerges in its withdrawal, insofar as it withdraws. More precisely, the giving of place is also and at the same time that which fails to provide a place, for the place that it is and translates is already not there at the moment it is walked upon. This movement by which something gives, "less than one and more than double," recurs so often, it is so numerously repeated in the case of the *Zohar*'s "ways," that its lack of centrality, its disappearance from any reading I am aware of, cannot fail to signify.[22] It signals the evanescence of a place upon which the rabbis, arriving and departing, are always "at our place," insofar as this place, their place, is also trans-lated. Moreover, this rhetorical movement recalls in a specific and different way the *Zohar*'s *ein-sof* ("there is no position at the end," in Mopsik's felicitous translation)—which we read earlier, and which insists nonetheless on naming itself as place—and the set of moments and movements of language by which a place inscribes itself as its withdrawal. This complex movement of translation also gives place in and to the *Zohar*'s language, as the *Zohar*'s language.

Taking the Byway

Rabbi Yose and Rabbi Ḥiyya were walking on the way.
While they were walking, night fell;
they sat down.
While they were sitting, morning began to shine;
they rose and walked on.

Two traditional versions, two narratives, have conveniently provided a way to locate the *Zohar*. They articulate the rudiments of a context within which to read the text. They constitute, in fact, readings of the text that continue to be told in family and academic circles, and have been preserved in this way. The two narratives concern themselves with the (re)emergence of the *Zohar* in the Western Mediterranean around the thirteenth century. Both traditions, but there are more, hold that the *Zohar* had, so to speak, "gone under." The ancient manuscripts are said to have been hidden after being written in the second century C.E. by a well-known rabbinic figure, Rabbi Shimᶜon bar Yoḥay, only to reemerge elsewhere a thousand years later. This "fact," shared by both traditions, is paradoxically enough the ground upon which the *Zohar* stands. It constitutes the basic account, a common explanation, that was provided as to why the *Zohar* "disappeared," why it left no literary trace in the centuries that followed its writing by Bar Yoḥay, why it was found to have been neither mentioned nor quoted until the time of its appearance or reappearance in the thirteenth century.

The two versions of this account do differ, however, and the divergence between them has to do with the book's peregrinations, its own travels, prior to its reappearance. Reproducing the narrative movement of a text that insistently and unsystematically thematizes displacing wanderings and constitutes itself as the travelogue of wandering rabbis in search of rare knowledge and of rare books, repeatedly reminding its readers that they are constituted by way of travel and displacement ("Rabbi Yose and Rabbi Ḥiyya were walking on the way . . . "), the two traditional accounts of how the *Zohar* was found again have the book itself on the way, walking and traveling to more than one place. With them, the text takes place as the deployment of questions of location and destination.

It is important to note that these narratives, which have preserved the story of the book, construe it as having traveled in too many directions at once. If the *Zohar* is one—but that is a weighty "if"—its origin and destination, both geographical (the land of Palestine, al-Andalus) and textual (the original manuscript, the message, the targeted audience and readership), should not find themselves already split. Yet a split origin—and we will turn, if not return, to a comparable feature of the destination, the goal, later on—is precisely how the *Zohar* "is," the manner in which it constitutes itself and enacts its own (lost) beginning: it is a place that withdraws from localization.

Hence, even though it is "unlikely that significant portions [of the *Zohar*] have been lost," it is also the case that no complete copy seems to have been distributed, "no complete manuscript has yet been found."[23] Both complete and incomplete, the *Zohar* does not enable us to locate it or its beginnings. How did the *Zohar* begin? "Where did the author begin and how ought one to picture his method of working?"[24] What came first in the diverse parts that, in the printed version, had constituted the complete and incomplete, lost and found manuscripts? What is the "real Zohar"?[25]

These appear to be the ultimate philological questions, but they are also questions that the text raised before its modern and scholarly readers—partly presenting itself, and also failing to do so, as commentary and therefore as derivative ("it is very far from constituting anything like a real commentary")[26]—but, moreover, these are questions that it refrains from answering. More precisely, the text offers its answers at the same time that it multiplies and reinscribes the questions that gave rise to those answers, and it does so in such a way that one cannot remain at the site of either question or answer. One has to read and assume repeatedly, therefore, as

Eliane Amado Lévy-Valensi explains, the "impossible grasping, *l'impossible saisie*," the failure of a "first grasping, *une saisie première*" directed at a "withdrawn beginning, *un commencement soustrait*, a subtracted, retreating beginning."[27]

Although the text makes clear that there are points of departures, that one could locate it according to such coordinates, between withdrawing questions, it also shows that there is no one point of departure. It is this multiplication of beginnings, and the multiplication of failures to grasp them, that offers itself in the printed versions, much as the *Zohar* "itself" offers other beginnings, its own version of repeated, and loose, commentaries on the biblical "In the beginning, *bereshit*."[28] Such beginnings constitute and deconstitute the book as a "dissemination"—a word used by Lévy-Valensi, but also by Betty Rojtman, in their respective descriptions of the *Zohar*—of beginnings: "These mysteries of the beginning, of the radiant point of the origin, find themselves disseminated in the zoharic text, *ces mystères du commencement, du point irradiant de l'origine, se trouvent disséminés dans le texte zoharique*."[29] It is not that there is no beginning, then, but rather that no unique place, no one "point" could therefore make itself available. *Plus de commencement*: Commenting on this (radiating point), Lévy-Valensi soon finds herself obligated to suspend her own inscription of such a "point," precisely, under quotation marks: "The originary 'point' is beyond reach, *le 'point' originel est hors de portée*" (29).

Gershom Scholem had already asserted the "comparative obscurity of [the *Zohar*'s] early beginnings,"[30] and Kabbalah scholarship has certainly proved him right in its incessant search for illumination, ecstasy, and clearer origins of the authorial and philological kind. Indeed, Scholem's remarks could not have been more appropriate if they had also been a reflection on the text "itself," but the "same" could be said, of course, of the "origin" of authorship ("Was there one author or were there several?" insists Scholem with a question, modalities of which remain at the center of current academic conversations that remain fixated on "leading figures"),[31] in a text that insistently figures itself as the impossible figure of a dissemination, as the impossibility even, of figuration and of localization ("At first sight, the existence of a multitude of writings of apparently very different character, loosely assembled under the title 'Zohar,' seems to leave no argument against the view that they do in fact belong to different writers and different periods" [159]). This is the text that is held to have canonized the doctrine of a multiple and fragmented divinity (the famous doctrine of the *sephirot*, or divine forces that interact within themselves and in response to the actions of this world). Here unity remains to be achieved and the task of uni-fying, as Charles Mopsik reminded us earlier, is hardly a given (it is a "relative unity" that "cannot attain the absolute . . . limited in its essence. It cannot go as far as the amalgam that embraces all the elements").[32] This is the text that is also held to have canonized the practice of pseudepigraphy in medieval Jewish letters.[33]

Along with the "points" of departures, the traditions of the *Zohar*'s reemergence also multiply the "points" of arrival of the *Zohar*, and are therefore not only close to the movement of the zoharic texts, but are also closer to academic conclusions than is often assumed. This is not only because they acknowledge—with the *Zohar* "itself"—the novelty of its being found again, "published," if one wills, in the Middle Ages, but also because they address, without resolving it, the ensuing need or at least the desire to account for the *Zohar*'s (new) location(s). The enigma of origins, of the originary place (or, indeed, places) of the *Zohar*, which have preoccupied its readers, traditional or academic, without giving them much rest, can therefore be shown as themselves emerging, translating—were the text to qualify as a "point" of departure—from the text. They are events of its translating occurrence.

Consider, for example, that this collective attempt at localization—which manifests itself perhaps most visibly in the early and recurring "mapping" of the divine (the famous maps of the *sephirot*) that enable the readers to locate themselves and to find their ways—constitutes the central and dominant figure of "the Kabbalah," the better known "Jewish" "mystical" tradition within which the *Zohar* itself has been exclusively located. The obsession with place that is, I argue, a determined but also contingent response to the text, and, indeed, a disjuncted continuation of its own translation, will be shown in this chapter, along with the withdrawal of place, correlative with this obsession, at work in—and as—the text. Place and placing, as well as *topoi*, common places and figures, will therefore persist here as the texts—otherwise than contexts—to be read.

The first version of the reemergence of the *Zohar* takes us to Palestine, where a wandering rabbi has been sitting, his wanderings suspended. But this narrative also begins as its place of origin—its original context—

withdraws: this is the decline, the catastrophic end, of "our place" in Acre. Rabbi Isaac, whose name is also the name of that place—he is Rabbi Isaac of Acre—"wrote that Acre had been destroyed in the year fifty [one] (i.e., 1291 C.E.), and that the pious of Israel had been slaughtered there. . . . In 1305 this Rabbi Isaac of Acre was in Navarre, in Estella, having escaped from Acre, and in the same year 1305, he came to Toledo." It is two hundred years later that Rabbi Abraham Zacuto writes down these words, (dis)locating Rabbi Isaac and explaining that he "found the diary of Rabbi Isaac of Acre" who "went to Spain to find out how the book of the *Zohar* . . . came to exist in his time."

So begins the reported story of the early search for the place of the *Zohar* in this time and place, the story of how a rabbi, coming from a place—Acre—that is no longer one, had heard of the appearance—not quite the publication—of a midrash, not necessarily anything that looks like a "real" commentary, as Daniel Boyarin has argued.[34] This midrash, rumor had it, although now found in the Iberian peninsula, would have emerged from, it would have lost its early place, where Rabbi Isaac sits, at our place in Palestine. Never having heard of it, Isaac takes the road, sets on his way to travel West after the book, in its pursuit and in pursuit of its place(s) and of its origin(s). The obsessive dimension of place—nothing is left unmarked by a place name—indicates the extent to which mapping and locating is everything. Yet the activity of locating has nothing to do with stability. At this very moment in this work, the multiplication of names effectively undermines the possibility of any stability of place.

I pursued it and asked the scholars . . . whence had come these wonderful mysteries. . . . Some said one thing and some said another. Some said in answer to my question that the faithful rabbi Nachmanides had sent it from the land of Israel to Catalonia, to his son, and the wind had brought it to Aragon, and others say Alicante, and it had fallen into the hands of the sage Rabbi Moses de Leon, who is also described as Moses de Guadalajara.[35]

Isaac, from Acre, then meets Moses, from León—or from Guadalajara, Wadi l-Ḥijāra—face to face: "When I came to Spain I went to Valladolid . . . and I found Rabbi Moses there." Multiplying places and place names, Rabbi Isaac is performing and repeating the very momentum offered by the text he pursues, as if the text were in fact in pursuit of him. Suggesting again and again that "in what is asked about there lies also that which is to be found out by the asking," there is an absolute coincidence at the level of statement and textual performance. The text engages movement and Rabbi Isaac gets on his way, at least thematically. In this pursuit, as it turns out, it is never a matter of reaching a goal.

There are named and nameless places, "real" or fictional, and there are entire libraries of "new and rare texts previously unknown in Spain"—books that seem occasionally to lead readers astray, Gershom Scholem among them. Scholem writes: "The whole book is full of fictitious quotations and other bogus references to imaginary writings which have caused even serious students to postulate the existence of lost sources for the mystical parts of the *Zohar*. . . . Not in a single instance are we confronted with genuine quotations from earlier writings which have since disappeared."[36] These imaginary writings also cover a land that is not one (for lands and worlds too are multiplied, above and below, *de-le^cela, de-letata, leit atar panuy mineih*, no place is void of Him and He is ten), all omnipresent, figuring and disfiguring, locating and dislocating, places of displacements. Is this a place about which the question "where?" can be asked? If it must be asked, (when) did its location ever coagulate into existence? Clearly Scholem is right when he says that the land here

> described in all its parts is not the real country such as it exists or existed, but an imaginary one. . . . Knowledge of the country was derived entirely from literary sources. Localities which owe their existence in literature to the misreadings of medieval Talmudic manuscripts. . . . [The] descriptions of the mountains of Palestine, for example, are of the most romantic kind and accord far better with the reality of Castile than with that of Galilee. (169)

Scholem thus insists on anchoring this indeterminate territory in "Spain [*sic*]" rather than Palestine, as if forgetting that he recognized that both are equally fictional and literary.

Scholem's referential drive is still something that needs to be interrogated, as well as the status of the fictional sites and their resolute proliferations.[37] There is also the question of the misreadings with which Scholem is concerned. Isaac, for his part, describes how Moses made him an offer. We do not know whether this was a trick, though it is certainly worthy of the picaresque exploits of any self-disrespecting *maqāma* rogue. Moses suggested that they not remain sitting where they were but that they rise and walk on. The two of them, the two rabbis, should proceed on the way—though not together—and meet in Avila, where Moses's house and the ancient manuscript are said to be found: "May God do so to me, and more also," said Moses, "if there is not at this moment in my house, where I live in Avila, the ancient book." Yet Avila and the ancient book as the explicitly stated goal hardly provide us with the end of a geography lesson that sent us on our way to the (homely?) place of the book's origin. Rabbi Isaac will continue in his travels, and, although we must soon leave him, we ourselves hardly remain sitting. Just when it seemed as if the two became one, having gathered from their multiple points of departure at a fusional, even *mystical*, point of convergence, there is yet another detour that testifies to the parting of ways: the "we" of the rabbis does not maintain itself in its unity, if there was one. "Rabbi Moses left me after this and went to Arévalo on his way home to Avila."

Why the detour within which they split ways? Why did the two not stay together as one on the way, or at least as companionable allies? What stood in the way of togetherness, in the way of the one (place, manuscript, goal, etc.)? The answer is not to be found in the text, nor is the place of origin, nor, finally, is the one goal ever reached. On the way—or rather on the ways—the author too is dead again, extraordinarily enough, something that still fails to put an end to traveling as such: Rabbi Moses "fell ill in Arévalo and died there. When I heard the news I was furious, and resumed my journey."

One can only speculate as to what the manuscript was—what manuscripts there were—that Moses would have shown Isaac, as to how the wandering rabbi met on the way would have revealed himself as righteous (or not), and as to what cunning strategy, rhetorical or other, he would have used in order to convince Isaac that it was indeed the one ancient manuscript of the *Zohar*, written eleven centuries before by Rabbi Shimᶜon bar Yoḥay in the cave. This too will remain subject to an uncomfortable lack of final resolution and relocation, subject to speculation. As we have just seen, Moses of León, also of Guadalajara, died before reaching the place of his home in Avila. At this point, Isaac of Acre—whose own testimony further thematizes and translates the traditional structure of Muslim *ḥadīth*, a chain of tradition of reported speech, and is reported, as I have said, in a later compilation that itself came from another place and is signed, therefore, under a different name, pseudo-epigraphically, as it were[38]—Isaac, then, brings another link in the chain of tradition, another rumor reported from hearsay—as Isaiah Tishby revealingly has it: "there are reasonable grounds for doubting [the story's] accuracy. Rabbi Isaac of Acre heard the story from a man who himself got to know of it in a roundabout way. It involves several hands with two women at the center."[39] This, now, would be the gossip of women, or so we are told, the expandable, negligible, and unreliable testimony of Moses's wife—but we do not know wherefrom she is—who, speaking to the wife of Rabbi Joseph of Avila (the latter reporting that conversation to Isaac of Acre), swears that there was no manuscript, not even one. Her husband, Moses—who did provide multiple copies of booklets for the asking, something which was taken as proof of the truth of his claims—did not have a con-text, and would have done all the writing and copying out of two or more distinct origins or places: "May God do so to me and more also if my husband ever possessed such a book. But he wrote what he did *out of his own head and heart, and knowledge and mind,*"[40] out of con-text.

It may be possible to understand why a few readers were led to wonder whether this was not the perfect way for a woman to hide her own hand in the process of writing the book. The writer/editor/publisher certainly enacted the art of dissimulation in ways that were worthy of the name de León (or de Guadalajara) and would thus have written as a woman—she would have been, in fact, a woman.[41] Although proverbial sayings relate a man's place, his home, to his wife (*ishto beito*), and the importance given by the *Zohar* to the feminine still requires an account that would not involve the mysterious operations of a Jungian archetype, it nonetheless remains difficult to locate that place, the place of the *Zohar*, as a feminine one.

It is true that some of the most impressive modern readings of the *Zohar* have shown that "*le féminin sert de maison, de demeure au masculin, et cela à tous les niveaux*, the feminine serves as home and abode to the masculine, and this at all levels," but it is also the case that there remains, as Corina Coulmas also asserts, the "ambiguity," indeed, the difficulty of locating the feminine as simply a locale.[42] Hence, rather than follow the dominant readings that have seen in the feminine a locatable principle (preferably and insistently *below*), I want to point out the way in which here too the attempt to locate is a response to the "ambiguity"—to use Coulmas's word—of the text and of its place, its author or redactor ("one is struck, on the contrary, by the essential absence of the redactor, *ce qui frappe au contraire c'est l'absence essentielle du rédacteur,*" writes Mopsik), and so on.[43] The suggestion of a feminine place (of the place as feminine) is a gesture of localization but it does less by way of resolving the question of place than it intervenes in remarking it, and so complicates even more the localization of the *Zohar* as part of a tradition, *kabbalah*, in which, Gershom Scholem tells us, "there were no women kabbalists."

> Rabbi Ḥiyya said, "See the face of the East, *anpoi de-mizraḥ*, how it shines!
> Now all the children of the East, *bnei madinḥa*,
> who dwell in the mountains of light, are bowing down to this light,
> which shines on behalf of the sun before it comes forth,
> and they are worshiping it.

But what of the second tradition and its account of the travels of the *Zohar*? We turn East, and West, again, to follow another route and another rumor with which this report begins ("They said that the book of the *Zohar* . . . ") toward Palestine (" . . . was hidden in Meron in a cave"), and from there toward the Western Mediterranean. But first, let us rather linger in the East and with the "Eastern ones," at our place in Palestine. Abraham Azulay, who writes this report, is a sixteenth-century rabbi whom Charles Mopsik credited for having understood the importance of peripatetic travels in the *Zohar*.[44] Azulay was born in Fez, Morocco, and wrote a book, among others, called *Or ha-Ḥamma, The Light of the Sun*. This book was written in Palestine whereas other books he had previously written in Morocco have been lost. It is in *The Light of the Sun* that Azulay reports the story of the *Zohar*, a story he had received from his teacher, Moses Cordovero. Since then, this story has become the most famous and accepted account of the *Zohar*'s disappearance and reappearance for North African (so-called "children of the Oriental communities, *bnei ͑edot ha-mizraḥ*," or "Oriental") Jews. Azulay, offering the *Light of the Sun* to read, turns us both East and West at the same time, toward the "Levant" and the "Couchant." He tells us that after Bar Yoḥay concealed the *Zohar* in the cave where he had been hiding, the text was found by an "Ishmaelite" ("and an Ishmaelite found it there"—Azulay would have meant a Muslim, much like Maimonides had when he said "an Arab," and, historically speaking, may also have referred to an Arab and/or a Bedouin). This individual proceeded to distribute and sell parts of the precious manuscript that subsequently served to wrap spices—recall that there is some evidence that, in Arabic culture, it was customary to write poetry or letters on scented manuscripts, but, according to scholarly opinion, "Jewish mysticism is not poetry," nor, we should rest assured, do Jewish letters bear any but distant and highly localized relations to Arabic.

The manuscript is never quite figured as whole, though there is no evidence that any page was in fact lost, and it hardly finds itself in one place. Rather, its pages are insistently dispersed throughout ("A few pages from it came into the possession of a scholar from the West. . . . he collected together every page from every merchant. He also searched in rubbish heaps and discovered that merchants were wrapping and selling spices in them"), and brought over, trans-lated, "perhaps" by the Arab or by another Moroccan sage, the descendants of whom are, as I have said, still often called "Orientals" (the West, this "other heading," *maʿarav* or *maghreb*, usually refers to Morocco, and it certainly does here). The *Zohar* would have passed over to Morocco, then, but it is not clear from the story how this trans-lation occurred.

The testimony becomes uncertain when it describes that the text, all the disseminated pages of which had been collected from decidedly unsacred rubbish heaps, appears not to have been later found but only to have then emerged, where the sun declines, sets, departs, and withdraws (Ar. *ġaraba*) at our place in the Maghreb (Ar. *maġrib*, from *ġaraba*)—it was only "perhaps" brought over—but only for the most part ("mainly") in one city (or two?) among others ("one of the cities of the West"). This recognizable place that the text may or may not have reached, though it did emerge from it, is the famous Moroccan town of Todgha, in the Atlas mountains, which may or not be the place where our Western scholar lived ("it emanated mainly from one of the cities of the West called Todgha, and perhaps this Western scholar had taken it to the city where he lived").[45]

> Of course once the sun comes forth,
> there are many who worship the sun;
> but there are those who worship this light,
> calling this light, the God of the shining jewel
> and their oath is, "By Allah of the shining jewel, *ve-umaʾa di-lehon*
> *be-Allah de-margela de-nahir.*"
> Now you might say: This worship is in vain!
> But since ancient primordial days they have discovered wisdom through it.

It is not merely the case that the *Zohar* is nowhere, then, nor that it has no place or simply fails to take place. Rather, it locates itself as it withdraws from location, dis-located out of a context that, like the sun, withdraws and declines, between its ancient origins and its medieval reappearance, between Bar Yoḥay and de León, Palestine and the Western Mediterranean, between the Jew and the Arab, Morocco and the Iberian peninsula. This translating movement that locates by withdrawing from place, that offers a place insofar as this place withdraws its context, is the movement of language that translates Kabbalah into literature. The movement itself demands a reading, the transit and translation as such demand to be read.

But what does reading mean here? The quasi-mystical task of unifying the *Zohar*'s different (authorial, geographical) origins and locations seems to be the major task that the *Zohar* itself continues to present to its readers. Yet the minimal consequence of the task that it sets itself involves the status of its narratives. Those narratives, taken as preserving the unreliable story of its disappearance, wanderings, and reemergence, must not only be seen as responding to the predicament of the text, as I have been arguing, but also as pursuing, carrying over, translating—if hardly continuously—its narrative movement. Rabbis on the way in search of a rare and unknown text, questions of origin and of place, are dis-located between East and West, between Arab and Jew, North and South. The striking narratives carried by and about the *Zohar* are also clear cultural assertions that concern themselves with the place of the *Zohar*, the importance, indeed, the necessity, of its Muslim, of Arab and Jewish, and, indeed, Arab Jewish intermediaries—of its Arab and Jewish carriers, readers, and trans-lators. All participate in turning our attention to those narratives of displacement as *readings* of the *Zohar*, as readings of Allah "in" the *Zohar*, readings of a translated and untranslated, a dis-located, name of God. These intense and profound readings *of* the *Zohar*—by the narratives *on* the *Zohar*—as the narrative movement of a translation, a movement of dis-placement, turn Kabbalah ineluctably into literature.

One cannot read the *Zohar* without repeating, without being recurrently carried and given over to, and translated by, the movement of the text and of its narrative receptions. Following, as Rabbi Isaac did, the paths and ways, then, the meanderings and wanderings, the walking on the way, and on the "ways of Torah," that it follows, the *Zohar* insistently appears to place and dis-place its readers onto a map (sephirotic, philological, or mystical) that does not merely converge in one place. Neither quite fully on the way ("while they were walking, night fell; they sat down"), nor ever more than temporarily resting between times and places ("while they were sitting, morning began to shine; they rose and walked on"), places that are themselves neither true nor fictional, the *Zohar* withdraws from its localization, from its classification as simply the repeated and repetitive story of wanderings that are never quite far from—nor quite locatable in—the

"East" ("Having disposed of all the fantasies about the various parts of the *Zohar* belonging to different periods, about its sources and its supposed derivation from the East").[46]

The *Zohar* can therefore hardly be reduced to "mysticism," understood as an ideal of experiential fusion aiming for a unitary goal. Rather, it multiplies and offers narratives of wandering that function as means of situating its commentary, locating (and obviously failing to locate) it in and as literature. The *Zohar* refers to its textual object or subject, but also to these peregrinations and commentaries, and finally to itself, as "ways." The "ways of Torah," literary ways if ever there were, are thus located within narratives that have yet to achieve the prominence they deserve. As with their Eastern and Arabic beginnings, these narratives do vanish historically, but they will have turned Kabbalah into the custody of literature. Until now, the literary has been dissociated, largely for ideological reasons, from the sacred origin of this text. This dissociative imperative belongs to a defensive strategy that views literature as an imminent danger and threat to the sanctity of its intention as a religious and mystical tract. Crossing borders, literature no doubt always brings the menace of an uncontrollable incursion that would disrupt the mystical experience and compromise the sacred, auratic standing of the *Zohar*.

> There is hardly another writer of the period whose personality is of such *arresting* interest to us.
>
> —Gershom Scholem, *Major Trends* (my emphasis)

The *Zohar* already functions as a translation of its "own" narratives of deceiving old men who, refusing to identify themselves in any direct way, conceal their (place of) origin, in narratives that have long declined and withdrawn as "narrative frames" and—this Orientalist but also zoharic *topos* —"empty rhetoric." The *Zohar*, a book that achieved the amazing feast of intensive narrativization while concealing it under the (in)famous veil of an ironic condemnation of biblical narratives, also functions as another translation of the *maqāma*, the rhymed-prose narrative that was so successfully translated from its Eastern (not quite) origins to al-Andalus, and later into "Jewish" letters. It is such a *maqāma* that will occupy us in the second part of this chapter, one that reveals and conceals, and tells the story-not-story of wandering rhetoricians. Like those Andalussī *maqāmāt*, the *Zohar* is uneasily situated in between departing and arriving, in the difference of the place (of arrival or departure) from itself, permanently displacing itself and its readers onto that place, a place that is not one, "our place in al-Andalus."

In what follows, there are two questions I want to address, where the issue of localization, the question of the place of language and the taking (and the giving) place of the language of the *Zohar* ("our place in al-Andalus") acquire a particular urgency. First is the question of the language "itself," the question of Aramaic (the language in which most of the *Zohar* is written): Aramaic fails to maintain its status as a language still used, as the ancient and normative language of study, but also, and more importantly, Aramaic remains—and also fails to remain—*marked as the vernacular language.* Aramaic comes to constitute an unavoidable moment in the movement of translation that the *Zohar* articulates. Second, I will try to read one of the *Zohar*'s recurring figures, the figure of the rose, in its relation to the question of genre (that is, also, the question of place and location) and of the title of the *Zohar.* The status of figuration in the text and of the text which is also figured by its title, of the text figured as its title in the mode of figuration that is—if not quite proper to it—peculiar to the way it takes and gives place.

De Arami Eloquentia: Vernacular and the Emergence of Prose

> We appreciate too little the enormity of the step taken when the vernaculars usurp the rightful place of the languages of power.
> —María Rosa Menocal, *Shards of Love*

First, then, is the question of the language "itself," namely the status of Aramaic, the language in which most of the *Zohar* is written, although it should be noted that in addition to not being the sole and exclusive language—there are also lengthy passages in Hebrew, as well as recognizable traces of Arabic and Romance languages—this Aramaic is distinct from other Aramaic forms known to philologists. It is a highly singular language, unique to the *Zohar*, and a language that, its eminent French translator Charles Mopsik suggests, *should* even to some extent be read out of context. This is a pedagogical imperative. The *Zohar* "is written to a large extent in an Aramaic that is peculiar to it, thus disposing of a language that is bequeathed to it alone and that one must learn in its singularity, without contamination from the proximity of Hebrew or even Aramaic, *est écrit en grande partie dans un araméen qui lui est propre, disposant ainsi d'une langue à lui seule échue qu'il importe d'apprendre dans sa singularité, sans se laisser contaminer par la proximité avec l'hébreu ou même l'araméen.*"[47]

The proximity of Hebrew, and most importantly of Aramaic itself, is, however, essential, if also misleading. With it, this singular—but also *revived*—Aramaic takes its distance from itself. On the one hand, it maintains the status of a language that is still used as the ancient and normative language of study. The *Zohar*'s Aramaic was therefore properly pointed out as part of an actively traditional "return" (underscored by the proclaimed antiquity of the newly found *Zohar*). Hence, to quote from Gershom Scholem's pertinent discussion "Tradition and New Creation in the Ritual of the Kabbalists," whatever "new creation" is occurring alongside, or even in tension with "tradition," it would appear that Aramaic is here on the side of a formal and conservative intent, indeed, on the side of a "deliberately conservative attitude of men" expressing their "piety toward tradition." If Aramaic did take part in the "ambivalence" that Scholem sees at work in the Kabbalah, it nonetheless remained on the side of "expression," and it was the expression of "a return to ancient images and symbols." Scholem valued, of course, not only this tension but the productive (and destructive), revolutionary dimensions of innovation. Still, it seems to have been clear to him that "the rejuvenation of religion repeatedly finds its expression in a return to ancient images and symbols."[48] Aramaic—and this means the Aramaic of the *Zohar*—remains on the side of the "return," something that is considered possible, at least formally, and that manifests itself clearly in spite or because of the numerous flaws ("misunderstandings and grammatical misconstructions . . . wrong forms"), mistakes ("simple misunderstanding of expressions"), and naive, unphilological, dead giveaways to their medieval origin ("he does not seem to have realized that the Hebrew of his day, which he tried to translate into Aramaic, totally differed as a language from that of the ancient books. With all his vast erudition he was anything but a philologist," and "it is evident that the author had no clear perception of the difference between the Old Midrash, whose tradition he tried to carry on, and the mediaeval homily which issued from his pen without his being aware of it").[49] Aramaic, then, is on the side of an in-different authorial intent, an intent that was quite unintelligent, but also profoundly conservative and reactionary.

On the other hand, and no less importantly, Aramaic remains *marked* as the vernacular language. The same authorial intent, Scholem further tells us, asserted itself in that direction as well: "The author apparently regarded the [Aramaic] language of the Targum Onkelos as the *dialect which was spoken* in Palestine in 100 A.D.").[50] And because this marking of Aramaic as "spoken" adds to, perhaps even exceeds, the alleged authorial intent toward historical accuracy in its conservative "return," the consequence becomes that the *Zohar* partakes of the invention, of "the beginnings of the vernacular literatures," and even of the "emergence of prose" that takes place in the Western Mediterranean.[51] That it has also failed to do so is, again, not an accident.

What I want to argue, in fact, is not only that Aramaic, as vernacular, here enables and simultaneously disables a contextualization in either "past" (the tradition toward whom one could allegedly "return") or "present" (the medieval emergence of vernacular literature), but indeed that it is an essential—and strictly speaking unlocatable—dimension of the translation of the *Zohar*, of the *Zohar* as translation, whose "context" declines and withdraws. Aramaic "itself" fails to be located as either Western or Eastern, conservative or revolutionary, or both conservative and revolutionary. Aramaic articulates an unavoidable moment (and/in the) movement of translation to which the *Zohar* gives place, as which it takes place.

The *Zohar* refers to Aramaic—whether its "own" or that of the rabbinic sources, real or fictive, that it quotes—by way of the established word *targum*, which, like *romançar* and *romanzare*[52] and like its Arabic cognate *tarjama*, means "translation"—the early translations of the Hebrew Bible into Aramaic (and Targum Onkelos among them) are referred to as *targumim*. *Targum* is also the second term in a binary couple, in which it is opposed to *leshon qodesh*, or "holy tongue," namely, Hebrew.[53] It is therefore accurate to consider it marked—and Scholem, uniquely, does—as "vernacular," and it is in fact called just so in Hebrew: *leshon ḥol*. The explanation implicitly offered in the zoharic texts regarding the use of this language for the divulgation of secrets is a traditional one—that Aramaic conceals from, and is not understood or cared for, by potentially harmful angels[54]—but because of such antecedents (for all intents and purposes "deliberately conservative," as Scholem has it), it is one that deserves some attention.

At a time when the *Zohar* had yet to be found, Aramaic, Joseph Yahalom explains, had already "become one of the hallmarks of Judaism."[55]

In addition to the fact that the language was widely used (that is, until its displacement by Arabic and its vernaculars), we know that it was marked as "popular" prior to the Islamic expansion and after. Yet it was a long time before "Aramaic itself gradually ceased to be the language of daily intercourse, especially after the Arab conquest" of Palestine. Prior to the conquest, Aramaic can only be described as having been "the common vernacular" (44). In the Talmud, Aramaic is the language of expression, even though there remain signs that it had not always enjoyed its vernacular status: Hebrew too was maintaining its once spoken status and was considered (proper) "speech." Aramaic, however, was not only the de facto vernacular, it was also a language of loss—something which already brings us closer to the *end*, at "our place in al-Andalus"—and was thought to be most appropriate for *eulogies.* Why eulogies? Because, said Saul Lieberman, "there is no true mourning and lamentation except in the mother tongue."[56] Indeed, it seems that in ancient Palestine, "on occasions centering on death and mourning, it was customary . . . to use the vernacular spoken by one and all—Aramaic." Hebrew, on the other hand, was used on those same occasions but only "for reciting the blessings over the mourners" (36).

Aramaic then is marked in the rabbinical sources upon which the *Zohar* was undoubtedly relying (as the reference to the angels' lack of understanding makes clear) as both the mother tongue and as a language of loss, a rhetoric of sadness. It is therefore not surprising that it was marked not only as "popular" and "lowly"—even if it was used "by one and all" as the vernacular—but was also figured by way of biblical metaphors that would reinforce that dimension. It is striking to note that this was done with the help of the figure that will occupy us later—namely, the rose—a figure that therefore already intervenes in the configuration of loss and displacement, of mourning and language, a configuration that has been looming over much of my discussion so far. While explaining that one must bless the mourners in Hebrew even if the rest of the service is conducted in Aramaic, the late antique rabbis testify to the rarity of Hebrew and contrast it with the widespread usage and popular knowledge of Aramaic: "It is like ten people who entered a house of mourning and did not know how to recite the blessing over the mourners. And if there was one who did know how to recite the blessing, he stands unto them *like the rose amongst the thorns*" [Song of Songs, 2:2] (36).

As a language of loss—which itself testifies to the loss of the "rose"—

Aramaic is then removed from itself, lost to itself as the language of loss. Aramaic is displaced by Arabic as the new Jewish vernacular but it remains culturally marked as the spoken language, even if it has stopped being practiced as such. When it appears in its singular form in the *Zohar*, it does so in the midst of an explosion of vernacular literatures, something that unsettles its localization as either ancient or modern: Aramaic (fails to) take(s) place as vernacular, it marks itself as such, because all the while signifying—though not succeeding, as Scholem makes abundantly clear—its return, its gesture toward itself as the lost language of loss. Aramaic thus cannot quite or simply be said to participate in one of the most profound and revolutionary changes undergone by the languages of Europe, with Arabic *en tête*, whose colloquial literary expressions were progressing in great strides. More precisely, Aramaic fails to appear as the vernacular it is nonetheless marked as insofar as the emergence of vernacular literatures (Ibn Quzmān and other *azjāl* poets, the troubadours, Chrétien de Troyes, the *Roman de la rose*, the *Libro de buen amor*, Dante's *De vulgari eloquentia*, etc.) *withdraws*, insofar as "literature" fails to achieve its status as context, and insofar as the *Zohar* disables its localization in such failing context. This greatly complicates the double movement of a "conservative" return and a revolutionary change that Scholem describes, for it affects the "place" —indeed the place of the language—of the *Zohar*. The text that has been documented as making its assertions with "new-ancient words," fails to let itself be contextualized either in terms of an ancient tradition, in terms of an ancient body of texts, or in terms of a revolutionary novelty.[57] It is insofar as it fails to locate itself in either but remains the occasion for a response that would seek its contextualization as either or both, the *Zohar*—that is, the language of the *Zohar*, the place of its language—exceeds the possibility of localization: "our place in al-Andalus."

Nonetheless, one must ask whether there is "another" tradition, one that, though it withdraws, would continue to mark—to mark and not to practice, though the distinction may cause more trouble than it resolves—Aramaic as vernacular (i.e., as "spoken"). Such a tradition would not necessarily have to be found "elsewhere," yet at "our place" it would have to be distinct from the traditionally recognized sources of the *Zohar*—sources in relation to which, one should note, the *Zohar* is "very far from constituting anything like a real commentary," at times no more than a "superficial imitation of the Midrash"—sources that "naturally . . . are not mentioned."[58]

Moreover, such a tradition, such sources, would have to show a usage and a conception of language that would disturb the "mystical" classification and themselves testify to the translating movement of al-Andalus, the displacing translation that loses us in "our place in al-Andalus" and that had begun—if it ever, in fact, began—earlier than Maimonides, and would continue to be at work "in" the *Zohar*. "The whole book," writes Scholem, "is full of fictitious quotations and other bogus references to imaginary writings which have caused even serious students to postulate the existence of lost sources for the mystical parts of the *Zohar*. . . . Not in a single instance are we confronted with genuine quotations from earlier writings which have since disappeared."[59] If there was a tradition that could have served as "context," it has in fact "ended" and "disappeared," though not necessarily in the impossible way here described by Scholem (for how could one ever be confronted with a verifiable, or better yet, "genuine," quotation from writings that have disappeared? Unless disappearance remains to be read?).

With Maimonides (and Naḥmanides) we have begun to contemplate the possibility of such translations as they indeed occurred, not only between philosophy and literature, but also between midrash and poetry. We recall that midrash turned into poetry under the translating project of Maimonides, and precisely at the moment when his text was engaged in classifications that should have remedied that predicament. We are now addressing the way language (Aramaic) "itself" carries the burden of a classification, a localization of a tradition that fails to maintain itself in (one) place. Aramaic, as faux vernacular (but is there a "true" one?) makes its place anew when, in sources that are hardly inaccessible—though they are neither "mystical" nor rabbinical—and that constitute themselves as key moments in the process that al-Andalus articulates, it dislocates the place of language.

These key moments are translations of and between Arabic and Hebrew poetry and prose, between high and sacred and low and popular languages. Consider the historiographical insistence with which the so-called Spanish Golden Age must at all cost be localized, bound and maintained as a passing "elite" event of which the always and unchangingly faithful "masses" would have remained blissfully unaware or against which they would have constantly rebelled, failing even to speak—or "worse," be affected by—the "high" Arabic language spoken by their neighbors, and incidentally by famous poets who wrote scores of *azjāl* and other vernacular poetry. Such localizing insistence interestingly repeats itself—as if one had to *respond* continuously to the translations of al-Andalus—when tremendous efforts are deployed in order to "protect" the youth of Israel from hearing poems the Hebrew of which is at the same time so complex and intertextually resonant, it could never be understood (though the risk of such understanding seems precisely what one attempts to prevent) by such a "popular (young, and easily influenced)" audience, and between other languages as well.[60]

Aramaic intervenes in medieval poetry and prose precisely as the marker of—indeed, as the name of—the vernacular. It is reinscribed in such a role, therefore, in the poetry of the major poets of the Andalusī Jewish tradition, namely that of Shmuel ibn Naghrīla ha-Nagid, that of Yehuda ha-Levi (in his most famous book, the *Kuzari*). Insofar as Aramaic also serves to *name* the vernacular of those speaking their "own" (foreign?) tongue around the speaker, it also functions as a translation of the Arabic *ʿajamiyya* and of the Hebrew *laʿaz*. In Arabic, as James Monroe explains, the

> *ʿajam* were the non-Arabs or "foreigners" in a very general sense, as opposed to the *ʿarab*, or Arabs. As the latter moved out of their peninsula and spread their empire in all directions, the word *ʿajam* came to acquire more specific meanings. In the East, it was normally used to designate the Persians. . . . In Andalus, however, the term *ʿajam* was consistently applied to the Romance-speaking populations of the Peninsula, and to the Mozarabs in particular, the Arabic term for whose language, *ʿajamiyya*, is the etymon for Spanish *aljamía*.[61]

Hence, when Maimonides uses the Arabic term, he means "Ibero-Romance." Much in the same way, when Yehuda ha-Levi, in a Hebrew *muwwaššaḥa*, compares a lover's words to that of a "doe" singing in that very same "Ibero-Romance" (and ha-Levi does proceed to "quote" from that Romance song), he writes that she sings in *Aramaic, ke-tsviya teshorer aramit.*[62]

Aramaic is therefore not simply "foreign" but insistently marks a vernacular speech. Indeed, in the poems of Shmuel ibn Naghrīla ha-Nagid, Aramaic is allocated the very role which Saul Lieberman described so eloquently about rabbinic times: "There is no true mourning and lamentation except in the mother tongue." The poet receives a messenger of ill news, and, terribly saddened over the loss of his brother announced to him, greets this messenger with a curse. Interrupting the flow of Hebrew verse, and prefiguring the role it took in modern Hebrew literature prior to a standardized "spoken" Hebrew, it is Aramaic that carries speech and the spoken curse. It is with Aramaic that the poet recalls the interruption that grief constitutes:

"Is Isaac alive?—Already dead," he answered. Then I cursed him 'Be deaf and have dust in your mouth [Aram. *ʿafra be-fumakh*].'"[63]

These small detours—interruptions by way of translations and losses—would have been more necessary, of course, had there been an alternative translation (one that would add to the displacement that Aramaic already undergoes and produces) to the word "Aramaic." But Ibn Naghrīla, Yehuda ha-Levi, and Ibn Tibbon (ha-Levi's medieval translator) produced bilingual evidence that they knew well enough that Aramaic not only "is" but also translates "vernacular": *al-siryaniyya leshon ḥol, ha-aramit leshon ḥol,* Aramaic is the vernacular.[64]

Al-Andalus gives place, then, to the vernacular and it does so at "our place" in the *Zohar.* Having repeatedly withdrawn from localization, the *Zohar,* at the place of its language, "our place in al-Andalus," is "itself" the movement of translation that I have been describing as al-Andalus. It has not come to "qualify" as a new literary object ("the new medievalism," "Arab Jewish studies," or "the new Jewish literature"), nor has it simply become locatable as literature; yet the linguistic events that constitute al-Andalus, a set of events that has been so far partly described as the emergence of vernacular literatures, offer themselves as a place that, declining and withdrawing as the place and context of the *Zohar,* was once again trans-lated. At "our place in al-Andalus," we need to linger with both the rose and its thorns, and with the possibility of figuring a beginning.

It is like ten people who entered a house of mourning and did not know how to recite the blessing over the mourners. And if there was one who did know how to recite the blessing, he stands unto them *like the rose amongst the thorns.*

Ce est li romanz de la rose / Ou l'art d'amours
est toute enclose.[65]

Death and life are perverted flowers. Their roots are in the mud of the sky and of being.
All rain is good for the soul, but bad for the eternity that has unraveled itself from life and death; the eternity that is air.
One of the contemporary disciples of Reb Simoni reports the dialogue of two twin flowers that had grown in his garden.
—I know not, said the disciple of Reb Simoni, whether my garden is Paradise or Hell.

DIALOGUE OF THE TWO ROSES

—So, audacious friend, you challenge me in your soul.

—I am faithful to love.

—Love loves only it/him/self, *l'amour n'aime que lui.*

—I am life. He/it is mine, *il m'appartient.*

—Not always. The lovers offer their life to me.

—The unhappy lovers. Not love.

—Love is the trap you set for men to dress yourself in their shivers, to drink their tears.

—Light in the eyes, that is what love is.

—Love devours the eyes which see.

—Cold friend.

—My accomplice.—Here, there occurred, writes the disciple of Reb Simoni, a long silence, then the voice turned supplicant.—Abandon Sarah and Yukel to me.

—I do not want to lose them.

—One day, you will have to yield.

—One morning, perhaps, when I feel gay; at the moment when they will have become unbearable to me.

> —Here, I believed I heard it/her laugh, *j'ai cru l'entendre rire,* writes the disciple of Reb Simoni.

—You will have a few hours or a few weeks, it will depend, in order to tear them from me.

—Cruel one, you know they are suffering.

—Love is my youth.

—You are life.

—Love is the master of my life.

—Abandon Sarah and Yukel to me.

—Why the hurry? Are they so pleasing to you? You crawl like a slave. Are you in love?

—I have nothing to do with love.

—Then, why wish to ravish my lovers?

—Because it is in the order of things and also because it is my job, *c'est mon métier.*

—You are racing through the stages. And my pleasure, don't you care for it anymore? You disappoint me.

—It happens to me, sometimes, to be tender with humans.

—Why?

—A little out of pity. I love to be believed good.

—You are jealous. You are dying with love.

—I kill everything I touch.

—Your body is drunk with caresses, your petals are moist from hoped-for kisses. But I am strong. I am stubborn. It amuses me to make you wait.

—You relentlessly wound me. But beware. I could avenge myself.

> —Here, it seemed to me, writes the disciple of Reb Simoni, that they had moved closer to each other, and their attitude was that of challenge.

—Admit that I am pleasing to you; that through the couples who exalt me, it is me you desire?

> —They gave their back to each other only to face themselves off a few moments later in their freed hatred, writes the disciple of Reb Simoni.

—Girl/Daughter/Slut, *fille.*

—The lovable avowal, *l'aimable aveu.*

—I am not at the end of my resources. You hurt me. You know it. My desire tears me entirely. Too bad. Too bad. Too bad. That concerns only me.

—I despise you.

—I love you with an impossible love. I remove those whose behavior keeps me from embracing you. I make, with their eyes, two skylights; with their body, a lost ship. The most sensual are the most vulnerable.

> —Lengthy minutes must have passed, writes, here, the disciple of Reb Simoni, which I am at pain to remember. Fragments of speech, the meaning of which escaped me, were reaching me; then I distinctly heard:

—Hush. You are chilling me.

—You are the snow that melts in April.

—I am the fever. I am the sun. I hate water, shrouds.

—You die for every birth. You prepare, with talent, beings, the world, for their announced end. Mad one who speaks to them of me. You are the antechamber. I am the bed. Your victims call to me for help. Their cries are pearls around my neck. I appear to them, then, in my inaccessible splendor. I appropriate their gaze for ever. I make it into a road, a rainbow.

—Let me live. Let me nourish myself on my life.

—Let me, my prodigal rose, relish my death.

> —When I approached them in order to assure myself they were truly real, writes the disciple of Reb Simoni, I found myself facing two roses offered to a bee's greediness and that had returned to their vegetal existence.

Edmond Jabès[66]

Ce est li romanz de la rose / Ou l'art d'amours est toute enclose

> *ZUHAR* pl. Qui commencent à briller, c.-à-d., les trois premières nuits d'un mois lunaire. ZAHRAH, pl. ZAHR, AZHÂR, AZÂHÎRU 1. Fleur, en gen.—ZAHRU LLAYLI Belle de nuit. 2. Fleur d'oranger. 3. Beauté, éclat. 4. Beauté, brillant des choses de ce monde. 5. Blancheur, blanc pur. ZUHRAH 1. Blancheur. 2. Beauté, éclat.
>
> —Biberstein-Kazimirski, *Dictionnaire arabe-français* (1860)

> From philosophy, rhetoric. That is, here, to make from a volume, approximately, more or less a flower, to extract a flower, to mount it, or rather to have it mount itself, bring itself to light—and turning away, as if from itself, come round again, such a flower engraves—learning to cultivate, by means of a lapidary's reckoning, patience.
>
> —Derrida, "La Mythologie blanche"

Notwithstanding the repeated assertions of Kabbalah scholarship about the figural ("symbolical") dimension of the book attributed to Reb or Rabbi Simon, Simeon, Shimᶜon (Simoni?), son of Yoḥay and his disciples—the *Zohar*—I will (only momentarily) concede that there is little ground to refute a description of that text (also known as *The Book of Splendor*) as a metaphorical "system" or organism, indeed, as the complex articulation of a "totality," one constantly traversed by roads, ways, and rainbows. In what follows, I nonetheless propose to raise anew the question of rhetoric—although not because there would be a ground to stand on at "our place in al-

Andalus," a privileged perspective in this garden from which to write about the figures and tropes (if that is what they are) of the *Zohar.* I propose to do so in order to consider, in fact, whether the "admission" of metaphoricity, and, even more so, of "symbolism," could counter the double, unsettling, and displacing movement that takes the *Zohar,* its stories, ways, and languages, into too many directions at once; inscribing its difference from itself, its taking and giving place and/as the withdrawing of its place and context; its failure to provide a ground, a place from which to read the *Zohar.* These considerations will thus continue, rather than conclude or bring to an end, the question of translation and displacement that constitutes the giving place of language at "our place" as it occurs in the *Zohar,* as its translation.

Let us temporarily admit, then, the metaphoricity of the *Zohar,* and agree that by metaphoricity one would mean that the *Zohar*'s language takes part in, or even fully constitutes, a "system" within which occur "these operations that share something which is characteristic of the metaphoric process," a process in which metaphor is at work. And metaphor "is to be understood here according to its classical definition as it appears in theories of rhetoric from Aristotle to Roman Jakobson, as 'an exchange or substitution of properties on the basis of resemblance.'"[67] This announces what Scholem claims about the *Zohar*'s language, a language that, he argues, articulates such an exchange or substitution.

Everywhere a term "stands" for another, and we find that, Scholem insistently tells us, "stylistic variations all play upon a single theme and never obscure the essential identity of the mind behind them. . . . every page displays a *rainbow* picture of linguistic eclecticism, the constituent elements of which . . . remain constant throughout."[68] The "formulae with which distinctions between different categories of the same general application are made are everywhere the same" (167), and "the figurants change, but the story remains the same." Following Scholem, the *Zohar*'s language would thus be a language in which "the author had no clear perception of . . . difference" (171), and in which every passage, even if loosely connected with the rest of the book, "is part of the same general picture that the author tends to repeat himself" (172). The "construction" of this language "is on the whole regular and systematic and exhibits recurrent characteristics. There is no difference" (171). Precisely because Scholem's analysis is here "literary," it would seem justified—and we are still within our provisional admission of metaphoricity—to assert that the *Zohar* presents us with a "metaphoric system" and with a consistent expression of a "totality" in which sameness is key. In other words, the *Zohar*'s constant "positing of resemblances between terms" seems too obvious (even too notorious if, at times, also too mysterious)[69] to be debated. The recurrence of the zoharic phrase "everything is one, *kola ḥada hu*" would (no doubt?) confirm such description and provides a satisfying anchoring moment to trust in it.

But how safely anchored, how safely sheltered and placed—and in which garden—can we remain?

In order to answer this question, one example (among many which could, therefore, be substituted for it) has already become familiar to us in another(?) context; thus it will, no doubt again, help to remain within its familiar vicinity. It can be read on the very first page of the *Zohar* as it is found in print (there are no complete manuscripts antedating the printed versions). There, the text could be said already to confirm and thematize the "substitutability" we have found, when it introduces two names for the rabbi who is reported, quite commonly in the *Zohar*, as having "opened" the verse. Indeed, since there is as yet no critical edition of the book, the printed, so-called traditional version supplies the reader with two distinct alternatives enabling (or forcing) one to read both or either: "Rabbi Ḥizkiah opened and said . . . " *or* "Rabbi Elʿazar opened and said . . . "[70]

In this text, however, and beyond that early, particular, exchangeability between rabbis, there is a more significant one: a rose (or, *alternatively* perhaps, a lily, *shoshana*) which momentarily appears only to be swiftly substituted for *knesset israel*, the community of Israel. The rabbi—whatever his name is—has opened and the text continues, by quoting from his speech.

> It is written "Like a rose among the thorns, so is my love among the maidens" [Song of Songs, 2:2]. What/who/which [is the] rose, *man shoshana*? It is the community of Israel (because there is a rose and there is a rose). Like the rose who is "among the thorns," in her are found red and white, so the community of Israel, in her there is justice and love. Like the rose in which there are thirteen leaves, so the community of Israel, in her are found thirteen measures/vessels of love around her from all sides. (ibid.)

Biblical commentators, and the *Zohar* among them, as we saw, were keenly aware of the arbitrariness of a beginning. The beginning of the Hebrew Bible, though quite explicit about itself ("In the beginning . . . "), did not alleviate the sense of this arbitrariness in its readers, or at least, their sense that there was nonetheless a need to justify this beginning rather than any other one. This became particularly acute in the Middle Ages, and in his commentary on the start of Genesis, Naḥmanides, for example, provides an elaborate, and somehow accessible, summary as well as an expansion on the debates that surround the different ways of reading (the beginning of what?) and the choice of that particular beginning (as opposed, for example, to the First Commandment). Distinct from this expository approach, the current edition of the *Zohar*, the early lines of which I have just quoted, *exemplifies* and multiplies—rather than countering and resolving—the difficulties surrounding beginnings. It does so by enacting, as I have described earlier, a multiplicity of beginnings, a multiplicity, in fact, of *bereshit* ("In the beginning"). This multiplication does not solve, nor does it explain or justify, why this rather than that beginning. It instead maintains the arbitrariness of the beginning by flooding the reader with a diversity of other, possible (readings of) beginnings.

Were one to ask how to begin reading the *Zohar* one would find, no doubt, that it was possible to begin somewhere else, that one could have substituted, as it were, many a beginning for the one presented at the moment. It is, moreover, quite likely, and all the more so in the case of the *Zohar*, that such substitutability of beginnings affects any given moment of the text (which could then just as well be the beginning), thus unsettling the certainty that one is in fact beginning at the beginning. Addressing the question of beginning, one is in fact already responding to the possibilities of many more dimensions of the text (and of other texts). In this process, "beginning" is translated, however, having ceased from being (never having been) identical to itself.

These remarks may complicate, although they certainly do not cancel, the question of, not how or where to begin, but of how to read this (or that) beginning(s), the beginning chosen by later editors, at a time when the *Roman de la rose* was quite famously well known: what/who/which (is the) rose? And about what is the question asking? What is the place of language—is there one?—figural and otherwise, in this question? Where is that "somewhere" of which Betty Rojtman speaks and which, difficult to grasp, locates or dislocates itself between "symbolization and concretization"? What does the *Zohar* have to say about the metaphorical? the linguistic? substitutability and its systematicity? What does the *Zohar* have to say about words—words like "rose"—which are, as Scholem wrote, "all within the limits of language and expression"?[71] What limits, what place, would such words set on language? Assuming that we can answer some of these questions, what does the *Zohar* here say it does with words, with figures and things? And, if it does, does it do what it says it does?

Aside from the awkward multiplication of slashes that split what should be one question (*man?*), and to which we will shortly return, the text says a few things at once. Continuing the rabbinical tradition that reads the Song of Songs allegorically, it considers the Song's protagonists to be figures for God and the community of Israel. Within this reading, the rose is never quite a rose—it was never a matter of reading the rose as rose—nor are the figurants (in the Song or, alternatively, in the *Zohar*) ever quite themselves, and we seem to be the farthest away from "concretization." Rather, we are provided with "keys," explanations or translations of metaphors (or of the simile), "rose" ("Like the rose," says the text). Having opened the distance between poles it has inscribed and identified, between the rose and the community of Israel, thus also distancing the word "rose" from itself, we can begin to read the text as making explicit the similarities between them, slowly eradicating the distance it itself has opened between the community of Israel (whether it is a what, a who, or a which) and the rose. Rodolphe Gasché's assertion, quoted earlier, about the "positing of resemblances" that strongly connects between two terms and establishes a unified totality could, then, hardly have found a more appropriate example: the rose appears as a figure, indeed, a metaphor (of the community of Israel).

Are we, then, reading a metaphorical text? Or more accurately, have we established that the *Zohar* is reading the words of the Song (and specifically, the word "rose") as metaphors? Do we know whether the sign is or is not the thing or a meaning derived from the thing and by what process?[72] Is it entirely clear that the *Zohar* has collapsed the distance between readings of the rose as figure, as thing, or as word? Is it promoting a form of ontology (but is it a floral, human, or divine ontology?) or is it keeping to a textual representation? What (who, or where), in other words, is the *Zohar* reading? Note the difficulty of the question on the linguistic—if not exclusively so—level: the text does not provide enough clues to let the question settle on (in whatever order) rhetoric, hermeneutics, or ontology, since it appears to ask, at the same time, so to speak, "who/what/which (is) (the) rose?"

The difficulty of translation that I am rendering by slashes and parentheses is therefore more than a play on words. It is, in fact, already and partly enacted in the work of translation done by two modern scholars. The more recent, by Charles Mopsik, translates the *Zohar* into French and renders the question *man shoshana?* into *qu'est ce que*, what is, *la rose*?[73] The other, slightly older translation is by Isaiah Tishby and it has, in Hebrew: *mi hi*, who is, *shoshana*?[74] Following *both* translations, and leaving aside for now the far from illegitimate possibility that they both left out (Which rose? or Which is the rose?), one could somehow arbitrarily distinguish the two questions in terms of their focus, and observe that what the text attends to is less the dimension of "likeness" ("like the rose among the thorns"), but is an ontological question that rather attempts to decode the text by uncovering the essence of a referent (What is the rose? The word "rose" here would not be just a name but would signify without equivocation or figuration, without interpretation, the thing, the flower rose and/or the community of Israel). Alternatively, the text may ask a hermeneutical question (assuming that there is a difference—but we would be here at "our place in mysticism," where differences matter little) that strives to translate the rose into another sign or into its literal meaning (Who is the rose? Insofar as personification is involved, the word "rose" would indicate the sign which, already figurative—even the rose of the verse was never, literally, quite a rose—also figures, in turn, the community of Israel) of the term. The "which" (no less possible a substitution for not having been considered by the translators) does not seem, at this point, to *add* to our understandings, or lack thereof, of the question(s).

What is crucial, though, is that the (word) rose could function, as well as not function, as a figure. Similarly (or not), the questions could be said to ask or to dismiss the questions of interpretation, lexical, figurative, or otherwise, and would thus locate themselves at distinct (though not quite distinguishable) levels of reading. These possibilities introduce a discrepancy between sign and referent, but they are perhaps still substitutable, gathered into a totalizing, unifying system, and would confirm the "semioticization of the created universe, *semiotisation de l'univers créé*," described by Betty Rojtman, a semiotization that "marks the symbiosis of the real and the sign."[75]

And yet, the distinction between real and sign, between word, figure, and thing, may have remained or become a source of confusion. It has become difficult to distinguish between the different possibilities and the difference they make or do not make. Allegedly, the confusion as to what is asked about, and whether "rose" is or is not a figure, a word, or a thing, could be dispelled by a teacher, a carrier of tradition, a translator (but we found two, and they disagreed). But that alone confirms that the text maintains the confusion and difficulty, that even the teacher, the translator, would have to resolve by deciding—or being informed upon—whether the rose, or the question of the rose, must in fact be interpreted or translated, whether it has anything to do with the thing rose, or whether "rose" is a word that partakes of figuration and whose meaning(s) can be distinguished between proper and figurative, whether it is *one* or has only one meaning, for example, simply "community of Israel," and whether "rose" is a "who" or a "what" (between a who and a what), whether it is a figure, a metaphor that stands in, that is substitutable for, the community of Israel. A metaphorical reading, in that sense, would here consider the word "rose" and the phrase "community of Israel" to be interchangeable, either by virtue of their referring to the same organic entity or by virtue of their having the same meaning. Could the teacher and translator decide? Could she make *one* decision? But who is "she"?

In spite of these difficulties, and in spite of the seeming "organic unity" and substitutability—or perhaps because of these difficulties, and because that unity is already disturbed by the multiple possibility of questioning and answering—there has emerged an open space, a "tiny, but vertiginous space that opens up between two words having the same meaning, two meanings of the same word: two languages in the same language."[76] There remains a not quite localizable "somewhere," some place given to ask whether or not the text produces what Gasché calls an "erasure of difference."

> The real world appears in [the image] as it were between parentheses or quote.
>
> —Emmanuel Levinas, "Reality and Its Shadow"
>
> In such examples as these, that which originally is itself only appearance, for instance, a rose, is being treated by the empirical understanding as a thing in itself, which nevertheless, in respect of its colour, can appear differently to every observer.
>
> —Immanuel Kant, *Critique of Pure Reason*

The community of Israel and the rose, much like some other textual moments we have touched on, do appear to have become, for all intents and purposes, interchangeable. However, the lack of unity between the three possible questions already suggests that the question *man?* hardly enables such coagulation of a figure of unity. And yet, the assumption of unity could still resolve the multiplicity of questions into an indifferent totality. Do not the three questions occur in *one* word? Isn't it the case that the multiple possibilities and the hesitation as to whether words or things are commented upon precisely the dimension of "symbolism," of "symbiosis between real and linguistic," that is attributed to the "mystical" *Zohar* that we are now reading? Yet, is it not also the case that prior to the way substitutability has become established, it was dependent upon a silent exclusion or erasure of the phrase "there is a rose and there is a rose, *ʾit shoshana veʾit shoshana*"? The phrase, a parenthetical addition, seems to belong—insofar as it is neither opaque to nor enables an elucidation of meaning—what Jerome McGann calls the "bibliographic" rather than the "linguistic" code.[77] It is "bibliographic" because it does not "elucidate meaning," nor does it "locate meaning . . . entirely in linguistic symbologies" (57). Rather, the phrase "calls our attention to other styles and scales of symbolic exchange" or exchanges, "places" that are not quite as locatable as meaning. Note that even without the parentheses, the form of the phrase (there is *x* and there is *x*, *ʾit milta ve-ʾit milta*) is so consistent with similar or other phrases found throughout the zoharic texts that it adds nothing to an understanding of the linguistic code, to an interpretation that strives for meaning.

If it is the case that to ask "what does something mean, the answer must take the form of 'bringing to light a resemblance,'"[78] then "there is a rose and there is a rose" comes precisely not to answer the question of meaning. Rather it reinscribes the opening of a space, that "tiny but vertiginous space that opens up" *within* one word (*man*, rose). The event of this opening, this giving place, does not maintain itself as place (though it does appear to cite the rose as *topos*), but it does raise the question of difference, the difference of that phrase from meaning. The phrase, then, makes *no difference*, but it gives, by opening, a path, a distance of the rose from the rose, and from a "linguistic," hermeneutic reading.[79] Remaining with McGann's levels of analysis, the phrase also functions like the question(s) "which," that add(s) nothing to "who" or "what" and could hardly be said to resolve the question of a metaphorical versus a literal or ontological reading. In a manner that recalls the nonidentity of Aramaic in the earlier section, the phrase "there is a rose and there is a rose" exacerbates the very problem of identity (is it this or that?): it opens and raises the question of difference between two roses, but also between the rose and "itself": the rose—but which?—translated.

"There is a rose and there is a rose" can be read, then, in many ways. In medieval Latin terms, we have been asking whether we have here a *figura verbum* or a *figura rerum*. On one level, then, and assuming it is now established that the community of Israel is indeed (like?) a rose—the sentence asserts that the rose-rose is one thing, and the rose-community of Israel is another thing. The phrase also tells us that though we read one word: the biblical word "rose," we should not be mistaken into thinking that it is actually the case that only one word (or only one thing) is found. According to this reading, there are not one but two words or two configurations thereof: the word "rose," and the word "rose." Duality, and at times even multiplicity, is a basic structural principle upon which zoharic texts articulate themselves; so much so, in fact, that it would seem difficult to dismiss any of the possible meanings of the phrase. Does this mean that "rose" is a figure and/or thing? Yes and no. There may very well be a difference. And even a difference from difference. Rather than an erasure of difference, then, what the sentence "there is a rose and there is a rose" introduces—or, rather, repeats and confirms, suspends and substitutes, between difference and indifference, such as was already at work in the question "who/what/which (is) (the) rose"—is the "nothing" of an incommensurable difference. Hence, it constitutes quite precisely a "revealing [of] the difference necessarily introduced by the substitution," the substitution of one thing for another, of one word for another, and so on.[80]

The distance opened by the parentheses between the two parts of the "commentary," by the parenthetical phrase between the rose and the rose, and finally between difference and indifference, between difference and itself, is a distance that cannot be measured by the means that the *Zohar* itself provides. But it is a distance "within" which, as which, the language of the *Zohar* takes place. The rose, the flower, and the brilliant splendor (*zohar, zuhra, zahra*), the *argument*, of the *Book of Splendor* open a space within which a path may be given, a way may be traced, that places and displaces that very book at "our place in al-Andalus."

Zohar, as the dialogue of two roses, in which the rose may be a sign of either identity or difference, but the difference between them is not there to be read but gives space to reading, has been most convincingly read, as well as translated, by Edmond Jabès ("On the Threshold of the Book") in the text I have reproduced at length at the opening of this section. It is a dialogue that occurs within the given space, the opening in the *Zohar*'s language and *within* its rose, as the title of a book that, once again, renders unlocatable the occurrence of an incommensurable difference. Between what/which/who and what/which/who? but also between "which" and "which" (which rose? which is the rose?), *man* and *man*—an answer to which would be dependent on asserting both points of departure and of arrival, a localization that would then enable the very contextualization, the inscription of contexts that ineluctably, as we have seen, withdraw.

For anyone familiar with the rich explanations that Kabbalah scholarship has generated in the past fifty years, the above discussion may appear to constitute (and succumb to) a perverse temptation, a gratuitous attempt to render obscure what has in fact already been clarified. It may therefore be necessary to summarize, once again, this "clarification" in order to profit further from its contribution toward the question of how to read—rather than how to interpret and locate—the *Zohar*. This concerns the possibility of asserting with certainty the location of the "garden" within which the "dialogue of the two roses" (fails to) take place.

The *Zohar* would be a "metaphorical system," and its privileged figure the "symbol." The *Zohar* would not, however, simply assert resemblance as a rhetorical gesture. Rather, it would establish (or recognize) a fundamental unity, an ontological, organic link, between different entities, between lower and upper worlds. In the text quoted above and translated by two eminent scholars, we would be offered the beginning of a chain of substitutable symbols. The rose and the community of Israel would be symbols that participate or are even identical to the feminine power or dimension of the plural divinity of the kabbalists. Kabbalah, in Charles Mopsik's words, would then be "*une pensée de la sympathie universelle . . . [qui] se déploie en opérant un glissement quasi permanent entre la notion de ressemblance et celle d'identité*, a thought of universal sympathy [that] deploys itself by means of a quasi-constant sliding between the notion of resemblance and that of identity."[81] The notion of "sympathy" and "organic unity" upheld by the *Zohar*, then, would not be a rhetorical event, a moment and a movement of translation, but the very motion of a thought of unity that expresses itself from the early lines of the *Zohar* onward toward a no less unitary and mystical goal. These lines would describe the resemblance, indeed, the identity, between the rose and the community of Israel.

This is a unity that articulates both meaning and added elements of an endless chain of ontological substitutions and upon which the curious reader can be further enlightened by looking at Isaiah Tishby's important footnotes in what remains the most important, and certainly voluminous, scholarly achievement concerning itself with the *Zohar*, Tishby's *Mishnat ha-Zohar* (*The Wisdom of the Zohar*, as it was published in English, though it would perhaps be more accurate to translate it as "the *doctrine* of the *Zohar*"). The reader would there learn that the "community of Israel" also resembles and symbolizes the divine presence, the Shekhinah.

Additional confirmation of the way words of Scripture would constitute figures and symbols of the divine reality can be found in the work of a major writer contemporary of (and perhaps contributor to) the *Zohar*, namely, Josef Gikatillia's *Gates of Light* (*Shaᶜarei orah*), a book that prefigures (and later will have inscribed on its cover) the "map" of the *sephirot*. Building on metaphors found in Scripture, or on later allegorical readings, we would be, with its help, *guided out of perplexity*, as it were, toward how the *Zohar* substantializes and unifies organically between the terms of these figurations and produces a transparent text that oozes an undifferentiated, totalizing unity, a "mystical" fusion.

Whatever its complexity—and no one would deny that the *Zohar* is anything but a difficult text, or that kabbalistic thought is anything but a rich and complex one—the rhetorical dimension would never disrupt the unity it is said to articulate, the connections and their naturalization that it would assert. Rhetoric could therefore be glossed over. Thematic, conceptual, and doctrinal readings would be in order, then, rather than sustained attention to what is after all only an external layer, an "outer shell."

Such readings consistently interpret by situating the meaning of the text in its doctrine or in its truth, and though they may address some of the linguistic and rhetorical problems at work in the text, they would rarely consider the language of the *Zohar*, or the giving or taking place of its language as a question that emerges from the text as translation. Such readings are not mistaken, they are rather fundamentally supported by a text that also makes profuse use of the image of the multilayered nut, and of the slowly undressing beloved whose clothing can be—and ultimately has been—discarded. A rhetorical reading, a reading that would attend to words and sentences, to grammar rather than to doctrine, and would have more to do with the mechanics of the text than with its alleged meaning, would appear therefore as a disjuncted translation, as "forced" or "imported" on, rather than supported by, the *Zohar.*

Whether or not all this is, in fact, the case, one still has to decide what to do with the phrase "because there is a rose and there is a rose." What is its place and how does it take place? Indeed, the phrase itself may have been the text's "own" contribution toward the necessity of a rhetorical reading, a philological and translating "import," then, that nonetheless unavoidably asks about the differences words make, that asks indeed, about difference. The very question of reading that this phrase suggests is not, or not only, a "*glissement quasi permanent entre la notion de ressemblance et celle d'identité,*" but also a less than smooth sliding from resemblance to difference.

We already considered that even if that phrase had not appeared—and although one may remain puzzled by a univocal conclusion, a reading, that seems to assert that words do not make any difference, that they, like clothing, can simply be discarded, that there is, in fact, no difference because "everything is one," but who, what, which "one"?—the question of difference, the failure of a question, of a "one," to be identical to itself, is insistently raised at the same time that it also fails *not* to decline.

Can the difference words would make—or not make if "everything is one"—begin to account for the bizarre omission, in both of the modern translations I have mentioned, of the phrase "because there is a rose and there is a rose"? Is it not somehow remarkable to note that this very phrase has, in fact, *simply disappeared from the translations*? There may be, of course, very sound philological reasons for that disappearance (some important commentaries, Cordovero's, for example, do not seem to know the phrase, but another Reb Simon, Rabbi Simon Lavi from the Iberian peninsula, from Fez, from Tripoli, "our place in the Maghreb," did know it and read it in his *Ketem Paz,* in the *beginning*), but would these reasons not need to be argued explicitly (which they were not), and to be justified doctrinally, philosophically, or otherwise?

As I have already said, but Scholem said it before, the phrase, in its form, is nothing less than typical in the zoharic texts. This hardly leaves it safely located as a purely "external" addition that would have nothing to do with the text. In fact, even in its seeming banality (quite different though from "a rose is a rose is a rose"), the phrase reinscribes or replays the question "what/who/which (is) (the) rose?" something else than—though not entirely different from—a so-called rhetorical question. Its erasure from translations could indicate that, if it was not seen as "adding" anything at all, then the very question that precedes it was also an "empty" rhetorical question; and that is especially the case if the question in question is "which rose?" or "which is the rose?" It was not asking about a rose at all, and certainly not about roses, romanced or not, and the insisting notion that words do not make a difference, supported by the idea that everything is, in fact, one organic unity, is still clearly expressed. In fact, if that is the idea supported by the words of the *Zohar*, the translators are quite justified in endorsing it and practicing its lack of attention to words and the difference they make, in such an enthusiastic way.

What can be noted, at any rate, is that in order to dispense with these words (there is a rose and there is a rose), it is necessary to privilege a certain ideal content. The minimal consequence of such privileging, however, is that there are two readings at work here, two readings so fundamentally incompatible that, choosing one of them, one dismisses the difference words make under the ideal justification that there is no difference (Kabbalah as "mysticism," a thought, a doctrine, a mysticism, of identity); and the other, were it possible, reads the difference that words make to the point that they disrupt the identity-ideal in question. The ideal or conceptual reading offered by the translators does seem to have gone further by dismissing from the text as it is printed before us, and as it has been read since the sixteenth century at least, just a few words, only words, that would support (un)equivocally the question of difference. Such words, needless to say, only add to the notion that words, as they make up the mechanics of the text, are the elements that establish the resemblance (or even identity) between terms, and that by virtue of their doing so also indicate that the resemblance requires doing and making: the organic link, the coagulated unity of word, figure, or thing, is therefore not given; it is an ideal that withdraws, *se soustrait.*

One question we may be left with at this point is whether the zoharic text "self-consciously" undermines its own assertion of identity, or whether it already exemplifies some kind of logorrhea, adding words that do not add anything. Invoking Paul de Man's notion of "ultimate figure," I would answer that, in the text above, the rose functions as such a figure. Consider what it does and how the language of the *Zohar* is affected by it. Consider that, if it makes a difference, the difference it makes is that it displaces (though, again, not entirely) the language of the text from being "mystical" to being "poetical." By virtue of what is no less than a "denunciation of the ultimate figure," of the totalizing figure, the language of the zoharic lines, at the very moment that "it asserts itself in the plenitude of its promise," also circumvents all possible recuperation in the form of thematic or aesthetic statements about itself, in the form of any knowledge it may confer about itself. Poetical language—what I have been calling literature throughout—is understood here as nothing "but the advent of the disruption" of its "self."[82] By asking "who/what/which?" the text is "denouncing" the "ultimate figure" of the rose as the word that marks and makes the difference between unity and disruption, as the word upon which the two readings (the ideal—thematic or aesthetic—and the rhetorical) hang in their assertion of identity and difference.

The word "rose" as both figure and disruption of figurality can therefore also be described as what moves (translates) the text from "mystical" to "poetical," hardly enabling a "self-consciousness," as if consciousness was an identity that one could leave and return to. The rose, now seen as also disruptive, is the motion that actively separates between identity and itself, between the two readings, and makes them "incompatible" (ibid.). The rose as "ultimate figure" becomes the movement of a literary text, the very movement from the unity-oriented or "mystical" reading, to the difference-oriented "poetical" reading. Both readings are staged by the text in its thematics and in its mechanics. With the rose, the text, saying and doing, has begun again, from one of its beginnings, to become literature, indeed, a "mystical novel," as Gershom Scholem called it. In the short passage I have only begun to read, the *Zohar* has become what Scholem already said it was (but was that assertion identical to itself?): a novel, a roman, the *Roman de la rose, Kitāb az-Zahra,* translating and translated, "our place in al-Andalus."

"What's the difference?" asked Paul de Man quoting Archie Bunker, demonstrating the intricacies of the "so-called rhetorical question."[83] Nothing, it would seem, has become more difficult to ask, given that we do not know whether the question is "who?" "what?" or "which?" (and which "which"?). And it is, in fact, quite significant that the *Zohar* "itself" also articulates the space of questioning between "who" and "what." The "which" as the silent question, as perhaps no question at all in terms of the zoharic space of questioning, is as incommensurable as the difference between a rose and a rose. A space of questioning that does not appear as such, a question that may not be a question, configures the possibility and the impossibility of this (this?) difference. Indeed, "what is the use of asking, I ask, when we cannot even authoritatively decide whether a question asks or doesn't ask?" (ibid.). The question, if it is one—but who asks?—opens perilous realms and forces us to address the literariness, the translations, of the zoharic texts.

"What's the difference?" the *Zohar* asks (perhaps). Nothing, it would seem, has become more difficult to grasp and locate—if grasping and locating were at all the goal, and if the goal was one. Nothing may even be the answer, since "everything is one," but who, what, which one? The difference, if there is one, may therefore not have anything to do with any *thing.* And yet, "there (is) a rose and there (is) a rose." More significantly, in the *Zohar,* this difference, if it is one, has no name whatsoever. Given the importance of names, the conception that the Torah is the name of God (one of which is also, as the *Zohar* reminds us, Allah), that all names, therefore, are his name, it becomes impossible to determine whether or not the nameless difference between a rose and a rose (between the way and the road, Aramaic and Aramaic, etc.) can at any point fall under the recurring promise of unity which asserts that "on this day, God will be one and His name will be one"—but where, and in what, in which and in whose, place?

Interrupted Dialogues: The Place of Genre

The translation of and between genres to which Maimonides had introduced us does not simply repeat itself here—as if it could remain identical to itself, as if al-Andalus were one—but does enact a displacing movement that, because it withdraws from localization, because it declines, also produces its repeated "ends"—attempts to determine its limits. Yet, this is a movement, a set of movements and events, with which philosophy becomes literature, midrash becomes poetry, and the *Zohar* becomes *maqāma.* Recall that Maimonides had also described the taking place of these translations when writing to his student of his high opinion of him. Maimonides writes, he says, "because of your strong desire for inquiry and because of what I had observed in your poems of your powerful longing for speculative matters. This was the case since your letters and *maqāmāt* came to me from Alexandria, before your grasp was put to the test. I said, however: perhaps his longing is stronger than his grasp."[84] Aside from this image of excess, of a desire that exceeds ability, much like an excess of knowledge of language that, we saw in Maimonides' text, exceeds and disrupts understanding, the importance of this passage is essential for the readings and translations of language at "our place in al-Andalus": poems, letters, and *maqāmāt*, not to mention the quasi-philosophical and philosophical texts to which the *dalāla* obliquely directs us, constitute and fail to constitute the very texts as which al-Andalus takes and gives place, as declining contexts, reading, out of context.

Consider, then, the following words of one of the foremost literary critics of medieval Hebrew letters, Dan Pagis, as he addresses this very occurrence of language as a field, and as a locatable object, "literature." Pagis provides us with an added clue as to the way declinations of context also take place as incompatible readings, agonistic dialogues, from Maimonides' *dalāla* to the zoharic "dialogue of two roses." This will prove instructive in our final turn to the *maqāma* "itself"—the importance of which, Pagis says, has been blown out of proportions—for it will also clarify the way in which the relations of language that have occupied us are, so often, dialogical. Incidentally, this also concerns what the *Zohar* refers to as readiness toward an encounter with the text as a "fight," a contest. Pagis writes about medieval Hebrew literature in general, and about *maqāmāt*, rhymed prose narratives, in particular:

> We should remember that much of this literature is given over to the delight of argumentation. Even in the poetry of the age, we have a constant pro and contra, praise and blame: poems praising patrons (eulogies), or the dead (dirges), or wine and women, or wisdom or the writer's pen; and conversely, poems denigrating misers, poetasters, Time, or the World. . . . In some works conflicting argument is even the main axis around which disparate stories and poems revolve.[85]

As he discusses the fragmented and fragmenting use, the translation, of medieval narratives in scholarly studies, Pagis himself engages in a dialogical disputation and argues that one cannot or should not isolate the distinct moments of these narratives or draw conclusions from them. To do so would mean ignoring their function and meaning within the whole narrative. Pagis thus opposes the quotation of "isolated poems or stories in praise of greed, pride, hate or sin, which were originally refuted by the main argument of the book. Quotations out of context may sometimes deceive; quotations contrary to context always deceive: they are misquotations" (94–95).

What is fascinating about Pagis's remarks, however, is that his description of the practice of scholarly discourses that he attacks also applies to the very practice of the texts he himself documents and discusses: deception and/or misquotations, citing out of context, mosaic style, use of other languages, translations, appeal to other, vanishing, contexts that may or may not be able to be recalled, retrieved, located, by discerning or undiscerning readers. I do not mean to belittle the importance of Pagis's criticism of modern scholarship, much of which is painfully to the point. What interests me here is rather the way he provides another description of a certain repetition and a translation of previous decontextualizing dialogues found in these and other, older texts. What Pagis's discussion suggests, then, is that the theoretical articulation of a reading of these texts reproduces a marked difficulty: that of distinguishing, if not the dancer from the dance, perhaps, the dance from the critic.[86] In this translation and enactment of dialogues, it is not just a manner of determining whether communication has or should occur, whether there have been mistranslations, misquotations (or as some scholars would have it, "better" quotations), nor of whether there is a good, successful dialogue (or a dialogue at all) as distinct from a bad one. Following Pagis's image of quotation vs. misquotation—a translation of what we have considered as reading out of context, in displacement and translation, at "our place in al-Andalus"—it becomes a question of how dialogues have been operating from the "beginning(s)."

In the remainder of this chapter, I turn to the way dialogue, another translation of the event of language, "our place in al-Andalus," is staged in one of the richest sources of (mis)quotations for those decontextualized and decontextualizing medieval narratives written at the place where we stand (*maqām*), at the "site, location, position, place, spot, point, locality, situation, standing, rank, dignity, tomb of a saint, sacred place, key, tonality (*mus.*), on this occasion, *maqām*," at our place called "sitting, session, meeting, a genre of Arabic rhythmic prose, *maqāmāt*."[87]

> His progeny are his helpers, dissolving union is his business.
>
> —Badīᶜ az-Zamān al-Hamad̲ānī, "The Maqāma of the Spindle"

What are the poles between which we find or lose ourselves? Who are the participants in these dialogues? And where do they meet? Where does the *maqāma* take place and what is its relevance to the language of al-Andalus? There will have been no beginnings that safely entrust us to the security of a point, a location, but we need to trace some of the displacing translations that already occur in an early in-stance of language, at our place in Persia. It is where the genre which is not one begins to exercise its powerful and displacing hold as a new event of language, one that will later be carried over and translated by Arab, Jewish, and Arab Jewish writers. According to Abdelfattah Kilito, one of its most sensitive readers, the *séance* (the French word for *maqāma*), the scene, falls into incomprehension. Such becomes the rule of this other scene, hardly a context—declinations of context.

Cette situation d'incompréhension se répète, sous une forme ou une autre, dans l'ensemble des Séances. Entre les interlocuteurs, il se crée constamment une coupure, une distance, qui rendent les échanges hasardeux et problématiques. Loin d'être un moyen de communication, un médiateur docile, le langage apparaît au contraire comme un obstacle à la compréhension. Le malentendu, l'équivoque, le "bruit" deviennent la règle de la conversation.[88]

At this point, one only needs to add to Kilito's remark that what is at work between the pro- or anta-gonists of the *maqāma*, the "noise" that is said to interfere between them, will also be seen at work "within" them. There is no stable partner in this "dialogue" of constant veiling and failing.

One of the most famous among the *maqāmāt* of the "Wonder of the Age" (Badīᶜ az-Zamān al-Hamaḏānī, the "inventor" of that style of writing) is the "Maḍīra," which offers a wonderful instance of the *maqāma*'s internal disruption and constant translation, as it literally scandalizes the character who embodies the *maqāma*'s essence, if it had one: Abū l-Fatḥ al-Iskandarī. In this *maqāma*, the image of words multiplying (dividing) themselves, breaking from their context and from themselves, is addressed in a scene that depicts the trickster sourly tricked at his own rhetorical ("empty" or "formal" rhetoric) games. Abū l-Fatḥ is introduced by name, in this particular *maqāma*, from the very beginning (in most cases, the revealing of the protagonist's name occurs at the end of the *maqāma*), and he is explicitly positioned within a dialogical frame, as "the man of eloquence who summons it and it responds to him, the man of rhetoric who commands it and it obeys him, *rajulu l-faṣāḥati yadᶜūha fatujībuhu wa-l-balāġati yaʾmuruha fa-tuṭīᶜuhu*" (109/E88). He will, however, quickly enough find himself "split" in two, and indeed commanded, by the very words of a pressing host, a man who convinces Abū l-Fatḥ that he should come and eat an exquisite dish called *maḍīra* cooked by his wife. It is by means of the very attributes, *ṣifāt*, of his wife that the man causes Abū l-Fatḥ's predicament: "He split me with his wife's attributes, *ṣadaᶜani bi-ṣifāti zawjatihi*" (112/E90).[89]

It is important to dwell on the verb "split" that appears here. Having begun his sorry story, Abū l-Fatḥ quotes the first lengthy speech of his host, giving us a sense of his garrulousness. Obviously, interruption is not going to be an easy feast in front of this unending flow of words. Rather than cutting in, Abū l-Fatḥ finds himself cut into: the verb *ṣadaᶜa*, in its first form, means: to split, cleave, part, sunder, crack, break, and so on. When joined to the particle *bi*, as in *ṣadaᶜa bi-l-ḥaqq*, it means: to come out openly with the truth. *Ṣadaᶜa bi-ʾamr*, however, also means: to execute an order, to comply with an order. In its passive form (*ṣudiᶜa*) it means: to get a headache. It seems plausible that, in some manuscripts, the verb was written in the second form (*ṣaddaᶜa*—reduplicated *d*), which, among other things, means: to give a headache. The absence in the Arabic text of the reduplication, *tašdīd*, enables the preservation of both senses, something quite common in a *maqāma* text. Moreover, it is important to note the further insistence on the "splitting" power of Abū l-Fatḥ's protagonist, who reveals himself to have indeed, "sundered" and snatched away a pearl necklace, *ᶜiqdu laʾālin*, from a previous victim (116/E93).

For many nights I had been sleeping in my house with those therein when lo! there was a knock at the door. I said, "Who is the wandering nocturnal visitor?" And behold it was a woman with a pearl necklace with a surface as clear as water, and fineness like unto the mirage, which she offered for sale! So I snatched it from her with a plundering snatch, *faʾaẖaḏtuhu minhā iẖḏata ẖalsin*, and bought it for a low price. (ibid.)

According to a reigning metaphor of Arabic literature to which I shall return later, pearls, indeed strung pearls, constitute the nexus of eloquence: poetry, *naẓm*, itself. Indeed, the overflowing speaker steals away all words from the master of eloquence himself, and pointedly tells of his rich experience in that matter. By the end of this "mighty matter and never-ending affair," Abū l-Fatḥ will have to run for his life, exposing in the process how he has lost the very control he is famed for throughout: his control over pearls and his ability to string (*naẓama*) them into rhetoric. After the rhetorical stabs of his host, Abū l-Fatḥ will no longer be able to disseminate (*naṯara*) pearls, but rather only stones ("He who has seen the pearl will not compare a stone with it," recites Abū l-Fatḥ in the "Maqāma of Kings" [173/236]).

Having been sundered from himself, and from his words, he has no control left over the result of this weak envoi. One will remember that this is one rare instance where Abū l-Fatḥ's name is unveiled from the beginning of the *maqāma*, yet even this name will be substituted, for another, substitute, "title." Here is the final scene of his desperate escape:

And I went out towards the door, quickened my pace and begun to run, while he was following me and shouting: "Abū l-Fatḥ! The Madirah!" And the boys thought Madirah was a title of mine, and took up his cry. So out of excessive vexation I threw a stone at one of them, but a man received it on his turban and it sunk in his skull. Therefore I was attacked with sandals, old and new, and with cuffs good and bad; and then I was placed in prison and remained in that unfortunate plight for two years. So I vowed not to eat Madirah as long as I lived. (123/E97)

This is how this *maqāma* ends—if it can be said to end. The characters only establish relations on the basis of a constitutive separation—a displacement, that is repeatedly enacted. There is an inconstant but repeated separation of desire from its object, speech from intent, words from context. Here, as in most *maqāmāt*, the moment of unveiling (here, the explanation of the plight of Abū l-Fatḥ) does not bring about a simple return to a point of beginning. More precisely, if there is such a return it is only constituted through, and always announces, separation. The distances that are opened, carrying away words as they turn into pearls or stones, such distances open only to be traversed (the *dia* of dia-logue) and never to rest for more than a moment. Such a moment and movement, like the characters, is never identical to itself and it only repeats itself with a difference. Here too, then, the poles between which space is given, between which and as which language takes place, fail to offer themselves as stable loci. The séance is a place, *un lieu*, then, but one that takes place insofar as it withdraws from identity, from localization.

Les séances de Hamadhânî . . . sont le lieu d'un dialogue dans lequel deux ordres, représentés chacun par un personnage, entrent en conflit. Chacun des deux protagonistes est la négation de l'autre, mais on observe parfois des échanges, des mutations, qui nuancent ce schéma rigide. Il n'est pas rare que la contradiction qui situe ᶜIsā ibn Hichām et Abū l-Fatḥ à deux pôles opposés, se manifeste chez chacun d'eux sous la forme d'une dissonance ou d'un comportement incohérent. Le danger d'une contamination subtile ne peut en effet être écarté.[90]

It is toward the translation of this contamination, the failure of identity of the "same place," the failure of the place of language of al-Andalus to offer itself as locatable either outside or inside, within boundaries or strings, conditions or systems, as it takes place at "our place in al-Andalus" that we now turn in conclusion.

APPENDIX

Ibn al-Aštarkūwī's *Maqāma* "On Poetry and Prose"[91]

Al-Sā'ib ibn Tammām said:

I was journeying in a certain caravan, ridden by anxiety, wary of failing, agonizing over my having spent money. I distanced myself from my traveling-companions and became suspicious of compassion, until the time came to make a brief night-halt. There alighted in my vicinity a person with a coarse appearance and a threadbare robe, and with him, were two youths who surrounded and treated him with respect and honor. When night descended and the stars turned their reins for the journey and reigned supreme, one of the two inquired of his partner, saying:

—O Ḥabīb, do you claim to possess understanding, and to be a physician able to cure the diseases of *adab*?

He replied:

—Not in the least, Ġarīb. What has baffled you to the point that you insult one who greets you and salutes you kindly?

He replied:

—A question that has baffled the first and the last, the earnest and the scoffer, namely, poetry and prose, *an-naẓm wan-naṯr*. What is the long and short of both, which is the sword blade and which is the luster? Which of the two follows in the tracks of its companion and which carries the day at its heels? Which makes a better impression on the soul, more fully quenches and alleviates the burning thirst? Which is more favored by rabble and kings, and makes embassies and messengers more efficient?

He replied:

—O Ġarīb, that is a simple question requiring a strange answer and a dubious distinction—by God's faith!—in which no ignorant or intelligent person has ever excelled. Perhaps it is a subject about which consensus, *ijmāᶜ*, has been solid, or before which ambitions have come to a halt, or perhaps it is a subject on which opinions have differed and about which Qurᵓānic reciters have followed their individual paths.

He replied:

—You have summarized, *jamaᶜta*, and encompassed the question, you have devoted yourself and confined yourself to the truth, drawn forth the different branches of the tree of discourse, and bent them down for their fruit. Tell me, however, what your own opinion is, for one like you can clarify and penetrate any doubt that might arise.

He replied:

—Verily, the matter is very clear, as dawn sheds light upon things. Do you not see that the heights of poetry are more difficult to climb, and a more unusual choice? That poetry is more given to rhetorical ornamentation in diction, quicker to be memorized, broader in metaphors, clearer in brevity, more tightly knotted, superior in mind, concise in its meaning, taller in constructions, more flowing upon the tongue, more appropriate for human beings, more pungent as to its aloes wood, more able to kindle fire, more conducive to joy, and that it more easily banishes worries? Have you ever heard of prose upon which melodies were applied, or over which drinking-cups and bowls were emptied, before which the collars of garments emerged from the secrets of their hiding places, by which ears were seduced and upon which resolutions were made ambiguous. It awakens ambitions and joys, repels sorrows and grieves. It is enough for you to consider that it is found among Arabs and non-Arabs, that its meadow is moistened and drenched by the rain of minds, while the Arabs used to consider it worthy on account of the nobility of their diction, their accomplishment in it, and their preservation of it. Moreover, the great and the powerful judged that no composer of poetry was incapable of producing prose, yet how many a composer of prose is incapable of producing poetry, and how can he be capable of doing so, if his fortune stumbles? Have songs not been adorned or dwelling-places mourned, great exploits written down, the prolix speaker silenced, ambitions resurrected, covenants tied with the likes of poetry and extended speech, even though it possesses conditions, requirements, aspects of speech that make it resolute or irresolute, stops the well-informed reader, and its mountains are climbed by the reciter. Long ago, it aroused the noble, protected the harem, and brought to trial the rival, while it mediated between subjects and kings. It was worn like necklaces and strands, and indeed, the cautious and the heedless, the lofty and the lowly considered it marvelous and astonishing. They esteemed its composer, held him in awe, included him among the learned, and considered him to be one of the wise. By it, rebellious passions are won over, distant hopes are brought closer, enmities and dislikes are resolved, accidents and trials are avoided, indifferent souls are chained together, abated resolutions are resurrected. It pierces as do arrows, flows with thoughts and imaginations, and travels by night with each rainbearing and rainless cloud. Posterity thrives on it, and the years do not diminish it. Often it travels the path of a star, and shoots projectiles like a meteor. Many an obscure person was raised by it and it intervened for many a reciter. Many a fame it has launched, and brought close a distant one. But as for prose, it is a loose bridle, eloquence unraveled, reins easily mastered, and a road well-traveled, a water hole easily reached, a tattered garment, a sanctuary treated as public property, an evening and a morning drink toward which the slow and the swift steed alternate in chasing one another. It treats equally the submissive and the rebellious slave. Its claims are disseminated, and its esoteric and exoteric meaning are the same. My words have brought out the truth openly and delivered judgment, and how many a wise statement do they contain!

He [the narrator] said: Then he replied:

—O compassionate one, you are worthy and deserving, for in you truth and its accomplishment, you have insightfully hit the mark—may our clan and people be your ransom! Nonetheless, would you mind hearing certain words, broadening your knowledge, turning a blind eye to, and concealing your imbecility? The composer of prose is able to declare upon investigating the subject: "Prose is assuredly easier to pursue, more rewarding, more obedient to the bridle, more piercing of the spearhead. Kingdoms are ruled by it, roads are traveled, government is served, policies are established, conditions are maintained, property is protected. By it, sciences are communicated, minds are weighed, demonstrations and arguments are presented, sweet and salt waters are distinguished. How different[92] is the case of one fettered by rhymes, from that of one, the forefeathers and hidden feathers of whose wings are unrestricted, and whose composer achieves his goal, while a springtime pasture and a camel-pasture of eloquence are not barren for him! How many a huge army did prose repel, extinguishing what flared up and burned because of it, making unnecessary the *mashrafī* swords and the heads of spears, startling wet nurses by its cries, and causing a miscarriage in pregnant women. Prose is as delicate as

> the spring breeze, and brings joy to the smiling mouth. By it, the sun is tamed and controlled, old hatreds and animosities are resolved, hard hearts are won over, withered flanks are made flexible, fortresses are recovered, the forelocks of the horses are mastered, the disobedient is reduced to obedience, and the distant is brought near. Of old, has it been a mediator and an intercessor, a herald and a warner. By it, epistles are adorned, measures are adopted, the student and researcher meet with success. By its eloquence news is transmitted; in it, both Islamic and non-Islamic scholars glory. It is incessantly free of its bridle and keeps up with the clouds. No racecourse baffles it; no manifestation or concealment eludes it, for it is the glory and tongue of the state, the rider and the superior man of the battle, the Luqmān and interpreter of wisdom, the oath and safety of the kingdom. With its wording, treaties are ratified, the witness and his testimony are recorded, chronicles are adorned and embellished, and events are recognized and clarified. It is the measure of eloquence and chaste speech, the probe of support and composure. Because of it, the very erudite man of Hamaḏān, who was most powerful in it, was named 'The Wonder of the Age,' in olden days and times of yore, while he won high rank and ever-increasing prizes, and trailed the hem of his glory over Saḥbān, while camel riders discussed his stories in their evening, leisure hours. By my faith, even though he produced innovations and wonders in the field of poetry and manifested eloquence of his ideas, expressing himself clearly, his fame is confined to his prose and restricted to the long and short of it. Minds bear witness to that fact and observe of it, what has been recorded and transmitted. There suffices prose as a virtue and as pre-eminent position, the fact that it encompasses all the other sciences, while their occurrence in versified speech is rare, over and above the fact that prose constitutes one of the inimitable miracles of the best man in creation—and how honorable that is as a mark of superiority in rank and a rank of superiority. If there were high rank to be acquired, or glory to be considered, through poetry, noble status would not have been denied to him, his august tongue would not have been prevented from using poetry and what would have been his answer, when he had baffled every traveler and wanderer?"

Thus the debate continued between the two of them, nor did they resort to orderly discussion. On the contrary, the partisan of poetry began to gain victory, nor did he tend toward abridgment and restraint. Instead, he elaborated and exaggerated, he raised aloft the pavilions of his prejudice and fastened down their tent ropes. He began to present counter-proofs and to destroy the arguments his brother had provided. The dispute between the two intensified, and the bonds of love came near to being sundered. In the course of it all, the old man awoke from his nap, sat up cross-legged in his seat, belched from the depths of his stomach, rubbed sleep from his eyes, and asked about the reason for the dispute between his two sons. So they told him their tale, recapitulating it from beginning to end. Thereupon he donned his robe, put on his sandals, and cleared his throat, after having coughed. Then, he said:

> —O my sons, know that debating and disputing bequeath hatred and spite, for often has disputing divided two brothers and bequeathed them disobedience of their parents, while you have exceeded the proper bounds in that area, traversed the roughest of roads, submitted to your desire, ridden in the trail of him who errs and goes astray, and thus deviated from your goal, wandered, and become lost. Do you not seek what agreement, *iṣfāq*, encounters and conformity provides, or that toward which a truthful investigation leads, or what truth and sincerity support?

They both responded:

> —Yes, that is what we seek, may our souls and hearts be your ransom! Yet, is there no explanation for these essences, no clarification of these clear matters, no pearls of wisdom to suit these brilliant points of interrogation?

He replied:

> —The matter is as clear as the dawn that illuminates. They are only levels and stairs, and refreshment and fragrance, for every protector has his possession and every dice-player has his success. A piece of jewelry and the sciences, even if the vicissitudes of Fortune affect them, are hardly such that Fortune can diminish or increase them, or harass them from in front or from behind. Therefore, avoid superficial appearances, for neither do they grow nor do they decrease. Only dullness and briskness of trade in the market lead to agreement, *wifāq*, whereas being and non-being do not require agreement, *ijmā*ᶜ, so abandon this subject for ties of relationship have been broken because of them, and minds have lost their way in considering them. Away with pure science and its core! Everyone, with regard to it, is driven to excel and considered one of the eloquent. Yet poetry is a sterile stud, an immobile group of travelers, a hateful person much beloved, a fair curly haired youth whose ringlets have been clipped, a thing to which people have become attached, and to which they have linked and bound their aspirations. If they have blended poetry with

falsehood and untruth, they have turned a blind eye on the fact. Indeed, its praise is more copious than its blame, its honey is greater than its poison, the one who uses it for unworthy ends is unworthy, and the one who turns it away from its true purpose is reprehensible and blameworthy. What a difference there is between a subject and a predicate, and between an agent and an object. Among positive traits is justice in the case at hand, for the essence of justice is that virtue be abstracted from its performer, and knowledge be removed from its servant or implementer. So, beware of disputation, and keep within the bounds of moderation, for discourse consists of pathways and mountain passes, and debating produces ease and hardship. As for prose, it is a fertile female, a flint stick that is neither too dull nor too hard to produce fire when struck. It is a flowing spring, and a kind mother. It enjoys rank and status, plus power tempered by humility. It is both sweet and bitter; it both comes and goes. It penetrates every circle and kindles every fire stick, be it nomadic or sedentary, withered or verdant. It is an inconstant beloved who nonetheless grants the love union, and a cutting sword that glances off its victim.

How different are words that constitute pleasant, superior speech! The latter are true pearls, whether they be couched in verse or in prose, whether they are a verdict to be rejected or accepted. It does no harm to the pearls of poetry if composers of poetry do not organize, *lam tanẓim*, them into poems, since the great and the powerful have preferred to employ them unstrung, in prose. Hence, neither of you two should prefer one type of composer over the other, save on the basis of the superiority of the better composer, and of the power of the stronger one. Artistic excellence is manifold: the sun rises and sets, the moon wanes and waxes, it is both ugly and beautiful. Man is good and evil, the earth contains gold and dung, and the crown is not superior to the anklet other than by reason of the superiority of the head over the foot. Therefore, consider my words, that you may both trust my judgment and rely on what I have transmitted, for I have spoken in person with men of great wisdom, held lengthy debates and discussions with them, become fond of knowledge, and gained forbearance. Hence, beware of strife and argumentation by analogy, *al-maqāʾīsa*, and of impatience. In all situations, adopt what is the fairer and juster stance, lean toward the path that is smoother and broader, and do not turn away from the even path that represents the golden mean, since "that is true constancy" [Qurʾān, 42:43], for you are urgently required to do the above. Furthermore, beware of partisanship; of appearing and striving to disagree, for that is a defect in character and a flaw of the will. Every situation has its adherents and partisans, and everything has its preservation and destruction. The arts have their masters, and virtues have their causes. This world has its lots and shares, its lance and its sword, its justice and its enmity, yet among the "serpents of the earth" is the tribe of ʿAdwān.

They both replied:

—May we be granted your mercy and satisfaction. May we never lack for your forgiveness and indulgence, and may we continue to derive light and fire from your knowledge, so that, with your guidance, we may ascend a summit and climb up to a light house, for you have calmed our hearts and brought good fortune not only to our lucky omens, but even to our unlucky ones. You have versified an opinion that was in prose, and handed down choice knowledge of yours that will henceforth be transmitted from father to son.

He said to them:

—May God grant you good fortune through reconciliation. May you dwell forever among friend and sympathizer. May knowledge uphold and adorn you with the robe of forbearance, strengthen you with contentment and skill, and declare you to be above greed and submissiveness, for you have brought me joy with your nobility, and paid the debt you owe me through your filial piety, save that in my soul there is, because of you, that which is more painful than the burning of a live ember and more pernicious than gambling, namely, that you possess no wealth in this age, nor occupy any lofty position from which wealth may be derived. You have devoted yourselves to *adab* and to knowledge, while neglecting the inevitable things that happen, the preordained realities of life. Meanwhile, I stand in front of you, aiming my arrows and struggling to defend both of you, while vying with, and besieging Time, despite the fact that destroyers have wrecked knowledge, and terrors have scared off its flock, as if that knowledge clamors for blood vengeance to the one whose duty is to avenge it, and assaults him with even and odd misfortunes.

Then he recited:

How plentiful is ignorance and how many adherents does it have!
Alas for Knowledge! How it has perished!
Knowledge ruined me, so I ruined it:
I bequeathed it to him among men who ruined it!

Do you not both see how many people who have learned from me, and conveyed what I have taught them, and who speak and act according to my knowledge, have betrayed me and forgotten my exertion and effort on their behalf? I bequeathed honor and glory to them, and they bequeathed grief and sorrow to me. I made them alight in the uplands and hilltops, whereas they deprived me of loyalty and profits. I sincerely advise both of you to associate only with generous individuals, and to ride only the backs of noble steeds; to strike fire only with the *nab*ᶜ wood, and to alight only in springtime pastures; to mount a camel only with provisions for the journey, and to enter the desert only with a water skin. Behold, we have camped in an open desert, and complained of the cold, night winds. We have spilled water and endured thirst. The milk skin has become empty and the juicy plants have withered, to the point that we have perished. We do not know anyone of importance, and do not enjoy the recognition of anyone of importance, while the stranger is always an object of suspicion and loathing.

He [the narrator] said:

—Then everyone hearkened to, and sympathized with his words. They agree to console him, clapping hands to seal the bargain, and distributing before him whatever he desired in the way of food, drink, and clothes to cover his nakedness since, he claimed, his own had been plundered from him. Then, they smoothed his bed, comforted his sleeplessness, wrapped him in mantle after stripping his Bedouin mantle, treated him as one does a person who is noble and generous, and said: "God forbid that we should neglect to show concern for this learned scholar, for we are eager to provide consolation and to comfort him in his misery," whereupon he prayed that he might earn a lavish reward and an abundant means of subsistence.

Al-Sāʾib said:

—So I looked attentively at him, and he at me. Then he sped toward me with a light foot which he had set in motion. So I said:
—Abū Ḥabīb, are you to be found even in the dark of night?

He replied:

—Welcome, O Sāʾib, have you learned that it is you who are confined whereas I am free to wander, *sāʾib*?

Then he recited:

Every day we bid each other hello, we are never bored by doing so and are

given no peace by it.
How often has Time bladed you, O youth who are subject to Time, as if censure and blame were of any avail.
How passionately fond is man of harsh treatment, neither the old man or the boy is righteous.
A dream-image suffices you as a companion, a dream-image that travels forth by night when gloom descends.
The safer of two alternatives regarding a friend is for you to remember him in his absence, and when he bade you farewell.

So I recognized what he was talking about, aiming at, and alluding to, and said:

—I welcome you, for you are faithful, yet, let there be no contact between us. Beware of marauding like a wolf, and be on your guard against trivialities.

And when the night grew dark and reached its midpoint, he chose and collected what was there, turned his reins to one side, set himself a new goal toward which to travel, turned toward the road, and went away. When I followed after him, he left me, saying:

—O goodly Sāʾib, give me avoidance and opposition.
And be kind, for mutual sincerity depends upon kindness and coming to terms.
The paths of others are too narrow to contain broad desires.
How many an unprecedented assault have I undertaken, like the assault of al-Barrād.
In it, I set the riding camels in motion by means of the girth-thong and saddle-girths.
Leave outlaws to quench their thirst in al-Jafr or al-Firād.
And be satisfied, by way of life, eventually, with a small pool of stagnant water, or a spring producing a mere trickle.
And be not one who gains riches, or contravenes people.
It has been said that Time is a loan: far from you be the debt I have incurred!
The arrow of Time is inescapable, so let it hit its targets.
The anger of my people causes me no harm, as long as God is pleased with me.

Al-Sāʾib said:

—So I marveled at his artistic excellence and proficiency, at his ability to roam up hill and down dale in his discourse, at the abundance of his material, at the clarity of his liberality, at his insights into truths, his investigation into subtle matters, his observation of the limits and divisions of speech, his handling of its branches and sources, his playing tricks on men's minds, his contempt for what has been handed down and transmitted by tradition, and, moreover, for his stooping to infamous tricks, after having attained splendid and valuable achievements in science. I concluded that his defects amounted but to freckles on the face of his perfection; to a blemish in his beauty, and that grieved me in him. I continued to erase and efface his shortcomings from my heart, until I longed for him to be the companion for whom I had hoped, and in whom I could trust and confide.

Part 2: Parting Words

> This breaking force, *force de rupture,* is not an accidental predicate but the very structure of the written text. . . . [T]he sign possesses the characteristic of being readable even if the moment of its production is irrevocably lost and even if I do not know what its alleged author-scriptor consciously intended to say at the moment he wrote it, i.e., abandoned it to its essential drift. . . . [B]y virtue of its essential iterability, a written syntagma can always be detached from the chain in which it is inserted or given without causing it to lose all possibility of functioning, if not all possibility of "communicating," precisely.
>
> —Jacques Derrida, "Signature, Event, Context"

> As Plato indicates, the fairest bond is that of continued geometrical proportion—in short, the union according to analogy.
>
> —Rodolphe Gasché, *The Tain of the Mirror*

Similar, *siwā,* are the horizons' darkening and the worry and apprehension over life departing, *ḏahāb al-ʿumr,* to words departing in vain, *waʾan yaḏhaba l-qawlu hadran,* which truth does not praise in their coming and going, *wirdan wa-lā ṣadaran,* even if they have only issued, *waʾin kāna lam yaṣdur*—as God be my witness—from a soul that hovers over truth . . . continually gives guidance toward righteousness, and constantly goes in the direction of repentance. (Ibn al-Aštarkūwī, *Al-Maqāmāt al-Luzūmīya)*

Quietly disrupting the image that would claim a clear connection, a straightforward analogy, between writing and dying, Ibn al-Aštarkūwī concludes his collection of *maqāmāt* by writing that the "departure of words" is related and not related to death. In spite of the appearances, the relation—if it is one—does not establish a simple parallel, an analogy, between the "departure of life" and the "departure of words." Rather, we are told, writing is similar to the "apprehension over life departing," to the growing anxiety of a being-toward-death, a being toward its end. Hence, it is "the darkening of horizons and the worry and apprehension over the departure of life," rather than the departure of life itself, that is said to be "similar to the departure of words." Neither life nor death, writing, or, more generally, the departure of words, is of that state or place that is between life and death. It is of that most fleeting condition, that mood, which figures the "darkening of horizons," and intervenes and disturbs as the "worry and apprehension over the departure of life." Writing appears, then, as the anxiety toward that utmost possibility that death is. This possibility—no more, but also no less than a possibility—is epitomized in the image or the thought of a separation, a departure that fundamentally threatens to separate between soul and words. Separation threatens what is already doubtfully related by way of an uncertain similarity with the toward-death, soul and words. Hence, rather than firmly establishing the common and the similar, the analogy, which was already disturbed by the lack of parallel between two departures, has now become as fleeting as these departures themselves. The analogy unsettles itself as what seemed at first obvious, the similarity between departures. It unsettles the stability of analogy as that which would rest on common grounds.

The hovering, evanescent, possibility of separation, rather than the separation "itself," is here also rendered as a "coming and going" of words. The phrase *wirdan wa-lā ṣadaran* inscribes the complex structure of the general departure and the anxiety associated with it in an important way. The two verbal nouns are based on verbs that etymologically relate to the notion of descent to and return from a well. More generally, and by extension, these words designate a walking motion. The negative particle (*lā*) complicates this description, however, as it also enables reading a "coming and not coming," thus both canceling and maintaining the gesture toward the back-and-forth motion rendered in the above translation. The negative particle signals a lack of symmetry between the two words, the absence of return. The verb *ṣadara*, which carries the meaning of appearing, can in turn be read as reflecting upon the whole expression, suggesting that the "coming and going" also means "appearing and not appearing."[93]

The expression "coming and going" concisely suggests a repetition and replay of the movement of departure carried by the passage of Ibn al-Aštarkūwī's colophon quoted above. It is a structure that articulates the inconstant possibility of being, if not out of place, neither here nor there; a peculiar mode of coming and going, then, that always possibly affects what links and separates words and souls. It is a rhetorical movement that cannot be reduced to the production of simple absence or of death. The coming and going of words that Ibn al-Aštarkūwī phrases is not the simple absence that death is. Rather, it is what works at maintaining words as they are and are not separated, as they are both coming and going, remaining yet departing, located but unlocatable, neither here nor there, neither life nor death, precariously hovering in the anxiety of the toward-death, following the declinations of the end.

The inconstant possibility of separation between words and soul, between doer and deed, between writing and its condition, and between text and context, does not cancel out any of the terms here articulated.[94] However, it is a possibility that shows an excess of the deed (the word) over the doer (the soul), a measure of dis-symmetry in the analogy that would simply connect between them. Beyond the doings of the soul, Ibn al-Aštarkūwī tells us, however well intended and close to God it may be, words do a little more than they were intended to do, they "depart in vain, and truth does not praise them, as they come and go." It is thus important to recognize in this possibility of excess, in this unsettling of analogy, that it is not contained in some kind of a liminal in-between. The coming and going cannot simply be seen as confined to an in-between that would not only be identical to itself as a location, but would also simply mediate between established terms. Rather, the movement that I am trying to follow affects and unsettles the very terms that could be seen as linked and separated by it. "Departure," as Ibn al-Aštarkūwī calls this movement of coming and going, can thus only be read in the complex relation it enables and disables between both soul and words, between intention and actions, between language and place. We will see that much like—and even as—the anxiety of the toward-death, this movement contaminates and unsettles both intention and actions, words and souls, in the *maqāma* "On Poetry and Prose," although, in this case too, it is probably not exclusively confined nor bound by this specific *maqāma.*

In *Les Séances,* Abdelfattah Kilito refers to the *maqāma* as "une tradition de pensée" (53). This suggests that beyond the normative separation of genres that may bind a medieval writer, and even though we have already seen how the *maqāma* is undoubtedly inscribed within determined literary genealogies, it is the way in which it exceeds these localizations that prevents reading it as hermetically distinct from other cultural endeavors, from the tradition of thought at work in medieval Arabic-speaking cultures. In an earlier article, Kilito had shown some connections of the *maqāma* to this tradition when he emphasized in it the importance of chains of reported speech, an attribution that repeats, with a touch of irony, the *isnād* (the chain of sources that enable the legitimation of a *ḥadīṯ* [saying of the Prophet]).[95] James Monroe has also insisted on both the necessity of reading the *maqāma* in its "literariness" and emphasized the connection between the writing of *maqāmāt* initiated by Hamḏānī in the tenth century and the development of increasingly complex techniques of interpretation (*taʾwīl*)[96] that are applied to Qurʾanic exegesis, legal argumentation, philosophical discussions, and so on. Yet, if words are that which uncertainly exceeds the chains of intention, it is difficult to miss the way their departure also affects not only what "tradition" means, but also the way they are located within such tradition. It becomes, therefore, quite significant to consider that Ibn al-Aštarkūwī, in his condensed exploration of intentionality and of the links (and lack thereof) between soul and words, author and work, doer and deed, is not only manifesting a concern over questions that were at work in literary and "nonliterary" endeavors; he is also engaged in a momentous reconfiguration of tradition.[97] Moreover, in this reconfiguration, he shows how different discourses are informing, but also disputing and disrupting, each other in ways that may be overt or, more likely, covert. Ibn al-Aštarkūwī is quite explicit about such "dialogue" with tradition, since he asks of his readers that they apply *taʾwīl* when reading his literary words. This should not be taken to amount to a simple interpretation that would establish the proper meaning of the *maqāma*, but suggests rather that one follow the movement of translation of the text, translations of, and/or into, philosophical, legal, or exegetical idioms that inform the tradition, and translations of the tradition and of the place of language. Ibn al-Aštarkūwī alerts us to the way these translated idioms intervene in the text we are about to read, as well as for the need to address this text thoughtfully, as a significant moment in a "tradition de pensée" whose continuity cannot be taken for granted, whose boundaries are far from fixed, and the "formality" and "empty rhetoric" of which may have to be, once again, questioned.

"The Essence of Justice Is That Virtue Be Stripped from Its Performer"

> La déconstruction est la justice.
>
> —Jacques Derrida, *Force de loi*
>
> Détaché de tout, y compris de son détachement.
>
> —Maurice Blanchot, *L'Écriture du désastre*

The tying of ties, but most importantly perhaps, their rupture, the constant traveling and departure of characters, constitutes one of the most recurring figures with which the reader of *maqāmāt* is faced. We find such figures at the very opening of our *maqāma* "On Poetry and Prose," whether indirectly represented in the words of the narrator ("I isolated myself from my traveling-companion, *fāᶜtazaltu ar-rafīqu,*" [372]) or explicitly mentioned in the description of the heated dialogue that takes place in this text ("the bonds of love came near to being sundered, *waqāribat ᶜurā l-wūddi l-infisāmi*").[98] Such a rupture of ties, the singularity and isolation of a character—or of a *maqāma*—is familiar enough and does not need, perhaps, to be dwelled upon. Perhaps it can even hardly be said to be a peculiar characteristic of the *maqāma,* insofar as images of separation and distance, of broken ties and loneliness, are too many to count in Arabic love poetry. Separation, however temporary, is, to a certain extent, a sine qua non condition for love poetry, a poetry in which the lover must express his longing. Still, it should be noted that upon that underlying necessity of broken ties, the poet and writer of Arabic recurrently articulates "necklaces and strands," organization and order, *naẓm.*[99] The poet adds, in short, poetry, *naẓm.*

Naẓm, the "stringing of pearls" as it relates to the poetic structure and organization of the poem, was long thought by scholars to have been limited to the isolated verse.[100] In contrast to that consensus, many are now claiming that poems in their entirety are, in fact, skillfully organized and arranged. James Monroe has further argued that such extended "stringing of pearls" also governs the writing of the *maqāma.* Monroe notes how Hamaḏānī's words make this call to order quite clear when he wrote to a disciple, "as for your writing, its wording is ample and its themes are eloquent, while its beginning is related to its end, and its end continuous with its beginning, and between them flows running water."[101] This circular and orderly view of poetry as the preservation or production of a flow, as the tying and securing of ties over the distance of (permanently or temporarily) broken ones, and as the guarantee of organization, can also be found in the following words attributed, by Ibn al-Aštarkūwī to our *maqāma*'s propoetry protagonist, Ḥabīb: "By it [i.e., poetry], the winning over of intractable inclinations is sought, remote hopes are brought nigh, enmities and dislikes are resolved, trials and tribulations are prevented, frozen spirits are made to flow, abated resolutions are resurrected. . . . [M]any a distant one has it drawn near" (374). The tying of ties, the collapse of distances, the promise of unbroken streams flowing harmoniously, that are of the essence of poetry, thus stand in stark opposition to the scattering, dispersal, and dissemination, *naṯr*, of prose, *naṯr*.

But as for prose, it is reins slackened, eloquence unraveled, a road well-traveled, a bridle easy to master, a water-hole well traveled to, *ḥawḍun mawrūdun*, a tattered garment, a forbidden precinct treated as public property, an evening and a morning drink toward which the slow and the swift steed alternate in chasing one another, and in which the submissive and the rebellious slave are equal. (ibid.)

Everything that the word *naẓm* here evokes, then, from the order that sustains words in poetry, to the order that sustains the hierarchical order of society in its entirety (*niẓām*),[102] is, therefore, shown to be thrown into question by prose as the figure of disorder. Ties, and everything along with them, have broken loose and the sources of flow and its circulation are in danger of becoming clogged when a multitude of unlikely equals is traveling the roads, drinking indiscriminately and unrestrained.

So goes the speech of Ḥabīb, who, in his defense of poetry, does remain near rather than distant from the meanings adjacent to the word *naẓm*, as well as near a tight and conservative emphasis on the importance of *naẓm*, of close order and organization. Ultimately, and though we find in his opponent and contrary brother Ġarīb some confirmation of his verdict on prose as the undermining of order (it is not "fettered by rhymes" but rather "incessantly free of its bridle"), the disagreement will however appear to be not so much about the very necessity of order and the tying and securing of ties, as much as about who should take and hold the reins, which form of speech would be more effective in that organizing and mediating, structuring, role. When he argues with his brother, Ġarīb praises the very same orderly qualities of prose and, in fact, the very same figures that we have seen praised in poetry, and more:

By it the sun is tamed and controlled, old hatreds and animosities are resolved, hard hearts are won over, withered flanks are made flexible, fortresses are recovered, the forelocks of the horse are mastered, the disobedient is reduced to obedience, and the remote is brought near. Of old, has it been a mediator and an intercessor, a herald and a warner. By it, epistles are adorned, measures are adopted, the student and researchers meet with success. By its eloquence news is transmitted; in it both Islamic and non-Islamic scholars glory. . . . With its wording treaties are ratified, the witness and his testimony are recorded, chronicles are adorned and embellished, and events are recognized and clarified. (ibid.)

Values that are fundamentally similar to the ones poetry was championing in Ḥabīb's speech are here defended by Ġarīb. The collapse of distance, the mediation and strength of order, the success of a meeting, the securing of tradition, and the taming of the unruly, although they do leave aside earlier considerations over the preservation of the flow, nonetheless all glorify quite clearly the privacy of water holes and ensure that their drinking will be as "sweet and salt water are distinguished" by virtue of prose's own organizing role. Underscoring what thus appears as the common ground shared by the brothers, it is significant to note that, when later asked whether they do "not seek what agreement, *iṣfāq*,[103] encounters and conformity, *wifāq*, provides," the two brothers immediately and (surprisingly) straightforwardly answer in the affirmative: "Yes, that is what we seek" (376).

The purpose of pointing out the way similar values are advocated by both brothers in this *maqāma* is certainly not to collapse the distance and differences that are found in and between their respective speeches. It is not to assert that, as they carry similar values, prose and poetry, at least in the way they are figured here, could not be said to be as distinct as one would perhaps think they are. It is quite possible, and perhaps even important, for such distinctions to be noted rather than passed over. Nonetheless, it remains difficult to avoid the common dimensions in the opponents' assertions. In both of their speeches, and each in their own way, they both glorify prose and poetry in the name of *naẓm*, in the name of the tying and securing of ties. This is the case even if poetry is more directly and forcefully associated with *naẓm* and *niẓām* (if only because of its "name") and with notions of organization and structure, even if it is closer to the sources, to the water holes, and if it therefore enables their highly directed, yet "natural," flow for the good of the privileged few. Hence, in the argument between the two brothers, and given that their values are recognizable as primarily the values defended by poetry, it is not entirely surprising to read that "the partisan of poetry began to gain victory, nor did he tend toward abridgment and restraint; instead he elaborated and exaggerated; he raised aloft the pavilions of his prejudice and fastened down their tent ropes."[104] In other words, doing what it does best (elaborating and exaggerating, fastening down ropes, etc.), poetry and its most direct spokesperson cannot but win the day. What is even more a cause for wonder is that whether or not it is correct to read both speeches as ultimately defending "poetry," what we are led to is not harmony and peace—the values that are after all defended by both brothers—but rather to the destruction of arguments ("he began . . . to destroy the arguments his brother had provided") and ultimately, to the danger, the perilous possibility of a severing of ties. So it is that in spite of a shared ground and goal of *naẓm,* "the bonds of love came near to being sundered."

It is at this point that the father of the two brothers, the old man, intervenes (by waking up and belching) in what appears as the unlikely role of retying or strengthening the now threadbare bonds between the brothers. He proceeds to do so by reminding them of the error of their ways, insofar as theirs are ways of disagreement and disharmony, ways that lead astray rather than to the continuous sharing of a common goal. Instead of considering their positions to be irremediably distinct, the old man suggests, as we tried to do earlier, that they should see the common threads that already connect them, that already bridge and fasten the bonds between their speeches. As they both seek "what agreement encounters and conformity provides," and as they share a common goal "toward which a truthful investigation leads, or . . . truth and sincerity support" (ibid.), the two brothers should come to understand that disharmony is only the product of appearances (hence, they should "avoid superficial appearances, *al-ᶜawāriḍi l-lāḥiqati*" [377]). Poetry and prose are not opposed, nor are they unrelated; rather, they should be considered in their interconnectedness. Not as opposites, then, but rather as "levels and stairs, and refreshment and fragrance, for every protector has his possession and every dice player has his success" (ibid.). Matters of agreement (or disagreement) are not determining, as Ḥabīb put it early on, "Perhaps it is a subject about which consensus, *ijmāᶜ*, has been solid . . . , or perhaps it is a subject on which opinions have differed" (373). What does appear determining, and that we learn from the old man, is that as soon as one makes the mistake of considering and setting things within such rigid oppositions, nothing can change their positions or conditions ("neither do they grow nor do they decrease" [377]). Even Fortune cannot change them since "even if the vicissitudes of Fortune affect them, [set things] are hardly such that Fortune can diminish or increase them, or harass them from the front or from behind" (ibid.). One must recognize the factuality of change in that it is more fluid, and that it can only occur when things are not set in stone, indeed, when they are recognized not to be like set stones, "a piece of jewelry and the sciences, *al-ḥulīyu wa-l-maᶜārifu,*" indeed "pure science, *al-maḥḍu min al-ᶜilmi,*" and its oppositions. The flow of Fortune does not occur in science, for it does not allow one "opposite" (a "stair" or a "fragrance") to turn into its "other." It is only where one avoids setting (things in) stones that change can occur. It is inherent to the logic of argument and its inner necessity for reified positions that it can only lead to disharmony and broken ties.

Therefore, avoid superficial appearances, for neither do they grow nor do they decrease. Only dullness and briskness of trade in the market lead to agreement, whereas being and non-being do not require agreement, *ijmā*ᶜ, so abandon this subject, for ties of relationship have been broken because of them, and minds have lost their way in considering them. (ibid.)

Such oppositions as "being and non-being, *al-wujūd wa-l-iḫfāq*," do not carry any necessity for agreement and harmony even if they maintain it as an ideal. It is as such that they have led to broken ties. And as we have established that broken ties are exactly what is opposed by both brothers, we may begin to feel the effects of the soothing, indeed, securing, words of the old man's speech.

Let us recapitulate, then, the lesson the old man seems to teach so far. The way to secure ties—the common goal of both prose and poetry—does not reside in oppositional arguments that establish unbridgeable and unresolvable sides and do not lead to agreement. Such dichotomous thinking (being and nonbeing) by definition "do[es] not require agreement," which is to say that it sets oppositions in stone and renders agreement expendable, if not impossible, at the very same time that it posits this very agreement as its goal. Such is the way of "pure science"; it resists "even the vicissitudes of Fortune," so much so that Fortune itself can neither "diminish [n]or increase," it cannot alter the dichotomies science sets for itself. Addressing his sons, the old man enjoins them not to practice this game, but rather to recognize the more continuous flow and fluidity, the "levels and stairs" that make these assumed opposites "diminish or increase" and show them to be under the sway of Fortune.

The old man goes on to develop this train of thought, arguing against people who "have become attached and [who have] linked and bound their aspirations" to poetry alone (ibid.). By fastening onto it exclusively, they are the ones who have rendered it unworthy. In a very dense and difficult passage of the old man's speech, we will follow the elements of an affirmation of justice against "disputation," and against what we have read as the dichotomous, oppositional, logic of argument as "dialogics." As we will also see, however, the soothing and conjoining effect of the old man's words may begin to dissolve.

Before addressing the intricate moves that govern the speech of the old man, it is necessary to indicate the very subtle shift that has already begun to operate in the course of his argument against arguments. We recall that we found a common element of prose and poetry to be the tying of ties. Though they may succeed in joining things to changing degrees, both poetry and prose—much like the two brothers—share in maintaining social, political, and linguistic order. It is possible to discern how the old man's words made manifest the way a common ideal, a common goal, was shared by both brothers and forms of speech from the outset. In both cases, the dominant purpose remains *naẓm.*[105] Convincingly endorsing that very goal, at least for the time being, the old man points out that the practice in which the two brothers have deeply involved themselves leads them away from their common, if ideal, goal of order and organization, their common goal of *naẓm* ("what agreement encounters and conformity provides"). He may therefore chastise them for not practicing what they themselves uphold as their ideal, for not doing what they say, and by extension, he can also criticize the major modes of discourse the brothers invoke for participating in the recurring failure to practice what one preaches.[106] These modes of discourse are thus all situated under the general heading of poetry (*naẓm*). Targeting the prominent among them, the old man will continue to chastise the brothers against the practice of science as a practice of strife and disharmony over against "trade in the market,"[107] which does "lead to agreement."

On a certain level, then, the old man appears to be telling the brothers what to do in order to remain joined, in order to secure the ties between them. They need to stay away from the dichotomous method of the "pure sciences." They need to not consider things as they have been considered up to that point, that is, in the case of—and here begins the subtle but momentous shift in the old man's speech—"a piece of jewelry and the sciences, *al-ḥulīyu wa-l-maʿārifu.*"

Let us postpone for a few more moments what I want to argue is an explanation that illuminates this puzzling expression, one in which the art of jewelry and the practice of the sciences are brought together. Indeed, in order to appreciate the weight of this expression, one needs to note that upholding, for all intents and purposes, the ideal of securing ties and the ideal of order, the old man actually criticizes this ideal as a practice—even if an unsuccessful one—of attachment. What the old man is saying is that even though it breaks "ties of relationship," pure science, as the practice of argument, is an attempt to fix and settle (to the point that even Fortune cannot shift) objects and positions, much like it sets and ties down, indeed, "fastens down tent ropes," positions and oppositions such as being and non-being. It causes strife, perhaps, but it is also the most far-reaching attempt to escape Fortune and its shifting, untying motions.

The Force of Rupture

What is it, then, that ties "a piece of jewelry and the sciences"? I have already begun to argue that it is precisely (and once again) the common practice, and the common goal, of "stringing pearls," of tying and securing ties, the common, organizing goal of agreement or *ijmā*ᶜ. Much as the two brothers were in fact in agreement over this goal even as they were failing to reach it, so is science in agreement with them (and with prose and poetry) in that it presents itself as pursuing that very same, if also ideal, goal. Bringing together science, prose, poetry, and jewelry, the old man hence shows one common and governing ideal to be equally active and dominant in all of them: the stringing of pearls. Insofar as they all share this ideal, insofar as they all seek order and agreement, the tying and securing of ties, whether they do so by setting stones in strings, by setting "being and non-being" in stone, or by setting words in strings, poetry, science, and jewelry, have more in common than they seem to recognize. They, of course, hardly succeed in their endeavor, as is made explicit in the case of science (and in the case of the brothers' dispute), but this does not alter the way agreement remains, in fact, the powerful and governing ideal that, if it can hardly be reached, nonetheless organizes and structures all of their discourses.

It may now become clearer why, while chastising the people who "have become attached" to poetry, the old man also criticizes poetry "itself." For he has shown that the lack of disagreement between prose, poetry, and the sciences was only a matter of appearances. His criticism, therefore, is not directed solely at these methods that seek agreement, order, and the tying and securing of ties, but at the governing goal of any practice that involves itself in the tying of ties, such as "becoming attached" and being "linked and bound." There is good and bad in both poetry and prose, the old man says, but considered from the perspective of the dominant and governing ideal of *naẓm*, it remains with it "a sterile stud, *faḥlun ʿaqīmun*, an immobile group of travelers, *safrun muqīmun*" (377), to which one becomes attached. Hence, there can hardly be more appropriate examples for the tying of ties and its opposition to what can only be described as language out of bounds, out of context.

Still, it is important to note that to consider poetry only in this way, to fix it in this position, would be no less than the faithful repetition of the stringing activity it itself engages in, a setting in stones that produces the same polarization poetry and its companions produce. Such a categorization of poetry would, therefore, be a mistake of the kind practiced by the pure sciences.

It could still be argued that by overtly praising prose ("it is a flowing spring") the old man is contradicting himself (or at least contradicting the role I have attributed to him so far). I want to emphasize that this is not the case, however, because the prose that he here praises is, in fact, quite distinct from the prose defended earlier by Ġarīb. Indeed, the old man's prose plays a very different role than the harmonizing, mediating, tying, and securing one prose had played in Ġarīb's speech. This time, far from securing and tying anything, it is the cutting and unpredictable side of prose that is praised. This distinct kind of prose can therefore be described as "an inconstant beloved who nonetheless grants the love union, and a cutting sword that glances off its victim, *wahājirun wāṣilun, wanābun fāṣilun*" (377–78). Such a discourse, if it is one, could hardly fit into a fixed setting; it could only with difficulty be inserted into either "being or nonbeing," strung into a permanent necklace or another piece of jewelry.

What, then, is the position of the old man? What, if not ties and bounds, is he defending? Though this can hardly be located as an opposite side, or even located at all, it seems possible to read the old man's words as the force of rupture that is, in fact, implicit in and underlies all attempts that strive for and toward *naẓm*. Insofar as it is what such attempts battle against and try to constrain and confine, the force of rupture of his words is what the old man has called prose (that "inconstant beloved who nonetheless grants the love union, and a cutting sword that glances off its victim"). More strikingly perhaps, we will see that it is also what he calls *justice*. Finally, insofar as prose alternates ("coming and going") between tying and untying, between union and separation, between *naẓm* and *naṯr*, it is related to Fortune as that which "diminishes or increases," "harasses from the front or from behind," as that which also alternates in-between.

But why justice? Here too, we must defer an answer in order to address in detail what the old man is saying (something which cannot simply be called defending a position, since we already saw that position is only one aspect of an alternating, inconstant, movement between, and determining of, both *naẓm* and *naṯr*).

We have not entirely left the field of jewelry, though this time we are not considering the modalities of ties and bounds within which stones can be set; rather, we are considering a different unit, one that is—if it is—prior to or elsewhere than *naẓm* and *naṯr*: the word.

How different are words, *al-kalāmu*, that constitute pleasant, superior speech! The latter are true pearls, whether they be couched in verse or in prose, *manẓūman aw manṯūran*; whether they are a verdict to be rejected or accepted. It does no harm to the pearls of poetry if composers of poetry do not organize them into poems, since the great and powerful have preferred to employ them unstrung, in prose. . . . Artistic excellence is manifold: the sun rises and sets, the moon wanes and waxes; it is both ugly and beautiful. Man is good and evil, the earth contains gold and dung, and the crown is not superior to the anklet other than by reason of the superiority of the head over the foot. Therefore, consider my words. (378)

Many of the unstrung stones and pearls we have tried to follow will almost be coming untied, scattered, disseminated. The word, prior to any *naẓm*—yet inevitably inserted, or "couched" in one—appears here as the condition of possibility and impossibility of any facile opposition that would claim to constrain it. A "true pearl," whatever its setting (and it cannot be found without one), is, because it can be fit and untied, a true pearl. It can be accepted or rejected, agreed upon or not, though this would be a setting that brings us back to the central notions of agreement, even consensus, and *naẓm*, that pure science articulates. One should therefore not consider words or pearls as being set in stones, but rather as stones that can always be set or reset. To engage in disputation (to limit the conversation to agreement vs. disagreement, prose vs. poetry, etc.) is to further tie and bind these pearls without recognizing the way they exceed their ties. Words, rather, are themselves to be considered as what enables pleasant speech, or for that matter any speech (both ugly and beautiful, good and evil, gold and dung), to occur, and it is as such (though they are never found "as such") that they must be considered. Enabling both being and nonbeing, and other dichotomies that follow, words can always be reset, they can always be separated from a particular setting, they can be spoken and written, out of context. "Therefore, consider my words."

Therefore, consider my words, *fāᶜtabirā maqūlī*, that you may both trust my judgment and rely on what I have transmitted, for I have spoken in person with men of great wisdom, held lengthy debates and discussions with them, become fond of knowledge, and gained forbearance. (ibid.)

To consider words, in order to trust a judgment, is significantly distinct from passing a verdict of agreement or disagreement. As the old man makes here explicit, to consider words is to consider them in their many settings, whether the person is, what we still call, present, "speaking in person," or whether his judgment, his words, are relied upon long after he is gone, long after the "departure of life." Indeed, to consider words, as distinct from (but not necessarily opposed to) passing a verdict, may be to consider words as both distinct from and couched in, indeed, as a changing setting. To consider words, finally, may have more to do with justice than it has to do with pure science and the dichotomies it establishes between, for example, poetry and prose.

Hence, beware of strife, of argumentation by analogy *al-maqāʾīsa*, and of impatience. In all situations, adopt what is the fairer and juster stance, *fī kulli l-āḥwāli bi-l-āᶜdali l-āqsaṭi*, lean toward the path that is smoother and broader, and do not turn away from the even path that represents the golden mean, since "that is true constancy" [Qurʾān, 42:43], for you are urgently required to do the above. . . . Every situation has its adherents and partisans, and everything has its preservation and destruction. . . . This world has its lots and shares, its lance and its sword, its justice and its enmity. (ibid.)

Justice ("the fairer and juster stance") does not consider things only in what links them to other things (argumentation by analogy [*al-maqāʾīsa*, from *qiyās*, analogy]) but rather widens the path of its considerations ("lean toward the path that is smoother and broader"). We have already read many hints regarding what may constitute such an attitude: indeed, this passage repeats the injunction to "consider my words," not only in the specific context in which they are set, but indeed, as pearls and stones that exceed their contexts, their many conditions and situations. Indeed, much like a word, "every situation has its adherents and partisans, and everything has its preservation and destruction" (ibid.). Preservation and destruction, like adherents and partisans, may either enhance or destroy. At any rate, they articulate a structure without which no word, no thing, could exist or move from context to context. Tying and untying, the prose before, or rather the prose that is broader than both poetry and prose, that which determines and enables oppositions (but is not opposed to oppositions, hence "*beware* of strife" and not "*oppose* strife"), that which enables analogy but is not exhausted by it, that which is always in a context, but can always be decontextualized, as well as that which considers things in such alternating motion, that is justice: "for the essence of justice is that virtue be abstracted from its performer, and knowledge be removed from its servant or implementer, *fawajhu l-ʿadlu an yujarrada l-faḍlu an ḥāmilihi, wayuzaḥzaḥa l-ʿilmu, an ḫādimihi aw ʿāmilihi.*" (377). This movement of abstraction and removal (*jarrada*, literally, ripping, tearing apart), this movement that unties, much as it recognizes the ties, does not have *naẓm* as its dominant goal, since it is what enables and disables both *naẓm* and *naṯr*. Justice is that which considers the always possible rupture between author and text, between virtue and performer, between knowledge and servant of knowledge, between knowledge and its implementer: the judge. It is that which enables both terms in their rupture and tie. It is justice as that "inconstant beloved who nonetheless grants the love union, and a cutting sword that glances off its victim." Justice is therefore also prose, but it is a prose that clearly cannot be said to stand in opposition to poetry; it is, in a sense "prior" to and as poetry, prose, and disputation.

The remainder of the *maqāma* can be read as a further illustration of the force of rupture that is always at work in words and contexts. For this knowledge that has now been transmitted by the old man cannot but be recited in the ways it was and is separated from its "servant" and "implementer." Indeed, it had to be so if words are words, and no *naẓm* could be considered set in stones. Hence, the recurrent appearance of betrayal, failure, and even destruction, of knowledge. "Do you not both see how many people who have learned from me, and conveyed what I have taught them, and who speak and act according to my knowledge, have betrayed me and forgotten my exertion and effort on their behalf?" (379). Can this be said to be an absolute destruction of knowledge, the complete absence of its death? Hardly so. First of all, because the text continues to illustrate, or rather to enact, precisely what the old man had taught. His words too, like everything else, have their "adherents and partisans," their "preservation and destruction." Neither presence nor absence, knowledge is separated from the old man in a way that he himself enacts. Like his words, like the stones he described, he describes himself as dependent upon, and disconnected from, his context, awaiting justice, rather than a verdict that will only consider agreement and disagreement, *naẓm* and *naṯr*: "we do not know anyone of importance, and do not enjoy the recognition of anyone of importance, while the stranger is always an object of suspicion and loathing" (ibid.). And so are words considered in their isolation, but they are also free, like the old man, more so than their listener, al-Sā᾿ib, who is already tied fast in ways he does not recognize: "have you learned that it is you who are confined whereas I am free to wander?" (380).

Like words that can be set in prose, poetry, or argument, the old man wanders into and repeatedly breaks free from texts and contexts. Neither being or nonbeing, his mode of departure, his coming and going, cannot be simply opposed to presence. Like the dream-image or the friend, he is neither here nor there. Hence, "the safer of two alternatives regarding [him], is for you to remember him in his absence, and when he bade you farewell, *ḏikrāhu bi-l-ġaībi was-salāmu*" (ibid.). We are again offered the notion that considers things (words, images, friends) as both present and absent, as neither present nor absent, as that which is the condition for both. Hence separation, departure, is necessary, it will always happen. Settings and contexts will always *decline*, be destroyed or disregarded and effaced ("let there be no contact between us" [ibid.], and later "I continued to erase and efface his shortcomings from my heart" [381]). Yet, that separation, the impossibility of presence, is also the possibility of the trust that the old man had invoked regarding judgment. It is, indeed, insofar as there is separation that there can be justice (which does not mean that justice was done), insofar as the other is already gone that "I longed for him to be the companion for whom I had hoped, and in whom I could trust and confide" (ibid.).

Let us note that such hope for ties and companionship, that is for a companionship of ties, was at no point expressed in the *maqāma* (at the beginning, the narrator had chosen rather to "isolate myself from my traveling companion and became suspicious of anyone who expressed any interest in me"). The now gone companion is rather the occasion, indeed, the condition of possibility of the hope and yearning for him. He is, quite literally, an impossible ("let there be no contact between us") companion. This impossibility is significantly thematized in the words of the old man, which were apparently addressed to his sons, with whom contact and success could have been taken for granted. The sons had promptly claimed to be the rightful heirs to the old man's teachings ("you have . . . handed down choice knowledge of yours that will henceforth be transmitted from father to son" [378]). However, as was bound to happen, here too the force of rupture ("justice") is at work: the old man leaves alone, and it is the accidental listener (one to whom the words were not addressed, to whom they were not intended) who pays tribute to his absence/presence, his memory. One could perhaps say that the sons are still considering words exclusively as knowledge ("pure science"), while it was justice and the way it affects knowledge that is offered to the consideration of the listener and that is enacted in the final words of the *maqāma.* "Artistic excellence is manifold, *wa-l-iḥsānu ḍurūbun,*" indeed, which demands justice with, rather than simply in opposition to, knowledge.

Justice, in the words of this Andalusī text, is never done. It is the event of trans-lation, that which reads the cutting off that separates, ineluctably, words from contexts, and deeds from doers. The event of this trans-lation is, here again, though distinctively and singularly, the occurrence of language, at "our place." With it, language, this language that defies identity and keeps eluding its localization, occurs as translation. Language displaced onto its place, declinations of contexts, "our place in al-Andalus."

REFERENCE MATTER

Notes

FRONTISPIECE

I owe thanks to Amnon Raz-Krakotzkin for giving me to read Mahmoud Darwish's poem "On the Last Evening on This Earth" (rendered below in my translation; all translations in this book are my own unless otherwise noted. References are either to the original text, whatever the language, or to the English translation alone. When referring to both the original and the English translation, the latter is indicated by the letter *E*.)

On the last evening on this earth, we cut off our days
From our shrubs, and we count the ribs that we will carry with us
And the ribs that we will leave behind, there . . . on the last evening
We bid farewell to nothing, and we do not find the time for our end
Everything remains as it is, the place changes our dreams
And changes its visitors. Suddenly, we are no longer capable of irony
And the place is ready to host nothingness . . . here on the last evening
We fill ourselves with the mountains surrounded by the clouds: conquest
    and reconquest
An ancient time grants to this new time the keys of our doors
Come on in, O conquerors, enter our homes, and drink the wine
Of our complacent muwaššaḥa. For we are the night when it splits
    in two,
No horse rider arriving from the last prayer call to deliver the dawn . . .
Our green hot tea—drink it! Our fresh pistachio nuts—eat them!
These beds are green made of cedar wood—surrender to drowsiness!
After this lengthy siege, sleep on the feathers of our dreams
The sheets are ready, the scents are at the door, and the mirrors are many
Enter them so that we can come out! Soon we will seek what
Has been our history around your history in the distant lands
And we will ask ourselves in the end: was al-Andalus
Here or there? On the earth . . . or in the poem?

INTRODUCTION: Declinations of Context

1. Hamacher, *Premises*, 5.

2. Monroe, "Al-Saraqusṭī, Ibn al-Aštarkūwī," 19.

3. Strauss, "The Literary Character," 52.

4. Septimus, *Hispano-Jewish Culture*, 1.

5. There were numerous conferences, cultural events, and publications to accompany the five hundredth anniversary of the highly loaded date of 1492. The combined effects of the expulsion of the Jews from Spain, the fall of Granada (the last major Muslim political enclave in the Iberian peninsula) and the conquests and "discoveries" of Columbus, were all celebrated in one way or another. Tzvetan Todorov's *The Conquest of America* was beginning to set the tone in the 1980s, and many collections followed by highlighting the undeniable dimension of loss and devastation. Collections of essays referred to the "heritage" and "legacy" of that which is no more, or, alternatively, celebrated the cultural richness of the *convivencia*, the living-together in both conflict and harmony as it took place before 1492.

6. Ronell, *Finitude's Score*, xiv.

7. I quote here from Jacques Derrida's discussion of "the end" ("What should be understood here *by the end*?") in "Finis," *Aporias*, 8.

8. Roskies, *Against the Apocalypse*, 1. Roskies focuses on modern times, not on medieval ones, but he establishes a genealogy of "responses to catastrophe," from the Bible to the Talmud and Eastern Europe via medieval Ashkenaz. The word "Jewish," therefore, finds its authority in ancient times but it already seems to translate—exclusively?—the word "Yiddish."

9. J. Boyarin, *Storm from Paradise*, 10. The community of which Boyarin speaks appears to require no further clarification: it is a "Jewish" community, where "Jewish" translates, even if in admittedly complicated ways, "Yiddish." At the time of *Storm*'s writing, Boyarin had not yet made clear the further and intentional collapse of the word "Jewish" that takes place in his later book *Thinking in Jewish*. Only a different translation of the word "Jewish"—were it simply possible or, indeed, simple—would make the difficulty of the sentence I quote apparent. This is also (that is to say, not only) a matter of language and of translation. In yet another instance of such (internal? external?) translation, the limits of "Judaism" (and the contribution of "Jewish studies" to a wider intellectual discourse) are staged, in a recent volume, between "the Jew," westernized Jews, and, finally, *Judentum*. Producing this seemingly unregistered displacement, the editors of the volume summarize the movement of their own introduction and the place of their "Jewish" language. "*Modernity, Culture and 'the Jew,'*" they write, referring to the title of the volume, "is a varied exploration of the fraught and continuing relationship between modernity and *Judentum*" (Cheyette and Marcus, *Modernity, Culture*, 18). What calls, and what is called, "Judaism"?

10. For an extensive discussion of Arab Jews and their "end," see Ella Shohat's

work, beginning with her *Israeli Cinema.* For a refocusing on the Middle Ages of the questions raised by Shohat and others, see Alcalay, *After Jews and Arabs,* and Raz-Krakotzkin, "The National Narration of Exile."

11. See Chapter 3.

12. Derrida, "Fors," xxi.

13. Alexander García Düttmann has articulated this necessity in terms that are fully relevant to the present project. "It is necessary," he writes, "to touch upon the limits of cultural evolution, upon the limits which, given that culture is disunited and not-one, are discovered historically, and which, in presenting themselves historically, show the being-not-one of culture" (Düttmann, *Between Cultures,* 27).

14. Derrida, *Aporias,* 11.

15. The disappearance, indeed, the exhaustion, of context that al-Andalus constitutes is a specific translation of the failure of any context to "determine meaning to the point of exhaustiveness." How much more so if exhaustion and disappearance is its mode of appearance. "Therefore the context neither produces nor guarantees impassable borders, thresholds that no step could pass [*trespasser*], *trespass,* as our anglophone friends would say" (ibid., 9). What needs to be shown, then, is how, in this specific instance, "this border of translation does not pass among various languages. It separates translation from itself, it separates translatability within one and the same language" (10).

CHAPTER 1: Maimonides, *Dalāla,* Midrash

1. Maimonides, *Guide of the Perplexed,* trans. Shlomo Pines, II: 29, 336. Unless otherwise indicated this is the translation I use throughout. I also follow the Arabic text established by Salomon Munk and revised by Joel, *Dalālat al-ḥāʾirīn* (1929), as well as Husein Atay's edition of the book (1972). The text is divided in three parts, indicated by Roman numerals. Each part is divided in a number of sections, indicated by the Arabic numbers that follow. The last or only number in the reference is always the page number and it is that of the English translation.

2. Agamben, *Language and Death,* 66; and see also Agamben, *Stanzas.*

3. I quote here from Maimonides' explanations on the composition of the *Guide,* in his introduction (*Guide,* 15).

4. Maimonides wrote in Arabic, Judeo-Arabic, and Hebrew. Leo Strauss refers to some of the language statistics in his "How to Begin to Study the *Guide of the Perplexed*" (*Guide,* xvi). The *Guide* was twice translated into Hebrew in the twelfth century, once by Samuel ibn Tibbon, and once by Yehuda al-Ḥarizi. Modern editions and translations are invaluable to scholars and most often used, whether in French (the first edition of the Judeo-Arabic text was made by Salomon Munk and was accompanied by a French translation and extensive notes), Arabic, English, or Modern Hebrew.

5. Conceivably, the opposition of meanings between the Hebrew and Arabic is

an instance of what Sigmund Freud discussed as "The Antithetical Meaning of Primal Words." Arabic has a technical term for such words, referring to them as *aḍḍād* (plur. of *ḍidd*). But to the extent that this word functions in Maimonides' text as a figure of language and of the "speech of the prophets," it can hardly be dismissed as just an example. And what is "just an example"? The problem of exemplarity is one that I want to address here precisely because of the difficulty in deciding what the representative and the figurative value of a word is.

6. This section and my ensuing reading of the problems of "communication" as I take them to occur in Maimonides' text rely on Jacques Derrida's "Signature, événement, contexte" in Derrida, *Marges de la philosophie*, 367–93/E309–30.

7. *Guide*, 3–4.

8. On the discontinuous history of the figurations and transfigurations of the word *figura* as implying continuity, historical or other, and as a concept from which the very notion of historical continuity and interpretation is, in fact, derivative, see Auerbach, "Figura." I am also quoting from Walter Benjamin's essay, "The Task of the Translator" (69). For an extended discussion of figuration in a wider sense than I use it here (and relevant for my use of the word through the book), see Bahti, "Figure, Scheme, Trope."

9. "When the middle of an opposition is not the passageway of a mediation, there is every chance that the opposition is not pertinent. The consequences are boundless" (Derrida, *Marges de la philosophie*, 306/E256).

10. Derrida, "La Loi du genre," 279/E244. At the beginning of this text, Derrida had already questioned—in ways that will be important for what follows toward understanding the "accidents" of Maimonides' words—the now all too common trope of "mixing," hybridity, and the like, when he writes about genres that: "if it should happen that they do intermix, by accident or through transgression, by mistake or through a lapse, then this should confirm, since, after all, we are speaking of a 'mixing,' the essential purity of their identity" (253/E225). It is both the purity and the mixing that the "law of genre" as "principle of contamination" problematizes (256/E227). As such, it also remains, as Derrida emphasizes, the question of a limit, a *trait*, and of an exposure.

11. Maimonides inscribes this constant possibility when he writes to his disciple that "certainty should not come to you by accident, *bi-l-ᶜaraḍ*" (*Guide*, 4). *ᶜAraḍ* refers to contingency, unessential accidents, and chance, as well as to symptoms of a disease. Contamination, and other medical problems, would have been, of course, the expertise of the "physician of Córdoba," yet the status of contamination is still debated regarding the medical knowledge of the time (see the fascinating discussion of leprosy and contamination in Jacquart and Thomasset, *Sexuality and Medicine*). It is important therefore to consider that "contamination" does not have to exclusively imply the field of medicine, but also philosophical problems of causality, contingency, and so on. For the purposes of the discussion, it is also significant that the word *ᶜaraḍ* is related to *muᶜāraḍa*, which means opposition, resistance, contradic-

tion, objection, and, in poetry, imitation (see S. M. Stern, *Hispano-Arabic Strophic Poetry*, esp. 45–49).

12. Hamacher, *Premises*, 1.

13. See the pages that Jean-Luc Nancy devotes to this "classical form" of interpretation in order to distinguish, in the rest of his discussion, between interpretation and *hermeneia* (Nancy, *Le Partage des voix*, 15–21). It is important to note that Nancy asserts the closest relation, *le rapport le plus étroit*, between the questions he pursues and the work of Walter Benjamin on language, translation, and literature (11n2). I will later address the way in which Benjamin's work is relevant to my own discussion here.

14. Strauss, "The Literary Character."

15. *Guide*, 5. Note, however, that science, *ᶜilm*, may be related to signs, and sign posts, functioning as a vector as much as a place of destination (see Rosenthal, *Knowledge Triumphant*, 8–11). This will become more relevant later on.

16. Derrida, "Signature, événement, contexte," 370/E311. But the notion of continuity is what is most insistently placed under interrogation throughout Derrida's essay.

17. "What is at stake, in effect, is exemplarity and the whole *enigma*—in other words, as the word *enigma* indicates, the *récit*—which works through the logic of the example, *il y va en effet de l'exemplarité avec toute l'énigme—autrement dit, comme l'indique le mot d'énigme, le récit—qui travaille la logique de l'exemple*" (Derrida, "La Loi du genre," 256/E227).

18. Benjamin, "The Task of the Translator," 71. For my understanding of Benjamin's text, I am here particularly indebted to Fynsk, "Translation as a Concept of Relation," in *Language and Relation*, 177–89; and see also Jacobs, "The Monstrosity of Translation: Walter Benjamin's 'The Task of the Translator,'" in *Telling Time*, 128–41. See also following note.

19. Chase, *Decomposing Figures*, 5.

20. Benjamin, "The Task of the Translator," 72.

21. See the introduction to the first part of *Guide*, 5–6, up to the paragraph ending with "That is why, *walidālika*, I have called this Treatise 'The Guide of the Perplexed.'" What the demonstrative pronoun "that" refers to is, conspicuously enough, difficult to determine.

22. Irene Harvey, addressing Derrida's work, articulates the relation between examples and law in terms that are quite relevant here. She writes that examples "reveal another *allegiance*, another legality, which can be seen as illegitimate only within the system that only apparently governs them" (I. Harvey, "Derrida and the Issue of Exemplarity," 197).

23. Hegel, *The Philosophy of History*, 234, quoted in Hamacher, *Premises*, 6 (Sibree's translation gives "watch" for *lauschen* which is here corrected. The centrality of hearing in Hegel's discussion is unmistakable). Note that, following this reading, the "Arab's" eavesdropping could become the very figure of philosophy's

response to wonder, of its response to the *aporon* described by Aristotle. Hamacher explains that, for Hegel, the relation of spirit listening is a relation to an aporia, and it "consists in a pause, a breakdown of knowledge, a mere 'eavesdropping' on something that communicates itself, and as Hegel then indicates, this relation expresses itself in a question about an unfamiliar meaning." We will see how this could also be said to be the (aporetic) case in the *dalāla.*

24. T. Cohen, "*Othello,* Bakhtin and the Death(s) of Dialogue," in Cohen, *Anti-Mimesis,* 31.

25. Not entirely impossible, of course, since it is known that the *dalāla* was, in fact, read in Arabic by Arab Muslims and not only by Arab Jews (a "historical fact" that remains underplayed in spite of evidence to the contrary). Yet, the book is persistently studied as if it was entirely, indeed fully, governed by an essentialized authorial intention that would have excluded Arab readers (by "Arab," I hope it is therefore clear, I refer not to ethnicity but to language). Leo Strauss's claim that the *Guide* is a "Jewish book" is one of the most prominent examples of this bias I am aware of. On Maimonides' Arab partners in conversations, and possibly Arab readers, see Pines, translator's introduction to the *Guide,* and see also ʿAbdurrahmān Badawi, "Méprises au sujet de Maimonide," and S. M. Stern, "A Collection of Treatises," esp. 64.

26. To that extent, it will not yet be possible to assert whether the text under consideration is, in fact, strictly speaking, exemplary. Is "conversation" the law of which this would be an example? or is the relation between conversation and this text, between, one could say, the *dalāla* here and the *dalāla* there, another kind of relation, perhaps no relation at all? The relation of and to the *dalāla* is therefore precisely what remains under interrogation here. Moreover, assuming that this specific passage is in fact peculiar, and particular (as if this could be thought without making reference to some form of exemplarity), what would enable the recognition of that "fact"? What language could absolutely assert or deny the exemplarity or the singularity of this passage, of this *dalāla*? Is there one *dalāla*?

27. As the "Epistle Dedicatory" makes clear, the *dalāla* is a letter, *risāla,* addressed to Rabbi Joseph ben Judah: "Your absence moved me to compose this Treatise which I have composed for you and for those like you, however few they are. I have set it down in dispersed chapters. All of them that are written down will reach you where you are, one after the other" (*Guide,* "Epistle Dedicatory," 4). Platonic literary echoes notwithstanding, the *dalāla* thus inscribes itself among many "literary" writings, some of which were produced by Rabbi Joseph and had earlier produced a strong impression on Maimonides: "I had a high opinion of you because of your strong desire for inquiry and because of what I had observed in your poems, *ašʿār,* of your powerful longing for speculative matters. This was the case since your letters, *rasāʾil,* and compositions in rhymed prose, *maqāmāt*" (ibid., 3). Whether, like Plato, Maimonides would have seen in these writings a "pedagogi-

cal" step, seems difficult to establish insofar as it would demand a resolution of generic distinctions (between letters and letters, in fact). In this letter, *risāla*, the reader continues to be addressed as "you" throughout.

28. Strauss, "Literary Character," and see also Strauss's introductory essay to the English translation of the *Guide*: "How to Begin to Study *The Guide of the Perplexed*." Joel L. Kraemer also observed that "the *Guide* is essentially a dialectical work." Kraemer also shows that alternative possibilities remain open when he writes that this dialectical dimension of the *Guide* does not imply "that it does not contain demonstrative arguments, or for that matter even rhetorical and poetical statements" (Kraemer, "Maimonides on the Philosophic Sciences," in *Perspectives on Maimonides*, ed. Kraemer, 102). Sara Klein-Braslavy writes that dialogue is the "ideal [teaching] situation" in the *Guide* (Klein-Braslavy, *Maimonides' Interpretation*, 34); and Hannah Kasher explores the oral dimension of the *Guide* as it is preserved in the linear development of the writing, a linearity that does not, however, preclude the repetition of reading (Kasher, "The Art of Writing").

29. Strauss, "Literary Character," 47.

30. Note how the following lines sustain this interpretation of conversation as the most efficient way of teaching (I quote more extensively, however, as the passage bears upon my discussion in more than one way).

> I do not say that this treatise will remove all difficulties for those who understand it. I do, however, say that it will remove most of the difficulties, and those of the greatest moment. A sensible man thus should not demand of me or hope that when we mention a subject, we shall make a complete exposition of it, or that when we engage in the explanation of the meaning of one of the parables, we shall set forth exhaustively all that is expressed in that parable. An intelligent man would be unable to do so even by speaking directly to an interlocutor. (*Guide*, 6, introduction to the first part)

31. Ronell, "Doing Kafka," in *Finitude's Score*, 186.

32. Ibid., 189.

33. The phrase "that there is language" is Christopher Fynsk's, in his *Language and Relation* (but it should also resonate with Giorgio Agamben's discussion of the occurrence of language in *Infancy and History*, to which I return in the next chapter). In another work, Fynsk notes that "the questioning relation provoked by the arrest of thought" is described by Martin Heidegger as "an astonishment or perplexity" (Fynsk, *Heidegger*, 16). As in Maimonides, and without pushing the analogy too much further, perplexity is that which "claims . . . thought and gives it its movement" (18). The movement of the word—one might say, of a language of—perplexity, is part of what I seek to explore here.

34. Benjamin, "The Task of the Translator," 69.

35. Arthur Hyman describes one of the school of interpretation of the *dalāla* as being "harmonistic" (A. Hyman, "Interpreting Maimonides," 26ff.).

36. Ronell, *The Telephone Book*, 63.

37. Louis Althusser, "Ideology and Ideological State Apparatuses"; and see Judith Butler, "Conscience Doth Make Subjects of Us All," in *The Psychic Life of Power*. On the call as "interpellation," see Ronell, *The Telephone Book*.

38. Derrida, *The Post Card*, 326. I have altered Bass's translation, which gives the English "murmur" for the French *rumeur* (rumor); see *La Carte postale*, 347.

39. As Werner Hamacher writes:

> Is it already settled that I will hear this call and hear it as one destined for me? Is it not rather the case that the minimal condition to be able to hear something as something lies in my comprehending it neither as destined for me nor as somehow oriented toward someone else? Because I would not need to hear it in the first place if the source and destination of the call, of the call as call, were already certain and determined. (quoted in Ronell, *The Telephone Book*, 420n25)

And see also Hamacher on "eavesdropping," in *Premises*, mentioned earlier.

40. It should be clear that these accidents cannot be seen as exterior to the "conversation" as it is construed by Maimonides. It is not a matter here of presuming a conversation "free" of accidents—as if this were possible. Note, therefore, that in following the "Arab's" question-and-response, we consider this and any reader who "acts as a kind of translating machine which at no point enjoys a direct line to a logos" (Ronell, *The Telephone Book*, 426n48).

41. The extent to which the *dalāla* could be said to "program" its readings and misreadings is perhaps most obvious in moments like this (remembering that Benjamin affirmed the connection between original and translation, but that this connection is not necessarily one of significance). Once again, the "Arab" is not simply an expandable accident, and neither are those which Raphael Jospe describes as "recreating Maimonides in [their] own image," as sharing with him the same *dalāla* (R. Jospe, review of *Interpreting Maimonides*). To follow Jospe here would suggest, against Benjamin as I read him here, that there is absolutely no connection, but rather a sheer novelty, creation out of nothing, and even an error, as it were, between the *dalāla* and its translations. I return to the matter of errors later on.

42. See ʿAbdurrahmān Badawi's comments on the question of Arabic vs. Hebrew script in his "Méprises," esp. 51–52. Badawi criticizes the way Hebrew script in texts by Arab Jews has been taken for granted. One way or another, the complications for a reading of our passage could hardly be minimized.

43. Jacques Derrida's remarks concerning the difficulties raised by the multiplicity of language as difficulties that exceed the translatability of the words, insofar as no translation can render the specific difference to be made *between* the particular languages and *in* any given language, are quite crucial to ponder in this context (Derrida, *Schibboleth*, 54–55; and see Benjamin on "the central reciprocal relationship between languages," in "The Task of the Translator," 72).

44. On contingency and the unaccountability of matter, the impossibility of its "thoroughgoing determination," see Goodman, "Matter and Form"; Funkenstein, "Maimonides: Political Theory and Realistic Messianism," in Funkenstein, *Perceptions*, 131–55; Guttmann, "Das Problem der Kontingenz"; and see also the very suggestive reading of "Maimonides' 'Ravings,'" by Jerome I. Gellman, who also criticizes the recurring attempts to determine Maimonides' "true positions," and, more to the point here, pays close attention to matter, as well as to the importance of addressing Maimonides' language on that matter. Alfred Ivry also discusses Maimonides' relation to matter in his "Providence, Divine Omniscience, and Possibility," esp. 177ff. I return to the question of matter below.

45. "Epistle Dedicatory," *Guide*, 4.

46. On the issues of address, destination, arrival and/or reception, that guide me here, see Ronell, *The Telephone Book*. One should consider the texts discussed by Ronell here, namely the conversation between Lacan and Derrida (but the entirety of Derrida's *Post Card* is here relevant), and see also Weber, "The Debts of Deconstruction and Other," in *Institution and Interpretation*. What is important here is that these works clarify not so much perhaps the legitimacy of the "Arab's" response, as much as that they ask us to consider the obligation, the indebtedness of the listener/reader, and thus the "Arab's" silent question and response to a voice, the origin of which is, to say the least, unclear. As Avital Ronell puts it, "there is no call that does not call forth responsible responsiveness" (*The Telephone Book*, 106). Such responsible responsiveness on the part of the "Arab" is also what prevents the assessment of his gesture in terms of a preexisting legitimacy.

47. Cadava, *Words of Light*, 61.

48. Ronell, *The Telephone Book*, 24ff. I am also relying here on Neil Hertz's "Lurid Figures," in Waters and Godzich, eds., *Reading de Man Reading*, esp. 96.

49. Abraham Nuriel, "Parables," 85. I take it that what Nuriel brings to consideration is the relationship, that is, the structure of the *mashal* as it articulates a relation. This recurs as what is to be read, therefore, whether the relation is between *mashal* and *nimshal*, or between revealed and concealed.

50. One translating illustration should suffice as to the difficulty produced by the word *maṯal* and its cognates. In a passage in which Maimonides uses the verb form for *maṯal* to refer to what he has just done, namely *maṯalna*, Munk translates, "dans tout ce que nous venons de citer pour exemple," whereas Pines offers "in all that we have said by way of parable" (*Guide*, I: 46, 98).

51. See David Stern's description of the rabbinic *mashal* in his *Parables in Midrash*, 8.

52. *Guide*, 12ff.

53. Most famous are perhaps Maimonides' "parable of the palace" (*Guide*, III: 51, 618) and his reappropriation of "Apples of Gold" (*Guide*, 11–12). See Frank Talmage's discussion in his "Apples of Gold." One significant exception to the general figuring out of Maimonides' own parables, if parables they are, is Josef Stern's

treatment of them in "Maimonides on the Covenant." See also Diamond, "The Use of Midrash."

54. Samuel Weber, *Institution and Interpretation*, 3–4. On "sharing" as partaking or *partage*, see Nancy, *Le Partage des voix*.

55. D. Stern, *Parables*, 3.

56. In this discussion, it should be obvious that I am less interested in the "truth" of the rabbinic *mashal* than in the structural problems that are raised by its reading, and in what can be learned from the effects of these problems toward a reading of Maimonides' *maṯal*. I have neither the intention nor the ability to adjudicate in the matter of the rabbinical *mashal*'s "true" form or genre, assuming there is such a thing.

57. Boyarin, "Take the Bible," 29. Underscoring what remains for me here a way of addressing an occurrence of language, Giorgio Agamben demonstrates the singularly linguistic, rather than ontic, dimension of the example in *The Coming Community*, 9–11.

58. It is not clear whether Boyarin's notion of indeterminacy falls under the critique of David Stern ("Midrash and Indeterminacy," and see also Daniel Boyarin, *Carnal Israel*, 27), mostly because Stern never quite addresses who or what it is that he so vehemently opposes ("If the difference between rabbinic polysemy and contemporary indeterminacy is fairly clear," Stern writes—and, by that point in the essay, that is a "fairly" large "if" [141]). Nonetheless, Stern's essay constitutes a possible qualification of Boyarin's "indeterminacy." Another moment of this debate does not mention indeterminacy explicitly but does bear relevance insofar as, in Boyarin's argument, there is an account of the relational, even reciprocal difficulty between *mashal* and *nimshal*, between interpretation and interpreted text, an account that is missing from Stern's emphasis on, and strict distinction between, narrative and exegesis. Insofar as this difficulty cannot be said to be fully solved, insofar as new "gaps" are produced in the very combination of texts into one, more than "polysemy," as Stern calls it, seems to me to be at stake (see D. Boyarin's review of Stern's *Parables*, "Midrash in Parables," and see also Boyarin and Stern, "An Exchange.")

59. Silver, *Maimonidean Criticism*. See also Kellner, *Maimonides*; Fox, *Interpreting Maimonides*, 7ff.; and Derrida, "Interpretations at War," esp. 65–66.

60. Boyarin suggests that the need for the *mashal* arises out of the conception of the biblical text (which he opposes qua "'true' story" to the *mashal*-as-fiction) as either "meaningless in itself" or as having meaning but "this meaning is not transparent by itself" ("Take the Bible," 46). See also Nuriel, who describes a parallel distinction at work in Maimonides, between reading the Bible as "historical event" or reading it as *mashal* (Nuriel, "Parables"). As useful as these distinctions are, they are also quite difficult to maintain.

61. This is not, of course, "the whole story," as Boyarin points out, but it is relevant enough that the distinction between early and late appears in his review of

Stern, where the question of ontological or logical primacy plays a major role (Boyarin, "Midrash in Parables," 127–29).

62. It seems to me that it is therefore neither insignificant nor accidental that the "rare and precious explicit rabbinic comment on hermeneutics" discussed by Boyarin ("Take the Bible," 32) turns out to be a "dugma of dugma" (33). Boyarin and others have, after all, shown that, with the *mashal*, "Scripture interprets Scripture" (see, for example, D. Boyarin and Stern, "An Exchange," 273). In order to explain what *dugma/mashal* is, "the rabbi gives an example of the literary form 'dugma,' that is to say, a dugma about dugma, indeed, a mashal of mashal" (Boyarin, "Take the Bible," 32). This moment of Boyarin's argument should be read together with Judith Butler's notion, in *Bodies That Matter*, of "materialization," which I take Boyarin to echo in his "concretization," especially where Butler stresses the ancient view of "matter as a site of *generation* or *origination*" (*Bodies that Matter*, 31ff.). I also rely heavily on Andrzej Warminski's introduction to de Man, *Aesthetic Ideology*, "Allegories of Reference," and on his discussion of what he calls "allegories of *of*," in ibid., esp. 18–19). See also Warminski's work on Hegel and *Beispiel*, which, I hope, has helped me avoid some pitfalls, if not gulfs, myself (Warminski, *Readings in Interpretation*).

63. J. Stern, *Problems and Parables*, 11.

64. Ivry, "Maimonides on Possibility," 71.

65. The figure or expression of "hermeneutic circle" must, however, be read with much reservation. Jean-Luc Nancy explains that, against the prevalent understanding, the circle should neither be seen as a figure of continuity nor as a figure of return to an origin (precomprehension, presupposition). Rather, presupposition is here what shatters the possibility of reaching the origin—or the end (Nancy, *Le Partage*; and see also Werner Hamacher's discussion of the hermeneutic circle in *Premises*, esp. 25ff.).

66. Warren Z. Harvey, addressing the question of the *Guide*'s reading of the Bible, describes this hermeneutic circle only slightly differently: "The Bible is our guide, therefore, a book of education for ourselves and for our children. Hence, we must read it carefully and dutifully, *be-hitbonenut u-be-meḥuyavut*, and interpret it according to our best religious and philosophical understanding. We must interpret it according to reason so that it can guide us according to reason" (Harvey, "How to Begin," 15). It is possible to read Leo Strauss's own (and earlier) "How to Begin," and its characterization of distinct readers, as also implying a hermeneutic circle, though Strauss's formulation would probably be more readily translated today as inscribing somehow essentialized "subject-positions," the place of the subject as the place of language.

67. Ronell, *The Telephone Book*, 151.

68. Strauss, "Literary Character," 94.

69. The validity of this dichotomy between readers is not quite convincing, even if one grants that it may serve, temporarily at least, some heuristic purposes,

and even if it has some textual basis (but we will see, as Strauss makes clear, that there are serious difficulties in the claim that one understands the dichotomy and could even situate oneself in it). Witness, for example, how Strauss both defends the esoteric thesis and writes, nonetheless, that the "teaching of the *Guide* is then neither entirely public or speculative nor is it entirely secret or exegetic" (Strauss, "How to Begin," xvi). Marvin Fox also made careful and qualified statements that do not amount simply and entirely to an exoteric view (Fox, *Interpreting Maimonides*, esp. 64ff.). Yet the terms of the dispute are set as if the divide was between exoteric and esoteric. Fox himself rejects the esoteric reading as barring access to a book that was, after all, exposed "to the general reading public" (63). Fox writes that the book is a "public document," and it is "much too important for us to accept passively the judgement that [Maimonides'] teaching is permanently inaccessible" (ibid., and see the general discussion of Strauss on 54–66). It should be noted at this point that I am indebted to many moments of Fox's stance on the problems of reading Maimonides. Most particularly, his insistence that Maimonides does not present a "synthesis at all," or some resolution of en-gulfing problems that would follow a logic of either/or. Rather, Fox continues, Maimonides' work is an "affirmation of 'both/and' with the elements interpenetrating each other as far as legitimately possible and being held in balanced tension when that becomes necessary" (23; and see also, 43ff. for a discussion of this "balanced tension"). There is reason perhaps to regret a certain passing of this tension when it is, as it were, suspended at the point when what is addressed is, precisely, a difficult conversation. Fox seems here to "fall back" onto a logic of either/or when he writes: "For any sentence we speak to be intelligible to others, both speaker and hearers must take basic rules of reason for granted. If we do not, we are in a world in which nothing is fixed, nothing is stable, and nothing is intelligible" (28). It would be, then, either all or nothing. But why only one speaker in opposition to multiple hearers? And why, here, such hermetic dichotomies? Finally, why such insistence on intelligibility and meaning as the a priori condition of possibility of language? Did Fox presume too much familiarity with ("Everyone today is familiar with . . . "), too much of the same meaning and recurring "enterprise" in some of the so-called modern "schools" ("such schools as the new critics, the structuralists, and the deconstructionists, among others") as having only "hermeneutic concerns" (64)? If Fox and other readers (this one included) are also disjunctive effects and translations of the text, then there is no reason to simply accept another, not unrelated, dichotomy he makes, between seemingly external, arbitrary "widely differing ways of reading," and "the substantive issues" (27). A direct polemical approach that situates itself ostensibly on the opposite side of all notions of esotericism can be found in Oliver Leaman, *Moses Maimonides*.

70. Benjamin, "The Task of the Translator," 69.

71. Strauss, "Literary Character," 49.

72. See for example, ibid., 75–76, where Strauss writes that Maimonides hides something "which only the learned . . . would miss," namely his true position

(again) on Aristotle and the sense of touch. It is a matter of readers, rather than of textuality. W. Z. Harvey seems to concur when he tends to ascribe the difficulty of what he calls "double lexicographic explanations" not to a linguistic problem, *beʿaya shel yediʿat ha-lashon,* but rather to an intellectual problem, *beʿaya shel maḥshava.* This, Harvey says, emerges out of the "suspicion . . . that according to Maimonides, the problem of the correct interpretation of Scripture . . . is fundamentally not a problem of a knowledge of the Hebrew language, but rather an intellectual problem" (W. Harvey, "How to Begin," 7). Language has been all figured out.

73. The doctrine of different intellects and different understandings is, of course, to be distinguished from what has been called the "doctrine of the double truth," though the later seems to have derived from the former (for a discussion of this *mythe de la double verité,* see de Libera, *Penser au moyen âge,* 122ff. On the distinction between intellects, that is, between readers, see Ibn Rushd, *Kitāb faṣl almaqāl*; see also Ibn Rushd's teacher, Ibn Ṭufayl, who in his *Ḥayy ibn Yaqẓān* writes of the character's error in thinking that all human beings have the same intellectual abilities (*Ḥayy ibn Yaqẓān,* 147), and see Maimonides himself, who describes a hierarchy of enlightenment at the beginning of the *dalāla.*

74. Strauss alludes earlier to the possibility of a hermetic esotericism, claiming that it would make the interpretation of the *Guide* "wholly impossible for the modern historian. The very intention of interpreting the *Guide* would imply an unbearable degree of presumption on the part of the would-be interpreter" (Strauss, "Literary Character," 58).

75. Strauss here quotes from Maimonides' *Mishne Torah.*

76. In his "How to Begin," Strauss does not follow Pines's translation, and refers to *amṯāl* as "similes" (xiv). Marvin Fox has also observed some inconsistencies in Strauss's use (or lack thereof) of Pines's translation (Fox, *Interpreting Maimonides,* 57). Regardless of the meaning of such inconsistencies, it is important to note that Strauss uses the very same word here and there.

77. Consider Marvin Fox's criticism of Strauss regarding the hurried way in which Strauss decided that Maimonides' contradictions were all logical ones: "Maimonides would be a far easier writer to understand if he had not strewn so many obstacles in our path. If he needed to include a deliberate collection of inconsistencies in his book, it would have been far easier to cope with them if they were all of a standard logical type" (Fox, *Interpreting Maimonides,* 88).

78. Such depths and gulfs have an uncanny way of inscribing themselves on attentive readers of the *Guide.* Fox quotes Yaakov Becker, who describes the *Guide* as deepening the "abyss" between Law and philosophy (ibid., 13). Aryeh Leo Motzkin is most interesting in this context. He sees the abyss, *tehom,* as historically recent and as coextensive with the attempt to bridge it. He does not seem to consider that his claim for a return to a medieval dualism, *shniyut,* also constitutes and covers an abyss that is constitutive of the poles (here philosophical theory and political praxis), not simply separating them (Motzkin, "On Maimonides' Interpretation"). On the

very first page of her book, Sara Klein-Braslavy writes of the open "gap, *paʿar*" that separates between the biblical text and the faithful, as they are represented in the book (*Maimonides' Interpretation*, 9). Klein-Braslavy concurs with those who see Maimonides' self-defined task as a bridging. In the context of the passage we are reading, which seems to warn against the dangers of consensual understanding, it is interesting that she goes on to describe this bridging activity as canceling this very gap, since there would be, according to Maimonides, a "perfect fit, *hatʾama gmura*" between philosophy and law (ibid., 10). The consensus would be total, and it would further have inscribed itself even in the other perfect fit that Simon Rawidowitz sees between literary form and philosophical content, between interpretation and philosophical exposition (Rawidowitz, "The Question"). There are no gaping or disjunctive holes. Yet, doesn't one still need to account for the wide divergence of interpretations in terms of the singular experience of language that the *dalāla* constitutes, in terms of the very gaps and gulfs it itself opens? What of the "concretization" of the text's theories and doctrines and its resistance to consensual interpretation?

79. Consider the effects of such a drive to resolution, to a covering and covering up of the gulf, on the following assertion: "And, of course, Maimonides' *Guide* is written for R. Joseph (and those like him) in order to lead him out of his perplexity. . . . [W]e need merely reiterate that the *Guide* itself is framed as an attempt to resolve the perplexity" (Frank, "The Elimination of Perplexity," 121). A not dissimilar distancing is at work in Hannah Kasher's argument for a general following of meaning and intention, as it must have been for Maimonides the author, in opposition to specific and over-interpretive faithfulness to the letter of his text into which "mistakes" may after all have fallen: "Detailed analysis may restore the crown [of Maimonides] to its proper place and bring about an over-interpretation, *havharat yeter*, of his doctrine's meaning" (Kasher, "The Guide of the Perplexed," 82; on intention and mastery of language, see p. 81). Interestingly enough, the alternative between reading the *Guide* as literary masterpiece or as holy script, as Kasher puts it, is also reader-based rather than text-based. Who the "radical modern interpreters" (81) are who read the *dalāla* as holy writ Kasher does not say. What is clear though is that their existence as an alternative does open yet another gulf, *paʿar*, which, here too, must be closed (75). One final note on the distancing between the textual difficulties and their localization in some distant reader or translator. Discussing the difficulties of figuring out figurative language, Joseph P. Cohen, who never once mentions the Arabic text, offers yet another systematic resolution of said difficulties. What is the source of the problem then? It is an external, perhaps even accidental, fault that has nothing to do with the "original": "Translators of Maimonides have unfortunately not found a standard set of terms to translate the logical or semantic terms [Maimonides] uses" (J. P. Cohen, "Figurative Language," 394n4).

80. On Strauss's early notion of nature as social nature, see Strauss, "Notes," esp. 89, where Strauss writes that "man is by his nature an *animal sociale*, the human nature on which culture is based is the natural social relations of men, that is,

the way in which man, prior to all culture, behaves toward other men." According to Martin Yaffe, it is this early discussion of Schmitt by Strauss that led to his turn to Maimonides and to the notion of "a higher, supramoral or suprapolitical authority" that could mediate and adjudicate social and political relations (M. Yaffe, "Autonomy, Community"). In the context of the "law of genre," it is interesting to note that Strauss approves of Schmitt's contribution as a renewed interrogation of the question of the political as the "genus question." The question of genre and of genus seem to have remained anthropological for Strauss, therefore, even anthropocentric. This is a clear point of disagreement not only with Benjamin ("It should be pointed out that certain correlative concepts retain their meaning, and possibly their foremost one, when they are not referred exclusively to man, *wenn sie nicht von vorne herrein ausschließlich auf den Menschen bezogen werden*" [Benjamin, "The Task of the Translator," 70]), but also, even if in different ways, with Maimonides.

81. Derrida, "Signature, événement, contexte," 381/E320. Jean-Luc Nancy makes what I take as a similar point when he discusses the passage from "a regime of interrogating principles" to the "establishment of principles," rather than preserving the incommensurability of one and the other and denying the *partage* constitutive of both and to which both are exposed (Nancy, *L'Expérience de la liberté*, 215). See also Tom Cohen's remark on the "social" in *Anti-Mimesis*, esp. chap. 1.

82. Derrida, "Signature, événement, contexte," 393/E330.

83. Aside from Strauss on Maimonides on sociality and the *polis*, see Kraemer, "Maimonides on the Philosophic Sciences," in *Perspectives on Maimonides*; his "Alfarabi's *Opinions of the Virtuous City*"; and "On Maimonides' Messianic Posture"; and see also Goetschel and Sirat, "Maimonide, la politique, le politique," in *Délivrance et fidélité*; and Funkenstein, *Perceptions*, esp. chap. 5.

84. Butler, *Excitable Speech*, 153.

85. The quote is from Fynsk, *Heidegger*, 194.

86. Ronell, *The Telephone Book*, 87.

87. As Philippe Lacoue-Labarthe and Jean-Luc Nancy remind their readers in "Le Dialogue des genres," the etymology of the Greek word *dialogos* has nothing to do with duality and everything to do with a notion of a passage, a crossing, a going *through* (*dia*); see also Guellouz, *Le Dialogue*, 79.

88. There is a striking tone of assurance in that moment of Strauss's argument, who had earlier asserted that the *Guide* is not a book at all, and now writes that it is a book after all. Not only that, it is one that is absolutely determined both in terms of its author and in terms of its readers. Hence, Strauss writes, "it is not a philosopher's book . . . but a Jewish book: a book written by a Jew for Jews" (Strauss, "How to Begin," xiv). As I have already suggested, such an assertion restricts and even reduces the complexities of the text and of reading by refusing to take into consideration the text's constitutive, necessary possibilities of "Arabs" (over)hearing, as it is articulated at least in the passage under discussion in this chapter.

89. Exodus, 14:3. This suggestive translation is from *The Jerusalem Bible*. See

also ad loc commentaries by Rashi and Ibn ᶜEzra. And see Faur, *Golden Doves*, which says that "ḥaira is the specific function of the Desert" (75).

90. In my attention to the title of Maimonides' book, which to some extent may be said to be the only text I am trying to read throughout this chapter, I have found most helpful Paul de Man's remarks on Keat's *Fall of Hyperion*, most relevantly de Man's assertion that (at least) two "readings are grammatically correct, but it is impossible to decide from the context (the ensuing narrative) which version is the right one." De Man also refers to the "impossibility" for the author "as for us, of reading his own title." De Man continues and writes that "it matters a great deal how we read the title, as an exercise not only in semantics, but in what the text actually does to us" (de Man, "The Resistance to Theory," in *The Resistance to Theory*, 16). Consider also Derrida, "Titre à préciser," in *Parages*, and Ronell's discussion of the title in *Finitude's Score*, 7–8.

91. Faur, *Golden Doves*, 74. I am indebted to José Faur for having so suggestively opened the question of the *dalāla*, the figuring out of which was so close to complete, it would in all likelihood have become invisible (and see also Faur's more recent *Homo Mysticus*). One should mention however, as Faur does, the short discussion by Salomon Munk about the problems of the title's translation (though Munk, oddly enough, addresses mostly the difficulties associated with *ḥaira* rather than with *dalāla*, ["Note sur le titre"], as well as Avner Giladi's "Note About the Possible Origin." I should say that there are other very important discussions of language in Maimonides that have been very helpful to me. Aside from those already referred to in these notes, I have found most helpful Blumenthal, "Maimonides on Mind and Metaphoric Language"; Hyman, "Maimonides on Religious Language," in *Perspectives on Maimonides*, ed. Kraemer; and J. Stern, "Logical Syntax."

92. In attending to the word *dalāla*, I also attempt to abide to Joel Kraemer's injunction regarding the attention that is required by the chain of citations at work in Maimonides' use of language (Kraemer, "Sharīᶜa and Nāmūs"). Aside from the meaning "signification," with which Pines translates *dalāla* in the passage I have been trying to read throughout this chapter, on *dalāla* as "significance," see Faur, *Golden Doves*, 173n66, and see references there; as "signification, indication du sens d'un mot, référence à l'idée qu'il représente," in Ibn Sīnā, for example, see Goichon, *Lexique de la langue philosophique d'Ibn Sīnā*, 125ff. And see also Abed, *Aristotelian Logic*, who reports that Alfārābī "flatly declares . . . that he is concerned with references, *dalālāt* and meanings, *maᶜānī*" (1); Lane, *An Arabic-English Lexicon*, under art. *dalla*, has, for *dalāla*, "signification, or indication of meaning," as well as "direction, right direction, or guidance." More directly related to logic, Josef van Ess explains that *dalāla* is a "proof in the sense of a scheme and a structure" and he claims that its "original" meaning is "demonstrative force of a sign," as when smoke is a sign that there is fire (the example is Sextus Empiricus's, which van Ess invokes connecting between derivatives of *dalla* and Stoic logic). Whether smoke reveals or hides may have to be asked, however (van Ess, "The Logical

Structure," esp. 26n25 and 27). For Al-Ghazālī, *dalāla* also means "argument" (see Jabre, *Essai sur le lexique de Ghazali*, 91). The root verb *dalla* generally means "to indicate," that is, to refer, but also to signify; in the *Guide* itself, it seems to me important not to miss or dismiss these meanings. Hence, Maimonides writes that "when we wish to indicate, *ad-dalāla*, that the deity is not many [we say] that He is one" (*Guide*, I: 57, 133). He also writes of divine names as having many meanings ("indicative of several notions, *maᶜna*"), or as having only one meaning ("being indicative of one notion only") (*Guide*, I: 62, 151). In case this does not provide enough of a range of both matter and spirit that may be referred to by *dalāla*, Maimonides also writes of the articulated name as giving "a clear unequivocal indication, *dalāla*, of His essence" (*Guide*, I: 61, 147), implying that a *dalāla* is not always clear and unequivocal. What should be clear, though, is that this dissemination of *dalla* (it serves for sign, proof, and demonstration, *dalīl*, as well as for reasoning and argumentation, *tadlīl*) also exceeds polysemy, and that its occasional univocality does not diminish the range of problems it produces. Needless to say, the word *iršād* (guidance), to which Strauss ascribes particular significance ("Literary Character," 87 and 87n144) is used quite often by Maimonides, and would have offered itself much more readily if all that was needed was, in fact, a *guide*. Guidance does appear as much straightforward if, at times, also as less reliable in its results: "there is an immense difference between guidance, *iršād*, leading to a knowledge of the existence of a thing and an investigation of the true reality of the essence and substance of that thing" (*Guide*, I: 46, 97). That the root *r-š-d*, one which Maimonides uses profusely in the *dalāla* and a prominent one in Arabic, in proper names or common references to the "guided Caliphs," for example, would not have been more immediately available to Maimonides in the context of Islamic culture, is difficult if not impossible to entertain.

93. *Guide*, 6.

94. *Guide*, 11. This "nothing" is not nothing enough, insofar as it "conceals, *ḫafiya*" and is multiplied into another *maṯal* of sort, a comparison, *tašbīh*, with the darkness of the night that forbids the finding of the proverbial pearl. Nothing functions, therefore, with peculiar force. In other words, nothing matters (see Faur's discussion of negativity in Maimonides in *Golden Doves*, 59–83). Incidentally, and for reasons that are not clear to me, the word *klum*, written in Hebrew rather than in Arabic, remains therefore marked as a citation in the *dalāla*. Maimonides had quoted it from the midrash, commenting that it is "literally what they say, *haḏa naṣuhum*, this is their text" (Munk translates "telles sont les paroles textuelles"). It seems therefore that *klum* remains a text, and therefore something to be pondered over and read.

95. Warminski, "Reading for Example," in *Readings in Interpretation*, 173.

96. *Guide*, 5.

97. Ronell, "Support Our Tropes: Reading Desert Storm," in *Finitude's Score*, 284.

98. On this expression, see Fynsk, *Language and Relation.*

99. J. Stern, "Logical Syntax," 145. For a more extended discussion of matter in Maimonides, see Jerome Gellman, who underscores Maimonides' relation to Galen, as well as the pervasiveness of matter related "problems." Gellman puts it suggestively when he writes that the matter of any individual "be such as to resist by its very nature the embodiment of the species-form in question in it" (Gellman, "Maimonides' 'Ravings,'" 313). For a very different reading of matter in Maimonides, one that focuses on the negativity of his views, see D. Boyarin, *Carnal Israel,* 57–60. However, as Boyarin himself puts it, it may be useful here too to "carefully tease out from these texts the different strands of discourse and counter-discourse which they preserve and suppress and sometimes preserve by suppressing—complicating our reading of ancient ideology and not simplifying it" (195).

100. *Guide,* III: 9, 436.

101. Ibid., 7.

102. Funkenstein, "Maimonides: Political Theory and Realistic Messianism," in *Perceptions,* 138–39. It should be noted that Josef Stern would seem to disagree with this interpretation of generalized indeterminacy in Maimonides ("The Idea of a Ḥoq," see esp. 102). In his argument about Law in Maimonides, Stern claims in fact that indeterminacy is restricted to an epistemological position rather than to an ontological one. It is not clear what status language and history have in this dichotomy for Stern. But be that as it may, there now seems to emerge yet another gulf, which generates, indeed, "considerable tension" (130n38). Lenn E. Goodman, on the other hand, presents a different argument that confirms Funkenstein's, if from a different perspective. Taking into account that the language of the *dalāla* takes place also as matter, Goodman's argument about the "finitude" of matter and form is very compelling (Goodman, "Matter and Form," 87). Goodman succinctly summarizes in words that converge significantly with what I am trying to show: "Matter is not a positive reality whose existence expresses a specific perfection; if it were, it would be a form. Rather it is that residuum of otherness not reducible to the categories of human intelligence, rational explanation, or purpose, but without which there could be no particularity" (94).

103. On relation, relating, and narrating, see Derrida, *Monolingualism of the Other,* 19.

104. See Shlomo Pines's comment, quoted in epigraph at the beginning of this chapter, but see also the heated debate over the "literary character of the *Guide,*" as it resonates, for example, in the bibliographic sources I have been addressing in the notes (see also, Warren Zev Harvey, "Why Maimonides Was Not a *Mutakallim,*" in *Perspectives on Maimonides,* ed. Kraemer, esp. 109–11).

105. Kraemer, "Maimonides on the Philosophic Sciences," in *Perspectives on Maimonides,* 102.

106. "*Genos* indicates, therefore, the place" (Derrida, "La Loi du genre," 259).

107. Strauss, "Literary Character," 48; my emphasis.

108. D. Boyarin, *Intertextuality*, 1.

109. Aside from Boyarin, there are only few cursory discussions of Maimonides' position on midrash apropos the peculiar passage that interests me here. Among them are: I. Heinemann, *Darkhe haᵓaggadah*, and Fraenkel, *Darkhe ha-Aggadah veha-Midrash*. Fraenkel also refers to Rabbi Avraham ben ha-Rambam, who reiterates this reference to poetics in midrash (see "Maᵓamar ᶜal ᵓodot derashot ḥazal," in Rabbi Avraham's *Milḥamot ha-shem*, esp. 91). Additional, if less direct, bibliographic references are provided below.

110. D. Boyarin, *Intertextuality*, 3.

111. As far as I could determine, this expression occurs one other time in the *Guide*, thus falling short of a *hápax legómenon*. It is important to note that Pines translated it in significantly different ways. In the context of a discussion of astronomy and an instance of a "true perplexity" that he does not claim to have solved, Maimonides offers a paraphrase for this avowed limitation of man's knowledge of the heavens, namely a verse from Psalms 115:16. Maimonides introduces this paraphrase, he says, "according to the way of *an-nawādir aš-šiᶜrīya*," which Pines translates, this time, as "poetical preciousness" (*Guide*, II: 24, 326; this is not said, of course, to diminish the value of Pines's translation on the whole, though it is interesting to note that this particular lack of consistency around the *nawādir* does seem to parallel the [necessary?] inconsistency of the translation of *dalāla*. Significantly enough, these specific problems were noted in neither praises nor reservations as formulated by Marvin Fox [*Interpreting Maimonides*, 47ff.]). Munk here translates *locution poétique*, and al-Ḥarizi has *melitsat ha-shirot*, whereas Ibn Tibbon is the only one who remains consistent with *melitsat ha-shir* in both cases. The word *nawādir* is the plural of *nādira*, which Mansour Ajami translates as "bon mot" or "witticism" (see Ajami, *The Neckveins of Winter*, 51; and see also Ajami's *The Alchemy of Glory*, 32). Joel Kraemer suggested "aphorisms" or simply "sayings" (personal communication, 18 May 1997), and Dimitri Gutas translates Ḥunayn ibn Isḥāq's *Nawādir al-falāsifa* as "Anecdotes of the Philosophers" (Gutas, *Greek Wisdom Literature*, 38). The expression *nawādir šiᶜrīya* appears in al-Jāḥiẓ, *Al-Bayān wa-l-tabīyn*. It is translated by van Gelder as "epigrams" (*Beyond the Line*, 40). It does not seem to have had a more specific, technical meaning. It will be important to note, for what follows, that the term *mashal*, used here by Yehuda al-Ḥarizi in his translation, is also the term with which he himself introduces *poems* in between the rhymed prose of his *maqāmāt*, in his *Taḥkemoni* (incidentally, al-Ḥarizi had translated Ḥunayn's *Nawādir* with the Hebrew *musarim* rather than *meshalim* in his *Sefer muserei ha-filosofim*). This recurring expression, also found in other medieval rhymed prose narratives, is *venassa meshalo*. Philosophy, translated, becomes literature.

112. *Guide*, III: 43, 573. Another expression used by Maimonides in the same passage is "poetical comparisons [*tamṯīlāt šiᶜrīya*; also, as Munk renders it, *allégories poétiques*]" in which we find the root *m-ṯ-l* (found in *maṯal*) again. However,

as Maimonidean allegories and allegoresis have been discussed over and over, it is the other poetical concepts, in fact, the poetical analogy in general, which he invokes here that seems to me of most interest. It should however be noted that, at the time Maimonides writes, *tamṯīl* was already a well-established term in Arabic literary criticism. It was, for example, at the center of al-Jurjānī's poetics, as Kamal Abu Deeb shows (Abu Deeb, *Al-Jurjānī's Theory*).

113. I thank Joel Kraemer for referring me to his discussion of this intertext; see his "Maimonides on the Philosophic Sciences," in *Perspectives on Maimonides*, and see also Kraemer's detailed discussion in "The Influence of Islamic Law." Al-Fārābī is the Aristotelian whom Maimonides, in the context discussed by Kraemer, quotes quite often (see also Kraemer's "Sharīᶜa and Nāmūs," 194n25). Maimonides went so far as to recommend to his translator Samuel ibn Tibbon to only read al-Fārābī in matters of logic. The possibility of classifying a particular form of discourse as "poetical" (rather than demonstrative, dialectical, sophistic, or rhetorical) is sustained by the cognitive classification that al-Fārābī develops in his *Introductory Treatise on Logic*; see also Black, *Logic and Aristotle's Rhetoric*. A later and important chain of translations of Aristotle and al-Fārābī in Arab Jewish and Sephardi Talmudic readings has been followed by Daniel Boyarin in his *Sephardi Speculation*.

114. Maimonides, *Introduction to the Mishna*, 54; see also Braude, "Maimonides' Attitude to Midrash," 81. Whether there is here an additional instance of what Shlomo Pines called "the limitations of human knowledge" is perhaps debatable, since the issue here is not necessarily governed by divine intent (Ar. *taᶜlīl*). Some kind of limitation, however, is clearly expressed (see following note).

115. That Maimonides held to a finite notion of understanding and knowledge is, of course, beyond doubt. See Shlomo Pines's discussion in "The Limitations of Human Knowledge" and see also J. Stern, "The Idea of a *Ḥoq*."

116. Quoted in D. Boyarin, *Intertextuality*, 3.

117. Weber, *Mass Mediauras*, 2.

118. Qudāma ibn Jaᶜfar, quoted in Scheindlin, "Rabbi Moshe ibn ᶜEzra," 114n2; and see also Yosef Tobi, "Aristotle's *Poetics*."

119. Leupin, *Fiction et incarnation*, 11. On the "epistemological rupture," see É. Balibar, "Le Concept de 'coupure épistémologique.'"

120. Mishnah, tractate Avot, 1:17.

121. It is to be noted that some scholars have emphasized the expansiveness with which Maimonides addresses this passage, multiplying words whereas he would usually be quite brief (see Monroe, and Kraemer, next note). As an experience of language, this text too would be asking its readers to linger with (its) language, to remain at "its place."

122. Maimonides, *Commentary on Mishna Avot, ad loc.*, translation (slightly altered here) by Norman Roth in his *Maimonides*, 53. Note that Maimonides applies to language the fivefold division of the Muslim law regarding actions. On this and other dimensions of this passage, see the discussions by Kraemer, "On Maimonides'

Messianic Posture" (132–33), and his "The Influence of Islamic Law" (232ff); and see also Monroe, "Maimonides on the Mozarabic Lyric."

123. Kozodoy, "Reading Medieval Hebrew Love Poetry," 111.

124. The third category includes "the majority of stories, *muᶜaẓam aḥādīṯ*, of people on what happened and what was, and how a certain king behaves in his palace, and what the cause of the death of so-and-so or the wealth of so-and-so" (Roth, *Maimonides*, 53). Under the generic "stories," Maimonides clearly includes history as well. However, this hardly seems exclusive of other kinds of narratives, since such "stories" could just as easily include fictional narratives. This is important to note because the Hebrew translation of M. D. Rabinowitz has *sipurim* also in the fourth category, but neither *aḥādīṯ* nor any apparent equivalent is used there. There is no reason to gloss over this semantic difference between the two categories. Roth, rather than doubling "stories," offers "prose and poetry" in the fourth category. I return to this expression below. For now it is sufficient to note that "stories" are not, or not exclusively, what Maimonides will speak about in the remainder of this passage.

125. Ibid.

126. Roth, following Baneth's Hebrew (*divrei mashal u- melitza*), offers a translation of the Arabic *ḫuṭab wa-l-ašᶜār* as "prose and poetry" (usually rendered *naẓm wa-naṯr*). *Ḫuṭab*, however, is, like the word *ašᶜār*, in the plural form. It is the plural of *ḫuṭba*, one important meaning of which is, in fact, sermons. Rhymed prose (more often called *sajᶜ*) is another of the meanings of the word *ḫuṭba*. The functional conflation of sermons and poetry here may perhaps explain why, in the *dalāla*, Maimonides can associate midrash with poetry. Functionally, for him, the two (or three) forms of speech are in fact analogous. As he puts it in the *dalāla*, in terms very similar to what we find here, the words of midrash "instill a noble moral quality" (III, 43). It is important, here too, to note the different readings of Maimonides and of Moses Ibn ᶜEzra. For Ibn ᶜEzra, rhetoricians and preachers [Ar. *al- bulaġāʾ wa-l-ḫuṭabāʾ*; Heb. *ha-melitzim veha-darshanim*] produce words that are of equal truth/fiction value (Maimonides' third category) (Ibn ᶜEzra, *Kitāb al-muḥaḏāra wa-l-muḏākara*, 118–19). For Maimonides, as we read here, they belong to the fourth category and have more (at least ethical) value than simply fictional stories. Needless to say, of course, there is nothing quite revolutionary in the assertion that *derashot* or midrash are sermons. The orality of the chain of tradition was inscribed in its very name—the oral Torah—and there is no reason to doubt that midrash was well known for having been, even if only partly, part of the "aggadic tradition [which] was transmitted chiefly by word of mouth, that is, by being related orally in the public sermon" (J. Heinemann, "The Nature of the Aggadah," 42).

127. Naḥmanides in *Otsar ha-vikuḥim*, 89; trans. [slightly altered here] in Chazan, *Barcelona and Beyond*, 149.

128. The connections between Maimonides and Naḥmanides, most particu-

larly on the status of aggadah, were recognized however, if not so much in the terms I am phrasing them. Most particularly, they were noted in M. Auerbach, "Die Ansichten des Maimonides und des Nachmanides"; Angel and Salomon, "Naḥmanides' Approach," esp. 43; and see also Fox, "Naḥmanides on the Status of Aggadot." Henri Atlan's discussion of the different kinds of "reasons" at work between Maimonides and Naḥmanides are also instructive (Atlan, "Mystique et rationalité autour de Maimonide," in *The Thought of Moses Maimonides*, ed. Robinson et al.). The connection of Naḥmanides to Andalusian culture is discussed most extensively in Septimus, "'Open Rebuke and Concealed Love,'" which also touches on the connection with Maimonides (see 22–24 and notes). My interest in philological demonstrations does not extend to the possibility of "proving" whether Naḥmanides could or could not have read Maimonides in the Arabic original (though the question has been interestingly discussed in Jospe, "Naḥmanides and Arabic"). An approach that differs from the philological and "influential" model regarding the question of cultural transmission, if transmission was in fact needed, is explored in Amos Funkenstein's *Perceptions*; most directly for what concerns me here, see his "History and Typology: Nachmanides' Reading of the Biblical Narrative," 98–121. One should also read Nina Caputo, "And God Rested," which offers a new synthesis of the debate around Naḥmanides; and see also Elliot R. Wolfson's illuminating discussion in "'By Way of Truth': Aspects of Naḥmanides' Kabbalistic Hermeneutic." Wolfson discusses Funkenstein (110ff.) and the relation of Naḥmanides to Maimonides (118n45), and his rapport to aggadah (173 ff.). More recently, Josef Stern also discussed aspects of the relations and translations between Maimonides and Naḥmanides in his "The Fall and Rise of Myth in Ritual," 225ff. (see now Stern's extensive book on the subject of this connection between the two writers, *Problems and Parables*).

129. There is no need to see Naḥmanides' classification as original, of course. In the context of discussing, and accessorily of beginning to diminish the value of aggadah, Hai Gaon had already insisted on the difference between the Talmud and the rest (i.e., midrash, etc.): "everything written in the Talmud is more correct than what is not included in it" (quoted in Saperstein, *Decoding the Rabbis*, 9; see also Goldin, "Freedom and Restraint," and Fraenkel, *Darkhei ha-Aggadah veha-Midrash*, 501). It is with the content and the governing principles of the classification that I am concerned, rather than with the classification itself.

130. This is also not an original contribution of Naḥmanides, since the question of belief, or trust, had surrounded the status of aggadic discourse since the Talmud period, and came to play a prominent role in Gaonic discussions of Aggada (see Goldin, "Freedom and Restraint"). Yet, the historical conflation of Naḥmanides' reiteration of the centrality of belief with Maimonides' work is what I claim produced a difference.

131. Ibn ᶜEzra, *Kitāb al-muḥaḍāra wa-l-muḏākara*, 116–19.

132. Fox, "Naḥmanides on the Status of Aggadot," 99.

133. See Derrida's comments on a mark "engendering" its context, as well as the important qualifications he provides to these comments in *Limited Inc.*, 79. This "outside" is therefore not to be taken as the object of a reference; rather, as Jean-Luc Nancy puts it, it is "exscribed within the text."

134. See Samuel Weber's "Genealogy of Modernity," esp. 472.

135. "Com-parution" is a term elaborated by Jean-Luc Nancy in his work, most notably *La Communauté désœuvrée*, and *La comparution.*

CHAPTER 2: "Our Place in al-Andalus"

1. Heidegger, "The End of Philosophy," 375.

2. Baer, *History of the Jews*, 1: 60.

3. Ibn ᶜEzra, *Dīwān*, no. 262; trans., slightly altered here, in Baer, *History of the Jews*, 61. This is from a Hebrew letter written by Ibn ᶜEzra in rhymed prose.

4. Brann, *The Compunctious Poet*, 62.

5. It is the very "style" of the Andalusī writers that allows for a description of their words as already translated. In his letter, as in his poems and other writings, Ibn ᶜEzra inserts biblical quotations that are thus de- and re-contextualized, translated, then, in the etymological sense (see also the medieval Hebrew: *haᶜtaqa*, taking from one place to another, translation). As T. Carmi describes this style, it consists of "an adroit and fluent weaving together of biblical quotations, from a short phrase to an entire verse. The quotation could be verbatim, slightly altered, or elliptical; it could create a broad spectrum of effects by assuming an altogether different, and even contradictory, meaning in its new setting." (Carmi, introduction to *Penguin Book of Hebrew Verse*, 27). The displacing difficulty created by this style (also used in exegetical texts) can be illustrated by the uncertainty of a scholar commenting on that other Andalusī writer, Naḥmanides, that "the reader is *perhaps* expected to remember" a previous interpretation (Septimus, "'Open Rebuke and Concealed Love,'" 26; my emphasis). Nonetheless, by way of this uncertain allusion, the text "elegantly constitutes its own prooftext" (ibid.; see also n50, where Septimus provides more references on the "mosaic style" of Andalusī writers).

6. Drory, "Literary Contacts," 283.

7. Blau, "'At Our Place in al-Andalus.'" See also the extended discussion of Maimonides' relationship to al-Andalus, in Blau's "Maimonides, Al-Andalus, and the Influence of the Spanish-Arabic Dialect on His Language."

8. See Hegel's famous discussion of deictics ("this, here, now") in the "Sense-Certainty" section of the *Phenomenology of Spirit*, 58–66.

9. De Man, "Semiology and Rhetoric," in *Allegories of Reading*, 5.

10. As pointed out in the previous chapter, I borrow this phrase from Ronell's *The Telephone Book*, 87.

11. Montrose, "Professing the Renaissance," 30. For Montrose, "not only the poet but also the critic," texts, practices, and students exist "*in* history," indeed,

"they themselves live in history, and . . . they *live* history" (25). That there is no "outside" is perhaps to be taken for granted, but whether the only place is "history," or an all-encompassing context (that may be dynamically, and even "dialectically," defined—"the dialectic between the text and the world" (24)—is the question I wish to raise. This question also applies to the "prior historical or ideological subtext" described by Fredric Jameson, one that "must itself always be (re)constructed after the fact" and which enables the literary or aesthetic act's "active relationship with the Real," if only because it is "doing something to the world" (Jameson, *The Political Unconscious*, 81). History—"the world"—remains the only determining context, the only place for language.

12. Hall, "Cultural Studies," 284.

13. Funkenstein, *Theology and the Scientific Imagination*, 206.

14. Said, "The Text, the World, the Critic," 170. For Said, texts are "beings in the world" that bear analogy with "a talking voice addressing someone" (163). Although he also suggests that this is a skewed perspective, which may be rectified by bringing "style" ("the result of some immediate contact between author and medium") into the picture, Said maintains that the mode of being of the written text is "silent": "Considered as I have been considering it, style neutralizes, if it does not cancel, the worldlessness, the silent, seemingly uncircumstanced existence of a solitary text" (163). This would suggest that "being in the world" is only one of the modes of "being" of the text. Rather than considering these other modes, however, Said—who is careful to assert that he opposes "any reduction of a text to its circumstances"—nonetheless conceives of the "solitary text" as "self-sufficient." He therefore rejects what he sees as the only alternative to such "reductions" and declares himself "not entirely satisfied with the idea of a self-sufficient text. Is the alternative to the various fallacies *only* a quite hermetic cosmos whose significant dimension of meaning is . . . a wholly inward one?" (166). As much as he opposes the dichotomy, Said nonetheless maintains it by refraining from considering the modes of "being" of the text that would be neither "self-sufficient" nor simply "placing" it(self) in "the world." Texts, Said writes, "*place* themselves—that is, one of their functions as texts is to place themselves—and they *are* themselves by acting, in the world" (171). Here too, however, this suggests that "placing," much like "being," can be considered a function that has different modes. It becomes possible to speak, alongside Foucault's "author-function," about the "placing-function" or "context-function" of the text (see next note).

15. Recall that Foucault describes how the "disappearance of the author" enables locating the author-function. It becomes possible, Foucault writes, to "locate the space left empty by the author's disappearance, follow the distribution of gaps and breaches, and watch for the openings that this disappearance uncovers" (Foucault, "What Is an Author," 105). As Foucault makes clear in the discussion that followed his lecture (reprinted in Foucault's *Dits et écrits*), to assert the disappearance, even the "death," of the author, does not amount to saying that the author

doesn't exist. Similarly, to question the "worldliness" of the text does not amount to an aesthetic "cutting off" or denial of the world, of the context, but to a rethinking of its (and the text's) modes of existence. I thank Jay Fisher for pointing out the relevance of Foucault's argument here.

16. Derrida, "Limited Inc. a b c . . . ," in *Limited Inc.*, 78.

17. Nägele, *Echoes of Translation*, 12.

18. Ibid., 12–13.

19. See Thomas F. Glick's concise but compelling discussion "A Question of Names," in his *Islamic and Christian Spain*, 13–15.

20. Chétrit, "Le Judéo-arabe," 710. For a more extended study of Judeo-Arabic see Hary, *Multiglossia in Judeo-Arabic*, and see bibliographies in both Chétrit and Hary. The academic study of Judeo-Arabic relies most heavily on the extensive work of Joshua Blau.

21. Having noted that the resemblance between Hebrew and Arabic letters is striking in manuscripts written in an Arabic cultural sphere, Colette Sirat adds that "*il est remarquable qu'en Espagne chrétienne, l'influence du style arabe, bien loin de s'effacer, se poursuit jusqu'au XVe siècle*, it is remarkable that in Christian Spain, the influence of the Arabic style, far from diminishing, continues until the fifteenth century" (Sirat, *Écriture et civilisations*, 12).

22. On the different languages and dialects of al-Andalus, and the difficulties they raise, see David J. Wasserstein's informative "The Language Situation in al-Andalus."

23. L. Harvey, *Islamic Spain*, 84; and see also Hegyi, "Minority and Restricted Uses." For a detailed study of *aljamiado*, see Wiegers, *Islamic Literature in Spanish and Aljamiado*.

24. Leonard Harvey quotes Ice de Gebir as referring to Spanish with the term *aljamía* (L. Harvey, *Islamic Spain*, 81; on the use of the word *ʿajamī* as an equivalent to *laṭīnī*, Latin or Romance, see also Wasserstein, "The Language Situation," 7ff., and see Monroe, "Maimonides on the Mozarabic Lyric." This is something that will be of considerable importance for my argument in the final chapter.

25. The *muwaššaḥa*, or "girdle song," is one of two "Andalusī innovations" (the other being the *zajal*) which have been described as "sister genres." James Monroe explains that "both forms are strophic, and both are closely related in structure. Second, both incorporate elements of vernacular diction to a varying degree. Third, both exhibit puzzling departures from the rules of classical Arabic metrics" (Monroe, "*Zajal* and *Muwaššaḥa*," 404). Monroe adds that whereas the *zajal* is "composed entirely in the vernacular Arabic dialect of al-Andalus, occasionally besprinkled with words or phrases in Hispano-Romance," the *muwaššaḥa* is written "in classical Arabic, with the exception of its final element [the *ḫarja*], which is normally in vernacular diction, either Arabic, Romance, or a combination of both" (ibid.). Hebrew versions of *muwaššaḥāt* reproduce most of these patterns, adding the Hebrew language to an already complicated linguistic and prosodic situation

that has yet to be "resolved." The dispute over alternate solutions and over the origins of the *muwaššaḥa* may therefore be less about origins than about the attempt to circumvent what Susan Einbinder described as the *muwaššaḥa*'s "most fascinating and portentous aspects," namely, its

> refusal to comply with historically delimited categories of knowledge, genre and "reading." A kind of platypus of poetry, the muwashshaḥ deserves the integrated efforts of interdisciplinary analysis. The question is less that of the disputed primacy of chicken or egg than that it is such a platypus laying them, whose properly situated place in the history of the European lyric, in the history of Arabic verse, and in the specific history of Hebrew literature, may shed light on them all. (Einbinder, "The Current Debate on the Muwashshaḥ," 174)

The *muwaššaḥa* as a linguistic (but also prosodic, critical, cultural, etc.) problem, as a linguistic event that raises the question of place to a level unheard of, is one of the major occurrences of al-Andalus as I seek to address it. However, its better known singularity should not obscure the ways in which there are other occurrences partaking of language at and as "our place in al-Andalus."

26. Although the Talmud and the Midrashim that constitute Rabbinic literature have come to hold a prominent place in the Jewish tradition, they never became holy or sacred. There is no "Holy Talmud." Only the Hebrew Bible and the *Zohar* have achieved such status. This, however, did not necessarily increase their legal, prescriptive value.

27. It is important in what follows to make a clear distinction between "Jewish mysticism" and the *Zohar*. Although the *Zohar* is the central text of the Kabbalah and of what continues to be called "the Jewish mystical tradition," I will have only very little to say about either of these two categories. Historically speaking, the term "Kabbalah" was used by those who saw themselves as part of the tradition. Jewish mysticism, on the other hand, is a recent term, and it is part of a discourse, mostly but not only academic, that constitutes kabbalistic texts and others as its objects while conducting on them a specific translation. Jewish mysticism is also a discourse and an event of language, one that I address in its specificity in the next chapter and elsewhere. Jewish mysticism and the *Zohar* are not completely independent from each other, of course, but they have a relative autonomy that makes it possible to speak of one without the other.

28. This is also the case in one area that I will not explore here, namely the parallel yet very different discussions of imagination that follow al-Andalus and that are considered by Giorgio Agamben, in *Stanzas* (I return to Agamben's work in more details below), and by Elliot R. Wolfson, in *Through a Speculum.*

29. Scholem, "The Name of God," 62.

30. For accounts of the operation of these two disciplinary fields (using history in a wide sense, that mostly includes, but is not exclusively limited to, the history

of ideas) in Kabbalah studies as they enable and limit inquiry, one should consult Moshe Idel's *Kabbalah: New Perspectives* and Idel's argument against history in his "Mystique juive et histoire juive." In this article, Idel calls for a certain evacuation of history, an evacuation the structure of which is not unsimilar to the translations that concern me in this study. Arguably, this evacuation of history determines even more the approach that Idel advocates as historical. See also Tirosh-Rothschild, "Continuity and Revision," and Liebes, "New Directions." On the "experiential" front, the importance of Mircea Eliade and Carl Jung, prominent as they are in religious studies, is well established in Kabbalah studies, even if not always acknowledged, and this importance, which has yet to be critically evaluated, has quite a lot to do with the continued focus on "psychological" rather than linguistic, literary, and/or rhetorical dimensions of the texts. As to the importance of language, a recent issue of the *Revue de l'histoire des religions*, vols. 213–14 (1996), is entirely devoted to the question of language in Kabbalah. I am therefore not denying that language occupies a central place, but I am interrogating the very construction of that place, the experience of language that is implied by this construction. Notable exceptions, if only in the distinctiveness of their attitude to language, in the field of Jewish mysticism are Janowitz, *The Poetics of Ascent*; Rojtman, *Feu noir sur feu blanc*; and Ouaknin, *Concerto pour quatre consonnes*. Ouaknin's proposal, in the early parts of the book, to read Kabbalah otherwise than mysticism, and his focusing less on ecstatic experiences and unification, and more on language and finitude, is quite noteworthy, but Ouaknin mostly stays away from the sephirotic Kabbalah, that is, from the *Zohar*, and he has little to say about languages other than Hebrew, and, occasionally, Aramaic.

31. Mopsik's text in "Notes complémentaires," which I will address here at some length, is probably the best introduction to the notion of *ein-sof*, a term that defies de-finition as should become clearer from what follows.

32. I return to the "silent voice" in the next chapter. In the meantime, on the *Zohar* attitude toward silence, see Liebes, "Zohar and Eros," 71–72.

33. In "Pensée, voix, et parole," and against his own description of a lack of one origin in the *Zohar* (discussed below), Mopsik refers to (one) "source silencieuse" of language, and also refers to "son point d'origine ineffable" (406)—regarding language then, for the *Zohar*, there would be one origin, one place at the end and beginning. Note that, as I will go on to show, this is precisely the logic that Mopsik has most convincingly shown *not* to be at work in the *Zohar*.

34. This gesture of translation parallels Mopsik's adoption of the phrase "profération de l'Ineffable," which Mopsik—not the *Zohar*—takes from John Scotus Erigena in order to illustrate the occurrence of language in the *Zohar*.

35. *Ein-sof* is said to be the name of some or even all *sephirot*. One source, however, may suggest that there are no "words" "at" *ein-sof*, which is the place, lodging (*tequ*; also: fastening) of all desires and thoughts, where "they do not stand with any word, *la qaiman be-mila klal*" (Margaliot, ed., *Sefer ha-Zohar* [henceforth,

Zohar], II: 244b). Whether this makes it "ineffable"—that is, beyond even the language of names, seems to me difficult to establish. At any rate, this is the only place where "words" are explicitly mentioned in an otherwise not rare naming and sets of sayings about *ein-sof.* That such saying has a familiar paradoxical form does not resolve the difficulty in any way.

36. Scholem, Idel, Mopsik, and others are quite clear on the fact that the language of Kabbalah is not simply "communicative language." They direct us, rather, toward its performative ("theurgic" and/or "talismanic") dimension (Scholem, "The Name of God"; Idel, "Reification of Language"; Mopsik, *Les Grands textes*). What I am trying to follow here is, however, something else than the performative/constative aspects of language.

37. See Giorgio Agamben's discussion of Benjamin in "Language and History," in *Potentialities.*

38. Agamben, *Language and Death*, 73.

39. Rojtman, *Feu noir sur feu blanc.* See also Rojtman's "Sacred Language and Open Text."

40. B. Rojtman, *Feu noir sur feu blanc*, 89/E68; and see also 97/E73.

41. Mopsik, "Notes complémentaires," 526.

42. Mopsik, "Pensée, voix, et parole," 396.

43. See de Man, *Aesthetic Ideology*; and see also T. Cohen, *Anti-Mimesis.*

44. Mopsik, *La Lettre sur la sainteté*, 16; see also Mopsik, "The Body of Engenderment."

45. In light of the "place" of *ein-sof* (which also helps "situate" the place of will and desire in the divine), it seems hardly necessary that the emphasis on the primacy of intention, and the entire notion of a mystical experience as a spiritual experience, would be somehow also dis-placed in its primacy, a primacy that is hardly asserted by the *Zohar* "itself" although most certainly by its modern readers.

46. Mopsik, "Notes complémentaires," 534.

47. Mopsik, "Avant-propos," 12.

48. Liebes, who sees his "primary role, *ᶜiqar tafqidi*," as the bringing about of an international recognition of the *Zohar* as literature (81), is often hailed as the path-breaking critic who has uncovered the importance of the literary dimension of the *Zohar*, and indeed, in this essay, he does much to question the notion that the literary form (what Liebes still calls, in order to counter its inscription—for it must still be countered—"the literary frame") is secondary to the "content" or to the "doctrine" (90). It is paradoxical then that the linguistic realm becomes, or remains, for Liebes, nonetheless derivative, as I try to show.

49. Hence Ecclesiastes' "vanities (*hevel*, also the vapor, the spirit that rises from the mouth)" or vain speech (Ecclesiates, 1:2) can be said by the *Zohar* to be the foundation upon which the world stands, even if "ironically" ("Zohar and Eros," 81).

50. Wolfson, "Beautiful Maiden," 172. The word *peshat* refers to one of the

four levels of interpretation; it usually translates "literal." On the irreparable (and its configurations in Kafka and others), see Agamben's *Coming Community* (esp. the appendix "The Irreparable").

51. Wolfson, "Erasing the Erasure," in *Circle in the Square*; and see also Wolfson's "Circumcision, Vision of God, and Textual Interpretation," in the same volume.

52. Wolfson, "Erasing the Erasure," 72.

53. Note that the logic of co-constitution, rather than of derivativeness from an origin, is the very logic described by Mopsik in much of his work, although the place of language suffers from what appears as a hiatus in that logic. A recent and concise formulation of this logic is found by Mopsik in the work of Moses de León, the presumed author of the *Zohar*, according to whom, Mopsik writes, "before God engaged in the creation of the world, before the process of emanation began in order to achieve creation, God had no existence" ("Pensée, voix, et parole," 393). Strictly speaking then, God is not "at" the origin.

54. Wolfson, who seeks to replace the model of the nut with that of the veil, here does fall back onto the language of "shells," something which may suggest that the distinction between the two is not strictly tenable.

55. Liebes, "Zohar and Eros," 97 and n182.

56. Benjamin, "Two Poems by Friedrich Hölderlin," in *Selected Writings*, 1: 21; Ger. original: "Zwei Gedichte von Friedrich Hölderlin," *Gesammelte Schriften*, II: 1, 108. There is something out of the ordinary in Benjamin's argument for a literary criticism that, though it addresses two poems that are already connected ("a certain relationship connects them, so that one could speak of different versions") nonetheless asserts as necessary, in order for the poems to be read, a demonstration of their comparability ("the method will demonstrate that the poems are comparable"). Comparability, though it may seem assured as a possibility, is thus not taken for granted. Like much else throughout this study, this section owes much to Christopher Fynsk's discussion of Benjamin's work (Fynsk, *Language and Relation*, 177–223).

57. Benjamin, "The Task of the Translator," 74.

58. Fynsk, "Translation as a Concept of Relation," in *Language and Relation*, 183.

59. Agamben, *Coming Community*, 2.

60. Agamben, *Language and Death*, 67.

61. For a different, though not opposed, account of the medieval reception of ancient rhetoric, see Curtius, *European Literature*. Unlike Curtius, Agamben does not restrict himself to the "Latin" Middle Ages, but notes that he is less making assertions about what the rhetorical tradition had truly been, and addresses rather the way in which it is translated in the occurrence of language that he reads.

62. Agamben, *Language and Death*, 67.

63. Agamben, *Stanzas*, 129.

64. On language and negativity, aside from Agamben's work, see Wolosky,

Language Mysticism, and see also Iser and Budick, eds., *Languages of the Unsayable*. Emmanuel Levinas makes a comparable diagnostic in the opening pages of *Totalité et infini*. Agamben acknowledges the comparison in *Language and Death*, 40.

65. Agamben, *Language and Death*, 69.

66. Ibid., 68; author's emphasis.

67. Agamben, "Language and History," in *Potentialities*, 182.

68. Agamben, "Pardes: The Writing of Potentiality," in *Potentialities*," 207.

69. See Derrida's remarks as to the conflation between "Jewish mysticism" and deconstruction, in Rötzer, *Conversations with French Philosophers*, 46–47.

70. Agamben, "Pardes: The Writing of Potentiality," in *Potentialities*," 209.

71. Agamben, *Coming Community*, 79–83; and see also *Moyens*, 91–101.

72. Agamben, *Coming Community*, 79.

73. Drory, "The Hidden Context." Interestingly enough, Drory's point is that the Hebrew-Arabic "context" is not the only relevant one in the study of al-Andalus, a point that is so well taken that one could hardly notice how quickly the Arabic context itself becomes a "hidden" one. On some of the uses of the notion of "decline" in Israeli historiography, see Gabriel Piterberg's informative discussion in "Domestic Orientalism."

74. L. Harvey, *Islamic Spain*, 85.

75. This is also described in David Wasserstein's "The Language Situation in al-Andalus."

76. For reasons that seem related to the availability of sources, most of the research has been done on Valencia and on the Crown of Aragon by Yom-Tov Assis, Ron Barkai, John Boswell, Robert Burns, Eleazar Gutwirth, Elena Lurie, Mark Meyerson, David Nirenberg, Norman Roth, and a few others. Thomas Glick and L. P. Harvey are among the rare historians who attempt to cover the issues of *convivencia*, the living-together in the Iberian peninsula, or at least not to presuppose a lack of contact when there is only a lack of sources. One should also consider in a different disciplinary space, the work of Ammiel Alcalay, Daniel Boyarin, Paul Fenton, María Rosa Menocal, James T. Monroe, all of whom indicate that different forms of translations from Arabic are originally at work in al-Andalus, even when viewed in historical perspectives, and in spite of the overwhelming majority of writings that inscribe "ends" and "decline."

77. See Shepard, *Shem Tov: His World and His Words*.

78. The obtuseness with which al-Andalus is thought of as an amalgam of hermetic cultural enclaves can be seen as well entrenched when considering what its opponents often have to argue against. Consider Jerrilynn Dodds's description of the Toledo El Transito synagogue, built in 1360, on the walls of which Qur^ᵓānic verses are inscribed. Dodds write that "various explanations have been offered for these last inscriptions. [One scholar] contends that they are due to the use of Muslim craftsmen on the project. There is little doubt, of course, that Muslims were among those who worked on the synagogue. However, the idea of their quietly slip-

ping long bands of Arabic writing into the design unbeknownst to [patron] Samuel Halevi, or that some carver added texts from the Qurʾān at his own whim . . . does not make any sense" (Dodds, "Mudejar Tradition and the Synagogues of Medieval Spain," 125).

79. Nirenberg, *Communities of Violence.* On the limits of the term "multiculturalism" see Hamacher, "One 2 Many Multiculturalisms."

80. Nirenberg, "Muslim-Jewish Relations," 249; and see also Nirenberg's *Communities of Violence.*

81. Castro, *The Spaniards,* 43. Note that Castro, in spite of all efforts, still refers here to Muslim and Arabic presence as an "occupation," as well as to the "Spain" that, he himself explains, did not quite yet exist.

82. De Libera, *Penser au moyen âge,* 150.

83. See Glick, "A Question of Names," in his *Islamic and Christian Spain,* 13ff.

84. De Certeau, *The Writing of History,* on mourning and the writing of history is most important to consider here. For a fuller discussion of the representation of Arab Jewish cultures in contemporary terms, see Shohat, *Israeli Cinema,* and Alcalay, *After Jews and Arabs.*

85. Baer, *A History of the Jews,* 1: 155. On Baer's work, see Myers, "Ytzhak Fritz Baer: Romanticism and Return in Jewish History," in Myers's *Re-Inventing the Jewish Past,* 109–28; Raz-Krakotzkin, "The National Narration of Exile" and "Exile Within Sovereignty"; and Piterberg, "Domestic Orientalism."

86. For a critique of this construction of the "essence" of "Spain," see Castro, *The Spaniards,* 20ff. And see Thomas F. Glick's description of the debate between Castro and Sánchez-Albornoz, in *Islamic and Christian Spain,* 314ff.

87. Baer's usage of the word "reconquest" and the general reading of "Spain" at work in his writings deserves a more extended discussion. Such can be found in Amnon Raz-Krakotzkin's "The National Narration of Exile" and "'Without Considering Others.'"

88. Bernstein, *Foregone Conclusions,* 9.

89. Septimus, *Hispano-Jewish Culture,* 2.

90. Drory, "Literary Contacts," 279. Consider however, Sadan, "Rabbi Yehuda al-Ḥarizi as a Cultural Crossroad," and its implicit criticism of Drory, for a more balanced picture.

91. Septimus, *Hispano-Jewish Culture,* 1.

92. O'Callaghan, *History of Medieval Spain,* 248.

93. Assis, "The Judeo-Arabic Tradition in Christian Spain," 115.

94. O'Callaghan, *History of Medieval Spain,* 305.

95. G. Cohen, ed., *The Book of Tradition,* xvi.

96. Stegner, quoted in Vizenor, *Manifest Manners,* 9.

97. Makki, "The Political History of al-Andalus," in Jayyusi, ed., *The Legacy of Muslim Spain,* 75.

98. Benjamin, "*Trauerspiel* and Tragedy," in *Selected Writings,* 1: 54.

99. "Différance" and "Signature, événement, contexte" appear in Nancy's footnotes in *Le Sens du monde.*

100. Nancy, *Le Sens du monde,* 38/E20.

101. Derrida, "Le Toucher," and see now, Derrida's book *Le Toucher, Jean-Luc Nancy.*

102. Alféri, *Guillaume d'Ockham,* 8.

103. On love as exposure to singularity and on love as "transport" that does not return, or only returns shattered, see Nancy, "L'Amour en éclats," in *Une Pensée finie*; Eng. trans.: "Shattered Love," in *The Inoperative Community.* Nancy broaches his discussion of *être au monde* in this essay, in the context of discussing Heidegger on love. Agamben extends the discussion of some of the same passages of *Being and Time* on *in-der-Welt-Sein* in "The Passion of Facticity," in *Potentialities.*

104. A "critique of mysticism" runs through Agamben's work that would deserve a separate treatment, though aspects of it are obviously directing the present discussion.

105. Agamben, *Language and Death,* 69.

106. Agamben, *Coming Community,* 83.

107. Rudolf Pannwitz, quoted in Benjamin, "The Task of the Translator," 81. Jacques Derrida points out the way "translation" in the "proper sense" is always taken to be *between* languages even when considering that there are other kinds of translation (see Derrida's discussion of Jakobson in "Des Tours de Babel," 217/E173). On love and translation, see ibid., 233/E190; and see also García Düttmann, "On Translatability." García Düttmann refers to Agamben's *Coming Community* in his discussion of love and/as translation.

108. Agamben, *Infancy and History,* 147.

109. Agamben, *Coming Community,* 106; and see also, 2.

110. Nancy, "L'Amour en éclats," in *Une Pensée finie,* 265; "Shattered Love," in *The Inoperative Community,* 108.

111. On translation as critical-poetic act, see Agamben, *Infancy and History,* 147; on "means without ends," see Agamben, *Moyens sans fin,* and see also Hamacher, "Afformative, Strike.'"

112. Agamben, *Coming Community,* 25.

113. Ibid., 1.

114. Benjamin, *Origin of the German Tragic Drama,* 235/E55. The German text is from *Gesammelte Schriften,* I: 1, 235. The English translation here has "periods of so-called decadence," which loses the importance of the naming of periods as such. I return to this naming below. It should be noted that the word *Verfall* is the same word used by Benjamin to describe the decline of the "aura." On the complexity of this notion of decline, as something that does not simply occur from without, nor only from within, and that seems to prevent a full disappearance, see Samuel Weber, "Mass Mediauras," 35ff.

115. Benjamin, *Origin of the German Tragic Drama,* 235/E55.

116. Walter Benjamin, "*Trauerspiel* and Tragedy," in *Selected Writings*, 1: 60. For an extended discussion of these issues, see Agamben, "Language and History," in *Potentialities.*

117. Benjamin, *Origin of the German Tragic Drama*, 218/E38.

118. See ibid., 226/E45, and see Weber, "Genealogy of Modernity," 470.

119. I am referring here to the distinct contributions of Ammiel Alcalay, Yom-Tov Assis, Thomas Glick, Leonard Harvey, María Rosa Menocal, Dan Pagis, and Ella Shohat, for example, as well as in still too rare attempts to address the meaning of Arabic and Andalusī culture in "Europe."

120. I refer here again to defenders of the so-called "Arabic" hypothesis, from Américo Castro to María Rosa Menocal (see the bibliography in her *The Arabic Role* and *Shards of Love*, and see Roger Boase, *The Origin and Meaning of Courtly Love*), but also to the slightly less nostalgic work of Alain de Libera (*Penser au moyen âge*, on the philosophical front) and Leonard Harvey (*Islamic Spain*, on the historical front). See also *The Legacy of Muslim Spain*, the sheer range and size of which indicates the remaining need for repetition even for the assertion that there is such a "legacy."

121. De Man, "Walter Benjamin's 'The Task of the Translator,'" in *The Resistance to Theory*, 91.

CHAPTER 3: Mourning Mysticism

1. The "voice of the friend" is a phrase used by Martin Heidegger in *Being and Time.* It is strikingly illuminated by Fynsk, who shows that it not only articulates a crucial moment for an understanding of what Heidegger calls "Being-with," or "*Mitsein*," but that it is also an instance of the attention to language required by Heidegger's language and by language in general. The voice of the friend intervenes in Heidegger's text at a moment when the relation to the other, to the voice of the other, is being discussed, and when "listening opens *Dasein* to the other" (Fynsk, 42). For more discussion, one should also read Ronell, "The Conference Call: Weber—Fynsk—Borch-Jacobsen," in *The Telephone Book*, 50–83; Derrida, *Politiques de l'amitié* (on Derrida's reading of the "voice of the friend," see 269–70 and 341–65); and see also Derrida, *Memoires.*

2. I borrow these formulations from Daniel Boyarin's discussion in "Reading Without the Phallus; or, Barter in a Midrashic Economy" (University of California, Berkeley, 30 August 1997), 23.

3. On the "sadness of the scholar," see Agamben, *Idea of Prose*, 65 (about Scholem, see 55ff.).

4. Scholem, "Revelation and Tradition as Religious Categories in Judaism," in *The Messianic Idea*, 296; see also Biale, *Gershom Scholem*, 131.

5. Abraham and Torok, "The Topography of Reality: Sketching a Metapsychology of Secrets," in *The Shell and the Kernel*, 160.

6. Scholem, "The Name of God," 194.
7. Biale, *Gershom Scholem,* 130.
8. Quoted in ibid.
9. Derrida reads this letter in "The Eyes of Language: The Abyss and the Volcano" and "Secularizing Language: The Volcano, the Fire, the Enlightenment," trans. Gil Anidjar, in *Acts of Religion.* There, Derrida alerts us not only to the importance of Scholem's letter, but also to the logic of haunting and spectrality at work in it (See also Derrida, *Monolingualism of the Other,* 78–93n9).
10. Scholem to Franz Rosenzweig, December 1926, quoted in Cutter, "Ghostly Hebrew, Ghastly Speech," 415–18.
11. Scholem, "Revelation and Tradition," 294; punctuation original.
12. Scholem, *Major Trends,* 249.
13. Scholem, "The Name of God," 194.
14. Ibid., 59.
15. Scholem, *Major Trends,* 8.
16. Ibid., 27.
17. Ibid., 7; author's emphasis.
18. Scholem, "Zehn unhistorische Sätze über Kabbala," 271.
19. Rotenstreich, "Symbolism and Transcendence: On Some Philosophical Aspects of Gershom Scholem's Opus," in *Essays in Jewish Philosophy,* 299.
20. Scholem, *Major Trends,* 247.
21. Cadava, *Words of Light,* 139n39.
22. For more on the "monumental legacy" which was "bequeathed to us" (but who us?) see Beinart, ed., *Moreshet Sepharad,* 7. The phrase "lachrymose conception of Jewish history" is derived from a 1928 essay by Salo Baron. It is discussed in an illuminating way by Mark R. Cohen in his *Under Crescent and Cross.* Scholem's view of 1492 as the governing event according to which one could make sense of Jewish history is best known from his study of Sabbatai Sevi. It is also in relation to 1492 that Scholem was addressing, in quite ominous terms, the rise of Nazism, also considered here as an opportunity to further understand history:

> The horrible thing about it, though, if one dares to say so, is that the human cause of the Jews in Germany only stands to benefit [*sic*] if a real pogrom were to take place, instead of the "cold" pogrom that they will be trying to restrict themselves to. It represents almost the only chance of bringing about something positive from such an eruption. For, although the extent of the catastrophe is of historic proportions, and it can teach us something about 1492, the stuff of which resistance is made has been reduced in German Jewry to a very small fraction. (Scholem to Benjamin, 13 April 1933)

More on some of these issues in Israeli historiography can be found in Myers, *Re-Inventing the Jewish Past,* and in Raz-Krakotzkin, "The National Narration of Exile."

23. Idel, *Kabbalah*, 12; Idel may be referring here to Scholem's own "hope of a true communication from the mountain" (quoted in Biale, *Gershom Scholem*, 32).

24. Idel, *Kabbalah*, 35.

25. It is important to note that, quite uniquely so far in the study of Jewish mysticism, Elliot Wolfson goes quite a long way toward abandoning the rhetoric of sadness, language as mournful longing for a lost experience. Wolfson suggests, for example, that the "experience" may be conceived as otherwise than lost when he argues that "the whole distinction between experience and interpretation from the vantage point of the mystical sources within Judaism cannot be upheld" (*Through a Speculum*, 54). Wolfson's work deserves therefore a separate treatment, which can only be broached here. Rather than mourning a lost object (ineffable, invisible, etc.), Wolfson interrogates the phonocentrism of the tradition as presented by Scholem and even questions the dominance of ineffability in kabbalistic texts (see Wolfson's "Negative Theology"). Wolfson rather insists on the "ocularcentrism" of the Jewish tradition. In this his work conjoins with Daniel Boyarin's. Both Wolfson and Boyarin interrogate the notion that the Jewish God would always have been considered invisible, from the Bible on (see chapter 1 in *Through a Speculum*, "Israel: The One Who Sees God," and see D. Boyarin, "The Eye in the Torah," and *Carnal Israel*. By reestablishing the primacy of vision, the textual experience becomes also a visual experience that has a value of its own and does not simply substitute for a voice that was lost. This positive attitude toward written language and toward language in general may seem to reflect what Scholem, Idel, and others have shown to be a more positive relation to language, one in which language would not be an obstacle but rather a means to reach the object of desire. There remains, however, a common ground, ultimately shared even by Wolfson, in the conception that language remains a means toward an end that is still conceived as remote and exterior. Language is only of value insofar as it points toward something other than itself, pushing to go elsewhere. Hence, there is maintained throughout a language of longing for a "home" beyond. Even if, in Wolfson's work, the figuration of loss is abandoned, there remains therefore the notion that there is "something of a 'core' experience that may underlie a significant portion of the tradition complexes that helped give shape to more distinctive redactional units" (*Through a Speculum*, 81). Having affirmed his reserved Kantianism (52–73), Wolfson may be neither mourning nor sad, but he does inscribe a longing for the *Ding an-sich*, and his preservation, even monumentalization, of a language of (psychological, individual) experience testifies to that longing. Wolfson recently added to this view and insisted that he has "emphasized the experiential underpinning of theosophic Kabbalah in [his] own independent voice" (Wolfson, "Coronation of the Sabbath Bride," 306n15). Although I would maintain that there are elements in Wolfson's work that show a different attitude to language than the one I am describing here as a rhetoric of sadness, here Wolfson tends to give priority to the "underpinning" object of study, one that is psychological, rather than textual, lin-

guistic; in other words, Wolfson is still after a nonlinguistic experience rather than attempting to read language as (nonpsychological) experience. Whether this is an effect of Wolfson's earlier testimony regarding his psychological affiliations ("My thinking has been influenced by . . . the work of C. G. Jung" [*Through a Speculum*, 6n8]) is perhaps difficult to establish conclusively and does not, therefore, diminish what I am trying to point out regarding the value of Wolfson's work on the importance of language and the necessity of reading, all of which indicate that one can, in fact, read differently, otherwise than by mourning mysticism.

26. Idel, "Universalization and Integration," 27.

27. Ibid., 28.

28. Agamben, *Language and Death*, 88.

29. "Anyone who writes a memoir, *Erinnerungen* . . . must take to heart the unmistakable warning presented to us by the publication of Gustav Janouch's *Conversations*," writes Scholem (*Walter Benjamin*, x).

30. Occurrences of the word *Gespräch* are so numerous in the story of this friendship that it would be difficult to count them. One will note, though, that it is on the very question of having heard Benjamin's voice, having conducted a conversation with him, that Scholem becomes haunted, as it were, by the risk of fictionality. After all, is it not slightly possible that, like Janouch's, Scholem's "conversations" constitute a work of "dubious authenticity that nevertheless was swallowed uncritically by a hungry world" (*Walter Benjamin*, x)? The editors of the recently published *Selected Writings* of Benjamin do not hesitate to quote Scholem's text profusely, as sound historiographic evidence in the chronology placed at the end of the volume. Yet Scholem's words seem to beg the question: Are these memoirs, *Erinnerungen*, truly conversations? Are they conversations at all? Why are Janouch's allegedly fictitious conversations even presented as a "warning," as the negative model which, Scholem says, one "must take to heart, *muß* . . . *beherzigen*"? Why does Scholem so harshly criticize Janouch for having provided "an unverifiable explanation of the delay, *einer unkontrollierbaren Erklärung für den Aufschub*," for publication? What is so important about "control" and how does it play with philological doubts of authenticity? Scholem himself, whose first text on Benjamin appeared only in 1964, does not offer any explanation for the thirty-five years delay of his own account of *Gespräche* (1975), though he does acknowledge that for the skeptic, "these recollections will remain mute, *bleiben diese Erinnerungen stumm*" (*Walter Benjamin*, 8/Ex). These (possibly mute) conversations—and not only the fact that "we subsequently had quite a number of conversations, *nicht wenige Gespräche*, about Goethe" (82/E63), conversations which here too turned out to have been "monologues, *Monologe*"; nor the fact that Benjamin, who signed a letter as "Goethe" (143/E112) may himself have therefore "taken" Goethe "to heart"—render indispensable a reading of Avital Ronell's discussion of Eckermann's *Gespräche mit Goethe* in her *Dictations*; and see also, Ronell on Alexander G. Bell and Thomas A. Watson in *The Telephone Book*, 226ff. In *Dictations*, Ronell also dis-

cusses Benjamin's link to Goethe as being related to a "vault" in Benjamin's *One-Way Street* (xxv). Part of what is intended in this chapter is a consideration of some of the less explored dimensions of the relationship between Benjamin and Scholem. Benjamin's "presence" in these "conversations" is still too problematic to warrant their description in terms of "double talk," as Wayne Koestenbaum defines it, even if some elements of Koestenbaum's study appear to be at work here too (Koestenbaum, *Double Talk*). More directly relevant perhaps is Daniel Boyarin's discussion of "the rise of heterosexuality and the invention of the modern Jew," which covers issues related to my discussion, namely, the matter of a different, more gendered, aspect of the "Jewish Sciences" (D. Boyarin, *Unheroic Conduct*). I mean here to extend Boyarin's descriptions to the specific case of a discourse I have tentatively referred to, after the work of Ella Shohat and Ammiel Alcalay, as "Jewish Orientalism" (Anidjar, "Jewish Mysticism Alterable and Unalterable," and see also Biale, "Sabataï Tzevi"). It is also important to mention here that Scholem himself was engaged in intensive reflections on some of these issues, discussing the possibility of another "double-talk," and of cultural (or, as he called it, "historical") dialogue, *Gespräch*. Here too, some of the dominant motifs are fictionality and "spectral" speech (cf. Scholem's contributions to the question of "the German-Jewish dialogue" in Gershom Scholem, *On Jews and Judaism in Crisis*). Though I occasionally allude to this, it would take much more space to unravel the perceived interconnectedness of the places and contexts provided by Germany and by Spain ("1492," the "end," etc.) in the work of Scholem and in Jewish historiography in general.

31. Martin Buber, quoted in Biale, *Gershom Scholem*, 1.

32. Gershom Scholem, "The Science of Judaism," in *The Messianic Idea*, 304; "Wissenschaft vom Judentum," in *Judaica*, 148.

33. "Even in times of narrowly prejudiced thought there was an inkling that life was not limited to organic corporeality," wrote Benjamin in "The Task of the Translator" (71).

34. Scholem, "The Science of Judaism," in *The Messianic Idea*, 152–53/E306–7. Whether or not this burial has "in fact" been expressed by representatives of the science of Judaism is here of course less relevant than the character of Scholem's (and others') response to, and perhaps fixation on, burial and mourning. The term "legacy" continues to be used, most specifically, if not exclusively, when referring to Spanish Jewry, though Scholem also refers to the legacy of that "living organism" which Judaism is said to be.

35. Scholem, *Major Trends*, 3.

36. Mourning and melancholia, the rhetoric of sadness constitutive of the study of al-Andalus and of Jewish mysticism, have not been discussed by critical readers of Scholem's work, nor by scholars of Jewish mysticism or of Jewish historiography. Biale, Bloom, Dan, Funkenstein, Handelman, Momigliano, Moses, Myers, and Schweid all insist on the foundational and restorative dimension of

Scholem's study of Jewish mysticism either to agree or, less often, disagree with Scholem. In his discussion of Benjamin's "Destructive Character," Irving Wohlfarth had already noted that to view Benjamin "à la Scholem . . . would be to reconstruct the traces instead of effacing them" (Wohlfarth, "No-Man's-Land," 63). That there is in Scholem a constructive and reconstructive process at work could hardly be debated, but what kind of building or monument is being built still deserves attention, as I hope to show.

37. Benjamin, "The Work of Art in the Age of Mechanical Reproduction," in *Illuminations*, 236; *Gesammelte Schriften*, I: 2, 500.

38. Consider Moshe Idel's own description of his "new perspective" as "Reconstruction" (see Idel, "An Appraisal for Reconstruction," in *Kabbalah*, 32–34). The governing principles of this scholarly endeavor are, I think, quite clear, as is the conception of the field or land upon which this construction takes place. Peter Fenves demonstrates how such a reconstructive project constitutes a "strenuous attempt to reconstruct the liberties and communities torn apart in wickedness" (Fenves, "From Empiricism to the Experience of Freedom," foreword to Nancy, *The Experience of Freedom*, xxix); and see also Ella Shohat's perspective on these issues in "Imagining Terra Incognita."

39. Scholem, *Major Trends*, vii.

40. The Freudian term "cathexis" translates the German *Besetzung*, a term that has connotations of placing and taking place. See "Investissement," in Laplanche and Pontalis, *Vocabulaire de la psychanalyse*; and see also, Weber, *The Legend of Freud*.

41. In the German version, Scholem writes of a *Trümmerfeld*, a field of ruins. This "field of ruins," or *Trümmerfeld*, also appears at the opening of *On the Kabbalah and Its Symbolism*. Benjamin's interest in ruins (*Ruine*) is well known from, among other places, the *Trauerspiel* book.

42. Scholem, *Walter Benjamin*, ix.

43. Scholem, *Major Trends*, viii.

44. I have already suggested that readers of Scholem will look in vain for information about the political and social situation of the Iberian peninsula at the time—for any account of "Spain" as anything but the barest of locations, indeed the most undetermined "context" as a thin conglomerate of place names—though they will read much about the little-known life and ("archaic") mind of Moses of León. I return to these issues in the next chapter.

45. Scholem, *Major Trends*, 190–91.

46. I refer here to the third of Scholem's "Ten Unhistorical Theses," which addresses the "character of knowledge in the Kabbalah" (*Judaica 3*, 265–66). Note that knowledge, *Erkenntnis*, and epistemology, *Erkenntnistheorie*, are the occasion of another "departure." It was the object of study from which Scholem says he withdrew: "When I was about to put on the hat of the philologian and withdraw from mathematics and epistemology into a much more dubious field, *und mich*

aus Mathematik und Erkenntnistheorie auf eine so viel zweideutigere Position zurückzuziehen" (Scholem to Zalman Schocken, 29 October 1937; quoted in Biale, *Gershom Scholem*, 31; the German text is on page 155 of Biale's book). Aside from the "Theses" and from very occasional remarks (such as the intuitive perception of the "mystical now"), I am not aware of any extended discussion of epistemology in Scholem's work.

47. Scholem, *Major Trends*, 156.

48. Scholem, *Judaica 3*, 265.

49. Scholem, *Major Trends*, vii.

50. Ibid., 226.

51. The word *Andenken* means "remembrance, souvenir." Scholem will later translate the English dedication into German as *Dem Andenken an*, "in memoriam." On friendship and the question of epitaphs, see Derrida, *Politiques de l'amitié*, 115ff., and de Man, "Autobiography as De-facement."

52. Though texts that Scholem had studied or discussed with Benjamin are amply mentioned, from Hermann Cohen to Molitor, von Baader, and more. Scholem even quotes Baader on Angelus Silesius, a figure he himself participated in later associating with Benjamin's name (*Major Trends*, 405n109). In respect to what I refer to as Benjamin's "silent voice," it is remarkable to note that Scholem did end up mentioning Benjamin's name, if belatedly, in reference to a moment that no doubt demanded Benjamin's intervention, namely, Scholem's discussion of symbol and allegory. The later German version of *Major Trends*, published by Scholem in 1957, includes a slightly expanded note (note 25 of lecture 1) that does not appear in any of the English versions (the original lectures were delivered, as Scholem writes, in English). In this note Scholem writes that "we owe the most significant explanations on this subject to Walter Benjamin's *Origin of the German Tragic Drama, die bedeutendsten Ausführungen über diesen Gegenstand verdanken wir Walter Benjamins* Ürsprung des deutschen Trauerspiels)" (Scholem, *Die Jüdische Mystik*, 388). There is perhaps some irony in that the connection to Benjamin occurs in an appropriating translation and is asserted to rest on a certain "significance, *Bedeutung*." Benjamin's assertion, in "The Task of the Translator," about the plausibility of a translation having no relation of significance to the original is, therefore, to be kept in mind. However that may be, it is clear that for fifteen years *Major Trends* insistently remains a "'*ci-gît' où le nom du décédé demeure longtemps illisible*, a 'here lies' on which the name of the deceased long remains unreadable" (Maria Torok, "Maladie du deuil et fantasme du cadavre exquis," in Abraham and Torok, *L'écorce et le noyau*, 247; *The Shell and the Kernel*, 121 [trans. altered]).

53. That there may be an important distinction to be made between "life and works" and friendship is suggested by Benjamin himself who, writing on Max Brod's biography of Kafka, says that "it is all the more memorable as the document of a friendship that is not among the smallest mysteries of Kafka's life" (Benjamin to Scholem, 12 June 1938; *The Correspondence . . . 1932–1940*, 223). Later on, in the

same letter, Benjamin indicates one of the directions of reading along which I am trying to read the ink (if not necessarily the print, as we will see) of Benjamin's friendship. Benjamin writes that Kafka's "friendship with Brod is to me above all else a question mark which he chose to ink in the margin of his life" (226). One should consider here the important remarks made by Eduardo Cadava regarding Benjamin's "identification with Kafka" (Cadava, *Words of Light*, 113).

54. Cadava, *Words of Light*, 130.

55. Insisting on the "intellectual symbiotic compact" constituted by Benjamin and Scholem, Gary Smith argues against the "resistance in Germany to reading Benjamin as a Jewish thinker," but also against "the falseness" of a view that sees Scholem as more indebted to Benjamin than the reverse. Most interestingly, and without providing more evidence than what supposedly meets the eye, Smith argues that the two shared "a rhetoric of silence" (Smith, "'Die Zauberjuden,'" esp. 237–39).

56. This essay was first delivered as a lecture in German. It can be found in Scholem's *On Jews and Judaism in Crisis.*

57. "Kabbalah," translated belatedly as "Jewish mysticism," made an even later entry onto the scene of the academic study of mysticism. Witness the oft-mentioned example of its absence from William James's *The Varieties of Religious Experience* and from Evelyn Underhill's *Mysticism*, where the phrase "Jewish mysticism" does not appear and where Kabbalah is mentioned only in the context of magic and experiences which are "far more occult than mystical in character" (Underhill, *Mysticism*, 155). Underhill's book, heavily praised by Scholem in *Major Trends*, was published in 1910 and revised in 1930.

58. Habermas, *Philosophical Discourse of Modernity*, 182–84. In an earlier article on Benjamin, Habermas was perhaps more nuanced in dealing with Benjamin's "mysticism," but here too he happily abandons to Scholem and to the mystical the "failure" of Benjamin, one which strangely conflates a drive for unity, which would have been Benjamin's, and what Habermas sees as "serviceable": "Benjamin did not succeed in his intention of uniting enlightenment and mysticism because the theologian in him could not bring himself to make the messianic theory of experience serviceable for historical materialism" (Habermas, "Walter Benjamin," 114). Other prominent examples are Terry Eagleton, who, among those "features of Benjamin's thought that prove for us the most intractable," quotes without hesitation from Scholem's (!) notion that "scriptural revelation is the voice of God . . . generative of meaning but in itself meaningless" (Eagleton, *Walter Benjamin*, 115–16); and see also Richard Wolin, who relies on the already sedimented tradition of Kabbalah/Scholem references, and therefore does not even provide a proof text when discussing it ("Experience and Materialism in Benjamin's *Passagenwerk*," in Gary Smith, ed., *Benjamin: Philosophy, Aesthetics, History*). Michael Jennings, who identifies the "curiously circular exercise in intellectual history" that consists in tracing Benjamin's Marxism or his influence on Adorno in terms of later interpre-

tations of Benjamin, fails to consider that any statement about Benjamin's mysticism will, most unavoidably, partake of the same circular structure (Jennings, *Dialectical Images*, 9n14). Finally, Gillian Rose seems to consider that the work of considering Benjamin's relation to Judaism has already been done in the "rich and substantial body of criticism already in existence in which reference to the Jewish dimensions of Benjamin's life and work helps to clarify precisely the tremendous scope of his interests" (Rose, "Walter Benjamin," 59). As Derrida generously remarks, it is not a question of avoiding mediated reading, but of acknowledging such mediation as the gesture common to both critique and enthusiastic appropriation, a gesture most visible when reference is made to so-called "lost sons of Judaism," where it is not clear what "Judaism" or "Jewish mysticism" there would be, for critics of Benjamin and Derrida and other "Jewish mystics," "behind" the mediation (see "Jacques Derrida," in Rötzer, *Conversations with French Philosophers*, esp. 47).

59. Most importantly here for my concerns are the works of Agamben, Cadava, de Man, Derrida, Fynsk, Hamacher, Lacoue-Labarthe, Nägele, Ronell, and Weber.

60. As I have already discussed in the previous chapter, in Benjamin's "Two Poems by Friedrich Hölderlin" he writes of a method that "will demonstrate that the poems are comparable, *Sie wird im Verlaufe die Vergleichbarkeit der Gedichte erweisen*, it will demonstrate their 'comparability'" (*Selected Writings*, 21; *Gesammelte Schriften*, II: 1, 108).

61. Derrida, *Of Grammatology*, 14.

62. I quote here from where Benjamin describes a childhood photograph of Kafka, in which "the model holds in his left hand an oversized, wide-brimmed hat of the type worn by Spaniards" (Benjamin, "Franz Kafka: On the Tenth Anniversary of His Death," in *Illuminations*, 118).

63. On the "mute word [*le mot muet*]," see Derrida, "Fors," in Abraham and Torok, *Cryptonymie*.

64. See Lacoue-Labarthe, "Œdipe comme figure," *L'Imitation des modernes*, 206.

65. Concerning figuring, Abraham and Torok write of *antimétaphore*, which should be strictly distinguished from a return to a literal sense, but is rather innovative, "a new figure of style," the impossible figure of a destruction of figuration (*The Shell and the Kernel*, 132). How the figuration, then, of Benjamin is the effect of a use of his name that seriously limits the possibility of figuring him otherwise should become apparent in what follows. And see also de Man, "Autobiography as De-facement." Concerning "agony," Derrida writes of "le travail d'agonie" of a tradition, an expression that, here, may be more suggestively translated as "the work of agony" than as "agonizing work," as the English translation has it (Derrida, *De la grammatologie*, 26/E14). Note the added meaning of agonism in agony (in and over against "friendship"). Consider also Philippe Lacoue-Labarthe's discussion of agony in "The Echo of the Subject." Underscoring the importance of the "name of the agonizing subject," Lacoue-Labarthe helps to orient the present inquiry toward

the "work of agony" in Scholem's text, from the question of mourning, *Trauerspiel*, the tomb, figuration, and autobiography (which is also, as he notes and as we will see, "*allothanatographie*, voire *hétérothanatographie*"): "autobiography, the biography of the dead other, is always inscribed in an agon, *l'autobiographie, la biographie de l'autre mort, s'inscrit toujours dans une agonistique*" (Lacoue-Labarthe, "The Echo of the Subject," 179; *Le Sujet de la philosophie*, 266). By maintaining the notion of a work of agony close to that of mourning as I articulate it here, I wish to suspend the question of distinguishing between mourning and melancholia, and to avoid the prescriptive dimensions regarding what would qualify as a "proper" or "adequate" work of mourning as it suggests itself, for example, in Eric Santner's discussion (consider how for Santner, the "error" of Paul de Man is that his response to grief "cannot be considered an adequate response," Santner, *Stranded Objects*, 29); and see also Gillian Rose, "Walter Benjamin." My reading of Scholem's text is not intended to adjudicate on what the adequate response (if there is such a thing) to grief may be.

66. Quoted in Scholem, *Walter Benjamin*, 281/E226.

67. Ibid., 255–66/E205–14.

68. Ibid., 281/E226. This is also the source of the text of Benjamin's epitaph.

69. Kant, introduction to *Critique of Judgement*, 12.

70. Torok, "The Illness of Mourning," in *The Shell and the Kernel*, 114.

71. Ibid.

72. Again, the later German version is somewhat different since its punctuation includes periods, and, instead of "unify" gives "meet themselves," *sich trafen*.

73. Momigliano, "Walter Benjamin," trans. M. Masella-Gayley, in *Essays on Ancient and Modern Judaism*, 199.

74. Scholem, *Walter Benjamin*, 224/E179.

75. *The Correspondance . . . 1932–1940*, 30 (13 March 1933). This letter is, strikingly enough, the first of the "Two-Way Correspondance" (Benjamin and Scholem, *Briefwechsel 1932–1940*, 45).

76. Scholem, *Walter Benjamin*, 7/Eix.

77. Scholem, *Von Berlin nach Jerusalem*. This partial autobiography (if that is what it is) was only published after the story of the friendship. Note that Scholem also refers to the story of his friendship as *Erinnerungen*, confirming that, for him, they both belonged to the same genre.

78. Momigliano remarks that this is one point where the English translation is disappointing, but he fails to note that this particular ending may be most faithful to the text than Momigliano allows (the German text ends on a quotation, Momigliano explains, from Wilhelm Busch: "So kam Lenchen auf das Land"). The text that Momigliano calls "Gershom Scholem's autobiography" is marked by a profound break between life and work, a break Momigliano himself would seem to want to reinscribe even more strongly (Momigliano almost chastises Scholem for making too obvious the connection between his scholarship and his under-

standing of Zionism). That Scholem would quote Wilhelm Busch, that he would quote, that is, another's voice, in order to indicate what may or may not be the continuation of his "life" (and which was not included in this "autobiography"), amounts to leaving undecided whether the beginning of a career ("thus began my academic career") is or is not part of his life. The English translation may therefore have been more faithful than Momigliano recognizes (Momigliano, "Gershom Scholem's Autobiography," in *Essays on Ancient and Modern Judaism*, 192).

79. Derrida, "Otobiographies," 19; and "Spéculer: Sur Freud," in *La Carte postale*; see also Ronell, preface to *Dictations*, ix–xix.

80. When telling of Hannah Arendt's testimony about Benjamin's resting place, Scholem may not have had much choice of words; nonetheless, it should be noted that though Arendt writes of a "spot, *Stelle*," he writes of a "place, *Ort*" (*Walter Benjamin*, 281/E226), a position that was certainly very stable.

81. Scholem, *Walter Benjamin*, 168/E133.

82. Quoted in ibid., 167/E133.

83. Scholem, *Major Trends*, 7–8.

84. Ibid., 4.

85. Nägele, *Theater, Theory, Speculation.*

86. Biale, *Gershom Scholem*, 124.

87. Scholem, *Major Trends*, 26.

88. Scholem, *Walter Benjamin*, 168/E134.

89. "If it is already a common phenomenon that one hardly accounts even vaguely, for example, for the gait of people, *vom Gang der Leute*, one is certainly completely unaware of the posture, *Haltung*, at any one fraction of a second of taking a step" (Benjamin, "A Short History of Photography," quoted and translated in Nägele, *Theater, Theory, and Speculation*, 105; *Gesammelte Schriften* II: 1, 371).

90. My discussion of "figures of imprint and printing" is indebted to Derrida, *Archive Fever.*

91. Scholem, *Walter Benjamin*, 16–17/E8–9.

92. On full and empty mouths, see Abraham and Torok, *The Shell and the Kernel*, esp. 127–28.

93. Benjamin, quoted in Nägele, *Theater, Theory, and Speculation*, 105.

94. This disruption takes various forms, of course. One is the insistent foreshadowing of Benjamin's death. Quite early in the story of the friendship, Scholem, who didn't see Benjamin during the last two years of his life, nonetheless ominously refers to Benjamin's death when he reports that he kept his hair "to the end, *bis ans Ende*" (*Walter Benjamin*, 16/E8). As detachable, as that which could have been lost but wasn't in the end, the hair is not unrelated to what Avital Ronell described as "Losing One's Quills" (*Dictations*, 166–75). On time and photography in Benjamin, see Cadava, "Words of Light." Cadava notes that for Benjamin, "rather than reproducing, faithfully and perfectly the photographed as such, the photographic images conjures up its death" (89). Photographs, or here, photographic descrip-

tions—what I think Cadava would agree on calling "words of light"—are, Cadava says, "memories of mourning" (90).

95. See Scholem, "Der Name Gottes," in *Judaica 3*. This is one of the rare occasions in which Scholem mentions Benjamin (translated as "The Name of God," but once again Benjamin's name does not appear in the English version). Scholem discusses at length his interpretation of Jewish exegetical history as the unfolding of the silent voice/word of God. As David Biale explains, the voice is meaningless but meaning-producing, *Bedeutung-Gebendes* (Biale, *Gershom Scholem*, 112–46).

96. Scholem, *Walter Benjamin*, 135/E105.

97. Note that, confirming the impression he repeatedly made on Scholem, one of the sources of this "imagery" may very well be Benjamin, who writes that "Kafka's female characters rise" from a "swampy soil, *Moorboden*" and that some, like Leni, are "swamp creatures, *Sumpfgeschöpfe*" (Benjamin, "Franz Kafka," in *Illuminations*, 130; *Gesammelte Schriften* II: 2, 429).

98. Heidegger, "The Origin of the Work of Art," 41.

99. Rickels, *Aberrations of Mourning*, 5.

100. Funkenstein, "Gershom Scholem," 137.

101. Abraham and Torok, *The Shell and the Kernel*, 160.

102. It may be Arnaldo Momigliano's reticence to take into account the difficulties surrounding autobiography, to consider the allo- and thanato-graphy rather than insist that he is reading an autobiography by Scholem, that makes him ask for what he calls a "deeper probing." One wonders what it is that Momigliano is longing for.

> Scholem avoids any deeper probing into his relations with Walter Benjamin and his wife Dora. The fact that Scholem had previously written a book and many papers on his friendship with Benjamin would not have made it superfluous to say something more definite in his *autobiographical account*, if the tone of the book in general had allowed it. (Momigliano, "Gershom Scholem's Autobiography," in *Essays in Ancient and Modern Judaism*, 193; my emphasis)

103. Bloom, introduction to Scholem, *From Berlin to Jerusalem*, xvi.

104. Recall here that Scholem was the teller of the parable reported by Benjamin and by Ernst Bloch, and discussed by Giorgio Agamben. This parable says that in the world to come "everything will be just as it is here. . . . Everything will be as it is now, just a little different" (Agamben, *Coming Community*, 53). Agamben's interpretation illuminates what Scholem seems not to have read, the "just a little different." Agamben writes that "the tiny displacement does not refer to the state of things, but to their sense and their limits" (54). Scholem's phonocentrism thus appears to be in solidarity with his drive for an ontological beyond, another stable position, another "state of things."

105. This extraordinary letter deserves a separate reading, which I cannot pro-

vide here. Suffice it to say that in this virulent attack on the German Jewish Youth Movement (the letter was originally published in the journal *Jerubaal: Eine Zeitschrift der jüdischen Jugend*), Scholem seems to depart from yet other rules he set to himself, one of which he both asserts and breaks in the letter: "Labor is oral teaching and nothing of it can be committed to writing except the method." Scholem's phonocentrism is not entirely distinct from his obsession with ineffability, showing both to be closely connected. Suggesting that youth is another silent voice ("Youth has no language"), Scholem appropriately ends the letter with the words: "and the rest is silence." (Scholem, "Farewell," in *On Jews and Judaism in Crisis*)

106. Benjamin, "The Task of the Translator," 69.

107. On the "expressionless" in Benjamin, see Hamacher, "Afformative, Strike," esp. 124ff.

108. Cadava, *Words of Light*, 7.

109. Scholem, *Walter Benjamin*, 7/Eix.

110. Scholem, *Walter Benjamin*, 107/E83.

111. As I pointed out earlier, "Walter Benjamin" was published in 1964 (reprinted in *On Jews and Judaism in Crisis*), the *Correspondence* in 1966, "Der Name Gottes und die Sprachtheorie der Kabbala" was given as an Eranos lecture in 1970, and *Walter Benjamin* was published in 1975.

112. Scholem, "The Name of God," 60; "Der Name Gottes," 7.

113. Scholem, *Walter Benjamin*, 241/E193.

114. Ibid., 51/E37.

115. Ibid., 80/E61.

116. Benjamin, *Origin*, 209/E29. On the writing surface, one should consider here Giorgio Agamben's first "Threshold," in *Idea of Prose*, 31–34, as well as his "Pardes: The Writing of Potentiality," in *Potentialities*; and see, of course, Derrida, "Freud and the Scene of Writing," in *Writing and Difference*.

117. This is the case for Scholem, assuming for now, quite arbitrarily, that he himself—as exposed as we found him—could still be maintained as absolutely distinct from any of the Benjamins. Scholem had to make sure of this when he said, "I am not Walter Benjamin. I am Gershom Scholem"; Scholem, "With Gershom Scholem: An Interview," in *On Jews and Judaism in Crisis*, 32.

118. Ronell, "Street-talk," in Nägele, *Benjamin's Ground*.

119. Benjamin, *Origin*, 234/E53; translation slightly altered.

120. Ronell, *The Telephone Book*; see also Eduardo Cadava's illuminating discussion of Ronell's "reading with one's ears" in his "Toward an Ethics of Decision."

121. Shoshana Felman's "Benjamin's Silence" appeared after this chapter was written. Although sharing her concern for the issue of silence, my argument remains distinct insofar as it focuses primarily on Scholem's text, on Benjamin's figure, rather than on Benjamin "himself." Moreover, my text hardly answers Felman's call "to return to Benjamin his silence" (234).

CHAPTER 4: *Zohar* and/as *Maqāma*

1. Gellens, "The Search for Knowledge," 59–61.

2. The failure of a generic—or consensual—definition as to what kind of texts *maqāmāt* are is not accidental, according to Abdelfattah Kilito, one of their foremost contemporary readers. The series of traits that would enable a generic definition is dependent on the possibility of "préciser la *place* des séances dans l'espace des genres de la littérature arabe" (Kilito, "Le Genre 'Séance,'" 51; author's emphasis). In his larger project, Kilito will go on to show how unstable, indeed unlocatable, this "place" is. Other arguments have been made that depart from a similar lack of fit, though the purpose was to curtail the possibility of comparison between *maqāmāt* as "the species of composition originated by or first associated with the name of Badīᶜ al-Zamān al-Hamaḏānī" and the European picaresque novel (Abu-Haidar, "*Maqāmāt* Literature," 1), but parallels, as James Monroe has convincingly shown, are in fact quite striking, unexplainable as they may be (Monroe, *The Art*).

3. Scholem, however, will enthusiastically call the *Zohar* "one of the most remarkable works of *Jewish* literature and of the literature of mysticism in general" (Scholem, *Major Trends*, 204). Not just *any* literature, then, though Scholem is thereby altering what each of these terms ("Jewish," "literature," "mysticism") means. I have tried to document some of these forays into literary and rhetorical criticism in Kabbalah scholarship in my "Jewish Mysticism: Alterable and Unalterable," and I return to these issues later in this chapter (as in that article, I do not intend to engage here the entire field of the study of "Jewish mysticism," but it is nonetheless important to refer to Peter Schäfer's work in which, discussing earlier so-called Jewish mystical literature, Schäfer also raised serious questions that parallel my own and often go further than I could. I refer the reader most notably to Schäfer's *The Hidden and Manifest God*, 150–57, and his "Jewish Mysticism"). For now, I will say that although Hava Tirosh-Rothschild generously attributes to the field of Kabbalah studies an extensive involvement with literary and theoretical issues and debates, the sign of such involvement rarely appears in bibliographies of Kabbalah studies. Among others affinities and sources, Tirosh-Rothschild finds American New Criticism (Tirosh-Rothschild, "Continuity and Revision," 166). Though this may have been institutionally true (through departments of Hebrew literature), it seems to me difficult to read much more than a familiar philology in the literary interests of Kabbalah scholars (Moshe Idel's Jungian "phenomenology" notwithstanding; see, for example, his *Kabbalah*, xix and 24–25). It is nonetheless important to note that many scholars of Kabbalah (and some scholars of Hebrew literature) make a point of recognizing (and joining) Liebes's work as taking the general direction of looking at the *Zohar* as "literature." Idel, again, whose approach may or may not be "decidedly French" (?), as Tirosh-Rotshchild puts it (174), has yet to reveal himself a literary critic, but does in fact seem to hold a distinctively antiliterary, antitextual—and more recently, antihistorical—viewpoint. In his view,

Scholem produced "an inert ideology of textology" (Idel, *Kabbalah*, 23). Idel, who recognizes that the philological tradition is "dominant," also thinks that it deserves the term "literary" (27; one may want to ask further what the meaning of the word "literary" is when Idel writes about the *Zohar* that "it is a literary work of art which assumes a symbolic interpretation" [Idel, "On Symbolic Self-Interpretation," 93]). Hence Idel's own "alternative" and "new" suggestions toward a study of mysticism within well-patrolled borders that would separate between "inner" and "outer" history. But none of these seem to include, in fact, "literature." After Idel's own post-textuality, posthistoricity?

There have been important steps made toward what literary readings of the *Zohar*, and of Kabbalah in general, could mean. However, as Eliezer Segal remarked, it is still the case that "whatever scholarly attention has been attracted by the literary merits of the *Zohar* seems to have been confined to the narrative structures" (Segal, "The Exegetical Craft," 32n3). I take Segal to mean the "literary frame," since hardly anything else is mentioned elsewhere, in spite of Yehuda Liebes's strong opposition to the word, nor has this opposition yet led to a discussion of the meaning of "literary," or of the poetics of the *Zohar* (the question of what "literature" is in the thirteenth-century Iberian peninsula has yet to be asked by philologists and historians alike, in this field). This holds true for the valuable work of Itamar Greenwald, Michal Oron (who promises that there is more to come in her forthcoming work), Mordechai Fechter, and Kurt E. Grözinger (in *The Age of the Zohar*, Joseph Dan., ed.), most of whom credit Liebes for his "path-breaking" article "The Messiah of the Zohar" (partly translated in Liebes, *Studies in the Zohar*; Hebrew original in The Israel Academy of Sciences and Humanities, *The Messianic Idea in Jewish Thought*). To this list should be added the work of Elliot Wolfson, who, though he unquestionably opens new venues in the matter of interpretation, also forcefully preserves the "basic concepts" of Kabbalah studies (namely "mysticism," "myth," and "symbol"), most notably on literary terms. Wolfson does extend the boundaries of Kabbalah to include poems, but he seeks there evidence of the "experiential" moments that govern much of his research (see Wolfson, *Through a Speculum*, *Circle in the Square*, and *Along the Path*). For the most part, those who advocate or proclaim their emerging interest in "literature" remain fairly silent about their understanding of a term they barely deploy critically. Moreover, they rarely relate to the literature of the time, unless it has already been identified as "Kabbalah" or as "mysticism." But why would the "religious" Ibn al-ʿArabi be more relevant than the "secular" Ibn Ḥazm's *Ṭawq al-Ḥamāma* (and otherwise than to show the ancient, purely Jewish, antecedents of kabbalistic prayer practices [see Idel, "The Prayer in the Kabbalah of Provence"; on Ibn Ḥazm, see esp. 276–77])? More relevant than Arabic and Hebrew "secular" poetry (not just Ibn Gabirol) and *maqāmāt* literature, the *Roman de la rose*, or the *Libro de buen amor*? What understanding of culture does this exclusive attention to "religious" and "mystical" texts, this hermetic separation between "sacred" and "profane," indicate? All it seems to produce is, once again, essentialism (of "mysticism" and of "Judaism") and a profuse use of a limited number of analytical categories such as form/content, and authorship. An additional attention is paid to very specific "literary" dimensions (midrashic, exegetical, and biographical) that insistently reinscribe and relocate the *Zohar* within a continuous chain of (*purely*?) "Jewish" traditions that would connect—without "outside influences"—the "inner history" that links Moses at Sinai with the late Rabbi Schneerson in Brooklyn. These and numerous references to Liebes's work as a kind of "last word" on literary issues still seem to me to sum up what is an important, if somehow slow, trend toward a "literary" reading of the zoharic texts. It is also important to note that in "Zohar and Eros" Liebes now writes of what he sees as his "essential role, *ᶜikar tafkidi*" as a scholar: the exposure of the *Zohar* as one of the greatest literary works in world literature (81). This is, indeed, a welcome indication of possible change in the configuration of disciplinary boundaries such as they still stand. Whatever "literature" means, it is important to emphasize that the term is meant here to open possibilities of reading, and to generate discussions toward a reflection on the very practice scholars and others engage in when "reading" a book such as the *Zohar*. As María Rosa Menocal reminds me, Harold Bloom's *Kabbalah and Criticism* is a significant example of how a literary scholar may be able to detect or underscore some of the intricacies of rhetoric and poetics in kabbalistic texts, as they transpired through Scholem's descriptions. For one, this again underscores the complexity and sophistication of Scholem's texts. Worth mentioning for its literary sensitivity is David Stern's short but illuminating pages on the *Zohar* (see Stern's *Parables in Midrash*, 227–32). One should also mention the questioning that emerges from the work of Matti Megged, whose essay "The Kabbalah as Poetry" and his *A Darkened Light* deserve more attention for pointing in a literary direction. A welcome addition toward the literary study of the *Zohar* is Lévy-Valensi, *La Poétique du "Zohar."* As she situates herself clearly outside of the field of Kabbalah studies, Amado Lévy-Valensi is important but clearly an exception in terms of the field itself. Finally, Charles Mopsik has recently argued that in the *Zohar* on Lamentations one finds not only the most striking rendition of its "theosophical system" but also that in it, the text uses a language that is "le plus universel de tous les langages, . . . celui de la littérature, de la poésie, de l'imagination, de la création artistique" (Mopsik, trans., *Le Zohar, Lamentations*, vol. 1, 9). A final remark as to the state of scholarship regarding the larger issue of the study of medieval rhetoric. Arthur M. Lesley has shown how we have very little knowledge of it and of the generic distinctions it practiced. Boundaries between texts and discourses have barely begun to be explored, hence the necessity of opening disciplinary borders rather than closing them (see Lesley, "A Survey of Medieval Hebrew Rhetoric"). We still have very few tools to determine where and how Kabbalah fits in the general picture, in the general production of texts in medieval cultures, let alone to assert that the only way they fit in these cultures is by way of "experiences," "influences," or "assimilation" (on the use and abuse of this last term, see Funkenstein, "Dialectics of Assimilation"). Still, all this persistently remains about localization, responding to dis-location.

4. It is enough for now to mark a few examples of the ubiquity of the ontological assertion in writings on the Kabbalah. Elliot Wolfson's distinction between "levels of discourse" and "ontological spheres" continues a long tradition ("Beautiful Maiden Without Eyes," 167; see also Wolfson's reference to "ontological graduations" in the kabbalistic hierarchy [169]). Elsewhere, Wolfson refers to the "evil realm" as "ontologically posterior" to the divine realm—as if God and Being were always coextensive, as if that had or could have been demonstrated—and attributes this terminology in a footnote to Tishby, *Wisdom of the Zohar* (32; cf. also 29n12). I have not attempted to trace the history of the "ontological" understanding of Kabbalah, but it could be noted that it appears already in David Neumark's *History of Philosophy*, where Neumark refers to kabbalistic symbolism as "ontological and historical symbolism, *ha-simbolismus ha-ontologi veha-histori*" (176). A condensed discussion of the current state of research can be found in Boaz Huss's dissertation, "*Ketem Paz*: The Kabbalistic Doctrine of Rabbi Simeon Lavi in His Commentary to the *Zohar*"; see esp. 113–19. Huss asserts that the "confusion, *ḥoser behirut*" regarding the ontological status of kabbalistic language revolves around problems of definition (*hagdarah*) of the symbol and its *essential link, kesher mahuti*, with the symbolized. Huss thus confirms that the question of essence ("what is?") governs the field in an exclusive way (114). For a forceful, if puzzling, alternative to ontological attributions, see Goldman, "On the Interpretation of Symbols." Finally, I have no disagreement with Yehuda Liebes's latest diagnosis as to the status of symbols in scholarly discourse (though I would and will express reservation as to the following lack of doubt: "Undoubtedly, many passages in the *Zohar* are consciously symbolic"). Yet it may be noted that the rationale Liebes offers for speaking instead of a "mythic language" is made in the name of the very same drive to reference: "Symbolic language . . . is quite different from what I shall refer to as 'mythic' language: that is, the direct reference to the divine entity itself" (Liebes, "Myth vs. Symbol," 213). This "direct" relation locates ever more effectively, of course, the language of the *Zohar*.

5. Kilito, *Les Séances*, 20.

6. *Zohar*, II: 94b–95a ("Saba de mishpatim"); Matt, trans., *Zohar: The Book of Enlightenment*, 121–22.

7. *Zohar*, III: 152a. In an already extended line of scholarly discussions of this statement, Stephen Benin recently reaffirmed the disdain of "mere stories" to which the *Zohar* would testify without any perceivable hint of irony (Benin, "Mere Stories," 91ff.). Interestingly, though, Benin makes a parallel with the famous zoharic parable in which a man from the mountains is offered a taste from a variety of wheat products (good bread, cakes kneaded in oil, royal pastry made with honey and oil) and thinks himself "the master of all these, for I eat the essence, *ᶜiqqara*, of all these: wheat!" The *Zohar* then continues: "Because of that

view, he knew nothing of the delights of the world; they were lost to him. So it is with one who grasps the principle, *kelala,* and does not know all those delectable delights deriving, diverging from that principle" (*Zohar,* II: 176a). The parallel established by Benin is interesting precisely because, if valid, it confirms that the *Zohar* recommends that one should not, in fact, dismiss and throw away the stories, and other garments and shells, in the mode of the proverbial bath water.

8. There lies in this one possible reason for the insistence on "myth" in recent scholarship, a "higher" substitute for the word "narrative" that the *Zohar* "condemns" in a highly ironical manner—myth translates narrative.

9. See Daniel Matt's comments on the dissemination of the *Zohar* and on the famous assertion on narrative and "secular compositions" in *Zohar: The Book of Enlightenment,* 3 and 204.

10. Matt, trans., *Zohar: The Book of Enlightenment,* 8.

11. Additional, if fragmented and partial, starting points by literary critics that gestured toward a literary-inflected reading of these provenances (while still too often deferring to the expertise of nonliterary scholars) were provided by Samuel Miklos Stern, in "Rationalists and Kabbalists in Medieval Allegory"; and David Stern, in *Parables in Midrash,* 227–33; and Matti Meged.

12. *Zohar,* I: 1b.

13. Azulay, *Ḥesed le-Abraham,* quoted in Mopsik, "Avant-propos," 12.

14. On this passage, see Matt, "'New-Ancient Words,'" 196.

15. *Zohar,* II: 215a.

16. *Zohar,* I: 1b.

17. Agamben, *The Idea of Prose,* 55.

18. I am borrowing this phrase from Homi Bhabha.

19. It is introduced with the general "we have learned, *taninan.*" No source is identified in the text, nor is there a rabbinical parallel that would provide an "author."

20. *Zohar,* I: 204b.

21. Bracken, *The Potlatch Papers,* 5.

22. I take Elliot Wolfson's discussion of "walking as a sacred duty," his attention to matters of paths and ways, to be both refreshing and indicative of the "declinations" of the place of the *Zohar.* Wolfson only mentions a late interpretation of the *Zohar* as a background, a context, to the practice of wandering in early Hasidism. I am not aware of a comparable discussion—and there are few who have studied the *Zohar* as extensively as Wolfson—on the wanderings of and in the *Zohar* (Wolfson, "Walking as a Sacred Duty: Theological Transformation of Social Reality in Early Hasidism," in *Along the Path*).

23. Matt, trans., *Zohar: The Book of Enlightenment,* 9.

24. Scholem, *Major Trends,* 181.

25. Ibid., 185.

26. Ibid., 157–88.

27. Lévy-Valensi, *La Poétique du Zohar*, 11. In what follows, I also rely on Betty Rojtman's (*Feu noir sur feu blanc*) unique and impressive study of what she calls "Jewish hermeneutics."

28. In an article that bears relevance here, Nina Caputo has convincingly described a different and distinct moment of such multiplied beginnings and failures in another instance, parts of which we have encountered earlier. At "our place in al-Andalus," Caputo explains, Naḥmanides "wrestled" with interpreting *bereshit*, in the beginning, attempting to produce a reading that would be "equally relevant for understanding the deeds of the patriarchs as . . . for understanding the vicissitudes of Jewish life in thirteenth-century Aragon" (Caputo, "*In the Beginning* . . . : Typology, History, and the Unfolding Meaning of Creation," 62). Doing so, Naḥmanides struggled with "the virtual impossibility of isolating any moment of time as the beginning of a narrative or event, all the more so when the event or story in question is the supreme act of divine creation" (66).

29. Lévy-Valensi, *La Poétique du Zohar*, 23.

30. Scholem, *Major Trends*, 156.

31. Ibid., 158.

32. Elie Munk, quoted in Rojtman, *Feu noir*, 113/E86.

33. See Scholem's discussion of pseudepigraphy in the *Zohar*, in *Major Trends*, 204; and see also Bernard Levinson's broaching of the subject as to the *Zohar*'s traditional antecedents in "The Right Chorale," 152. I am not aware of any discussion that would raise, in a comparative setting, the general question of the relation between this practice in the *Zohar* and what Marcia Colish called "one of the most striking innovations in Latin literature," namely "the production of texts, purporting to be classical, invented out of whole cloth by twelfth-century writers" (Colish, *Medieval Foundations*, 178). Declinations of contexts.

34. D. Boyarin, "Reading Without the Phallus."

35. I quote from the narrative of Isaac of Acre as reproduced in Isaiah Tishby's introduction to *The Wisdom of the Zohar*, 13–15.

36. Scholem, *Major Trends*, 174. How is it possible to establish that no "genuine quotation" could be found from "earlier writings" said to "have since disappeared"? Scholem never seems to question the remarkable philological achievement that would be involved here.

37. I have begun an interrogation of the referential drive that governed Scholem's readings or misreadings, and that continues to operate in the field of Kabbalah studies, in my "Jewish Mysticism Alterable and Unalterable."

38. The testimony of Isaac of Acre is preserved in a fifteenth-century book, *Sefer ha-yuḥasin*, by Abraham Zacuto. According to the *Encyclopedia Judaica*, Zacuto too was interested in mapping space: "Various passages in *Sefer ha-yuḥasin* testify to his interest in the burial sites of the pious in Ereṣ Israel" (*Encyclopedia Judaica*, 16: 906).

39. Tishby, *Wisdom of the Zohar*, 16.

40. Ibid., 15.

41. I am referring here to the work of Nitsa Kahn in particular. Note that the claim made by Moses de León's wife already locates her within medieval literature as it reproduces a recurring feature of *maqāma* literature, where narrative developments often end with a version or other of an authorial "admission" that all was invented (see for example *Minhat Yehuda Sone ha-Nashim*, by Judah Ibn Shabbetai, where the ostensible reason for writing-as-invention is also, as in Mrs. de León's "testimony," the gain of fame and money. The narrator turns to his patron and says: "The whole story was composed only in order to bring it to pass that I might stand before you in order to find your favor. For a man's wit gives him relief from his labors and leads him into the presence of the great." In D. Stern and Mirsky, eds., *Narrative Fantasies*, 289).

42. Coulmas, "Principes masculin et féminin dans le *Zohar*," 52 and *passim*. Although feminist readings of the *Zohar* have yet to come, it should be noted that the impact of feminist studies and gender studies are producing some of the most exciting work to date in Kabbalah studies, of which Coulmas is a striking example, but Charles Mopsik had led the way with his reading of the "Holy Letter." More recently, Elliot Wolfson is developing complex and new lines of research in these directions. The violent reactions that Wolfson's work—not just his conclusions—has elicited in Israel provide an interesting indication of the comforting places in which some would seem to want (sexuality) to remain.

43. Mopsik, "Avant-propos," 11.

44. Ibid., 12; referring to Azulay, *Ḥesed le-Abraham*, 4: 28.

45. This too is quoted in Isaiah Tishby's introduction to *Wisdom of the Zohar* (19). But see also the extended discussion of this story and of the significance of the *Zohar* in Morocco in Zafrani, *Kabbale vie mystique et magie*.

46. Scholem, *Major Trends*, 189.

47. Mopsik, "Avant-propos," 16. Whether or not the "purity" suggested by Mopsik could in fact be achieved, it is important to note that the *Zohar*'s Aramaic is also not Aramaic. Much as in the case of Maimonides' *Guide*, which obligates its readers to forget the language they already know, the *Zohar*'s Aramaic requires that one forget the Aramaic one already knows.

48. Scholem, "Tradition and New Creation in the Ritual of the Kabbalists," in *On the Kabbalah and Its Symbolism*, 118–19.

49. I quote from Scholem's discussion of the *Zohar*'s author and his "style" in *Major Trends*, 164–71.

50. Ibid., 164; my emphasis.

51. On the emergence of vernacular literatures, see Menocal, *Shards of Love*; focusing on the romance tradition, see Curtius, *European Literature*, 383ff.; and see Kittay and Godzich, *The Emergence of Prose*.

52. See Curtius, *European Literature*, 32. As Curtius explains, the words "*Enromancier, romançar, romanzare* mean: to translate or compose books in the vernacular."

53. See for example *Zohar*, II: 129b and 132b.

54. See for example *Zohar*, I: 9b, and I: 88b ("Sitrei Torah").

55. Yahalom, "Angels Do Not Understand Aramaic," 34.

56. Lieberman, quoted in ibid., 35.

57. See Matt, "'New-Ancient Words.'" True enough, as Matt writes, "the composer of the Zohar has assembled an alternative Rabbinic literature" (184) and she/he/they are clearly committed to the tradition, but what this tradition is, and how the text fits (or does not fit) in this tradition is the question raised by its "ancient-new" endeavor. From the perspective of current readings—overwhelmingly diachronic ("historical") and locating the text within "mysticism" (however qualified and defined) and other experiential realms—one must ask whether the accent has not been placed too exclusively on a very particular kind of contextualization.

58. I quote here from Scholem, *Major Trends*, 157–58, 171, and 173.

59. Ibid., 174.

60. For a description of this more recent chapter in translation, see Brann, *The Compunctious Poet*, esp. chap. 1; and see Dan Pagis's own description of the state of things in his *Hebrew Poetry of the Middle Ages*, 70–71.

61. Monroe, "Maimonides on the Mozarabic Lyric."

62. On these issues see Monroe, "Maimonides on the Mozarabic Lyric," and see also ha-Levi, poem 113 (*ᶜOfer ben enosh*) in Brody, *Dīwān des Abū-l-Hasān Jehuda ha-Levi*, 2: 322–23; and Samuel M. Stern's comments on this poem in *Les Chansons mozarabes*, 12. Stern briefly discusses this poem again in *Hispano-Arabic Strophic Poetry* (142). For "Aramaic," Stern translates "in the tongue of the Christians." Tova Rosen-Moked discusses the introduction of the final verses (*kharja*) of such poems and cites this poem as an example of an introduction of "Arabic or Mozarabic [i.e., Hispano-Arabic or Hispano-Romance]." She brings additional examples of the poets' introduction of the *kharja* by calling attention to its distinctive dimension as either "foreign" or spoken (Rosen-Moked, *Hebrew Girdle Poem*, 196–97). Finally, note that the Arabic term *ᶜajamiyya* was a synonym for *laṭīnīya*, another name for a vernacular (see Monroe, "Maimonides on the Mozarabic Lyric," 29n16; and see also Wasserstein, "The Language Situation in al-Andalus," 7ff.).

63. Ha-Nagid, "Belekhti laḥazot aḥi," in Yarden, *Dīwān Shmuel ha-Nagid*, 237; Cole, trans. and ed., *Selected Poems of Shmuel ha-Nagid*, 22.

64. *Kuzari*, 2: 68. It is to be noted that this understanding of Aramaic—not Hebrew—as vernacular was historically renewed, if not quite continuously maintained. Benjamin Harshav describes what is by now familiar, the practice of renewing "literature" by appealing, if partly, to the vernacular, and naming this vernacular, again, "Aramaic." In the case of eastern European Jewry, then, and "with the revival of Hebrew literature in Diaspora, Aramaic received a special position and an important stylistic function . . . it signaled living speech, that is, Yiddish" (Harshav, *Language in Time of Revolution*, 168).

65. Guillaume de Lorris and Jean de Meun, *Le Roman de la rose*, ll. 37–38.

66. Jabès, *Le Livre des questions*, 145–49; *The Book of Questions*, 129–32 (trans. slightly altered).

67. Gasché, "'Setzung' and 'Übersetzung,'" 42.

68. Scholem, *Major Trends*, 164.

69. "The exact nature of these references, which is difficult to grasp, is located somewhere at the intersection of a symbolization and a concretization, *la nature exacte de ces références, difficile à saisir, se situe quelque part au croisement d'une symbolisation et d'une concrétisation*," writes Betty Rojtman in *Feu noir* (93–94/E71).

70. *Zohar*, I: 1a.

71. Scholem, *Major Trends*, 26.

72. Is there anything, in other words, to *interpret*? I am relying on Paul de Man here, who describes how, for Charles Sanders Peirce, "the sign is to be interpreted if we are to understand the idea it is to convey, and this is so because the sign is not the thing but a meaning derived from the thing by a process here called representation." De Man, "Semiology and Rhetoric," in *Allegories of Reading*, 8–9.

73. Mopsik, trans., *Le Zohar*, vol. 1, 29.

74. Tishby, *Wisdom of the Zohar*, 235/E391. This could of course also be translated as "who is Shoshana [or Suzanne]"—indeed, who could she be? The English translation does not consider the proper name but understands the *shoshana*, against medieval usage, as "lily." On the understanding of this verse as *rosa inter spinas, la rosa de entre las espinas* as a topos of medieval Spanish literature, see McGrady, "More on the Image of the 'Rose Among Thorns' in Medieval Spanish Literature."

75. Rojtman, *Feu noir*, 94n12/E176n12.

76. Genette, "Figures," in *Figures of Literary Discourse*, 59.

77. McGann, "What Is Critical Editing," in *The Textual Condition*, esp. 53–57.

78. Bland, "Medieval Jewish Aesthetics," 548; quoting Foucault.

79. See Scholem, *Major Trends*, 167 (and n60), where Scholem refers to "formulae with which distinctions between different categories of the same general application are introduced" as being "everywhere the same" (167). The illustration, made in the footnote that follows this sentence, brings two specific examples of the use of *'it ve-it'*, a phrase that occurs, Scholem says, "in hundreds of places" (389n60). How such words became "categories" is never quite made clear by Scholem.

80. De Man, *Allegories of Reading*, 62.

81. Mopsik, *Les Grands textes de la Cabale*, 68–69.

82. Gasché, 44; quoting de Man, *Allegories*, 56.

83. De Man, *Allegories*, 9.

84. Maimonides, *Guide*, 3.

85. Pagis, "Variety in Medieval Rhymed Narratives," 94.

86. See de Man, *Allegories*, 11–13.

87. *Hans Wehr Dictionary of Modern Written Arabic*, 3rd ed., see under qām (qawm).

88. "This situation of incomprehension repeats itself, in one form or another, in the whole of the *Séances*. What is constantly created between the interlocutors is a cut, a distance, both of which make any exchange hazardous and problematical. Far from being a means of communication, a docile mediator, language appears rather as an obstacle to comprehension. Misunderstanding, equivocation, and 'noise' become the rule of conversation." Kilito, *Les Séances*, 214.

89. Prendergast has "He bored me with his wife's virtues," a translation that I alter for reasons that will become clear.

90. "The séances of Hamaḏānī . . . are the site of a dialogue in which two orders, each represented by a character, enter a situation of conflict. Each of the protagonists is the negation of the other, although one witnesses at times exchanges, mutations, which nuance this rigid scheme. The contradiction that situates ᶜIsā ibn Hichām and Abū l-Fatḥ at two opposite poles is often manifested in each of them under the form of a dissonance or of an incoherent behavior. The danger of a subtle contamination can never be avoided." Kilito, *Les Séances*, 65.

91. Al-Saraqusṭī, Abū l-Ṭāhir Muḥammad ibn Yūsuf Al-Tamīmī ibn al-Aštarkūwī, *Al-Maqāmāt al-Luzūmīya*. I am gratefully using James T. Monroe's unpublished translation of this *maqāma*. I have made slight changes to Monroe's translation, mostly to underscore the reading of the text I follow in my argument. With Monroe, I follow al-Warāglī's edition, which, for the most part of the *maqāma* "On Poetry and Prose" and for my purposes, is not significantly different from Ḍayf's edition, upon which Monroe's translation was originally based (see Ḍayf, ed., *Al-Maqāmāt al-Luzūmīya*). There is one significant exception, however, to the general lack of difference between the two editions, namely regarding the section that describes the final part of the debate between the two brothers, when prose is, in its turn, praised. The main difference between the two editions resides in the choice of the main text. Both editors, however, choose to preserve the full, alternative version (see next note). For my discussion, I have followed the choice made by Ḍayf in terms of the version foregrounded (it is in that version, for example, that the "founder" of the *maqāma* "genre" [if it is one], Badīᶜ az-Zamān al-Hamaḏānī, is mentioned). For the biographical, bibliographical, and historical background and more on Ibn al-Aštarkūwī, see Monroe, "Al-Saraqusṭī, ibn al-Aštarkūwī."

92. Or: [How different] are the serious from the playful and the gentle from the weary! What is poetry and the poet? Lies and noises, pure lie and upside-down. How different is the rank of the poet from the writer of prose, the prize from mere wages. This stands on one leg and he is satisfied with tears, while that one sits on a soft seat, and settles down in a preferred place. He walks on flat land and the earth unfolds for him like a carpet. Ranks rise toward him, and the saddlebag is open in front of him. He is clothed with distinction, and he meets power face-to-face. He confides in the king and shares his riddles. He is entrusted with his secrets, the treasurer of his good and wrongdoings. He has delegation to give

orders, and to roar the king's roar. He clothes with meaning the jewelry of his words, and his commands are covered with the mantles of his honor and protection. Perhaps, he disseminates speech and dilutes it, acts justly or unjustly. He has the privilege of dos and don'ts. He drinks from power's sweet basin and pond. He enters first and leaves last, brings hope close. He straightens and projects, disseminates styles and sends gambling arrows, he dispatches writers, and brings close the docile beast. He administers the states and owns horses and servants. Verily, the poet and the writer are like the satisfied and the censor, rank of lies and rank of beauty. [Poetry is] a lowly rule, a walking in shackles. It is never feared but when it ridicules, nor is it content, unless it fulfills hopes. Doors are closed in front of it, and garments are folded away from fear of meeting it. God's name is invoked against its importunity. Doubts are aroused because of its lavishing, it is called upon for no reason. It took away Imru-l-Qais's kingdom and brought upon it ruin. It did not save him as he deserved and distracted him for his coming and going. It demanded his home from him and stood in the way of his power. How many qualities prose has, indeed. Here judgment stops silent and judges.

93. There are recurring examples in the *Maqāmāt al-Luzūmīya* of expressions in which two words contrast or confirm each other. As James Monroe points out, the second term of such an expression often provides the reader with a lead toward clarification. The second word is thus often akin to a synonym. Following that insight, it seems to me important to recognize that the two words are on some level antonyms (*warada* evokes the descent to the well, while *ṣadara* evokes the ascent from it), but also synonyms: they both carry a sense of walking, but also of appearing, somehow suddenly. Biberstein-Kazimirski offers for *warada*, "Prendre, surprendre quelqu'un," as in the case of a fever, for example (*Dictionnaire arabe-français*, 2: 1517); and, for *ṣadara*, "Sortir, émaner, paraître," as well as "Toucher, frapper, blesser quelqu'un à la poitrine" (1: 1318). Hans Wehr has "to appear" for both verbs. The verb *ṣadara* occurs again in Ibn al-Aštarkūwī's text, immediately after our expression, referring to the way the words that are coming and going issue or emerge out of a God-fearing soul.

94. Binary oppositions, as Abdelfattah Kilito points out, are in fact necessary, structural elements in the discourse of the *maqāma* as Ḥarīrī developed it (Kilito, *Les Séances*, 213ff.).

95. Kilito, "Le Genre 'séance.'"

96. Monroe, *The Art*, 163–64. It is worth mentioning that the argument made by Monroe regarding the determining role of Mu^{c}tazilite exegesis in the development of a new literary discourse is advanced again in a very significant way by Susan Stetkevytch, in a different perspective and about another literary development. Specifically, Stetkevytch argues that practices of exegesis that were becoming dominant in Arabic culture in the ^{c}Abbāsid period were also significant in the development of the *badī*^{c} style (see Stetkevytch, *Abū Tammām*, esp. chap. 1).

97. The problem of divine intention (*ta*^{c}*līl*) was an important site of con-

tention in the dispute over methods of legal judgment. The possibility of making inferences or drawing analogies from intention was taken by some Ẓāhiris to be as elusive in the case of God as it was in the case of the law-giver: "They considered it unjustifiable to try to guess the *intention* of the law-giver on the basis of subjective judgement" (Goldziher, *The Ẓāhiris*, 52; author's emphasis). In the context of exegesis, intention was also of major importance. Jaroslav Stetkevych describes how *taʾwīl* is the expression of concern with "covert, or virtual meaning, or it reduces meaning to its ultimate *intent*" (Stetkevych, "Arabic Hermeneutical Terminology," 92). In many ways, then, it is also the question of intention and of the possibility of settling on an "ultimate intent" that is raised in this section.

98. The explicitness I speak of here may have to be qualified, as the sentence I quote does not appear in Warāglī's edition of the *Maqāmāt*, but only in Ḍayf's edition.

99. "On sait que le mot *nazm* signifie arrangement, organisation, mise en ordre (des mots à l'intérieur d'un énoncé); dans un sens particulier, il signifie *poésie*" (Kilito, "Le Genre 'séance,'" 28n2).

100. For a discussion, and to some extent a continuation, of these issues, see van Gelder, *Beyond the Line.*

101. Al-Hamadhānī, quoted in Monroe, *The Art*, 22n11.

102. Writing in the eleventh century, Avicenna (Ibn Sīnā) refers to the creation as the emanative process that brings about the "existence of a cosmic 'virtuous system (*niẓām li-l-ḫair*)'" (Heath, *Allegory and Philosophy*, 37).

103. I follow Ḍayf, who read *iṣfāq*, rather than Warāglī, who has *iḫfāq*.

104. Most of this passage is only found in Ḍayf's edition (555).

105. In contemporary terms, one would want to say that the most general terms of agreement—even if not achieved—were already settled between them: the brothers can be said to move toward "agreeing to disagree."

106. This is of course one of the longest-standing criticisms against poets. It is found, among other places, in the famous description of poets as "liars" who "preach what they never practice" (Qurʾān, 26:226).

107. The connections made by James Monroe between mercantilism and the development of the *maqāma* may help us to see in this marginal comment a significant repetition of the affirmation of commercial versus more traditional, intellectual practices. "By the tenth century, . . . the simple faith of the early days of Islam had been replaced by more worldly values derived from the needs of a complex commercial culture of international dimensions. Urban Muslims must have become increasingly aware of the ever widening gap separating Islamic practice from Islamic theory and ideals: *ad-dunyā* or *al-āḫīra*? The characters of the *maqāmāt*, significantly, function very much within a mercantile context, and it is mercantile goals that guide their actions" (Monroe, *The Art*, 129–30).

Bibliography

Abed, Shukri B. *Aristotelian Logic and the Arabic Language in Alfārābī.* Albany: State University of New York Press, 1991.

Abraham, Nicolas, and Maria Torok. *Cryptonymie: Le Verbier de l'homme aux loups.* Paris: Aubier-Flammarion, 1976. Trans. Nicholas Rand as *The Wolfman's Magic Word: A Cryptonymy.* Minneapolis: University of Minnesota Press, 1986.

———. *The Shell and the Kernel: Renewals of Psychoanalysis.* Trans. Nicholas Rand. Chicago: University of Chicago Press, 1994.

Abu Deeb, Kamal. *Al-Jurjānī's Theory of Poetic Imagery.* Warminster, Eng.: Aris and Phillips, 1979.

Abu-Haidar, Jareer. "*Maqāmāt* Literature and the Picaresque Novel." *Journal of Arabic Literature* 5 (1974): 1–10.

Agacinski, Sylviane et al., eds. *Mimesis desarticulations.* Paris: Flammarion, 1975.

Agamben, Giorgio. *The Coming Community.* Trans. Michael Hardt. Minneapolis: University of Minnesota Press, 1993.

———. *Idea of Prose.* Trans. Michael Sullivan and Sam Whitsitt. Albany: State University of New York Press, 1995.

———. *Infancy and History: Essays on the Destruction of Experience.* Trans. Liz Heron. London: Verso, 1993.

———. *Language and Death: The Place of Negativity.* Trans. Karen E. Pinkus and Michael Hardt. Minneapolis: University of Minnesota Press, 1991.

———. *Moyens sans fin: Notes sur la politique.* Paris: Bibliothèque Rivages, 1995.

———. *Potentialities: Collected Essays in Philosophy.* Trans. Daniel Heller-Roazen. Stanford, Calif.: Stanford University Press, 1999.

———. *Stanzas: Word and Phantasm in Western Culture.* Trans. Ronald L. Martinez. Minneapolis: University of Minnesota Press, 1993.

Ajami, Mansour. *The Alchemy of Glory.* Washington: Three Continents, 1988.

———. *The Neckveins of Winter.* Leiden: E. J. Brill, 1984.

Alcalay, Ammiel. *After Jews and Arabs: Remaking Levantine Culture.* Minneapolis: University of Minnesota Press, 1993.

Alféri, Pierre. *Guillaume d'Ockham: Le Singulier.* Paris: Minuit, 1989.

Althusser, Louis. "Ideology and Ideological State Apparatuses (Notes Toward and Investigation)." In Althusser, *Lenin and Philosophy and Other Essays,* 127–86. New York: Monthly Review Press, 1971.

Angel, Marc, and Herman P. Salomon. "Naḥmanides' Approach to Midrash in the Disputation of Barcelona." *American Sephardi* 6, nos. 1–2 (1973): 41–51.

Anidjar, Gil. "Jewish Mysticism Alterable and Unalterable: On Orienting Kabbalah Studies and the '*Zohar* of Christian Spain.'" *Jewish Social Studies* 3, no. 1 (1996): 89–157.

Arié, Rachel. *Etudes sur la civilisation de l'Espagne musulmane.* Leiden: E. J. Brill, 1990.

Ashtor, Eliyahu. *The Jews of Moslem Spain.* Vols. 1–3. Trans. Aaron Klein and Jenny Machlowitz Klein. Philadelphia: Jewish Publication Society, 1992.

Assis, Yom Tov. "The Judeo-Arabic Tradition in Christian Spain." In *The Jews of Medieval Islam: Community, Society, and Identity,* ed. Daniel Frank, 111–24. Leiden: E. J. Brill, 1995.

Atlan, Henri. "Mystique et rationalité autour de Maimonide." In *The Thought of Moses Maimonides: Philosophical and Legal Studies,* ed. Ira Robinson et al. Lewiston, N.Y.: Edwin Mellen Press, 1990.

Auerbach, Erich. "Figura." In Auerbach, *Scenes from the Drama of European Literature,* 11–76. Minneapolis: University of Minnesota Press, 1984.

Auerbach, M. "Die Ansichten des Maimonides und des Nachmanides über die Bedeutung des Midrasch für die Halacha." *Jeschurun: Monatschrift für Lehre und Leben im Judentum* 24 (1924): 356–63.

Azulay, Abraham. *Ḥesed le-Abraham.* Jerusalem, n.p., 1968.

Badawi, ʿAbdurrahmān. "Méprises au sujet de Maimonide." In *Délivrance et fidélité: Maimonide* (texts of talks held at UNESCO in December 1985), 47–54. Paris: Erès, 1986.

Baer, Yitzhak. *A History of the Jews in Christian Spain.* Philadelphia: Jewish Publication Society of America, 1961.

Bahti, Timothy. "Figure, Scheme, Trope." In *The New Princeton Encyclopedia of Poetry and Poetics,* ed. Alex Preminger and Terry V. F. Brogan, 409–12. Princeton, N.J.: Princeton University Press, 1993.

Balibar, Étienne. "Le Concept de 'rupture épistemologique' de Gaston Bachelard à Louis Althusser." In Balibar, *Ecrits pour Althusser,* 9–57. Paris: La Découverte, 1991.

Barkai, Ron, ed. *Chrétiens, musulmans, et juifs dans l'Espagne médiévale: De la convergence à l'expulsion.* Paris: Cerf, 1994.

Beinart, Haim, ed. *Moreshet Sepharad: The Sephardi Legacy.* Jerusalem: Magnes Press, 1992.

Benabu, Isaac, ed. *Circa 1492: Proceedings of the Jerusalem Colloquium: Litterae Judaeorum in Terra Hispanica.* Jerusalem: Magnes Press, 1992.

Benin, Stephen D. "Mere Stories and Ordinary Words." *Jewish Social Studies* 6, no. 1 (1999): 83–97.
Benjamin, Walter. *Gesammelte Schriften.* 7 vols. Ed. Rolf Tiedemann and Hermann Schweppenhauser. Frankfurt am Main: Suhrkamp, 1974–89.
———. *Illuminations.* Trans. Harry Zohn. Ed. Hannah Arendt. New York: Schocken, 1968.
———. "N, 9, 4 [Re The Theory of Knowledge, Theory of Progress]." In *Benjamin: Philosophy, Aesthetics, History,* ed. Gary Smith, 43–83. Chicago: University of Chicago Press, 1989.
———. *The Origin of the German Tragic Drama.* Trans. John Osborne. London: Verso, 1985.
———. *Selected Writings.* Vol. 1. Ed. Marcus Bullock and Michael Jennings. Cambridge, Mass.: Harvard University Press, 1996.
———. "The Task of the Translator." In Benjamin, *Illuminations,* trans. Harry Zohn, ed. Hannah Arendt, 69–82. New York: Schocken, 1968.
Bernstein, Michael André. *Foregone Conclusions: Against Apocalyptic History.* Berkeley: University of California Press, 1994.
Biale, David. *Gershom Scholem: Kabbalah and Counter-History.* Cambridge, Mass.: Harvard University Press, 1982.
———. "Gershom Scholem's Ten Unhistorical Aphorisms on Kabbalah." In *Gershom Scholem,* ed. Harold Bloom, 99–123. New York: Chelsea House, 1987.
———. "Sabataï Tzevi et les séductions de l'orientalisme juif." *Les Cahiers du judaïsme* 2 (1998): 13–22.
Biberstein-Kazimirski, Albert de. *Dictionnaire arabe-français.* Rev. ed. 2 vols. Paris: Maisonneuve, 1960.
Black, Deborah. *Logic and Aristotle's Rhetoric and Poetics in Medieval Arabic Philosophy.* Leiden: E. J. Brill, 1990.
Blanchot, Maurice. *L'Écriture du désastre.* Paris: Gallimard, 1980.
Bland, Kalman. "Medieval Jewish Aesthetics: Maimonides, Body, and Scripture in Profiat Duran." *Journal of the History of Ideas* 54, no. 4 (1993): 533–59.
Blau, Joshua. "'At Our Place in al-Andalus,' at Our Place in the Maghreb." In *Perspectives on Maimonides,* ed. Joel L. Kraemer, 293–94. Oxford: Oxford University Press, 1991.
———. "Maimonides, Al-Andalus, and the Influence of the Spanish-Arabic Dialect on His Language." In *New Horizons in Sephardic Studies,* ed. Yedida K. Stillman and George K. Zucker, 203–10. Albany: State University of New York Press, 1993.
Bloom, Harold, ed. *Gershom Scholem.* New York: Chelsea House, 1987.
Blumenthal, David R. "Maimonides on Mind and Metaphoric Language." In *Approaches to Judaism in Medieval Times,* ed. David R. Blumenthal, 123–32. Chico, Calif.: Scholars Press, 1985.

Boase, Roger. *The Origin and Meaning of Courtly Love: A Critical Study of European Scholarship.* Manchester, Eng.: Manchester University Press, 1977.

Boyarin, Daniel. *Carnal Israel: Reading Sex in Talmudic Culture.* Berkeley: University of California Press, 1993.

———. "The Eye in the Torah: Ocular Desire in Midrashic Hermeneutic." *Critical Inquiry* 16 (1990): 532–50.

———. *Intertextuality and the Reading of Midrash.* Bloomington: Indiana University Press, 1990.

———. "Midrash in Parables." Review of *Parables in Midrash: Narrative and Exegesis in Rabbinic Literature,* by David Stern. *AJS Review* 20, no. 1 (1995).

———. "Reading Without the Phallus; or, Barter in a Midrashic Economy." University of California, Berkeley, 30 August 1997.

———. *Sephardi Speculation: A Study in Methods of Talmudic Interpretation* (in Hebrew). Jerusalem: Ben Zvi Institute, 1989.

———. "Take the Bible for Example: Midrash as Literary Theory." In *Unruly Examples: On the Rhetoric of Exemplarity,* ed. Alexander Gelley, 27–47. Stanford, Calif.: Stanford University Press, 1995.

———. *Unheroic Conduct: The Rise of Heterosexuality and the Invention of the Jewish Man.* Berkeley: University of California Press, 1997.

Boyarin, Daniel, and Stern, David. "An Exchange on the Mashal." *Prooftexts* 5 (1985): 269–80.

Boyarin, Jonathan. *Storm from Paradise: The Politics of Jewish Memory.* Minneapolis: University of Minnesota Press, 1992.

———. *Thinking in Jewish.* Chicago: University of Chicago Press, 1996.

Bracken, Christopher. *The Potlatch Papers: A Colonial Case History.* Chicago: University of Chicago Press, 1997.

Brann, Ross. *The Compunctious Poet: Cultural Ambiguity and Hebrew Poetry in Muslim Spain.* Baltimore: Johns Hopkins University Press, 1991.

———, ed. *Languages of Power in Islamic Spain.* Bethesda: CDL Press, 1997.

Braude, W. "Maimonides' Attitude to Midrash." In Charles Berlin, ed., *Studies in Jewish Bibliography, History, and Literature in Honor of I. Edward Kiev,* 75–82. New York: Ktav Publishing, 1971.

Brunschvig, Robert. "Valeur et fondement du raisonnement juridique par analogie d'après al-Ghazālī." *Studia Islamica* 34 (1972): 57–88.

Buijs, Joseph A., ed. *Maimonides: A Collection of Critical Essays.* Notre Dame, Ind.: University of Notre Dame Press, 1988.

Burns, Robert I., ed. *Emperor of Culture: Alfonso X the Learned of Castile and His Thirteenth-Century Renaissance.* Philadelphia: University of Pennsylvania Press, 1990.

Butler, Judith. *Bodies that Matter: On the Discursive Limits of "Sex."* New York: Routledge, 1993.

———. *Excitable Speech: A Politics of the Performative.* New York: Routledge, 1997.
———. *Gender Trouble: Feminism and the Subversion of Identity.* New York: Routledge, 1990.
———. *The Psychic Life of Power: Theories in Subjection.* Stanford, Calif.: Stanford University Press, 1997.
Cadava, Eduardo. "Toward an Ethics of Decision." *Diacritics* 24, no. 4 (1994): 4–29.
———. *Words of Light: Theses on the Photography of History.* Princeton, N.J.: Princeton University Press, 1997.
———. "Words of Light: Theses on the Photography of History." *Diacritics* 22, nos. 3–4 (1992): 84–114.
Caputo, Nina. "'And God Rested on the Seventh Day': Creation, Time, and History in Medieval Jewish Culture." Ph.D. diss., Department of History, University of California, Berkeley, 1999.
———. "*In the Beginning* . . . : Typology, History, and the Unfolding Meaning of Creation in Naḥmanides' Exegesis." *Jewish Social Studies* 6, no. 1 (1999): 54–82.
Carmi, T., ed. *The Penguin Book of Hebrew Verse.* New York and London: Penguin, 1981.
Castro, Américo. *The Spaniards: An Introduction to Their History.* Trans. Willard F. King and Selma Margaretten. Berkeley: University of California Press, 1971.
Certeau, Michel de. *The Writing of History.* Trans. Tom Conley. New York: Columbia University Press, 1988.
Chase, Cynthia. *Decomposing Figures: Rhetorical Readings in the Romantic Tradition.* Baltimore: Johns Hopkins University Press, 1986.
Chazan, Robert. *Barcelona and Beyond: The Disputation of 1263 and Its Aftermath.* Berkeley: University of California Press, 1992.
Chétrit, Joseph. "Le Judéo-arabe et ses stratégies d'existence." In *La Société juive à travers l'histoire,* ed. Shmuel Trigano, 521–31. Paris: Fayard, 1993.
Cheyette, Brian, and Laura Marcus. *Modernity, Culture, and "the Jew."* Stanford, Calif.: Stanford University Press, 1998.
Cohen, Gerson D., ed. *The Book of Tradition (Sefer ha-Qabbalah), by Abraham ibn Daud.* Philadelphia: Jewish Publication Society, 1967.
Cohen, J. P. "Figurative Language, Philosophy, and Religious Belief: An Essay on Some Themes in Maimonides' *The Guide of the Perplexed.*" In *Studies in Jewish Philosophy,* ed. Norbert Samuelson, 367–96. Lanham, Md.: University Press of America, 1987.
Cohen, Mark. *Under Crescent and Cross: The Jews in the Middle Ages.* Princeton, N.J.: Princeton University Press, 1994.
Cohen, Richard. *Elevations: The Height of the Good in Rosenzweig and Levinas.* Chicago: University of Chicago Press, 1994.

Cohen, Tom. *Anti-Mimesis from Plato to Hitchcock.* Cambridge, Eng.: Cambridge University Press, 1994.

Cole, Peter, trans. and ed. *Selected Poems of Shmuel ha-Nagid.* Princeton, N.J.: Princeton University Press, 1996.

Colish, Marcia L. *Medieval Foundations of the Western Intellectual Tradition 400–1400.* New Haven, Conn.: Yale University Press, 1997.

Coulmas, Corinna. "Principes masculin et féminin dans le *Zohar* ou la rigueur d'une méthode." *Cahiers d'études juives* 1 (1986): 41–70.

Courcelles, Dominique de. *La Parole risquée de Raymond Lulle: Entre le judaïsme, le christianisme, et l'islam.* Paris: Vrin, 1993.

Culler, Jonathan. *On Deconstruction: Theory and Criticism After Structuralism.* Ithaca, N.Y.: Cornell University Press, 1982.

Curtius, Ernst R. *European Literature and the Latin Middle Ages.* Trans. Willard Trask. New York: Harper Torchbooks/Bollingen, 1963.

Cutter, William. "Ghostly Hebrew, Ghastly Speech: Scholem to Rosenzweig, 1926." *Prooftexts* 10, no. 3 (1990): 413–33.

Dan, Joseph, ed. *The Age of the Zohar.* Jerusalem Studies in Jewish Thought 8. Jerusalem: Magnes Press, 1989.

Darwish, Mahmoud, *Eleven Planets* (in Arabic). Beirut: Dar al-Jadid, 1992.

———. *The Tragedy of Narcissus/The Comedy of Silver.* Syracuse, N.Y.: Syracuse University Press, 2000.

de Man, Paul. *Aesthetic Ideology.* Ed. Andrzej Warminski. Minneapolis: University of Minnesota Press, 1996.

———. *Allegories of Reading: Figural Language in Rousseau, Nietzsche, Rilke, and Proust.* New Haven, Conn.: Yale University Press, 1979.

———. "Autobiography as De-facement." *Modern Language Notes* 94 (1979): 919–30.

———. "Conclusions: Walter Benjamin's 'The Task of the Translator.'" In de Man, *The Resistance to Theory,* 73–105. Minneapolis: University of Minnesota Press, 1986.

———. *The Resistance to Theory.* Minneapolis: University of Minnesota Press, 1986.

de Vries, Hent. "Anti-Babel: The 'Mystical Postulate' in Benjamin, de Certeau, and Derrida." *Modern Language Notes* 107 (1992): 441–77.

de Vries, Hent, and Samuel Weber, ed. *Violence, Identity, and Self-Determination.* Stanford, Calif.: Stanford University Press, 1997.

Délivrance et fidélité: Maimonide. Texts of talks held at UNESCO in December 1985. Paris: Erès, 1986.

Derrida, Jacques. *Acts of Religion.* Ed. Gil Anidjar. New York: Routledge, 2001.

———. "Of an Apocalyptic Tone Newly Adopted in Philosophy." In *Derrida and Negative Theology,* ed. Harold Coward and Toby Foshay, 25–71. Albany: State University of New York Press, 1992.

———. *Aporias.* Trans. Thomas Dutoit. Stanford, Calif.: Stanford University Press, 1993.

———. *Archive Fever: A Freudian Impression.* Trans. Eric Prenowitz. Chicago: University of Chicago Press, 1996.

———. *La Carte postale: De Socrate à Freud et au-delà.* Trans. Alan Bass as *The Post Card: From Socrates to Freud and Beyond.* Chicago: University of Chicago Press, 1987.

———. *L'Écriture et la différence.* Paris: Seuil, 1967. Trans. Alan Bass as *Writing and Difference.* Chicago: University of Chicago Press, 1978.

———. "Fors." In *Cryptonymie: Le Verbier de l'homme aux loups,* 8–73. Trans. Barbara Johnson as the foreword to "Fors: The Anglish Words of Nicholas Abraham and Maria Torok," in Nicolas Abraham and Maria Torok, *The Wolfman's Magic Word: A Cryptonymy.* Minneapolis: University of Minnesota Press, 1986.

———. *Glas.* Paris: Denoel/Gonthier, 1981. Trans. John P. Leavey, Jr., and Richard Rand as *Glas.* Lincoln: University of Nebraska Press, 1986.

———. *De la grammatologie.* Paris: Seuil, 1967. Trans. Gayatri C. Spivak as *Of Grammatology.* Baltimore: Johns Hopkins University Press, 1976.

———. "Interpretations at War: Kant, the Jew, the German." *New Literary History* 22, no. 1 (1991): 39–95.

———. *Limited Inc.* Trans. Samuel Weber. Evanston, Ill.: Northwestern University Press, 1988.

———. "La Loi du genre." In Derrida, *Parages,* 249–87. Paris: Galilée, 1986. Trans. Avital Ronell as "The Law of Genre," in *Acts of Literature,* ed. Derek Attridge, 221–52. New York: Routledge, 1992.

———. *Marges de la philosophie.* Paris: Editions de Minuit, 1972. Trans. Alan Bass as *Margins of Philosophy.* Chicago: University of Chicago Press, 1982.

———. *Memoires: For Paul de Man.* Trans. Cecile Lindsay et al. New York: Columbia University Press, 1989.

———. *Monolinguisme de l'autre; ou, La Prothèse de l'origine.* Paris: Galilée, 1996. Trans. Patrick Mensah as *Monolingualism of the Other; or, The Prosthesis of Origin.* Stanford, Calif.: Stanford University Press, 1998.

———. "Otobiographies: The Teaching of Nietzsche and the Politics of the Proper Name." In Derrida, *The Ear of the Other,* 3–38. Lincoln: University of Nebraska Press, 1988.

———. *Parages.* Paris: Galilée, 1986.

———. *Politiques de l'amitié.* Paris: Galilée, 1994. Trans. Georges Collins as *Politics of Friendship.* London: Verso, 1997.

———. *Schibboleth pour Paul Célan.* Paris: Galilée, 1986.

———. "Le Toucher." *Paragraph* 16, no. 2 (1993): 122–57.

———. *Le Toucher, Jean-Luc Nancy.* Paris: Galilée, 2000.

———. "Des Tours de Babel." In *Difference in Translation,* trans. and ed. Joseph F. Graham, 165–248. Ithaca, N.Y.: Cornell University Press, 1985.

———. *La Vérité en peinture.* Paris: Flammarion, 1978. Trans. Geoff Bennington and Ian McLeod as *The Truth in Painting.* Chicago: University of Chicago Press, 1987.

Diamond, James A. "The Use of Midrash in Maimonides' *Guide of the Perplexed*: Decoding the Duality of the Text." *AJS Review* 21, no. 1 (1996): 39–60.

Dodds, Jerrilynn D. "Mudejar Tradition and the Synagogues of Medieval Spain: Cultural Identity and Cultural Hegemony." In *Convivencia: Jews, Muslims, and Christians in Medieval Spain,* ed. Vivian B. Mann et al., 113–31. New York: George Braziller and the Jewish Museum, 1992.

Drory, Rina. "The Hidden Context: On Literary Production of Tri-Cultural Contacts in the Middle Ages" (in Hebrew). *Peᶜamim* 46–47 (1991): 9–28.

———. "Literary Contacts and Where to Find Them." *Poetics Today* 14, no. 2 (1993): 277–302.

Düttmann, Alexander García. *Between Cultures: Tensions in the Struggle for Recognition.* Trans. Kenneth B. Woodgate. London: Verso, 2000.

———. "On Translatability." Trans. Dana Hollander. *Qui Parle* 8, no. 1 (1994): 29–44.

Eagleton, Terry. *Walter Benjamin; or, Towards a Revolutionary Criticism.* London: Verso, 1981.

Einbinder, Susan. "The Current Debate on the Muwashshaḥ." *Prooftexts* 9 (1989): 161–94.

Eisenstein, J. D., ed. *Otsar ha-vikuhim.* Israel: n.p., 1969.

Ess, Josef van. "The Logical Structure of Islamic Theology." In *Logic in Classical Islamic Culture,* ed. G. E. von Grunebaum. Wiesbaden, Ger.: Otto Harrassowitz, 1970.

Ibn ᶜEzra, Moses. *Dīwān.* Ed. Haim Brody. Berlin: Schocken, 1935.

———. *Kitāb al-muḥaḍāra wa-l-muḏākara* (The book of conversation and discussion). Jerusalem: Mekize Nirdamim, 1975.

Faur, José. *Golden Doves with Silver Dots: Semiotics and Textuality in the Rabbinic Tradition.* Bloomington: Indiana University Press, 1986.

———. *Homo Mysticus: A Guide to Maimonides's "Guide for the Perplexed."* Syracuse, N.Y.: Syracuse University Press, 1999.

Felman, Shoshana. "Benjamin's Silence." *Critical Inquiry* 25, no. 2 (1999): 201–34.

Fishbane, Michael, ed. *The Midrashic Imagination: Jewish Exegesis, Thought, and History.* Albany: State University of New York Press, 1993.

Foucault, Michel. "What Is an Author." In *The Foucault Reader,* ed. Paul Rabinow, 101–20. New York: Pantheon, 1984.

Fox, Marvin. *Interpreting Maimonides: Studies in Methodology, Metaphysics, and Moral Philosophy.* Chicago: University of Chicago Press, 1990.

———. "Naḥmanides on the Status of Aggadot: Perspectives on the Disputation at Barcelona, 1263." *Journal of Jewish Studies* 11, no. 1 (1989): 95–109.

Fraenkel, Yonah. *Darkhe ha-Aggadah veha-Midrash* (The ways of Aggadah and Midrash). Jerusalem: Yad la-Talmud/Masada, 1991.

Frank, Daniel, ed. *The Jews of Medieval Islam: Community, Society, and Identity.* Leiden: E. J. Brill, 1995.

Frank, Daniel H. "The Elimination of Perplexity: Socrates and Maimonides as Guides of the Perplexed." In *Autonomy and Judaism: The Individual and the Community in Jewish Philosophical Thought,* ed. Daniel H. Frank, 121–42. Albany: State University of New York Press, 1992.

Freud, Sigmund. "The Antithetical Meaning of Primal Words." In *The Standard Edition of the Complete Psychological Works of Sigmund Freud,* ed. James Strachey, 2: 155–61. London: Hogarth Press, 1953–74.

———. "Mourning and Melancholia." In *The Standard Edition of the Complete Psychological Works of Sigmund Freud,* ed. James Strachey, 14: 239–58. London: Hogarth Press, 1953–74.

Funkenstein, Amos. "Dialectics of Assimilation." *Jewish Social Studies* 1, no. 2 (1995): 1–14.

———. "Gershom Scholem: Charisma, Kairos, and the Messianic Dialectic." *History and Memory* 4, no. 1 (1992): 123–40.

———. *Perceptions of Jewish History.* Berkeley: University of California Press, 1993.

———. *Theology and the Scientific Imagination.* Princeton, N.J.: Princeton University Press, 1986.

Fynsk, Christopher. *Heidegger: Thought and Historicity.* 2nd ed. Ithaca, N.Y.: Cornell University Press, 1993.

———. *Language and Relation . . . That There Is Language.* Stanford, Calif.: Stanford University Press, 1996.

Gasché, Rodolphe. "'Setzung' and 'Übersetzung': Notes on Paul de Man." *Diacritics* 11 (1981): 36–57.

———. *The Tain of the Mirror: Derrida and the Philosophy of Reflection.* Cambridge, Mass.: Harvard University Press, 1986.

Gelder, G. J. H. van. *Beyond the Line: Classical Arabic Literary Critics on the Coherence and Unity of the Poem.* Leiden: E. J. Brill, 1982.

Gellens, Sam. "The Search for Knowledge in Medieval Muslim Societies: A Comparative Approach." In *Muslim Travelers: Pilgrimage, Migration, and the Religious Imagination,* ed. Dale F. Eikelman and James Piscatori, 50–65. Berkeley: University of California Press, 1990.

Gellman, Jerome I. "Maimonides' 'Ravings.'" *Review of Metaphysics* 45 (December 1991): 309–28.

Genette, Gérard. *Figures of Literary Discourse.* New York: Columbia University Press, 1982.

Giladi, Avner. "Note About the Possible Origin of the Title 'Guide of the Perplexed'" (in Hebrew). *Tarbiz* 48, nos. 3–4 (April–September 1979): 346–47.

Glick, Thomas F. *Islamic and Christian Spain in the Early Middle Ages.* Princeton, N.J.: Princeton University Press, 1979.

Godzich, Wlad, and Jeffrey Kittay. *The Emergence of Prose: An Essay in Prosaics.* Minneapolis: University of Minnesota Press, 1987.

Goichon, A. M. *Lexique de la langue philosophique d'Ibn Sīnā.* Paris: Desclée de Brouwer, 1938.

Goldin, Judah. "The Freedom and Restraint of Haggadah." In *Studies in Midrash and Related Literature,* ed. B. L. Eichler and J. Tigay, 253–69. Philadelphia: Jewish Publication Society, 1988.

Goldman, Steven Louis. "On the Interpretation of Symbols and the Christian Origins of Modern Science." *Journal of Religion* 62, no. 1 (1982): 1–20.

Goldziher, Ignaz. *The Ẓāhiris: Their Doctrine and Their History.* Trans. W. Behn. Leiden: E. J. Brill, 1971.

Goodman, Lenn E. "Matter and Form as Attributes of God in Maimonides' Philosophy." In *A Straight Path: Studies in Medieval Philosophy and Culture: Essays in Honor of Arthur Hyman,* ed. Ruth Link-Salinger et al., 86–97. Washington: Catholic University of America Press, 1988.

Guellouz, Suzanne. *Le Dialogue.* Paris: Presses Universitaires de France, 1992.

Guillaume, de Lorris, and Jean de Meun. *Le Roman de la rose.* Paris: Le Livre de Poche, 1992.

Gutas, Dimitri. *Greek Wisdom Literature in Arabic Translation.* New Haven, Conn.: American Oriental Society, 1975.

Guttmann, Julius. "Das Problem der Kontingenz in der Philosophie des Maimonides." *Monatsschrift für Geschichte und Wissenschaft des Judentums* 83 (1939): 406–30.

Habermas, Jürgen. *The Philosophical Discourse of Modernity.* Trans. F. G. Lawrence. Cambridge, Mass.: MIT Press, 1987.

———. "Walter Benjamin: Consciousness Raising or Rescuing Critique." In *On Walter Benjamin: Critical Essays and Recollections,* ed. Gary Smith, 90–128. Cambridge, Mass.: MIT Press, 1988.

Hall, Stuart. "Cultural Studies and Its Theoretical Legacies." In *Cultural Studies,* ed. Lawrence Grossberg et al., 277–94. New York: Routledge, 1992.

Hamacher, Werner. "Afformative, Strike: Benjamin's 'Critique of Violence.'" In *Walter Benjamin's Philosophy: Destruction and Experience,* ed. Andrew Benjamin and Peter Osborne, 110–38. New York: Routledge, 1994.

———. "One 2 Many Multiculturalisms." In *Violence, Identity, and Self-Determination,* ed. Hent de Vries and Samuel Weber, 284–325. Stanford, Calif.: Stanford University Press, 1997.

———. *Premises: Essays on Philosophy and Literature from Kant to Celan.* Trans. Peter Fenves. Cambridge, Mass.: Harvard University Press, 1996.

al-Hamaḏānī, Badīᶜ az-Zamān. "The Maqāma of the Spindle." In *Maqāmāt Abī l-Faḍl Badīᶜ az-Zamān al Hamaḏānī,* ed. Muḥammad ᶜAbduh. Beirut, 1908.

Trans. W. J. Prendergast as *The Maqāmāt of Badīᶜ az-Zamān al Hamadhānī.* 1915. Reprint, London and Dublin: Curzon Press, 1973.

Hanssen, Beatrice. "Philosophy at Its Origin: Walter Benjamin's Prologue to the Ursprung des deutschen Trauerspiels." *Modern Language Notes* 110 (1995): 809–33.

———. "On the Politics of Pure Means: Benjamin, Arendt, Foucault." In *Violence, Identity, and Self-Determination,* ed. Hent de Vries and Samuel Weber, 236–52. Stanford, Calif.: Stanford University Press, 1997.

———. *Walter Benjamin's Other History: Of Stones, Animals, Human Beings, and Angels.* Berkeley: University of California Press, 1998.

al-Ḥarizi, Yehuda. *Sefer Taḥkemoni.* Ed. Y. Toporovski. Tel Aviv: Maḥbarot lesifrut, 1952. Trans. Victor Emmanuel Reichert as *The Tahkemoni of Judah al-Harizi.* Jerusalem: Raphael Haim Cohen's Press, 1965.

Harshav, Benjamin. *Language in Time of Revolution.* Stanford, Calif.: Stanford University Press, 1999.

Hartman, Geoffrey H., and Sanford Budick, eds. *Midrash and Literature.* New Haven, Conn.: Yale University Press, 1986.

Harvey, Irene. "Derrida and the Issue of Exemplarity." In *Derrida: A Critical Reader,* ed. David Wood, 193–217. Oxford: Basil Blackwell, 1992.

Harvey, Leonard P. *Islamic Spain: 1250 to 1500.* Chicago: University of Chicago Press, 1990.

———. "The Survival of Arabic Culture in Spain After 1492." In *La Signification du bas moyen âge dans l'histoire et la culture du monde musulman,* 85–88. Aix-en-Provence: Edisud, 1978.

Harvey, Warren Z. "How to Begin to Study the *Guide of the Perplexed* I: 1" (in Hebrew). *Daat* 21 (1988): 5–23.

———. "Why Maimonides Was Not a Mutakallim." In *Perspectives on Maimonides,* ed. Joel L. Kraemer, 105–14. Oxford: Oxford University Press, 1991.

Hary, Benjamin. *Multiglossia in Judeo-Arabic.* Leiden: E. J. Brill, 1992.

Ibn Ḥazm. *Ṭawq al-Ḥamāma fi-l-ulfa wa-l-ullāf.* Ed. Léon Bercher. Algiers: Éditions Carbonel, 1949.

Heath, Peter. *Allegory and Philosophy in Avicenna.* Philadelphia: University of Pennsylvania Press, 1992.

Hegel, Georg Wilhelm Friedrich. *Phenomenology of Spirit.* Trans. A. V. Miller. Oxford: Oxford University Press, 1977.

———. *The Philosophy of History.* Trans. J. Sibree. New York: Prometheus, 1991.

Hegyi, O. "Minority and Restricted Uses of the Arabic Alphabet: The Aljamiado Phenomenon." *Journal of the American Oriental Society* 99, no. 2 (1979): 262–69.

Heidegger, Martin. *Being and Time.* Trans. J. Macquarrie and E. Robinson. New York: Harper and Row, 1962.

———. "The End of Philosophy and the Task of Thinking." In *Basic Writings,* ed. David Farell Krell, 373–92. New York: Harper and Row, 1977.

———. "The Origin of the Work of Art." In Heidegger, *Poetry, Language, Thought*, 15–87. New York: Harper and Row, 1971.

Heinemann, Isaak. *Darkhe ha'aggadah* (The ways of the aggadah). Jerusalem: Magnes Press, 1970.

Heinemann, Joseph. *Aggadot ve-toldotehen* (Aggadah and its development). Jerusalem: Keter, 1974.

———. "The Nature of the Aggadah." In *Midrash and Literature*, ed. Geoffrey H. Hartman and Sanford Budick, 41–55. New Haven, Conn.: Yale University Press, 1986.

Huss, Boaz. "*Ketem Paz*: The Kabbalistic Doctrine of Rabbi Simeon Lavi in His Commentary to the *Zohar*" (in Hebrew). Ph.D. diss., Hebrew University, Jerusalem, 1992.

Hyman, Arthur. "Interpreting Maimonides." In *Maimonides: A Collection of Critical Essays*, ed. Joseph A. Buijs, 19–29. Notre Dame, Ind.: University of Notre Dame Press, 1988.

Idel, Moshe. *Kabbalah: New Perspectives.* New Haven, Conn.: Yale University Press, 1987.

———. "Mystique juive et histoire juive." *Annales HSS* 5 (1994): 1223–40.

———. "The Prayer in the Kabbalah of Provence" (in Hebrew). *Tarbiz* 62, no. 2 (1993): 265–86.

———. "Reification of Language in Jewish Mysticism." In *Mysticism and Language*, ed. Steven T. Katz, 42–79. Oxford: Oxford University Press, 1992.

———. "Universalization and Integration: Two Conceptions of Mystical Union in Jewish Mysticism." In *Mystical Union and Monotheistic Faith: An Ecumenical Dialogue*, ed. Moshe Idel and Bernard McGinn, 27–57. New York: Macmillan, 1989.

Iser, Wolfgang, and Sanford Budick, eds. *Languages of the Unsayable: The Play of Negativity in Literature and Literary Theory.* New York: Columbia University Press, 1989.

Israel Academy of Sciences and Humanities, The. *The Messianic Idea in Jewish Thought: A Study Conference in Honor of the Eightieth Birthday of Gershom Scholem.* Jerusalem: Magnes Press, 1982.

Ivry, Alfred. "Maimonides on Possibility." In *Mystics, Philosophers, and Politicians: Essays in Jewish Intellectual History in Honor of Alexander Altmann*, ed. J. Reinharz et al., 67–84. Durham, N.C.: Duke University Press, 1982.

———. "Providence, Divine Omniscience, and Possibility." In *Maimonides: A Collection of Critical Essays*, ed. Joseph A. Buijs, 175–91. Notre Dame: University of Notre Dame Press, 1988.

Jabès, Edmond. *Le Livre des questions.* Paris: Gallimard, 1963. Trans. Rosmarie Waldrop as *The Book of Questions.* Middletown, Conn.: Wesleyan University Press, 1976.

Jabre, Farid. *Essai sur le lexique de Ghazali.* Beirut: Publications de l'Université Libanaise, 1970.

Jacobs, Carol. *Telling Time: Lévi-Strauss, Ford, Lessing, Benjamin, de Man, Wordsworth, Rilke.* Baltimore: Johns Hopkins University Press, 1993.

Jacquart, Danielle, and Claude Thomasset. *Sexuality and Medicine in the Middle Ages.* Trans. Matthew Adamson. Princeton, N.J.: Princeton University Press, 1988.

Jameson, Frederic. *The Political Unconscious: Narrative as a Socially Symbolic Act.* Ithaca, N.Y.: Cornell University Press, 1981.

Janowitz, Naomi. *The Poetics of Ascent: Theories of Language in a Rabbinic Ascent Text.* Albany: State University of New York Press, 1989.

Jayyusi, Salma Khadra, ed. *The Legacy of Muslim Spain.* Leiden: E. J. Brill, 1992.

Jennings, Michael W. *Dialectical Images: Walter Benjamin's Theory of Literary Criticism.* Ithaca, N.Y.: Cornell University Press, 1987.

Jospe, Raphael. "Naḥmanides and Arabic" (in Hebrew). *Tarbiz* 57, no. 1 (1987): 67–93.

———. Review of *Interpreting Maimonides: Studies in Methodology, Metaphysics, and Moral Philosophy,* by Martin Fox. *AJS Review* 20, no. 1 (1995): 207–10.

Kant, Immanuel. *Critique of Judgment.* Trans. J. H. Bernard. New York: Hafner Press, 1951.

———. *Critique of Pure Reason.* Trans. Norman Kemp Smith. New York: St. Martin's Press, 1965.

Kasher, Hannah. "The Art of Writing in the *Guide of the Perplexed*" (in Hebrew). *Daat* 37 (Summer 1996): 63–106.

———. "*The Guide of the Perplexed*—Literary Masterpiece or Holy Writ?" (in Hebrew). *Daat* 32–33 (1994): 73–83.

Kellner, Menahem. *Maimonides on the "Decline of the Generations" and the Nature of Rabbinic Authority.* Albany: State University of New York Press, 1996.

Kemal, Salim. "Philosophy and Theory in Arabic Poetics." *Journal of Arabic Literature* 20 (1989): 128–47.

Ibn Khaldun. *The Muqaddimah: An Introduction to History.* Trans. F. Rosenthal. New York: Bollingen/Pantheon, 1958.

Kiener, Ronald. "The Image of Islam in the *Zohar.*" In *The Age of the "Zohar,"* ed. Joseph Dan, 43–65. Jerusalem Studies in Jewish Thought 8. Jerusalem: Magnes Press, 1989.

Kilito, Abdelfattah. "Le Genre 'séance': Une Introduction." *Studia Islamica* 43 (1976): 25–51.

———. *Les Séances.* Paris: Sindbad, 1983.

Klein-Braslavy, Sarah. *Maimonides' Interpretation of the Story of Creation* (in Hebrew). Jerusalem: Reuven Mass, 1987.

Koestenbaum, Wayne. *Double Talk: The Erotics of Male Literary Collaboration.* New York: Routledge, 1989.

Kozodoy, Neal. "Reading Medieval Hebrew Love Poetry." *AJS Review* 2 (1977): 111–29.

Kraemer, Joel L. "Alfarabi's *Opinions of the Virtuous City* and Maimonides' *Foundations of the Law.*" In I. Navon et al., *Studia Orientalia Memoriae D. H. Baneth Dedicata,* 107–53. Jerusalem: Magnes Press, 1979.

———. "The Influence of Islamic Law upon Maimonides: The Five Qualifications" (in Hebrew). *Studies in Judaica (Teᶜuda)* 10 (1996): 225–44.

———. "On Maimonides' Messianic Posture." In *Studies in Medieval Jewish History and Literature,* ed. Isadore Twersky, 109–42. Cambridge, Mass.: Harvard University Press, 1984.

———. "Sharīᶜa and Nāmūs in the Philosophical Thought of Maimonides" (in Hebrew). *Studies in Judaica (Teᶜuda)* 4 (1986): 185–202.

———, ed. *Perspectives on Maimonides: Philosophical and Historical Studies.* Oxford: Oxford University Press, 1991.

Lacoue-Labarthe, Philippe. "The Echo of the Subject." In *Typography: Mimesis, Philosophy, Politics,* ed. Christopher Fynsk, 139–207. Stanford, Calif.: Stanford University Press, 1998.

———. "Oedipe comme figure." In Lacoue-Labarthe, *L'Imitation des modernes (Typographies II),* 203–25. Paris: Galilée, 1986.

———. *Le Sujet de la philosophie: Typographies I.* Paris: Aubier-Flammarion, 1979.

———. *Typography: Mimesis, Philosophy, Politics.* Trans. and ed. Christopher Fynsk. Stanford, Calif.: Stanford University Press, 1998.

Lacoue-Labarthe, Philippe, and Jean-Luc Nancy. "Le Dialogue des genres." *Poétique* 21 (1975): 148–75.

Lane, Edward William. *An Arabic-English Lexicon.* London: Williams and Norgate, 1863.

Laplanche, Jean, and Jean-Baptiste Pontalis. *Vocabulaire de la psychanalyse.* Paris: Presses Universitaires de France, 1973.

Lavi, Shimᶜon. *Ketem Paz* (in Hebrew). Jerusalem: Ahavat Shalom, 1981.

Leaman, Oliver. *Moses Maimonides.* London: Routledge, 1990.

Lesley, Arthur M. "A Survey of Medieval Hebrew Rhetoric." In *Approaches to Judaism in Medieval Times,* ed. David. R. Blumenthal, 107–33. Chico, Calif.: Scholars Press, 1985.

Leupin, Alexandre. *Fiction et incarnation: Littérature et théologie au moyen âge.* Paris: Flammarion, 1993.

ha-Levi, Yehuda. *Dīwān des Abū-l-Hasān Jehuda ha-Levi.* Vol. 2. Ed. Haim Brody. Berlin: Mekize Nirdamim, 1909.

———. *The Kuzari* (in Judeo-Arabic). Ed. David Baneth. Jerusalem: Magnes Press, 1977.

Levinas, Emmanuel. *Autrement qu'être ou au-delà de l'essence.* The Hague: Martinus Nijhoff, 1974. Trans. Alphonso Lingis as *Otherwise Than Being or Beyond Essence*. Dordrecht: Kluwer Academic Publishers, 1978.

———. "La Réalité et son ombre." *Les Temps modernes* 38 (1948): 771–89. Trans. Alphonso Lingis as "Reality and Its Shadow," in *The Levinas Reader*, ed. Sean Hand, 129–43. Cambridge, Mass.: Basil Blackwell, 1989.

———. *Totalité et infini*. The Hague: Martinus Nijhoff, 1961. Trans. Alphonso Lingis as *Totality and Infinity*. Pittsburgh: Duquesne University Press, 1969.

Levinson, Bernard. "The Right Chorale: From the Poetics to the Hermeneutics of the Hebrew Bible." In *Not in Heaven: Coherence and Complexity in Biblical Narrative*, ed. Jason P. Rosenblatt and Joseph C. Sitterson, Jr., 129–53. Bloomington: Indiana University Press, 1991.

Lévy-Valensi, Eliane Amado. *La Poétique du "Zohar."* Paris: Éditions de l'Éclat, 1996.

Libera, Alain de. *Penser au moyen âge*. Paris: Seuil, 1991.

Liebes, Yehuda. "Myth vs. Symbol in the *Zohar* and in Lurianic Kabbalah." In *Essential Papers on Kabbalah*, ed. L. Fine, 212–42. New York: New York University Press, 1995.

———. "New Directions in the Study of Kabbalah" (in Hebrew). *Peʿamim* 50 (1992): 150–70.

———. *Studies in the "Zohar."* Trans. Arnold Schwartz, Stephanie Nakache, and Penina Peli. Albany: State University of New York Press, 1993.

———. "*Zohar* and Eros" (in Hebrew). *Alpayim* 9 (1994): 67–119.

Maimonides (Ibn Maimun), Moses. *Dalālat al-ḥāʾirīn*. Ed. Husein Atay. Ankara, Turk.: Maktabat aṯ-Ṯaqāfat ad-Dīnīya, 1972.

———. *Dalālat al-ḥāʾirīn*. Ed. I. Joel. Jerusalem: J. Junovitch, 1929.

———. *The Guide of the Perplexed*. 2 vols. Intro. Leo Strauss. Trans. Shlomo Pines. Chicago: University of Chicago Press, 1963.

———. *Introduction to the Mishna* (in Hebrew). Ed. I. Shilat. Jerusalem: Maaliot, 1992.

Margaliot, Reʾuven, ed. *Sefer ha-Zohar*. Jerusalem: Mosad ha-Rav Kook, 1984.

Matt, Daniel. "'New-Ancient Words': The Aura of Secrecy in the *Zohar*." In *Gershom Scholem's Major Trends in Jewish Mysticism, 50 Years After: Proceedings of the Sixth International Conference on the History of Jewish Mysticism*, ed. Peter Schaefer and Joseph Dan, 181–207. Tübingen: Mohr, 1993.

———, *"Zohar": The Book of Enlightenment*. Ramsey, N.J.: Paulist Press, 1983.

McGann, Jerome. *The Textual Condition*. Princeton, N.J.: Princeton University Press, 1991.

McGrady, Donald. "More on the Image of the 'Rose Among Thorns' in Medieval Spanish Literature." *La corónica* 17, no. 2 (1988–89): 33–37.

Meged, Matti. *A Darkened Light: Aesthetical Values in the Book of Splendor* (in Hebrew). Tel Aviv: n.p., 1980.

———. "The Kabbalah as Poetry." In *Proceedings of the Xth Congress of the Inter-*

national Comparative Literature Association, ed. Anna Balakian, 558–64. New York: Garland Publishing, 1985.

Menocal, María Rosa. *The Arabic Role in Medieval Literary History: A Forgotten Heritage.* Philadelphia: University of Pennsylvania Press, 1987.

———. *Shards of Love: Exile and the Origins of the Lyric.* Durham, N.C.: Duke University Press, 1994.

Momigliano, Arnoldo. *Essays on Ancient and Modern Judaism.* Trans. M. Masella-Gayley. Chicago: University of Chicago Press, 1994.

Monroe, James T. *The Art of Badīᶜ al-Zamān al-Hamadānī as Picaresque Narrative.* Beirut: American University of Beirut, 1983.

———. *Hispano-Arabic Poetry.* Berkeley: University of California Press, 1974.

———. *Islam and the Arabs in Spanish Scholarship (Sixteenth Century to the Present).* Leiden: E. J. Brill, 1970.

———. "Maimonides on the Mozarabic Lyric (A Note on the Muwwaššaḥa)." *La corónica* 17, no. 2 (1988–89): 18–32.

———. "Al-Saraqusṭī, ibn al-Aštarkūwī: Andalusi Lexicographer, Poet, and Author of *Al-Maqāmāt al-Luzūmīya.*" *Journal of Arabic Literature* 28 (1997): 1–37.

———. "*Zajal* and *Muwaššaḥa*: Hispano-Arabic Poetry and the Romance Tradition." In *The Legacy of Muslim Spain*, ed. Salma Khadra Jayyusi, 398–419. Leiden: E. J. Brill, 1992.

Montrose, Louis A. "Professing the Renaissance: The Poetics and Politics of Culture." In *The New Historicism*, ed. H. Aram Veeser, 15–36. New York: Routledge, 1989.

Mopsik, Charles. "Avant-propos." In Mopsik, trans., *Le Zohar*, vol. 1, 7–19. Paris: Verdier, 1981.

———. "The Body of Engenderment in the Hebrew Bible, the Rabbinic Tradition, and the Kabbalah." In *Fragments for a History of the Human Body*, ed. Michel Feher, 49–73. New York: Zone Books, 1989.

———. *Les Grands textes de la Cabale: Les Rites qui font Dieu.* Paris: Verdier, 1993.

———. "Le Judéo-araméen tardif, langue de la Cabale théosophique." *Les Cahiers du judaïsme* 6 (2000): 4–14.

———. *La Lettre sur la sainteté: Le Secret de la relation entre l'homme et la femme dans la Cabale.* Paris: Verdier, 1986.

———. "Notes complémentaires." In Mopsik, trans., *Le Zohar*, vol. 2, 513–54. Paris: Verdier, 1984.

———. "Pensée, voix, et parole dans le Zohar." *Revue de l'histoire des religions* 213–14 (1996): 385–414.

———, trans. *Le Zohar, Lamentations.* Paris: Verdier, 2000.

Motzkin, Arieh L. "On Maimonides' Interpretation" (in Hebrew). *Iyyun* 28, nos. 2–3 (1978): 186–200.

Munk, Salomon. "Note sur le titre de cet ouvrage." In Munk, *Le Guide des égarés*, 379–80. Paris: Maisonneuve et Larose, 1960.

Myers, David. *Re-Inventing the Jewish Past: European Jewish Intellectuals and the Zionist Return to History*. Oxford: Oxford University Press, 1995.

Nägele, Rainer. *Echoes of Translation: Reading Between Texts*. Baltimore: Johns Hopkins University Press, 1997.

———. *Theater, Theory, Speculation: Walter Benjamin and the Scenes of Modernity*. Baltimore: Johns Hopkins University Press, 1991.

———, ed. *Benjamin's Ground: New Readings of Walter Benjamin*. Detroit: Wayne State University Press, 1988.

Nancy, Jean-Luc. *La Communauté désœuvrée*. Paris: Christian Bourgeois, 1986. Trans. Peter Connor et al. as *The Inoperative Community*. Minneapolis: University of Minnesota Press, 1991.

———. *Etre singulier pluriel*. Paris: Galilée, 1996.

———. *L'Expérience de la liberté*. Paris: Galilée, 1988. Trans. Bridget McDonald as *The Experience of Freedom*. Stanford, Calif.: Stanford University Press, 1993.

———. *Le Partage des voix*. Paris: Galilée, 1982.

———. *Une Pensée finie*. Paris: Galilée, 1990.

———. *Le Sens du monde*. Paris: Galilée, 1993. Trans. Jeffrey S. Librett as *The Sense of the World*. Minneapolis: University of Minnesota Press, 1997.

Nancy, Jean-Luc, with Jean-Christophe Bailly. *La Comparution*. Paris: Christian Bourgeois, 1991.

Neumark, David. *The History of Philosophy in Israel* (in Hebrew). Vol. 1. New York: Stybel, 1921.

Nietzsche, Friedrich. *Untimely Meditations*. Trans. R. J. Hollingdale. Cambridge, Eng.: Cambridge University Press, 1983.

Nirenberg, David. *Communities of Violence: Persecution of Minorities in the Middle Ages*. Princeton, N.J.: Princeton University Press, 1996.

———. "Muslim-Jewish Relations in the Fourteenth Century Crown of Aragon." *Viator* 24 (1993): 249–68.

Nuriel, Abraham. "Parables Not Explicitly Identified as Such in the *Guide of the Perplexed*" (in Hebrew). *Daat* 25 (1990): 85–91.

O'Callaghan, Joseph F. *A History of Medieval Spain*. Ithaca, N.Y.: Cornell University Press, 1975.

Ouaknin, Marc-Alain. *Concerto pour quatre consonnes sans voyelles: Au-delà du principe d'identité*. Paris: Balland, 1991.

Pagis, Dan. *Hebrew Poetry of the Middle Ages and the Renaissance*. Berkeley: University of California Press, 1991.

———. "Variety in Medieval Rhymed Narratives." *Scripta Hierosolymitana: Studies in Hebrew Narrative Art Throughout the Ages* 27 (1978): 79–98.

Pines, Shlomo. "The Limitations of Human Knowledge According to Al-Farabi, Ibn Bajja, and Maimonides." In *Studies in Medieval Jewish History and Literature*, ed. I. Twersky, 82–109. Cambridge, Mass.: Harvard University Press, 1979.

———. "The Philosophic Sources of the *Guide of the Perplexed*." Translator's introduction to *The Guide of the Perplexed*, trans. and ed. Shlomo Pines, lvii–cxxxiv. Chicago: University of Chicago Press, 1963.

Pines, Shlomo, and Yirmiyahu Yovel, eds. *Maimonides and Philosophy*. Dordrecht: Martinus Nijhoff, 1986.

Piterberg, Gabriel. "Domestic Orientalism: The Representation of 'Oriental' Jews in Zionist/Israeli Historiography." *British Journal of Middle Eastern Studies* 23, no. 2 (1996): 125–45.

ha-Rambam, Abraham ben. *Milḥamot ha-Shem* (The wars of the Lord). Jerusalem: Mosad ha-Rav Kook, 1952.

Rawidowitz, S. "The Question of the Guide's Structure" (in Hebrew). In *Studies in Maimonides [Likkutei Tarbiz V]* 41–89. Jerusalem: Magnes Press, 1985.

Raz-Krakotzkin, Amnon. "'Without Concern for Others': The Question of Christianity in Scholem and Baer" (in Hebrew). *Jewish Studies* 38 (1998): 73–96.

———. "Exile Within Sovereignty: Toward a Critique of the 'Negation of Exile' in Israeli Culture" (in Hebrew). *Theory and Criticism: An Israeli Forum* 4–5 (1993): 23–56, 113–32.

———. "The National Narration of Exile: Zionist Historiography and Medieval Jewry" (in Hebrew). Ph.D. diss., History Department, Tel Aviv University, 1996.

Rickels, Laurence A. *Aberrations of Mourning: Writing on German Crypts*. Detroit: Wayne State University Press, 1988.

Robinson, Ira, et al., eds. *The Thought of Moses Maimonides: Philosophical and Legal Studies*. Lewiston, N.Y.: Edwin Mellen Press, 1990.

Rojtman, Betty. *Feu noir sur feu blanc: Essai sur l'herméneutique juive*. Paris: Verdier, 1986. Trans. Steven Randall as *Black Fire on White Fire: An Essay on Jewish Hermeneutics, from Midrash to Kabbalah*. Berkeley: University of California Press, 1998.

———. "Sacred Language and Open Text." In *Midrash and Literature*, ed. Geoffrey H. Hartman and Sanford Budick, 159–75. New Haven, Conn.: Yale University Press, 1986.

Ronell, Avital. *Crack Wars: Literature, Addiction, Mania*. Lincoln: University of Nebraska University Press, 1992.

———. *Dictations: On Haunted Writing*. Lincoln: University of Nebraska Press, 1993.

———. *Finitude's Score: Essays for the End of the Millennium*. Lincoln: University of Nebraska Press, 1994.

———. "Street-Talk." In *Benjamin's Ground: New Readings of Walter Benjamin*, ed. Rainer Nägele, 119–45. Detroit: Wayne State University Press, 1988.

———. *The Telephone Book: Technology—Schizophrenia—Electric Speech*. Lincoln: University of Nebraska Press, 1989.

Rose, Gillian. "Walter Benjamin: Out of the Sources of Modern Judaism." *New Formations* 20 (1993): 59–81.

Rosen-Moked, Tova. *The Hebrew Girdle Poem (Muwwašsaḥ) in the Middle Ages* (in Hebrew). Haifa: Haifa University Press, 1985.

Rosenthal, Franz. *Knowledge Triumphant: The Concept of Knowledge in Medieval Islam.* Leiden: E. J. Brill, 1970.

Roskies, David G. *Against the Apocalypse: Responses to Catastrophe in Modern Jewish Culture.* Cambridge, Mass.: Harvard University Press, 1984.

Rotenstreich, Nathan. *Essays in Jewish Philosophy in the Modern Era.* Amsterdam: J. C. Gieben, 1996.

Roth, Norman. *Maimonides: Essays and Texts: 850th Anniversary.* Madison: Hispanic Seminary of Medieval Studies, 1985.

Rötzer, Florian. *Conversations with French Philosophers.* Trans. G. E. Aylesworth. Atlantic Highlands, N.J.: Humanities Press, 1995.

Ibn Rushd, *Kitāb faṣl al-maqāl.* Ed. Georges Hourani. Leiden: E. J. Brill, 1959.

Sadan, Yosef. "Rabbi Yehuda al-Ḥarizi as Cultural Crossroad" (in Hebrew). *Peᶜamim* 68 (1996): 16–67.

Said, Edward. "The Text, the World, the Critic." In *Textual Strategies: Perspectives in Post-Structuralist Criticism,* ed. Josué V. Harari, 161–88. Ithaca, N.Y.: Cornell University Press, 1979.

Santner, Eric. *Stranded Objects: Mourning, Memory, and Film in Postwar Germany.* Ithaca, N.Y.: Cornell University Press, 1990.

Saperstein, Marc. *Decoding the Rabbis: A Thirteenth Century Commentary on the Aggadah.* Cambridge, Mass.: Harvard University Press, 1980.

Al-Saraqusṭī, Abū l-Ṭāhir Muḥammad ibn Yūsuf Al-Tamīmī ibn al-Aštarkūwī. *Al-Maqāmāt al-Luzūmīya.* Ed. Ḥasan al-Warāglī. Rabat, Morocco: Maṭābiᶜ Manšūrāt ᶜUkāẓ, 1995.

———. *Al-Maqāmāt al-Luzūmīya.* Ed. Badr Aḥmad Ḍayf. Alexandria: Al-Hayʾa al-Miṣrīya al-ᶜĀmma li-l-Kitāb, 1982.

Schäfer, Peter. *The Hidden and Manifest God: Some Major Themes in Early Jewish Mysticism.* Trans. Aubrey Pomerance. Albany: State University of New York Press, 1992.

———. "Jewish Mysticism in the Twentieth Century." In *Jewish Studies at the Turn of the Twentieth Century,* ed. Judit Targarona Borrás and Angel Sáenz-Badillos, 2: 3–18. Leiden: E. J. Brill, 1999.

Scheindlin, Raymond. "Rabbi Moshe ibn ᶜEzra on the Legitimacy of Poetry." *Medievalia et Humanistica* 7 (1976): 101–15.

Schirmann, Hayyim. *Hebrew Poetry in Spain and Provence* (in Hebrew). Jerusalem: Bialik Institute, 1960.

Scholem, Gershom G. *Von Berlin nach Jerusalem.* Frankfurt am Main: Suhrkamp, 1977. Trans. Harry Zohn as *From Berlin to Jerusalem.* New York: Schocken, 1980.

———. *On Jews and Judaism in Crisis: Selected Essays.* Trans. Lux Furtmüller. New York: Schocken, 1976.

———. *Judaica.* Frankfurt am Main: Suhrkamp, 1963.

———. *Judaica 3: Studien zur jüdischen Mystik.* Frankfurt am Main: Suhrkamp, 1970.

———. *Die jüdische Mystik in ihren Hauptstromungen.* Frankfurt: Alfred Metzner Verlag, 1957.

———. *Zur Kabbala und ihrer Symbolik.* Zurich: Rhein, 1960. Trans. Ralph Manheim as *On the Kabbalah and Its Symbolism.* New York: Schocken, 1965.

———. *Major Trends in Jewish Mysticism.* New York: Schocken Books, 1974.

———. *The Messianic Idea in Judaism and Other Essays in Jewish Spirituality.* New York: Schocken, 1971.

———. "The Name of God and the Linguistic Theory of the Kabbalah." *Diogenes* 79–80 (1972): 59–80, 164–94.

———. "Revelation and Tradition as Religious Categories in Judaism." In Scholem, *The Messianic Idea in Judaism and Other Essays in Jewish Spirituality,* 282–303. New York: Schocken, 1971.

———. *Walter Benjamin: Die Geschichte einer Freundschaft.* Frankfurt am Main: Suhrkamp, 1975. Trans. Harry Zohn as *Walter Benjamin: The Story of a Friendship.* New York: Schocken, 1981.

———. "Zehn unhistorische Sätze über Kabbalah." In Scholem, *Judaica 3: Studien zur jüdischen Mystik,* 264–71. Frankfurt am Main: Suhrkamp, 1970.

Scholem, Gershom G., and Walter Benjamin. *Briefwechsel 1932–1940.* Frankfurt am Main: Suhrkamp, 1980. Trans. Gary Smith and Andre Lefevere as *The Correspondence of Walter Benjamin and Gershom Scholem, 1932–1940.* Cambridge, Mass.: Harvard University Press, 1992.

Scholem, Gershom G., and Theodor W. Adorno, eds. *The Correspondence of Walter Benjamin 1910–1940.* Chicago: University of Chicago Press, 1994.

Seeskin, Kenneth. *Searching for a Distant God: The Legacy of Maimonides.* Oxford: Oxford University Press, 2000.

Segal, Eliezer. "The Exegetical Craft of the *Zohar.*" *AJS Review* 17, no. 1 (1992): 31–49.

Septimus, Bernard. *Hispano-Jewish Culture in Transition: The Career and Controversies of Ramah.* Cambridge, Mass.: Harvard University Press, 1982.

———. "'Open Rebuke and Concealed Love': Naḥmanides and the Andalusian Tradition." In *Rabbi Moses Nahmanides (Ramban): Explorations in His Religious and Literary Virtuosity,* ed. I. Twersky, 11–34. Cambridge, Mass.: Harvard University Press, 1983.

Shepard, Sanford. *Shem Tov: His World and His Words.* Miami: Ediciones Universal, 1978.

Shohat, Ella. "Imagining Terra Incognita: The Disciplinary Gaze of Empire." *Public Culture* 3, no. 2 (1991): 41–70.

———. *Israeli Cinema: East/West and the Politics of Representation.* Austin: University of Texas Press, 1989.

Silver, Daniel J. *Maimonidean Criticism and the Maimonidean Controversy 1180–1240.* Leiden: E. J. Brill, 1965.

Simon, Larry J., ed. *Iberia and the Mediterranean World of the Middle Ages.* Leiden: E. J. Brill, 1995.

Sirat, Colette. *Écriture et civilisations.* Paris: Centre National de la Recherche Scientifique, 1976.

Smith, Gary. "'Die Zauberjuden': Walter Benjamin, Gershom Scholem, and Other German-Jewish Esoterics Between the World Wars." *Journal of Jewish Thought and Philosophy* 4 (1995): 227–43.

———, ed. *Benjamin: Philosophy, Aesthetics, History.* Chicago: University of Chicago Press, 1989.

———, ed. *On Walter Benjamin: Critical Essays and Recollections.* Cambridge, Mass.: MIT Press, 1988.

Stein, Kenneth. "Exegesis, Maimonides, and Literary Criticism." *Modern Language Notes* 88, no. 6 (1973): 1134–51.

Stern, David. "Midrash and Indeterminacy." *Critical Inquiry* 15, no. 1 (1988): 132–61.

———. *Parables in Midrash: Narrative and Exegesis in Rabbinic Literature.* Cambridge, Mass.: Harvard University Press, 1991.

Stern, David, and Mark Jay Mirsky, eds. *Narrative Fantasies: Imaginative Narratives from Classical Hebrew Literature.* Philadelphia: Jewish Publication Society, 1990.

Stern, Josef. "The Fall and Rise of Myth in Ritual: Maimonides Versus Nahmanides on the Huqqim, Astrology, and the War Against Idolatry." *Journal of Jewish Thought and Philosophy* 6 (1997): 185–263.

———. "The Idea of a Ḥoq in Maimonides' Explanation of the Law." In *Maimonides and Philosophy,* ed. Shlomo Pines and Yirmiyahu Yovel, 92–130. Dordrecht: Martinus Nijhoff, 1986.

———. "Logical Syntax as a Key to a Secret of the *Guide of the Perplexed*" (in Hebrew). *Iyyun* 38 (1989): 137–66.

———. "Maimonides on the Covenant of Circumcision and the Unity of God." In *The Midrashic Imagination: Jewish Exegesis, Thought, and History,* ed. Michael Fishbane, 131–54. Albany: State University of New York Press, 1993.

———. *Problems and Parables of Law: Maimonides and Nahmanides on Reasons for the Commandments (Taᶜamei Ha-Mitzvot).* Albany: State University of New York Press, 1998.

Stern, Samuel M. *Les Chansons mozarabes.* Palermo: U. Manfredi, n.d.

———. "A Collection of Treatises by ᶜAbd al-Latif al-Baghdadi." *Studia Islamica* 1 (1962): 53–70.

———. *Hispano-Arabic Strophic Poetry.* Oxford: Oxford University Press, 1974.

———. "Rationalists and Kabbalists in Medieval Allegory." *Journal of Jewish Studies* 6 (1955): 73–86.

Stetkevytch, Jaroslav. "Arabic Hermeneutical Terminology: Paradox and the Production of Meaning." *Journal of Near Eastern Studies* 48, no. 2 (1989): 81–96.

Stetkevytch, Suzanne P. *Abū Tammām and the Poetics of the ʿAbbāsid Age.* Leiden: E. J. Brill, 1991.

Strauss, Leo. "How to Begin to Study *The Guide of the Perplexed.*" In Maimonides, *The Guide of the Perplexed,* intro. Leo Strauss, trans. Shlomo Pines, ix–lvi. Chicago: University of Chicago Press, 1963.

———. "The Literary Character of the *Guide of the Perplexed.*" In Strauss, *Persecution and the Art of Writing,* 38–94. Chicago: The University of Chicago Press, 1988.

———. "Notes on the Concept of the Political." In Carl Schmitt, *The Concept of the Political,* 83–107. Chicago: University of Chicago Press, 1996.

———. *Persecution and the Art of Writing.* Chicago: The University of Chicago Press, 1988.

Talmage, Frank. "Apples of Gold: The Inner Meaning of Sacred Texts in Medieval Judaism." In *Jewish Spirituality from the Bible Through the Middle Ages,* ed. Arthur Green, 313–55. New York: Crossroads, 1989.

Tirosh-Rothschild, Hava. "Continuity and Revision in the Study of Kabbalah." *AJS Review* 16 (1991): 161–92.

Tishby, Isaiah. *The Wisdom of the Zohar: An Anthology of Texts.* Trans. David Goldstein. Oxford: Littman Library and Oxford University Press, 1989.

Tobi, Yosef. "Aristotle's *Poetics* in Medieval Hebrew Poetry" (in Hebrew). *Dapim le-Mehkar be-Sifrut* 8 (1992): 107–22.

Ibn Ṭufayl. *Ḥayy ibn Yaqẓān.* Ed. Léon Gauthier. Beirut: Imprimerie Catholique, 1936.

Underhill, Evelyn. *Mysticism: A Study in the Nature and Development of Man's Spiritual Consciousness.* New York: Meridian Books, 1955.

Vizenor, Gerald. *Manifest Manners: Postindian Warriors of Survivance.* Middletown, Conn.: Wesleyan University Press, 1994.

Warminski, Andrzej. *Readings in Interpretation: Hölderlin, Hegel, Heidegger.* Minneapolis: University of Minnesota Press, 1987.

Wasserstein, David J. "The Language Situation in Al-Andalus." In *Studies on the Muwwašša and the Kharja,* ed. Alan Jones and Richard Hitchcock. Reading, Eng.: Ithaca Press, 1991.

Waters, Lindsay, and Wlad Godzich, eds. *Reading de Man Reading.* Minneapolis: University of Minnesota Press, 1989.

Weber, Samuel. "Genealogy of Modernity: History, Myth and Allegory in Benjamin's 'Origin of the German Mourning Play.'" *Modern Language Notes* 106 (1991): 465–500.

———. *Institution and Interpretation.* Minneapolis: University of Minnesota Press, 1987.

———. "Lecture de Benjamin." *Critique* 267–68 (1969): 699–712.

———. *The Legend of Freud.* Minneapolis: University of Minnesota Press, 1982.

———. *Mass Mediauras: Form, Technics, Media.* Stanford, Calif.: Stanford University Press, 1996.

Wiegers, Gerard. *Islamic Literature in Spanish and Aljamiado.* Leiden: E. J. Brill, 1994.

Wohlfarth, Irving. "No-Man's-Land: On Walter Benjamin's 'Destructive Character.'" *Diacritics* 8 (1978): 47–65.

Wolfson, Elliot R. "Beautiful Maiden Without Eyes: Peshat and Sod in Zoharic Hermeneutics." In *The Midrashic Imagination: Jewish Exegesis, Thought, and History,* ed. Michael Fishbane, 155–203. Albany: State University of New York Press, 1993.

———. *Circle in the Square: Studies in the Use of Gender in Kabbalistic Symbolism.* Albany: State University of New York Press, 1995.

———. "Coronation of the Sabbath Bride: Kabbalistic Myth and the Ritual of Androgynisation." *Journal of Jewish Thought and Philosophy* 6 (1997): 301–43.

———. "Left Contained in the Right: A Study in Zoharic Hermeneutics." *AJS Review* 9, no. 1 (1986): 27–52.

———. "Negative Theology and Positive Assertion in the Early Kabbalah." *Daat* 32–33 (1994): v–xxii.

———. *Along the Path: Studies in Kabbalistic Myth, Symbolism, and Hermeneutics.* Albany: State University of New York Press, 1995.

———. *Through a Speculum That Shines: Vision and Imagination in Medieval Jewish Mysticism.* Princeton, N.J.: Princeton University Press, 1994.

———. "'By Way of Truth': Aspects of Nahmanides' Kabbalistic Hermeneutic." *AJS Review* 14, no. 2 (1989): 103–78.

Wolosky, Shira. *Language Mysticism: The Negative Way of Language in Eliot, Beckett, and Celan.* Stanford, Calif.: Stanford University Press, 1995.

Yaffe, Martin. "Autonomy, Community, Authority: Hermann Cohen, Carl Schmitt, Leo Strauss." In *Autonomy and Judaism: The Individual and the Community in Jewish Philosophical Thought,* ed. Daniel H. Frank, 143–60. Albany: State University of New York Press, 1992.

Yahalom, Joseph. "Angels Do Not Understand Aramaic: On the Literary Use of Jewish Palestinian Aramaic in Late Antiquity." *Journal of Jewish Studies* 57, no. 1 (1996): 33–44.

Yarden, Dov, ed. *Dīwān Shmuel ha-Nagid—Ben Tehilim.* Jerusalem: Hebrew Union College, 1966.

Zafrani, Haïm. *Kabbale vie mystique et magie: Judaisme d'occident musulman.* Paris: Maisonneuve et Larose, 1986.

Cultural Memory in the Present

Gil Anidjar, *"Our Place in Al-Andalus": Kabbalah, Philosophy, Literature in Arab-Jewish Letters*

Hélène Cixous and Jacques Derrida, *Veils*

F. R. Ankersmit, *Historical Representation*

F. R. Ankersmit, *Political Representation*

Elissa Marder, *Dead Time: Temporal Disorders in the Wake of Modernity (Baudelaire and Flaubert)*

Reinhart Koselleck, *Timing History, Spacing Concepts: The Practice of Conceptual History*

Niklas Luhmann, *The Reality of the Mass Media*

Hubert Damisch, *A Childhood Memory by Piero della Francesca*

Hubert Damisch, *A Theory of /Cloud/: Toward a History of Painting*

Jean-Luc Nancy, *The Speculative Remark: (One of Hegel's Bons Mots)*

Jean-François Lyotard, *Soundproof Room: Malraux's Anti-Aesthetics*

Jan Patočka, *Plato and Europe*

Hubert Damisch, *Skyline: The Narcissistic City*

Isabel Hoving, *In Praise of New Travelers: Reading Caribbean Migrant Women Writers*

Richard Rand, *Futures: Of Derrida*

William Rasch, *Niklas Luhmann's Modernity: The Paradoxes of Differentiation*

Jacques Derrida and Anne Dufourmantelle, *Of Hospitality*

Jean-François Lyotard, *The Confession of Augustine*

Kaja Silverman, *World Spectators*

Samuel Weber, *Institution and Interpretation,* second edition

Jeffrey S. Librett, *The Rhetoric of Cultural Dialogue: Jews and Germans in the Epoch of Emancipation*

Ulrich Baer, *Remnants of Song: Trauma and the Experience of Modernity in Charles Baudelaire and Paul Celan*

Samuel C. Wheeler III, *Deconstruction as Analytic Philosophy*

David S. Ferris, *Silent Urns: Romanticism, Hellenism, Modernity*

Rodolphe Gasché, *Of Minimal Things: Studies on the Notion of Relation*

Sarah Winter, *Freud and the Institution of Psychoanalytic Knowledge*

Samuel Weber, *The Legend of Freud,* expanded edition

Aris Fioretos, ed., *The Solid Letter: Readings of Friedrich Hölderlin*

J. Hillis Miller / Manuel Asensi, *Black Holes / J. Hillis Miller; or, Boustrophedonic Reading*

Miryam Sas, *Fault Lines: Cultural Memory and Japanese Surrealism*

Peter Schwenger, *Fantasm and Fiction: On Textual Envisioning*

Didier Maleuvre, *Museum Memories: History, Technology, Art*

Jacques Derrida, *Monolingualism of the Other; or, The Prosthesis of Origin*

Andrew Baruch Wachtel, *Making a Nation, Breaking a Nation: Literature and Cultural Politics in Yugoslavia*

Niklas Luhmann, *Love as Passion: The Codification of Intimacy*

Mieke Bal, ed., *The Practice of Cultural Analysis: Exposing Interdisciplinary Interpretation*

Jacques Derrida and Gianni Vattimo, eds., *Religion*